"Evil" Arabs in American Popular Film

"Evil" Arabs in American Popular Film

ORIENTALIST FEAR

Tim Jon Semmerling

UNIVERSITY OF TEXAS PRESS
Austin

Requests for permission to reproduce
material from this work should be sent to:
    Permissions
    University of Texas Press
    P.O. Box 7819
    Austin, TX 78713-7819
    www.utexas.edu/utpress/about/bpermission.html

♾ The paper used in this book meets
the minimum requirements of
ANSI/NISO Z39.48-1992 (R1997)
(Permanence of Paper).

Library of Congress Cataloging-in-Publication Data

Semmerling, Tim Jon, 1961–
"Evil" Arabs in American popular film : orientalist fear /
Tim Jon Semmerling. — 1st ed.
    p.   cm.
Includes bibliographical references and index.
ISBN-13: 978-0-292-71341-3 (cloth : alk. paper)
ISBN-10: 0-292-71341-x (cloth : alk. paper)
ISBN-13: 978-0-292-71342-0 (pbk. : alk. paper)
ISBN-10: 0-292-71342-8 (pbk. : alk. paper)
    1. Arabs in motion pictures.   2. Motion pictures —
United States — History.   I. Title.
PN1995.9.A68S46   2006
791.43'6529927 — dc22

                        2005034326

Contents

The Water by Giuseppe Arcimboldo (1566). Courtesy of Kunsthistorisches Museum, Wien.

*T*HE painting hangs on the museum wall. At first sight, it simply appears to be another portrait like any other portrait. The Renaissance artist painted a god or goddess, a prince or princess, maybe a refined and
wealthy patron. There is nothing new here, and there is nothing exciting.
Even its title is banal. We are, as Roland Barthes describes, in the grip of
studium.[1]

But as we recock our heads, furrow our brows, and focus our eyes, we
discern that the sitting subject looks too disheveled and unkempt, the features are too swollen, the construction lacks the beauty of proportion, and
the adorning jewelry is overly ostentatious against the rough and weathered skin—all atypical of European portraiture. The subject looks crude
rather than sophisticated, more savage than civilized, more Other than
Self. Maybe the artist has painted an exotic indigene from the New World,
Africa, or the Orient? Step closer now. We can see the subject in more
detail. Our curiosity builds.

We see a fish, a ray, a crustacean, a coral, a mollusk, a marine mammal,
and even an amphibian. As we discern each creature, the human we once
saw disappears. The headdress, the cheek, the nose, the mouth, the jaw, the
chin, the neck, and the shoulders—all of them dissolve into distinct and
beautiful organisms worthy of new attention and appreciation. The portrait vanishes into a seafood still life, the body melds into a bouillabaisse,
and the individual becomes a marine ecosystem.

But the looking event is not over. As we investigate each creature, we
quickly notice the existence of its sequential relation to the others. And as
we open our visual field to accommodate more creatures into our attention, the human features reappear. The ray passes by the shark, the shark
passes over the squid, and the goatfish hides underneath—the cheek, the
mouth, the jaw, the chin and its whiskers. The painting becomes an illu-
sionist's game of hide-and-seek, and it is delightful. We scrutinize each
still-life creature just to find its anatomical function for the portrait, taking
turns again and again. *Punctum* is achieved. How marvelous and creative

this artist is! How beautiful nature is! How wonderful we are in solving the artist's puzzle and in our appreciation of his art! Does he make more?[2] Let's do it again.

Then we step back and wonder more deeply about the portrait. Did such a subject ever exist? Ichthyoid Man? Impossible! But maybe there was an original subject who actually did come and sit for the artist or one the artist had in mind. If so, then we must consider the sadism of the artist who has maliciously disfigured his subject. What grudge did he have against the subject anyway? We imagine the human being whose image must eternally exist behind this amusement, just as we imagine the sleek and beautiful ship that once sailed before it sank to the ocean's floor: its organized deck and smooth hull are no longer discernible now that it is a host, a home, a hiding place, and a feeding and breeding ground for this other world. It is hauntingly sad and a cruel joke. The human subject has been transformed into a monster. Boney fins; sharp teeth; gripping tentacles; slithering, slimy, and scaly bodies; and pinching claws are assembled to make us recoil from their creepiness and painful affliction — and ultimately to retreat from the subject underneath. The bodily image behind is now outwardly grotesque, the inner spirit is weighted down and can no longer break through, and the subject is powerless and cannot wipe away or pull the creatures off of itself.

We eventually abandon the pitiful prisoner to its fate. What can we do about it anyway? The original subject and artist are long gone, the picture is completed and hung on the museum wall, and the critics consider the painting one of the most ingenious displays of artistic talent in the history of Western art. There is much more in the museum to see, but for the time being *punctum* has reinvigorated us. We may move on, but we are now motivated to approach, consider, and scrutinize the other portraits and still-life paintings differently and with more acute perception.

Acknowledgments

I am proud to set aside this page to thank the following people and organizations for their help in making this book possible:

Nihad Awad, Joel R. Ayala, Dr. Richard Bauman, Jim Burr, Dr. John R. Clarke, Dr. Allen Douglas, Dr. Johan Elverskog, Dr. Liljana Elverskog, Cherie Lambourne, Dr. Fedwa Malti-Douglas, Joyce Mayer, Ellen McNamara, Stephen M. O'Connor, Dr. Tony Pilch, Anonymous Reader, Lynn Richter, Dr. Judith Roof, James and Marion Semmerling and family, Jeff M. Semmerling, Dr. Lee M. Semmerling, Jill Semmerling-Smith, Dennis P. Smith, Dr. Jack G. Shaheen, Paul Spragens, Dr. Beverly Stoeltje, Faye Thompson, and Dr. Renate Wise.

The Ablah Library at Wichita State University, the Bellevue Regional Library, the British Film Institute, the Richard J. Daley Library at the University of Illinois at Chicago, the Film Archive at the Academy of Motion Picture Arts and Sciences, the Fondren Library at Southern Methodist University, the Inside Out Art Studio, the Keller Public Library and its staff, the Kunsthistorisches Museum, the John C. Murphy Memorial Library at the College of Lake County, the Northeast Library at Tarrant County College, and the University of Texas Press and its staff.

Additionally, I wish to acknowledge the inspiration provided to me by Atticus Semmerling and Haedyn, Wyatt, and Drew Smith.

"Evil" Arabs in American Popular Film

Introduction

ORIENTALIST FEAR

*T*HE "evil" Arabs of American film are illusions. Much like those perplexing and ambiguous paintings of the celebrated Renaissance artist Giuseppe Arcimboldo (1527–1593), or those more simplistic drawings that are developed for entertainment and perception analysis in books featuring optical puzzles, the "evil" Arabs are also constructions for entertainment and have implications for the perceptions of the American cinematic audience. Samuel Tolansky has provided us with a useful term when discussing the type of illusions similar to that of the "evil" Arabs: illusions of "oscillating attention." Tolansky notes,

> These are cases where the diagram is designed such that attention can alternately be concentrated on one of two possibilities. In some instances the mind seems actually to oscillate between the two possible interpretations in rapid succession, and it is difficult to decide just what is being seen.[1]

While Tolansky cites concentration, attention, and distinguishing between light and dark as the causes of oscillating attention, writers like Patricia Ann Rainey, J. R. Block, and Harold E. Yuker believe that the driving force of what the viewers see first in an illusion of oscillating attention is "perception." Rainey tells her viewers/readers that perception is simply how people see things, or how people look at the world. She adds,

> Differences in religion, ideology, political beliefs, and even prejudice can be explained in terms of how people perceive. Thus knowledge of perception will give an understanding of human beings.[2]

Many of the portrayals of Arabs, at first glance, give the impression of cultural and ethnic traits that are inherently inimical to Western civilization. Even so, are not "evil" Arabs actually fictional characters that we have devised and, as such, not at all about the real Arabs and their multidimensional and deeply contoured cultures or ethnicity? Our filmic villains are narrative tools used for self-presentation and self-identity to enhance our own stature, our own meaning, and our own self-esteem in times of our own diffidence. Therefore, are the "evil" Arabs in American film actually oblique depictions of ourselves: the insecure Americans? And while we depict ourselves through them, do we not do so at the expense of the Arab Others?

"Evil" Arabs in American Popular Film is a film study written to encourage the American cinematic audience to look with a more critical eye at the depictions of the "evil" Arabs. It is written to promote a new way of thinking about the "evil" Arabs and to call forth a differentiation between the Arabs as-they-are-portrayed and the Arabs as-they-are. This book encourages its readers, when seeing or hearing of the "evil" Arabs, to scrutinize the characters and to discover our self-interested construction of the visual or the narrative: to see visual tropes that are often made through intertextuality and polarities of good and bad, and to identify narrative structures that adhere interstructurally to meaningful morphological formulae. Block and Yuker state of their illusions of oscillating attention, "Once one sees both pictures, it is impossible to focus on only one without the other 'popping' into your vision from time to time!"[3] Here, I seek to achieve an analogous effect with, however, the more serious implications of cultural prejudice and racism in mind. I ask the reader to reconsider the "evil" Arabs and to think about the way in which the Arabs are devised to produce fear, and at times solace, in an American cinematic audience. With this reconsideration, the illusion will manifest itself, thus making prejudices inculcated through our popular culture more clearly perceptible, more easily isolated, and more likely to be dismantled.

Jack Shaheen is well known for his lectures, written work, and media appearances that challenge the stereotypes of Arabs used in Hollywood film and in Western television. Shaheen's emphasis on stereotypes is essential as a beginning foray into understanding the construction of the "evil" Arabs in film. Fundamentally, he calls our attention to the first image of the illusion. For example, he has identified the "Arab kit," or "instant Ali Baba kit," as a quick and easy assembly of the stereotypical Arab character in Hollywood:

Property masters stock the kits with curved daggers, scimitars, magic lamps, giant feather fans, and nargelihs [*sic*]. Costumers pro-

vide actresses with chadors, hijabs, bellydancers' see-through panta-
loons, veils, and jewels for their navels. Robed actors are presented
with dark glasses, fake black beards, exaggerated noses, worry beads,
and checkered burnooses.[4]

Offering historical perspective, Shaheen reminds us that "when one ethnic, racial, or religious group is vilified, innocent people suffer" and that
"cinema's hateful Arab stereotypes are reminiscent of abuses of earlier
times" (i.e., cinematic abuses of Asians, Native Americans, blacks, and
Jews).[5] He has taken on the difficult task of documenting a plethora of
stereotype abuses and entreats the readers of his comprehensive tome of
Hollywood films, cleverly titled *Reel Bad Arabs,* to join him in continuing
to expose racism against Arabs in film—what he calls "The New Anti-
Semitism"[6]—and to find new ways of solving this problem. Shaheen states
of his objective, "To see is to make possible new ways of seeing."[7]

"Evil" Arabs in American Popular Film has been greatly inspired by Shaheen's impressive and important work. I, therefore, accept his challenge
and would like to expand upon his work at a new level: essentially, to un-
veil the other image in the illusion of oscillating attention. To do so, we
must consider Shaheen's work as an introduction to the topic of the prejudiced portrayals of the Arabs. *Reel Bad Arabs* is an indispensable reference
tool to find films that abuse Arab characters. But, because of its cumulative
nature, Shaheen's book does not reveal what it could about these films. In
fact, the book overlooks important and unique "how" and "why" performances and strategies used in the construction of "evil" Arab characters in
these films. For example, Shaheen's discussion of *The Exorcist,* given only
two inches of text, is by far too "lite."[8] While the author makes us aware of
our obsessive cultural use of "evil" Arabs, and the Foreword to his book
elucidates the Arabs as replacement villains for the Soviet Communists,[9]
I find my inquisitive appetite unsatisfied with his discussion confronting
our cultural needs and desires to enlist these characters. As a result of
Shaheen's focus on stereotypes, he, for example, promotes *Three Kings* in
his "Best List" because he sees it as an improvement in stereotyping, even
though it still denigrates the Arab character.[10] We must look deeper, beyond the "Arab kit," at how the Arabs' images are misused. Shaheen has
provided us significant opportunities to think further and to find the path
for deeper self-assessment in our construction of "evil" Arabs. What is
now needed is for scholars interested in the topic of cultural prejudice and
racism in film to delve into these films, to scrutinize filmic visual tropes

and narrative structures, and to investigate possibilities of why we keep using "evil" Arabs for our entertainment.

I enlist the work of Gordon W. Allport, who points out in his famous book *The Nature of Prejudice* that an attack on stereotypes alone will not eradicate the root of prejudice. The stereotype is but one of the keys on the ring that are needed to open the door holding the understandings of prejudice. Since an approach to prejudice must be a multitheoretical approach, Allport encourages us to delve deeper than the mere thought of the stimulus object (the Arab) and its phenomenology (how the Arab is perceived). One way of understanding the prejudicial act is to look at the character structure of the persons who employ the stereotype. We must discover their socially acquired personalities, attitudes, and beliefs; the structure of the society in which they live; long-standing economic and cultural traditions; and national and historical influences of long duration.[11] This methodology turns the spotlight of the prejudicial act away from the hated object and concentrates on the haters. It can, therefore, help us discern the alternative image in the illusion of an "evil" Arab.

It makes sense, then, to consider those ideologies, and the myths that illustrate them, of the prejudiced persons' world. I borrow from Louis Althusser's notions of ideology as the individuals' imaginary relation to the real relations in which they live.[12] Ideology, as Althusser explains, is an *illusion* considered as a truthful representation of reality that at the same time makes an *allusion* to reality. The human being is ideological by nature in that a concrete individual has already been and continually is transformed into a subject within the ideological frameworks at work and within the rituals of ideology. Ideology, the *illusion* based on *allusion*, causes the subject to culturally recognize and acknowledge raw occurrences and experiences in such a way that s/he will exclaim, "That's obvious! That's right! That's true!" What also occurs is the formation, through a process of "interpellation" (being hailed/called), of the individual's idealized self-image, or what Henry Krips acknowledges as a Freudian "ideal ego,"[13] that constantly rediscovers itself in the application of ideologies. When the individual is hailed/called, s/he should respond, nine times out of ten, to the interpellation as a subject by saying, "That's me. That's who I am." The stories humans tell to illustrate their ideologies, i.e., myths, go further in informing the individual of her/his subjective being, her/his connection to society, and her/his society's connection to the rest of the world and then the cosmos. Myths illustrate to the subject how to live a lively, healthy, and culturally meaningful life. They provide instructions, standards of value, and interpretive frameworks for experience, and, at the same time, power over existence. Myths, therefore, help to interpret and visualize the "truth" set forth in ideology. For example, while the individual may acknowledge her/himself as a subject existing in American capitalism, and American capitalism as *the* proper economic system at that, the success story of the American entrepreneur is the myth that illustrates the virtues of this capitalist ideology and the rules for the subject to follow.

Kaja Silverman acknowledges ideology as a suturing device in cinematic viewing. She sees that the filmic narrative is laden with ideological stances that interpellate individual viewers and thereby suture them into subjective positions within the film. Ideologies are often challenged in the film, but are also reaffirmed, strengthened, and proven righteous in the end.[14] Susan Mackey-Kallis uses mythic structure as a way of analyzing Hollywood films to unlock the American cinematic audience's psyche and its love of film and thereby explain the successful popular appeal of particular films in our culture.[15] To unlock prejudiced persons' ideologies and the myths through which they have been socialized and from which their society is structured, to see how that society has been formed from long-standing traditions and historical experience, is to properly apply Allport's approach to prejudice and can be enlightening when analyzing the "evil" Arabs in film. Ideologies and myths can inform us of our preconceptions, to which we cling when our vision and mentality confront these Arab characters on film. Or to borrow from Melani McAlister, these ideologies and myths can enlighten us as to how the Arabs and the Middle East come to make "common sense" when geographic and experiential spaces are too wide and, therefore, we must rely upon the medium of culture as surrogate.[16]

Orientalism is one such ideological structure and a basis of the inquiry at hand. Edward Said's seminal book *Orientalism* looks at the European colonial period's portrayals of the Arabs, their cultures, and their Middle Eastern land as Western discourse. Orientalism dominates the way that we in the West see, anticipate, and react to the Arab world in our past, today, and likely in the future. Said shows how Western portrayals of the Arabs became an issue of disciplining power, a particular Western knowledge of the East that divides the world into a conceptually evolving, modern, and superior Occidental "us" versus a static, backward, and weakened Oriental "them." To use Orientalism as a basis of this inquiry is an appropriate way of understanding our preconceptions of the Arabs in terms of the methodology supported by Allport. It helps in providing a vantage point to see the other image, our Self, in the illusion of an "evil" Arab. After all, as Said has taught us, "Orientalism is—and does not simply represent—a considerable dimension of modern political-intellectual culture, and as such has less to do with the Orient than it does with 'our' world."[17]

One of the possible roots of prejudice, as noted by Allport, is the prejudiced persons' fears and anxieties, and such a consideration of fears and anxieties can better narrow our own inquiry. When the prejudiced persons can no longer control their fear, chronic anxiety will result. It puts them on alert and predisposes them to see all sorts of stimuli as menacing. While social pressures force them to control and repress their personal anxieties, they tend to project their fear onto Others; and if this phobia is socially allowable, it provides them psychic release, as they are rescued by the "impression of universality."[18]

It becomes evident that discussion of stereotypes alone will not help us here. According to Allport, stereotype offers prejudiced persons a clear-cut structuring of the world, a way of imposing order where there is none, a lifeline to tried and tested habits when new solutions are called for, and an opportunity to "latch onto what is familiar, safe, simple, definite."[19] In essence, then, prejudiced persons utter or consume the stereotype for its functional significance. They do so for consolation, comfort, the pleasure derived from classificatory order, and an adoption of the law of least effort when aspects of the Other seem ambiguous and disrupt "logical" order. Similarly, the Orientalists work within a repertoire of stereotypes. As part of the exercise of power over those foreign peoples and objects that they confront, the Orientalists use language and methods of control to assign Others into classification schemes that protect the Orientalist self. Therefore, to discuss films only in view of their stereotypes or Orientalist tropes would suggest a discussion that looks more at our derivation of comfort from the Arabs. Once the stereotype is effectively articulated, the anxiety is, for the short term, ameliorated. Stereotype is the response to anxiety, not the anxiety itself, and as such it is only a partial view of the illusion. Moreover, I believe, concentration on stereotype alone dangerously encourages us to leave the images of the "evil" Arabs as they are rather than to scrutinize them for our prejudicial roots and risk our own psychic comfort.

To get at a better understanding of the construction and use of "evil" Arabs in film, we must upset the prejudiced persons' project, overturn their applecart, and peel the skin of their personalities in order to see their ideal egos lying underneath. We must find out what makes them squirm to really expose the nerve of their fear — the raw source and the full weight of the prejudiced act. To do so, I propose that we find instances in which their ideological and mythic structures are threatened and placed in jeopardy. This will give these persons no refuge as they flail about, grab anything they can, accept any explanation, and use their ingenuity, and will expose what methods they employ to set their ideologies and myths right again. We must look for instances when the Orientalist project is disrupted or when the Arabs refuse to be disciplined — or at least are perceived as doing so. David D. Gilmore points out that interstitiality, or the flagrant refusal to be categorized or to accept categories, is a cause of human discomfort and fear for the categorizer.[20] Likewise, Robert G. Lee states in his study of Asian Americans in popular culture that objects or people are designated as alien when their "presence disrupts the narrative structure of the community."[21] An approach to our prejudicial portrayals of the Arabs, particularly Arab wickedness, in film requires that we look at our fears, in addition to our comforts, where threatened ideologies and myths are important features.

Such fears have become common and intriguing entertainment themes in our cinematic portrayals of "evil" Arabs from the 1970s on into the present and, as such, have added to our socially allowable phobia toward the Arabs. These films, however, are reflections of our real-life fears of the Arabs in our everyday cultural and political lives. The post-Vietnam decade became an era in which seemingly undisputable truths informed by American ideological and mythic narratives had become destabilized, and, hence, the confidence of the American national self was in peril.

David Frum's cultural study of the 1970s points out that this American decade is notable for our society's loss of trust in our institutions and institutional practices. Whereas after World War II Americans generally trusted their government and military, the bases and advances of Western sciences, the economic structure and practices of the free market system, and the words and guidance of paternal leaders, in the 1970s many of these postwar "givens" had become undermined and an atmosphere of mistrust, skepticism, malaise, and pessimism flourished. As Frum states, "[B]etween 1967 and 1981, the United States sank into a miasma of self-doubt from which it has never fully emerged."[22] Frum does not blame the experiences of the 1970s themselves for this but rather the interpretation of experiences through the lens of overly zealous hopes and dreams, in the 1960s, that a postwar society would be great, just, and caring. This echoes Daniel J. Boorstin's description of American culture made earlier, in 1961. As Boorstin saw it then, Americans expected more than the world could offer. "We are ruled by extravagant expectations: (1) Of what the world holds . . . (2) Of our power to shape the world . . . We tyrannize and frustrate ourselves by expecting more than the world can give us or than we can make of the world."[23] These hopes, dreams, and expectations, galvanized by the confidence of democracy, seemingly proven victorious in great military conflicts, came to a crashing halt in the 1970s. And so, refracted through such myths, the experiences of the 1970s seemed all the more suspicious, trust-breaking, and devastating. Therefore, Watergate, Vietnam, the Pentagon Papers, inflation, economic stagnation, unemployment, the Equal Rights Amendment (ERA) movement, and the rise in crime, to mention but a few of the important experiences of the decade, gained their reputations of notorious cultural importance because they usurped long-standing mythic structures and institutionalized ways of thinking in our American culture and/or dashed the postwar hopes and dreams.

Likewise, the rising power of the Middle East and the perceived threat of the Arabs became another infamous theme of the 1970s. The Middle East loomed as an evolving "global imaginary," to borrow from Christina Klein,[24] that became a region often contextualized in an adversarial relationship with America, and, in turn, the Arabs were reduced to an ethnic imaginary that earned our prejudicial anger. For example, the Middle East became a nemesis in American foreign policy, and foreign policy, according to Melani McAlister, is a meaning-making activity that helps "to frame our ideas of nationhood and national interest," i.e., our ideologies.[25] McAlister argues in her book *Epic Encounters* that in order to understand our cultural perceptions of the Middle East, we must consider our encounters through the nexus of foreign policy. From this vantage point, we can also see how our cultural perceptions make conventional wisdom of this policy.[26] In particular, McAlister highlights the policies of "liberal developmentalism" before World War II, the "benevolent supremacy" theme of the 1950s, and the Nixon Doctrine of the 1970s. Liberal developmentalism promotes the economic influence of U.S. capitalism as an alternative to military conquest. In connection with Manifest Destiny egoism and self-interested commercial gains, the United States prior to World War II envisaged that all nations could and should replicate the U.S. model of economic, political, and cultural development. As McAlister describes it, by making mass products (sewing machines, condensed milk, cameras) available cheaply, [Americans] would help increase living standards in Latin America, Asia, or Africa, while also improving the U.S. strategic position and making money for American businesses.[27]

Benevolent supremacy is the ideology that calls for American international power, policy, and diplomacy to be used to promote democracy and the liberty of all nations as a morally preferable approach in comparison to slavery, referred to as being more like Soviet Communism, and arrogance, referred to as being more like European colonialism.[28] The Nixon Doctrine sought to fund and arm friendly governments, which would then serve as proxies for the protection of American interests.[29] The Middle East as global imaginary, in the 1970s, came to challenge these very ideologies and political policies through the discourses of oil, wealth, and violence. While the Middle East has been by no means exempt from ill-spirited American portrayals in the past,[30] in the 1970s the reputation of the Arabs was assigned a new level of popular American contempt in light of these policies.

According to Frum, oil lay in wait for half a billion years until humans could imagine a use for it, and then, through the mysterious processes of mass hysteria, they "terrif[ied] themselves that they were running out of it."[31] Daniel Yergin points out in his authoritative study of oil that the industrial nations' rising standard of living, the growing manufacture and consumption of newer and bigger products, the cheap cost of oil, and the high levels of oil production and supply drove a worldwide surge in oil consumption.[32] In 1971, the Middle East was supplying the industrial nations with much of the oil necessary to fuel their growing industrial economies. *Time* magazine reported that 85 percent of Europe's, 91 percent of Japan's, and 18 percent of the United States's oil came mainly from the wells in the Middle East. Whereas oil-producing countries of the Third World could at one time be diplomatically played off of one another for Western benefit, the Organization of Petroleum Exporting Countries (OPEC) was now seen as aggressively uniting in its effort to defend oil prices, demanding more of a share of the price per barrel, and becoming increasingly unhappy about Western support for Israel.[33] The West saw oil revenues as reward for Western ingenuity finding a use for the viscous liquid. At the other end of the spectrum, OPEC viewed oil as an indigenous resource driving the economic destinies of the producing nations. Therefore, these producing nations believed that oil should be under their own conservatorship and not under the control of the executives of Western oil companies. Weeks later, *Time* began reporting that the Shah of Iran, an emergent leader of the Middle East nations, was now calling for OPEC-like consortiums for producing nations of other commodities, such as coffee, tin, and rubber, in order to wield power over consumer countries. The Middle East seemed to be calling forth the Third World to take on the Western nations.[34] The OPEC countries were also demanding more control in the ownership of Western companies that were pumping oil in their nations, as if, in the American view, price increases were not enough to satisfy "their relentless search for new reserves of green."[35] In response, American political policy began to group these nations into spheres of "oil arrogance," with Libya and Iraq being radical, and Iran and Nigeria being considered more moderate, and henceforth the Arab Middle East was being considered an area that was politically unstable for the West.[36]

In the meantime, the rising wealth of the Arab oil nations was becoming increasingly more disconcerting in the American view. For an American culture that saw itself as economically fortunate from and morally deserving of the postwar economic boom, Arab wealth was a windfall of riches into the immature and irresponsible hands of Third Worlders. Arab wealth became an object of American jealousy, rivalry, and fear. For example, the $2.4 billion of Libya's annual oil income was depicted as coming in faster than the extremist Gaddafi could spend it on his Pan-Arabism dreams,[37] the de-Westernization/Christianization of his nation, and its replacement with Islamicization.[38] The oil reserves of the Middle East and the energy shortages of the West created an imbalance that, as it was believed, "may very well lead to significant redistribution of the world's monetary wealth."[39] Some imagined the future of the International Monetary Fund (IMF) as being not "run by the suave, dark-suited Americans and Europeans, but by white-robed sheiks from the Middle East."[40] Expectations were that America would increasingly rely on the Middle East in the future (up to 50 percent of its oil imports coming from the Arab nations).[41] Americans would be spending more just to keep their lifestyles, while the Middle East nations would gather funds almost twice as fast as they could spend them. There was a fear that the Arabs were likely to be irresponsible and untrustworthy with this new monetary wealth, maybe even using blackmail against America, and, thus, it was feared that America was funding its own demise. In the meantime, as a State De-

It happened to us once.
It can happen again.
And again.

This cartoon was used in an advertising campaign of the American Electric Power System, a consortium of energy companies based in the Midwestern states. The copy of this full-page ad discourages the importation of oil because such imports will make America vulnerable to embargoes and "will create a shortage of electric power that will touch the life of every American and plunge our country into economic chaos." Instead, the ad promotes the use of domestic coal as an energy source. Cartoon published in *Newsweek*, April 15, 1974.

partment spokesman stated, "With the possible exception of Croesus, the world will never have seen anything like the wealth which is flowing and will continue to flow into the Persian Gulf."[42]

Before the outbreak of the October War and the Arab oil embargo of 1973, Arabs were seen as purveyors of violence that threatened the balances of power in the world. The Arab-Israeli conflict became an imbroglio that threatened to bring the United States and the USSR into an arena where the two superpowers could clash, and almost did in 1973. Egyptian President Anwar Sadat was seen as recklessly courting the Russians to break the standoff between his country and Israel. The increase of arms flowing from the USSR and the United States to Arabs and Israelis at the same time Sadat was declaring 1971 the "Year of Decision" was "like stockpiling gasoline around an open fire."[43] And with his frustration over Israeli intransigence, Sadat made his move toward a new Pan-Arabism through a federation composed of Egypt, Libya, and Syria in 1971 and began to call for war against Israel. An ensuing joint Arab surprise attack on Israel during its period of holy observance in 1973 was designed to catch the Israelis when they were least prepared.

Meanwhile, factions of the Palestinian Liberation Organization (PLO) — the Popular Front for the Liberation of Palestine (PFLP) and Black September Organization, in particular—were committing skyjackings and acts of terror in airports, embassies, and trains. In an effort to draw the most attention to the Palestinian plight, Palestinian terrorist groups more frequently attacked specific, large, and valuable enemy targets, took advantage of shock value to make bold political statements via the broadcast airwaves, and used international travel to recruit international supporters and to export the conflict to countries outside of the Middle East. On September 5, 1972, Black September gunmen stormed into the Israeli athletic dormitory at the Olympics in Munich. The images and news coverage of this terrorist event riveted a worldwide audience, created shock and grief with the killing of eleven Israeli team members, and brought global condemnation of Palestinian terror tactics. Ironically, it was a great publicity coup for the Palestinian cause, as it used violence to bring the presence and grievances of the Palestinians into worldwide consciousness and showed that their militance was a force that had to be reckoned with and that could no longer be denied. *Time* reported that "eight young Palestinians managed to expose every weakness in the forces of law and in the helpless governments involved in the crisis."[44] The PLO proved violence as a successful method, which others wanted to copy to gain worldwide attention for their causes. Moreover, the attack showed that the violence of the Middle East was no longer containable within the region, but that it had been exported to the rest of the world—"first to Western Europe, and maybe eventually even to the U.S."[45]

Israelis and Palestinians continued their fighting on European soil. The War of Attrition, a term used to describe the deadly standoff between Egyptians and Israelis with military strikes on Israeli positions in the Sinai and attacks on Egyptians deep into Egypt itself, was now being used to describe Arab-Israeli violence that had spilled over into Europe. There were kidnappings, more skyjackings, hostage takings, and letter bombs. Assassination hits on Israelis and Arabs became commonplace in what *Time* called a "Deadly Battle of the Spooks," an underground warfare conducted anytime, anywhere, facelessly, and without warning, that scared the Western public and created a fear that the conflict would begin to find fertile ground in the United States. As one PLO spokesman was quoted as saying, "We don't have to occupy Tel Aviv to make our point. . . . We should fight the enemy anywhere in the world because every country bears the guilt of Palestine."[46] Moreover, approximately six months later, reports were coming in that innocent people were getting in the way and, in at least one case, being killed.[47] When Israeli commandos killed three PLO leaders in Beirut in early 1973, the PLO blamed U.S. intelligence for helping the Israelis. The PLO called on Arabs "to strike everywhere at American interests and embassies and kill and assassinate everyone who is American."[48] Arabs had now been reported to be threatening the American public with terrorist violence. As Frum notes of these terrorist events, "The United States was no longer able to protect its citizens from international anarchy. And through the 1970s, international anarchy obtruded itself ever more terrifyingly into American consciousness."[49]

By 1973, Arab governments began to demand of the Americans that they change U.S. foreign policy toward Israel. Americans came to learn that not meeting Arab demands would lead to Arab oil-producing nations enacting an oil embargo against the United States and ultimately exacting even further pressure on Washington through embargoes on Western Europe and Japan.[50] Americans viewed this as oil blackmail. Libya's Gaddafi reportedly announced in May of that year, when he demanded 100 percent control over oil companies in his nation, that "the day will come when oil will be used as a weapon by the Arabs in self-defense."[51] In a period of economic vulnerability, when inflation was on the rise and the dollar was falling in relation to foreign currency, a shortage of oil and a rise in oil prices were predicted to be surely devastating to an already ailing American economy, and Russian involvement with the Arabs in such a plan was already being feared.[52] In fact, Stephen Paul Miller states in his cultural analysis of the 1970s that the Arab-enacted oil embargo was an economic equivalent of Vietnam. While Vietnam created a credibility gap, a breaking down of public belief in official reality, "[t]he embargo changed many people's sense of America's self-reliance, and the threat of another embargo would hang over America for the rest of the seventies."[53]

The dreaded embargo did begin with the outbreak of hostilities be-

"So much for your bankroll . . . now fork over your Israeli policy . . .!"

By 1973, Arab governments began to demand change in U.S. foreign policy toward Israel. Americans came to learn that not meeting Arab demands would lead to an oil embargo by the Arab oil-producing nations against the United States. Americans viewed this as oil blackmail. Cartoon printed in *Time*, November 5, 1973.

tween Egypt and Israel in the October War. The Arab leaders rallied to the support of Sadat's surprise attack on the Jewish nation and, by October 29, it was reported that all oil shipments to the United States from Saudi Arabia, Abu Dhabi, Libya, and Algeria had been cut off.[54] In early November, reports intimated that Moscow might be the real winner in the oil embargo. Americans were told that the USSR was encouraging other Arab nations to fight Israel, America's ally. Concurrently with the embargo weakening America, the Soviet Union was broadening and developing its influence with the oil-rich nations.[55]

As the 1973–1974 winter approached, and America, north and south, was depicted as entering the cold, dark season, it was the images and stories of American lifestyles under Arab siege that stirred ever more anger and fear of the rising "New Arab." Take, for example, the introductory paragraphs of the *Time* article "The Arabs' New Oil Squeeze: Dimouts, Slowdowns, Chills," which deserve to be quoted here at length:

> Rushing to work last week, John Doe, American, swung his car onto the freeway — only to discover that the posted speed limit had been reduced from 60 m.p.h. to 50 m.p.h. When he stopped at a gas station for a refill, he learned that overnight the price had gone up 2¢ per gal. At his office he felt unusually cool because the thermostats had been pushed down a couple of degrees, to a brisk 68°. Later, when he finished work and was driving home, he noticed that the lights on outdoor advertising signs had been doused. In his living room he was greeted by his children, who gleefully reported that their school would be closed for a month this winter — in order to save oil.
>
> In the backward but wakening desert kingdom of Saudi Arabia, there was plenty of oil, and the wealth that it brought was beginning to show. Building cranes stuck their necks up everywhere in the few cities; Ferraris and Mercedes glistened in the showrooms, and the markets bulged with imported consumer goods. The national treasury was overflowing with foreign exchange, and there was talk of starting new industries to be fueled and financed by oil: petrochemicals, aluminum, steel. Indeed, Saudi Arabia was strong enough that it could afford to cut back oil production in order to make the rest of the world pay a higher price for it — in more ways than one.[56]

Although the story is a fictionalized account that juxtaposes a deteriorating, average American life and the ostentatious, ill-deserved lifeways of the Arab desert, it presents the relationship between the United States and the Arab world as a global imaginary of an Orientalist bipolar relationship; albeit this time it gives the Arabs the upper hand and the Americans the subordinate position. It is an account that was constructed to inspire fear and ire in Americans and to cultivate the roots of an "evil" Arab character. Later images and stories of America described a man having to resort to making gasoline from wood, leaves, brush, and garbage; Christmas lights being fewer and dimmer; carillon bells at churches cut off; gasoline ration cards imagined to be in the works; town meetings being conducted by candlelight; a professor teaching class in a raccoon coat; women buying long johns; people resorting to attending shelters for heated living; children going to school in the darkness of morning, due to the alteration of time itself under the daylight savings program, and shivering at their desks; motorists waiting and fighting amongst themselves in endless lines for gasoline; an American fighter jet taking off, with the caption stating, "Will they have enough to fly?"; and graphs and maps depicting paltry oil reserves of nations dwarfed by bulging reserves of the Middle East. The Arabs, in contrast, were shown as laughing, gloating, unified, plotting, and powerful enough to push America backwards in the modern industrial period that it worked so hard to achieve.[57] A kind of siege mentality was taking hold of America.[58] Old routines of work, play, celebration, and joys of travel, along with the stamina to sustain new patriotic reductions in energy consumption, were in jeopardy.[59] Western Europe and Japan were seen as faring far worse with oil and standard products manufactured with oil energy technology: Sunday driving bans were spread across the Continent; Italy put curfews on stores, restaurants, theaters, and even television stations; and a woman was reportedly trampled to death in a toilet paper stampede in Osaka.[60] European unity with and support for the United States were shown to be faltering as nations fought to get Arab oil,[61] a worldwide depression was forecast as possible, poor nations of the Third World allegedly could no longer continue their industrialization projects, and the Arabs reportedly contended most coldly, "Price concessions to the poor nations would amount to a kind of foreign aid—and foreign aid is the business of the [Western] industrialized world."[62] Saudi Arabia's Prime Minister of Petroleum and Mineral Resources Sheikh Ahmed Zaki Yamani was noted as wielding "greater influence over the lives of consumers in the U.S., Europe, and Japan than some of their own elected officials."[63] Meanwhile, the Arab nations were shown to make their own bilateral pacts with other nations,[64] to play states against one another,[65] to create a new sense of geopolitical order that meant Israel would have to be dismantled, to establish an international censorship of news agencies that chose to speak ill of Arab leaders,[66] and to take advantage of international disarray for their own benefit.[67]

The Arab reawakening, a discourse of powerful and vicious Arab resurgence based on oil production, obscene wealth, heinous acts of surprise attacks and brutal violence, and world economic dominance with the use of oil embargoes, seemed to flout the certainty and feel-good American self-image of liberal developmentalism, benevolent supremacy, and the

Mauldin © 1973 Chicago Sun-Times

Big Gun

Europe as well is shown vulnerable to the "evil" Arab in this cartoon from *Newsweek*, November 12, 1973.

Nixonian doctrine of the postwar decade that McAlister has explained for us. As noted by *Newsweek*, "A people once maligned as 'wogs' and nations long dismissed as backward deserts are now treated by the rest of the world with deadly seriousness."[68] One letter to the editor of *Time* said, "Hail to the rulers of the world—the Arab oil kings."[69] And the mayor of Rensselaer, Indiana, was quoted in his defense of turning off the town's 425 lights for patriotic reasons, "People thought I was a son of a b. for dousing the lights, but what do I care? If everyone in the country would make this kind of effort, we could tell the Arabs to go to hell."[70] The political events of the early 1970s gave the American popular consciousness a new nemesis, villain, and culprit that deserved to be defeated. McAlister points out that Americans lived vicariously through the tough-guy image of the Israeli soldier who courageously stood up to counteract the Arab threat during the 1976 Entebbe rescue. The discourse of this swift, decisive, and victorious use of military force thereby became a positive answer to the Vietnam syndrome and an example to the American nation.[71] The role of the "evil" Arabs wreaking havoc on America and the struggle to vanquish them were now poised as a plausible plot for popular film.

Throughout this decade, America felt ill at ease about the Middle East. American fears and feelings of impotence brought about sweeping generalizations that easily engulfed many non-Arab countries (Iran in particular) within a threatening global imaginary and thereby lumped vast populations, cultures, economies, landscapes, political events, and Islamic practices erroneously into an amorphous Otherness that was often symbolized by the image of the oil-rich, Islamic terrorist Arab. By the summer of 1979, another oil shock hit the world. The American policy of unending support for the Shah of Iran, our deputized policeman in the Middle East, had failed.[72] The Shah was losing control of his economy, his modernization program, his brutal secret police (the National Organization of Information and Security, known as SAVAK), his corrupt underlings, and, ultimately, his people and his legitimacy. The Ayatollah Khomeini, living in exile in France, called for his overthrow, a turn away from secularism, and a reorientation toward Islam. Massive riots rocked Iran, and its oil fields were closed down by striking workers, who opposed the Shah and supported Khomeini. Meanwhile, OPEC members no longer restricted the price of oil among themselves: any price that could be gained by any producing nation was fair game — a practice Yergin refers to as "leapfrogging" or a "free-for-all."[73] Price hikes were higher than the Carter administration considered reasonable. In America's time of despair, the Arabs seemingly celebrated and later even blamed us for our overuse of energy and our poor economic performance.[74] A scramble for the available supply among purchasers ensued because the price on any given day would be worse on the morrow.[75] Despite Saudi Arabia's disavowal of such pricing tactics, Americans once again viewed OPEC (popularly synonymous with the Arabs)[76] as taking advantage of a bad situation. By mid-1979, President Jimmy Carter and the leaders of the industrialized nations called new price increases "unwarranted" and the situation looked as if OPEC had "the industrial world over a barrel."[77] America, it was predicted, would have the sourest Fourth of July ever, and gas lines, frustrations, and riots would bring Americans to fisticuffs among themselves.[78] And by October 1979, the prediction became that "consuming countries can do little but swallow further price increases and almost nothing at all to ward off the possibility of future shortages."[79]

In the meantime, Zbigniew Brzezinski, President Carter's national se-

HERBLOCK—WASHINGTON POST

Leader of the Free World

In 1979, OPEC refused to cap the price of oil. President Carter denounced the price increases, and America was predicted to have the sourest July 4th ever. By October of that year, predictions were that consumer nations could do little but swallow further price increases and accept the possibility of future shortages. Cartoon published in *Time*, June 25, 1979.

curity advisor, announced a new cognitive map for America: "The Crescent of Crisis." This crescent of crisis was envisaged as those states that stretched along the shores of the Indian Ocean—from Turkey all the way to India—and, more frighteningly, were either close to or shared borders with the USSR. It was an area in which Moscow could make headway against Washington, and in which the Soviets had designs for the oil they would need in the future. Iran, the citadel of U.S. military and economic strength in the Middle East, was centered at the borderline of the spheres of the two world powers. Here, a new Kiplingesque "great game" was at hand: now between the United States and the USSR, and the new big prize was oil. "I'd have to be blind or Pollyannish not to recognize that there are dark clouds on the horizon," stated Brzezinski.[80] The eventual loss of Iran was considered a great blow to the United States. It was another failure, weakness, and inability of an unsophisticated American policy to protect national interests. *Time* magazine brought together seven policy experts to discuss U.S. policy in the crescent of crisis, and the tone of their discussion conveyed that "the U.S. has long since lost its power to do almost anything it wanted around the world, the kind of overwhelming role it enjoyed in the aftermath of World War II."[81] The Carter administration's attempts at brokering peace between Egypt and Israel were seen as preoccupations that squandered opportunities to foresee the fall of the Shah, and, at the same time, only united many Arab states in their drive to destroy such a peace.[82]

Then, the American hostage crisis in Tehran of November 1979 came as a new low in the American self-image in relation to the Middle East. Although Iran is not an Arab country, the hostage crisis created another, albeit erroneous, global imaginary for Americans. This map, according to McAlister, trumped oil wealth as a symbol and lumped Arabs and Iranians into a total realm of terrorism, wherein Islam became the new signifier of the region, and an inimical "Islamic World" seemed to be the new categorical label of the Middle East that even threatened the Middle East itself. Facing this new Islamic World, America, "the mightiest power on earth[,] found itself engaged in a test of will with an unruly gang of Iranian students and an ailing zealot of 79 [Khomeini]."[83] At issue was America's decision to grant the Shah, ill with cancer, a temporary visa for medical treatment in the United States. The new Iranian government saw this as political asylum and demanded the Shah's return to Iran for trial. If the Shah was not returned, the fifty-two captured Americans would be put on trial for espionage, with possible death sentences threatened. America, as it viewed itself, was being blackmailed for a decision looked upon as a humanitarian exercise of sovereignty. Moreover, it was a decision that upheld our ideological view that America is a haven for refugees.[84] Under a new siege, "the most serious international crisis for the U.S. since Viet Nam,"[85] emanating from the Middle East, and lasting over 444 days, America could not seem to achieve its former experiences of triumph. During this time, American embassies in the Islamic world were attacked, leading to a reduction in personnel for reasons of security, and travel to eleven Muslim countries was discouraged. Muslims were thought to hate Americans.[86] Americans had to endure televised pictures of Middle Easterners burning the U.S. flag and their president in effigy, blindfolding and binding their compatriots, causing emotional pain to families of the hostages, and chanting death calls and threats to their nation. With the failure in April 1980 of a rescue attempt known as Operation Eagle Claw, the president of the United States "was forced to live out his term against a televised backdrop of unending captivity and humiliation that seemed to highlight American impotence."[87] The impotence Americans felt with respect to this global imaginary and in the face of this humiliation gave rise to a powerful desire to take revenge on the Middle East[88] and, I might add, the "evil" Arab image, which had become convincing to them through their discourse on foreign policies.

Against this backdrop, my inquiry begins into the prejudicial portrayals of "evil" Arabs in American film. It begins with this new image of the "evil" Arabs and the Middle East of the 1970s, according to which they, along with the realizations resulting from Vietnam, Watergate, the Pentagon Papers, and the other notorious events of the decade, upset the place, policies, limitlessness, and strength that America had envisioned for itself in the postwar world. Our perception of their ransacking our self-confidence was an overturning of our American mythic structure as it related to our ideologies of politics, economics, and security. I shall look at those instances in which popular films, in step with this way of perceiving the Arabs in "real life," find ways to plausibly portray them wreaking such havoc through the narratives and images of the stories these films present. And unlike many films wherein good overrules evil in the end, in films of Orientalist fear the lines of victory are not so certain (*The Exorcist, Rollover,* and *Black Sunday*).

In the 1980s and 1990s, America declared a struggle against terrorism and retaliated against the global imaginaries of the Middle East, which further emphasized the ethnic imaginary of the "evil" Arabs. America under Ronald Reagan professed to stand firm on terrorism. However, with the killing of 241 U.S. Marines in a bomb attack in Beirut in 1983, it pulled out of Lebanon as a professed peacekeeping force. Furthermore, with the hijacking of TWA 847 in 1985, it, too, found itself unable to end the standoff with a decisive victory. American response to the hijacking of the *Achille Lauro* by Palestinian terrorists was different. When the hijackers surrendered the ship in exchange for safe passage, the Reagan administration used American fighter jets to force the Egyptian airliner carrying the terrorists to land in Sicily. Italian authorities took the Palestinian terrorists into custody.

In reaction to the bombing of a Berlin nightclub frequented by American soldiers, the Reagan administration bombed Libya in the name of self-defense against Libya's state-sponsored terrorism against the West. "I warned that there should be no place on Earth where terrorists can rest and train and practice their deadly skills. I meant it," Reagan told Americans in an address to the nation on April 14, 1986, to explain the attacks on Libya.[89] However, Washington's secret deals with Iran in the Iran-Contra affair blurred the administration's hard-line, blanket approach to states that sponsored terrorism. Violence in the Middle East continued to fill U.S. news programs and newspapers throughout the 1980s and early 1990s: Beirut was now at the center of a civil war and became a battleground of destruction; Iraq and Iran were fighting a costly war and causing oil prices to soar again; and Israelis and Palestinians were clashing in the popular uprising of the Intifada. The bombing of Pan Am 103 close to the Christmas holiday of 1988 once again shattered America's sense of civilian immunity from Arab terrorism, thereby emphasizing the continuing and close threat of the "evil" Arabs.

Ultimately, the first war with Iraq (1991) during the Bush administration would convince many that America had finally kicked the Vietnam syndrome, and, according to McAlister, at the same time vanquished the experience of Tehran even if only through an intertextual use of media coverage practices.[90] The benevolent myth that the United States stood up against tyranny over the helpless was employed in a narrative of the arrogant Arab despot (Saddam Hussein) waging war against his Arab neighbors. The administration painted a picture in which the United States had to stand up to this despot to save the Middle East and the world of nations along with the principles of honor, freedom, democracy, justice, and peace. For many, the victory in the Gulf War only proved that Vietnam and Tehran had been incidents in which America could have won if only American leadership had allowed America to win. America could now engage the worst of the world's dictators, in this case an "evil" Arab dictator, whenever and wherever, swiftly, in league with allies, and with the lowest number of casualties on its side. And yet, the "evil" Arabs continued to wreak havoc in popular films. The "evil" Arabs now undermined America in ways that were less overtly inimical, but rather made Americans question themselves in this newfound self-esteem, and lines drawn between good and evil continued to be ambiguous because the methodologies of our triumphs remained in question. The Vietnam period still

haunted us, postmodernism undermined our certainty, and multiculturalism broke down metanarratives (*Three Kings* and *Rules of Engagement*).

The new, improved, and coordinated terrorist attacks of al-Qaeda on
American targets at home and overseas during the Clinton period, and its
sublime attacks of September 11, 2001, begat a new era of fear of the "evil"
Arabs that broadened this fear to Muslims everywhere. The fears of the
1970s of Middle East violence coming to America had finally been realized: the "evil" Arabs have arrived; they live among us and are funded with
the wealth of the oil economy; and they meticulously plan against us and
wait patiently to commit the most heinous of crimes. Steven Emerson's
exemplary description of an Islamic terrorist convention, which called for
the destruction of Israel and the United States and took place in (of all
places) Kansas City, aims at convincing us that the violence of the Middle
East has taken root within our borders. In the United States, according
to Emerson, these Arabs use our principles of democracy and liberties
to plot against us.[91] But to assure the American public that America is
strong, the administration of George W. Bush has embarked on a campaign that recaptures and wields American ideologies and myths of heroism and righteousness to show that the "evil" Arabs have not won and
cannot win. In the new era of "evil" Arabs, the most bizarre, yet real,
images of destruction are made rational in the contextualization of narratives in which the Arabs threaten our ideological and mythic structures,
but ultimately these structures must prove to be too strong for total annihilation. Through this conventional method we confront and understand
the horrific events and perpetrators of September 11th (*America Remembers*). Despite our military retaliations, once again the clear victor, the
righteousness of the American or the wickedness of the "evil" Arabs, remains to be determined.

As we can see from the above recollections of American popular political discourse since the 1970s, Americans have experienced an atmosphere of fear in their real lives pertaining to the Arabs and the Middle
East. The Arabs and the Middle East did not and do not always respond
to our desires as we expect them to in our political designs and schemes,
i.e., our ideologies and myths. Put another way, this ambivalence of the
"evil" Arabs upsets the entire binary system of our Orientalist project,
thus creating a sense of Orientalist fear. And yet, this very cause of fear
is why stereotype is not a good enough anchor for the prejudicial act.
Homi Bhabha's work on the colonizer's use of stereotype shows that the

stereotype never successfully fixes the colonized as the colonizer hopes.[92] Stereotyping is a continual attempt to fix the Others because we sense a "lack" within ourselves of our own stable identities. It redirects attention away from us and onto them; hence we rely on the "evil" Arabs to be as they are (*outside* Others) because their fixed being *is* what we are not (our identifiable Self, our ideal ego). And so the issue at hand might not be that the Arabs are not conforming to our expectations, but rather that we ourselves are not upholding standards or are unable to achieve expectations dictated by our ideologies and myths (as per the discussion above of the 1970s, the effectiveness and righteousness of our political policies). Our self-reliant confidence, our independence from the Other, and our self-mastery are in jeopardy.

Likewise, I suggest that the films to be analyzed in the following chapters demonstrate that we are not as stable in our ideological and mythic structures as we might profess to be, and, consequently, these films frighteningly and sadomasochistically entertain us. These structures are highly fragile, easily contested, fraught with instability and contradictions, and sometimes impossibly demanding of the world. After all, as Althusser has made us aware, they are *illusions* of our relations to reality that are only built on *allusions* to reality. The "evil" Arabs, as plausible dramatis personae of *outside* Others, bring this to light for us. This creates for us a relationship of reliance upon the Arabs and brings them ever so dangerously *inside* the identity of our Self. Since, as noted by Shaheen, filmmakers stereotype the Arabs as "evil," with anxious repetition for fixation and, following Bhabha, as a cover for our own lack, this explains why we are more likely to see the first image of the illusion of the "evil" Arab rather than accept the second image. And once the second image of our lacking Self is discernible — a source of anxiety — the perceptual slide, or the oscillating attention, between the two images is very slippery, making a fixation on the first image an ameliorative device for acknowledgment of the second.

Jack Shaheen has shown us an array of films that produce anti-Arab stereotypes, which emphasize Hollywood's racist tendencies toward the Arabs. Matthew Bernstein and Gaylyn Studlar have coordinated the identification of Orientalist films as a genre to emphasize Western fascination with the East.[93] Furthermore, Kaja Silverman has informed us that film's narrative can lure us in through ideology and make us take subjective stances. The ideology may be challenged, but many times the ideological structure is revalidated in the end.[94] Continuing this line of reasoning, I

"As Adam Smith so aptly put it . . ."

The Arabs wield Adam Smith's theory of economics against Westerners, an act of mimicry, to justify the use of the oil embargo, as shown in this cartoon from *The New Yorker,* February 25, 1974.

suggest that we look deeply at specific films' visual tropes and narrative structures and see a hybrid genre of Orientalist fear. In the chapters to follow, I will discuss only six films.[95] We can find cinematographic attempts to depict the ethnic imaginary of Arabs and the global imaginary of the Middle East in Orientalist binary tropes and stereotypes, but in these films the Arabs and their landscapes are written about and depicted in ways so as to refuse such discipline. Instead, the Arabs go on the offensive to attack not only Orientalist structures but also other American ideological and mythic structures of national Self. The heroes' victories over the Arabs are as ambiguous as the Arabs' adherence to the Orientalist binary binds. The ideological and mythic structures are threatened and placed in jeopardy, and in the end they never fully recover their previously perceived assuredness. In the meantime, the American viewing audience senses exposure of its cultural truths and self-sufficiency and is left with feelings of anxiety, but also it experiences a sadomasochistically entertaining visual and narrative ride. Like the 1980s genre of slasher films, in which the perpetrator disappears after his showdown with the hero/heroine, allowing the villain to lurk on the fringes and providing a period for him to regain his strength to come again in a sequel, the films of Orientalist fear provide no clear defeat of the Arabs, or at least no clear victory for the Americans, and keep the "evil" Arabs as recurring characters and continual objects of the prejudicial act. The absence of a decisive resolution most likely produces a shared fear in an American audience, and thereby supports prejudicial perceptions of the "evil" Arabs with an impression of universality—in our depictions of them and acceptance of such depictions.

While not all audience members may read these films in the same way, it should be acknowledged that the ideological and mythic structures are known and shared among Americans through cultural inculcation. Therefore, I agree with Francesco Casetti's belief that films prefigure and presuppose their audiences. Through their narratives and visual tropes we can discern ideologies and myths at work and, therefore, an implied viewer or the one to be interpellated. Films rely on the audience to be an interlocutor, or one with a competence of intertextual application and a repertoire of knowledge that can weave symbols and narratives to restore the richness underlying production and reception. The audience partici- pates in the film by recognizing itself therein,[96] or, as Althusser points out, by answering to being "hailed." The structural usages of Orientalism and other American ideologies and myths in this hybrid genre interpellate an audience, which I shall call an "Orientalist audience."

The Orientalist audience that I define in this book is an American audi- ence, and oftentimes I refer to this audience with "our," "we," or "us." This requires two points of clarification regarding inclusion. First of all, I in- clude in this audience all American viewers of these films that have been culturally wired with, or interpellated through, the discourses of Ameri- can politics, ideologies, myths, Orientalism, and popular culture—and this even includes those of us scholarly trained in Near East Studies. I do not intend to outwardly call us "racist" by this means, but rather wish to enlighten all of us to our human proclivities, weaknesses, and frail- ties in making sense of the world and of Others. As human beings we are all susceptible to and capable of committing the prejudicial act: dis- criminating against, scapegoating, or hating Others. When watching these films, particular audience members may discern and reject the prejudicial act put forth on the screen, I hope more often than not. This may mo- mentarily dismiss them from inclusion, making them Althusser's one out of ten not answering to the hail. Nevertheless, we all have been inculcated through our cultural ways of seeing, and so we are susceptible to lapses of clinging to these realms of "truth" for meaningful order when we do not understand or cannot comprehend the world. The chaotic and emotional experiences of September 11, 2001, may have been such a time. There- fore, I mean to encourage a self-assessment of our thoughts and actions when seeing and representing Others and to bring forth the continual self-evaluating questions of "Am I being prejudiced? Was that racist?" whenever we make or are confronted by our representations of the Middle East, the Arabs, and their cultures. To see and acknowledge our Orientalist fear and to analyze these films in this way can be instructive. Not only does such analysis provide an opportunity to flesh out the second image of the illusion, but it can make us more sophisticated in our viewing and understanding of a variety of cultural performances that profess to represent the Arabs for us. It should make us more aware of the prejudicial act as it pertains to our representations of Arabs and help in ending this pernicious habit.

Second, by defining an American Orientalist audience I do not exclude my readers of other national identities. I believe that this book can help these readers understand American films, some of our ideological and mythic structures, and our thought processes better. In the meantime, I encourage them to apply similar methodologies to their own representations of Others and to create their own self-assessments.

My methodology is clear in the following chapters. First, I choose a limited number of films so that I may devote each chapter to the scrutiny and discussion of one film. Readers should be aware that my choice of films is not based on the "quality" of the film as reflected through critical acclaim, box office success, the film studio's reputation, budget, or the celebrity of its stars, producers, and directors. I choose films that were made, released, and viewed in the period between the 1970s and the millennium years, that use Arab characters as villains, and that provide excellent examples of "evil" Arabs attacking American ideologies and myths. Second, I introduce each chapter by selecting and describing a scene that I feel captures the essence of Orientalist fear in the film. Third, I identify those ideologies and myths that the film narrative concentrates on and that the "evil" Arabs will jeopardize. From there, I tackle the film, analyzing the narrative and visual tropes with appropriate scholarly theories that help make sense of the film as a narrative of threat and exposing the prejudicial act. Readers will note that my analyses refrain from stars' and directors' experiences, behind-the-scenes events, and in-depth celebrity interviews. While I acknowledge that these sources may have their place in other film studies discussions, I choose to bring Orientalist fear to light through analyses of narratives and images as seen on the screen and contextualized with scholarly theories rather than through entertainment trivia and gossip.

Additionally, I use two approaches when discussing ideologies and myths in the chapters. Both approaches cite scholars' research into ideologies and myths and follow their summarizations of the structure, but they do differ. The first approach includes scholars who create a narrative of the myths taken from the similarities that all retellings share. Most of these scholars simply summarize the myths for their readers, describing the myths in paragraph form, and cite examples of retellings as they go along in their analyses. The second approach includes scholars who create a narrative through the Proppian method: enumerating lists of functions and sorting out paradigmatic structure from syntagmatic structure. This latter approach is useful when comparing a number of retellings of a story, when trying to pinpoint exact points of deviance from the structure, when discussing a number of dramatis personae in relation to the mythic structure, and when readers are unacquainted with narrative studies. Although this Proppian approach can be instructive in the beginning chapters (Chapters 1 and 2), I do find that it can be cumbersome for readers who must slog through and remember long lists of functions for every chapter. Even the most attentive of readers are likely to fatigue. Therefore, in Chapter 3 and the following chapters, I revert to the first approach: the paragraphed summarization of a myth. However, my discussions are still structured on narrative syntagma and character paradigms, and I expect that readers will keep these ideas in mind.

I wish to further add that not all films in this book are Hollywood productions intended first for cinematic viewing. CNN's *America Remembers,* discussed in Chapter 6, is a case in point. Projection lives in the theaters are getting shorter, and many productions extend their viewing lives through television programming and play-on-demand technology. The age of VHS and DVD, the marketing of home theater, and the production and distribution capability of media powerhouses have blurred the lines of film being consumed first or only in the movie houses. On the other hand, news compilations and documentaries have come to mimic film art. They now can incorporate and exploit the pictorial, the dramatic, the narrative, and the moods of music just like film. They, too, have made their way into the popular display cases and libraries along with other films, can mask and market themselves as blockbuster movies with scenes more real than those boasting Hollywood special effects, and as such are edited and consumed as popular film. *America Remembers*'s narrative employs the structures similar to and some of the same visual tropes as Hollywood film in order to make sense to and to match and titillate the aesthetic expectations of the Orientalist audience. Thus, the real events of September 11, 2001, have been reinvented to play like Hollywood film. Therefore, I choose to include *America Remembers* among my analyses of American popular film.

The creation of the "evil" Arabs in American popular film relies on their characteristic confrontations with our ideologies and myths, and so the Arabs, as such a set of Others, are imagined only to exist and act in relation to our ideologies and myths. We have, in a sense, distorted the Arab image with a veneer of our own concerns and self-interests. Consequently, I declare, and am certain that my readers will come to see, that when it comes to "evil" Arabs in American popular film, we have indeed crafted our very own version of Ichthyoid Man.

1 | *The Exorcist*
ASSAULT ON AMERICAN CONFIDENCE (1973)

*T*HE *Exorcist* is often considered, or at least marketed to be, the most frightening horror film in American cinema.[1] In one of its many memorable and chilling scenes, Father Karras (Jason Miller) interrogates the demon that has possessed the young girl, Regan (Linda Blair). As the screenplay notes:

> The howling ceases, and Regan's head falls back on the pillow. The whites of her eyes are exposed, as her eyes roll upward into their sockets. She rolls her head feverishly from side to side, muttering an indistinct gibberish.
> Karras: "Who are you?"
> Regan/Demon: "eno on ma I. eno on ma I."[2]

Two scenes later, Karras, having recorded these sounds, reviews them with a language lab director at Georgetown University. Karras and the film's audience learn that this "indistinct gibberish" is, in fact, English spoken backward. With a reverse play of the tape, the demon is heard to be declaring, "I am no one. I am no one."

In spite of this demon's protests, the audience should not have been, nor continue to be, fooled. The demon is simply a character constructed from our Orientalist fear. I assert in this chapter that this demon is another disturbing caricature, what Jack Shaheen calls the "Hollywood Arab."[3] This demon may confuse the audience because it is not clad with the obvious costume of the "Arab kit."[4] Nonetheless, its identification as such results from the scrutiny of the film's narrative of the Western Self and the Oriental Other. The demon is recognizable as the "evil" Arab when considering that *The Exorcist* is both a threatened colonial discovery fantasy and an aborted narrative of the American cowboy hero. This Orientalist-imagined struggle between an Eastern bogeyman (the Arab demon) and the Western hero (the exorcist), turned upside down, creates suspense, fear, and panic throughout the plot of the film. The failure of the American cowboy figure (again the exorcist) is also a source of consternation at the film's end.

Critics have discussed the source of *The Exorcist*'s capacity to terrorize the psyche of American society. They seem to agree on the interpretation that the film echoes the temper of the 1970s era, when the American public had lost faith in its institutions, changed its moral structure, become more self-indulgent, found its fascination with the paranormal, and become enthralled with apocalyptic endings of the world. In explaining this film and its meaning, these critics look toward a demonized self that is inter-textualized with the scandal of Watergate; the terror, guilt, and shame of Vietnam; the moral disintegration associated with ever-increasing di-vorce rates; a generation of rebellious and disrespectful youths; the attack on male dominance by the women's rights movement; the seeming loss of religious faith; and the ineptitude of positivism when confronted with the unexplainable.[5] Most readings of the film are well argued and worthy of consideration.

In principle, I agree with these critics that the narrative is about our struggles with our ideal egos, but I believe that they miss the film's strategy of using the "evil" Arab to expose the precariousness of our identity. I sense that these critics arrive at their particular conclusions without con-sidering the narrative of *The Exorcist* in its entirety. The conventional ap-proach of critique is to sever the film in two: the Iraq prologue or sequence (the first 10 minutes of the film) and the Georgetown scenes (the remain-ing 102 minutes).[6] The former, though, is ignored because of the assump-tion that it is lacking in importance relative to the latter. I suggest that the reason for this omission is that the Georgetown scenes contain an easily understandable and recognizable self-narrative within familiar surround-ings and provide the most dialogue (i.e., upper-middle-class America and speaking in English). It is also the portion that includes the focal event of the film, as implied by the film title: possession and exorcism; and it thus seems to beg for interpretation.

That is not to say, however, that the critics do not show an awareness of the presence of the Iraq prologue. Mainly, they hail the Iraq prologue for the setting up of recognizable noises and symbols that are repeated later in the film. This is an important point, as it ties the demon in Regan's bedroom to characteristics of evil portrayed in the Middle East. However, these critics tend to drop this issue much too soon. Mark Kermode's study of the film is a telling example. Kermode points out that the Iraq prologue sets up not only reverberating sounds and symbols, but a battle between an ancient past and a modern present. Regardless of all that occurs here, he suggests that it is "material of only minimal narrative value."[7] Tony Williams provides shot-by-shot details of the prologue in his explanation of the film.[8] But he fails to analyze many of the very events he takes the time to enumerate, and his sketchiness in describing them may exasperate the more inquisitive reader. Then, he dismisses the symbolically packed prologue as a disjunctive narrative, or rather a failure to support his own reading of the film, i.e., a chronicle of the breakdown of the American family.

Will Wright's approach to film narrative may help us in the conceptualization and contextualization of the Iraq prologue. Wright shows that myths communicate conceptual orders and modes of action to those societies that use them. Two points are worth borrowing from Wright: First, Wright stresses the importance of symbols presented in binary oppositions because they create and distinguish characters of social types. This he likens to paradigmatic structure. But Wright further insists that syntagmatic structure must also be part of the analysis. He points out that syntagmatic structure tells how these social types interact and what they communicate to the society as socially acceptable actions and relationships for everyday life.[9] To make his point clearer, Wright uses the analogy of language, where paradigmatic social types and the symbols that represent them act as words, while syntagmatic narrative is the grammar that links them into a sentence of meaning. Second, Wright emphasizes that all narratives describe change. Therefore, he argues, events are arranged into a beginning, a middle, and an end to explain how a situation moved from one state to the next. Many narratives require the use of "complex middles," which are stories embedded within the story, but all such inner narratives are important to understanding the broader, outermost change. Wright is ardent in his belief that the story presents all of the information necessary to understand the change: "That is, everything in a story is important to the story. Unlike life, there is no extraneous information. If there were, the story would become boring (unsuccessful), so that later we would ask, 'What was the point of that, or that?'"[10]

In following Wright's theory (and I shall return to him again later in this chapter), critics like Kermode see the Iraq prologue as a paradigmatic structure, but they do not discuss how and why the symbols interact to create the narrative. Instead of analysis, Kermode's discussion of narrative becomes a detailed retelling of the film's events. To disguise this shortcoming, Kermode cleverly peppers his review with behind-the-scenes trivia to keep his readers interested. Williams's approach, in contrast, is more analytical, but it cuts out the narrative's beginning, relies upon its complex middle and end, and points out the unsuccessful story line of the film. Without a more concerted reconciliation of the Iraq prologue with the remainder of the movie, critics are missing its importance as a contextual frame that director William Friedkin and the novel's and screenplay's author William Peter Blatty so meticulously put before the audience during the first ten minutes. The practice of reading the Georgetown scenes as separate from the Iraq prologue changes the meaning of the film. Where such an approach would make more sense is in the film that was never produced, but initially put forth, in William Peter Blatty's original screenplay.[11] The Iraq prologue is eliminated from this version, and the proposed film begins with a series of images of landmarks in Georgetown and Washington, D.C. This "Washington prologue" would have placed the reason for the focal events solely within the United States. Previous knowledge of the demon, otherwise gained in the Iraq prologue, would have been withheld from the audience members, who would now have to spend their time searching to discover its evil origin domestically. Culpability for disturbance and murder would be fully cast upon the characters of the story as they deal with their own inner psychological demons. The audience members would be finding themselves watching a mystery or detective film rather than a film that is recognizable as a thrilling horror movie.

One possible reason that the Iraq prologue has been ignored is the critics' lack of awareness of, or reluctance to use, the critical approach of postcolonial studies. To be sure, Edward Said's book *Orientalism* and the flood of scholarly studies that followed came five years after the film debuted. However, these studies, known under the genre of postcolonial studies, have become powerful keys to unlocking deeper readings and reevaluations of classic works of literature. Postcolonial studies encourages us to reread canonical texts while questioning their established modes of representation of colonized subjects, their perspectives of realism, and their constructions of power in service to the colonists in narrative. As a result, postcolonial studies has provided old works with new and enlightened interpretations. As many scholars have shown, the postcolonial approach can be applied to visual studies as well.

Ella Shohat is one of the creative scholars who have taken the awareness of postcolonial studies into the cinematic realm. Her article "Gender and Culture of Empire" sets forth a structural format of Western films that picture Western power over colonized territories and bodies. The structural format asserts that the allegorical Western hero, being of virile stature, travels to and engages the outside world, i.e., the Orient. Oftentimes, and important to this discussion, the American version of the hero is depicted with the disposition of the archetypical cowboy. This hero exerts his sex appeal, colonialist gaze, scientific knowledge, authoritative language, technology, inclination to civilize, astuteness, and rectitude over people that are his binary opposites. The Orient is, for him, the other side of the looking glass, and its cultures are the antitheses of his own. The Orientalist film creates a masculine/feminine aspect to the story. Here, the Western hero uses his phallic powers as he travels to an awaiting, virginal locale. He then rightfully penetrates into the feminized body of the Oriental land. He strips the land of its enigma as he opens it up to discovery, appropriates its mysterious treasures that its indigenes cannot fully appreciate, and saves it from its own fate of physical and mental disorder.[12]

Shohat's structural format identifies an Orientalist myth, or what I would call a classical "Orientalist fantasy," of the audience's own imagination of Self and Other through film. When in balance, it can celebrate Western achievement, justify Western expansion, and assuage Western doubt. But when it is askew, it can produce anxiety for the audience. It can render our self-image questionable, weaken our imagined stature, and expose the paradoxes of our cultures. The mere thought of the fantasy in jeopardy incites Orientalist fear. *The Exorcist,* the most acclaimed horror film of 1970s America, accomplishes this exactly as a threatened narrative. It crafts its horror through the threat to mythical fantasy, to which we have become culturally accustomed but which we have only recently been able to explain with the advances in postcolonial studies. The film puts its viewers on the defensive by upsetting their visions of Orientalism, those ideological "facts" in their minds. It teaches us, as the viewers, to fear the possibility of such a reversal coming true to life. Moreover, it identifies the culprit as Arab. The tactic is to disenfranchise us from our concepts of place; powers of gaze, knowledge, and language; and ultimately our superior self-images. It leaves us flailing to regain control but always keeps such control just out of our reach.

Primarily, the film's strategy seems to create a visual scenario of an Orientalist Hell, a proper Oriental demon, and a weakened Western hero. Hell, Satan's kingdom in the underworld with its demonic inhabitants, is much like the far-out galaxies and their inhabitants in science fiction films, inasmuch as both must be constructed by the human mind. *The Exorcist* uses some of the Western conventions of Hell and the Orient that have become embedded in our minds. The concept of Hell traditionally starts with, as Piero Camporesi suggests, the opposite of what one knows, what one values, and what one desires.[13] If the Orientalist dominates and colonizes place, then Orientalist Hell must be that topsy-turvy land that the Orientalist cannot control with his powers of gaze, knowledge, and language, and moral and physical superiority. Here, the order of nature, as known to the Orientalist, is nonexistent. Confusion undermines certainty. The five senses are assaulted at every turn. The distinctions between "us" and the demons, the dwellers of Hell, are not only blurred but also redrawn so that these demons may overpower us, control us, and speak for us. The film establishes this Orientalist Hell in the Iraq prologue and then perpetuates this image in the Georgetown scenes. What happens in the Georgetown portion of the film is therefore narratively linked to the Iraq prologue. Separation between the two segments is feasible only when based upon geography, but not when based upon narrative integrity.

The film begins with the establishment of place in the Iraq prologue. Like the Orientalist fantasy, views of this non-Occidental place are shown to be otherworldly. The audience is taken to the Middle East with a performance of the muezzin's call to prayer. It is peculiar that the sun shines differently in this land. As an Orientalist trope, the other world is always trapped in a state of timelessness. The sun, when shown in the film, does not move here, although the sky does change color from the grayish morning light to the blazing high noon to the redness of twilight. The sun, as a marker of time, is always in the same place.

The viewers' sight is drawn to the colossal ruins of an ancient Mesopotamian site and sublime desert rock formations with the change of scenes. The land is parched, dusty, and monochrome. It is filled with stones and jagged rock formations, scarred with pits, and linked by confusing labyrinths. It is properly staffed with the Oriental icons of shepherds and their flocks, along with a camel caravan.

However, this place is not a blissful, virginal, and agricultural scene of Orientalist fantasy. Its chance at fecundity seems long past. It is, as the audience is informed, Northern Iraq, and it captures the fantasized characteristics of medieval Hell. It is a wretched land, scorched by that strange and fiery sun disk, and seemingly still smoldering. When one approaches the land from outside, the sky glows with a reddish hue while inside the sun shines a brilliant day light. The audience may recall Dante's description of his entry into the City of Dis. When Dante approaches the city of Lower Hell in Canto VIII, he converses with his guide Virgil:

But lamentation smote mine ears upon,
Whence I look forward with mine eyes dilate.
And the good Master [Virgil] said: "Now, O my son,
The city named of Dis is nigh at hand,
With heavy citizens, great garrison."
And I: "Already in the valley stand
Its mosques, O Master, and to me they show
Vermilion as if issuing from the brand."
And he made answer: "The eternal glow
Of inward flame kindles that ruddy glare,
As thou perceivest in this Hell below."[14]

Northern Iraq is a place of whirlwinds, noise, and probably strong smell. It further fits a medieval description of Hell as "the great workshop of pain where devils, those indefatigable metal workers[,] hammer without a moment's respite."[15] An amorphous legion of bodies, shabbily dressed with kaffiyeh-covered heads and faces, feverishly strike the land and break away rocks with the overhead swings of their hammers, shovels, and pick-axes; some scrape away the soil with their trowels. They exist among the echoes of indecipherable yells, songs, and chants that come from all of them but, because they have little facial recognition, not from anyone in particular. Thus, these beings are part of this place's scenery. They are the inhabitants of this Hell.

In this place there is only one white man: Father Lankester Merrin (Max von Sydow). His white skin is shown to matter in this place when his visual introduction to the audience is presented contrastingly through a darker body's legs that frame his body. Moreover, he is the first human face that the camera lens permits us to scrutinize. He wears the costume of a Western archaeologist and the wide-brimmed hat of a cowboy. In this landscape that is devised to alienate the Orientalist audience, these signifiers become familiar and welcomed signposts that heighten the audience's identification with Merrin. They act as the initially articulated "hailings" of interpellation, a point of suture, for the Orientalist audience. The audience can easily discern him as the hero: He will be the exorcist.

Shohat states that the audience will approach the land through the hero's experiences, stripping the land of its enigma through his eyes.[16] If this holds true, we are, through him, even further sutured into the film. We will identify with him, since he holds the keys to our imagined ideological self. His experiences will become ours. This symbiosis, then, as it relates to *The Exorcist,* is the beginning of our spiral into a hellish abyss. Orientalist fantasy is not found here. Merrin is not the archetypical hero viewers would like, but he is the only hero provided. His is unlike the youthful and quick body of the Arab boy that has led us to him, here being akin to the rabbit that led Alice down the rabbit hole. Merrin's body is a contrast to the strong bodies that move the earth. Merrin, this vicarious image of ourselves, is slow, old, and sickly. He has difficulty getting up, and he walks unsteadily about the pits. Even his hat, distinct from the kaffiyehs, is shaken by the whipping whirlwinds, and he fumbles to keep it in place.

As Shohat notes, the Oriental desert is a metaphor of a world ruled by the "out-of-control *id.*"[17] When Merrin penetrates the dry and dark orifice of this aggressive, feminine land, he is unlucky, because this place does not conceal or give birth to great treasures. It is a decaying land, as tritely signified by the fly that lands upon his hand. At best it holds broken shards of lamps, some arrowheads, and coins from its former inhabitants. A Saint Joseph's medallion that seems out of place is found, and its presence shows that Merrin is not even the first Westerner to penetrate the land. Its real treasure is not to be treasured at all. The jagged cavity, like a *vagina dentata,* contains an earth-covered amulet of evil. Merrin unleashes its spirit when he pries open the clay egg, and it escapes with the whirling wind.

An Orientalist audience needs a stronger man than Merrin to act as a hero in this place. The film has taken away one of the greatest of Orientalist powers: the gaze.[18] From the start of the film, the audience has been left in the dark with a blackened screen. We could only find our way with the help of our ears. The sounds of an eerie drone, the nerve-grating squeaks of glass pieces rubbing against one another, and the red signposts of credits were our only reference points. The muezzin's call to prayer, incomprehensible to non-Arabic-speaking Americans, is the only other guide into this place. Although the audience's sight is temporarily restored when viewing icons and a land that it can assemble and recognize as the Middle East, the audience is at the same time kept from categorizing and taking control over it. The continual sweep of the camera does not allow a moment to fix upon the land, and it does not allow scrutiny of or a chance to compartmentalize a face.

When the viewers are finally able to see Merrin, they can see that he, like them, does not have the power of gaze either. Linda Steet's study of traditional *National Geographic* images finds the normative relationship in archaeological digs is one in which the Western archaeologist stares down upon the landscape and the Arab diggers. The Western man is "the monarch-of-all-I-survey."[19] Here, in *The Exorcist,* the Arab boy stands above Merrin and stares down upon him when Merrin is first introduced to the audience. Merrin must look up, squinting under the boy's gaze. In a later scene in a teahouse, he trembles and fumbles for his medicine. The pounding of drums and the incessant beating of metal weigh down on him. Merrin suffers from a weak heart that is particularly vulnerable in this environment, and we can feel the added pressure that he is under from the panoptical view of the Arabs. Much like John Ellis notes, our cinematic experience tells us that we, the audience, *are* the voyeurs. We should be able to see without being seen.[20] Our voyeurship should give us security in our relationship to those in the images. Here, however, our voyeurship is put into question and even threatened. We think we are looking at the Orientalized Arabs, but the two old Arab men in the teahouse may actually be boring into us with their eyes. Merrin sits in the café almost comatose, with an unconscious look into space. When he diverts his eyes from the scruffy waiter, this waiter keeps him within his gaze. In the next scene, Merrin, together with the audience, is implied to be as sightless and as helpless as an elderly Arab who is led up a steep incline by a more agile and assuredly sighted Arab.

The Arabs continually and maniacally beat at shoe leather, at iron, and at wood. Steet points out that it is a common Orientalist trope to show Arabs in frenzy, placing them always within the realm of volatility.[21] Like the demons of medieval Hell, this essentialized activity is presented to us as the Arabs' profession. When the Arabs are not doing this, they stare at Merrin or, even worse, act indifferent to his existence. Even when they look at him, and us, they do so with an intimidating gaze and show their menacing physical features. The blacksmith stares with one eye. The milky white of the other eye captures our sight, forcing us to look at him, but always in submission to his good eye. His gaze upon Merrin seems to snatch away Merrin's breath. Merrin's already frail condition is weakened even further. He wanders through the labyrinths of the village, whose buildings resemble the ruins of the dig. Here, an Arab woman stares at him from above through her black shroud while other shrouded and phantomlike women pass by without acknowledging him. While he is in the café, the street activity of horse carriages and pedestrians goes on as if he is not there. Later, in the village labyrinths, a rumbling carriage knocks him off balance, almost killing him. The black-shrouded body inside, a woman featured with darkened eyes and smirking grin, chills us. This is not only because of her physical appearance that surprises us but also because she is indifferent to his condition. She invades our visual space and disappears just as we are getting a visual fix on her. To the audience, this covered woman appears and disappears, as frighteningly as a Halloween ghost.

Language, too, has been taken from the audience and from the hero. The hero should, according to Shohat, walk through the land "blessed with the divine prerogative of naming the elements of the scene about him."[22] But from the very beginning we were robbed of speech. The film plays on our lack of knowledge and familiarity with the Middle East and the Arabic language. The muezzin's words are, for many, incomprehensible, and subtitles are *not* supplied. The muezzin's call pierces our ears. At the same time, the film's title, so associated with horror, appears on the screen and affronts our eyes. The foreign cadence of his voice over the film's title and landscape is highlighted, not the meaning of his call. Norman Daniel's study of Western views of Islam tells us that the muezzin's call is traditionally, and quite ignorantly, resented by the West as a triumphant proclamation of an alien faith to the world.[23] Since such viewers do not comprehend the call, it becomes just another strange and odd sound attributable to this Hell. Merrin is not the first to speak in the film. In fact, he only speaks when confronted first in Arabic. He responds with hesitancy, without breath, in submission, and only in Arabic. Those in the audience who do not speak this language reach for the familiar to create "normalcy." Rumbling wheelbarrows, rhythmic hammering, tumbling rocks, and growling dogs locked in struggle become natural signifiers to their signifieds for us, far more than the words of these strange utterances to their subtitled ideas.

Even the clock on the wall appears odd. For an Orientalist audience, the numbers are almost readable. Attempting to reconcile them to our knowledge, we can distinguish that some sevens appear backward and the zero is in the place of the five. The number one is rightly positioned and so is the nine, but a seven is in the place of the six. Words, too, are written in this other world, but the Arab hand writes it backward in comparison to our own writing. The words look twisted, but we know that they mean something. As we struggle to make sense of the writing, we scan the Arab curator's paper and pick out the most recognizable shapes. For a moment, two drawings seem to almost represent the shape of the United States. Paranoia grabs us as we try to figure out what he is stating about us in his writing above and underneath these familiar shapes. Then, when he flicks his left wrist, we realize his writing is in relation to a broken piece of tablet. And with the mention of "evil," the clock abruptly stops. Time in this place is abstract. While the audience and the hero notice the abrupt stopping of the clock, the Arab curator only keeps his gaze upon the hero and thereby dismisses the disruption of time, marked on this strange clock and in the context of evil, as normal.

As Merrin drives his weathered jeep, his view of the road appears obscured. The crack in the windshield must obstruct his sight, again keeping him from the full powers of gaze. The Arab guards with piercing eyes rush at him and the audience with the barrels of their guns aimed at both. Once Merrin acknowledges them, they walk away without returning his wave, or a spoken greeting in kind, and apparently annoyed. He follows a difficult and rock-cluttered pathway down a hill and up to a mound. There, he finds himself caught in a crossfire of gazes. An old Arab watches him from behind, while the statue of a half-man/half-beast, the ancient demon Pazuzu, catches him from the front. The demon statue displays an erect male organ in phallic contrast to Merrin's perceived impotence. Its gaping and jagged-toothed maws, reminiscent of the previous *vagina dentata,* give Pazuzu a monstrous appearance and threatening character. Then the camera shot pulls away and shows the hero in a familiar setup of a staged Wild Western showdown.

The Iraq prologue has much to do with the story to come. As we can now see, it is more than just the assemblage of reverberating sounds and visuals noted by Kermode and Williams. It sets up the origin of evil by creating a world of evil. Paul Oppenheimer has identified the motifs of evil worlds as depicted in film, text, and paintings. First among these motifs are a landscape and environment "that [appear] exotically torn, wrenched, and shredded, in which time seems not only out of joint but absent, or reversed, or anachronistically jumbled."[24] In the second motif, there is a surrealistic mixing of straight naturalism with fantasy, and these mesh until one no longer knows what one can and cannot do, or what in fact may happen. In the third motif, there is a sense of helplessness in this geography. The fourth motif includes a collapse of language. Here the evil figures take command over language. The protagonists, in the meantime, lose control over language and succumb to the point that they are rendered speechless. Another motif is the extremity of the evil world, which denies the existence of typical, average, and middle-class settings. Only the extremes of lavish wealth, magnificent opulence, abject poverty, and shocking depravity rule here. The final motif is the repetitious behavior of demons and victims, who always seem to do the same sorts of things, governed by their unquenchable appetites.[25]

If Northern Iraq is depicted as the land of evil, then its inhabitants, the Arabs, must be its demons. Unlike our hero, the Arabs have not been given much facial recognition. The moving camera prevents us from looking at them and recognizing them as human beings. Similar to the recovered stone faces from the archaeological dig and the amulet head, whose detailed features have disappeared, many of the faces of the Arabs wearing their Oriental garb are only partially seen because of the swift camera movements. When their faces are seen, they are often shown to be physically repulsive, like the Pazuzu statue and its vicious-looking mouth. Hence, they become amorphous, seemingly sharing characteristics, heredity, and race. Everything in this Hell, except for our hero and ourselves, belongs in this land. The language of the inhabitants is disarming, their world is full of peculiar sounds, their activities are limited in scope but frantic, their faces are menacing, and their gaze is overpowering. The hero, in comparison, appears weak. He has little voice and displays little knowledge. Together with the hero, we also become weaker as the story progresses into this Hell. Merrin is not the dominant figure here, as Marsha Kinder and Beverle Houston maintain. Rather, I suggest, he is the dominated.[26]

The Georgetown scenes continue the threat to Orientalist fantasy, but now at a slower pace. The fantasy, as stated earlier, involves the hero traveling to and encountering the Orient. The hero is the masculine character who penetrates this female land and saves it from its inherent chaos. He overcomes and overpowers the indigenes with his masculinity, gaze, knowledge, language, technology, inclination to civilize, and moral rectitude. Now, the overpowering evil that was cultivated and set free in the Iraq prologue will penetrate our Western land, render us feminine, drive us into disorder, leave us speechless, and bring us to the brink of despair. It will attempt to create an environment similar to the one from which it originated. As with *The Exorcist*'s technique in the Iraq prologue, the film portrays the acts of the Arab demon by dismantling our sense of place, suspending our gaze, deconstructing our knowledge, attacking our language, and destroying the images we have of ourselves as being superior. This technique assaults the certainty of America's self-image as a modern, civilized, righteous, and secure place.

The viewers feel rescued from this Middle East Hell when the Georgetown scenes depict the familiar scenery of the American middle class that we recognize, or wish to recognize, as "home." It is a place where motorized traffic passes in an orderly way and emits a soft humming sound. It is a place where friendly dogs bark, bacon sizzles, coffee brews, and beds are comfortable. Here, the sun rises and sets within the workday as expected, lights turn on with the click of a switch, and the days of autumn are invigoratingly crisp and picturesque. The buildings are strong and symmetrical stone, brick, and wooden structures that are well maintained and remain intact. Green lawns surround these structures, and paved walkways weaving through them are clearly marked, orderly, and accommodating. People have discernible faces, differing names, relationships with each other, and distinct occupations. Moreover, they communicate with one another, and with us, in English. Their intentions are, therefore, well displayed. They often acknowledge the presence of each other. They live in our nation's capital, a metropole of power and civilization. The Georgetown home is clean, bright, and tastefully furnished. Clocks are readable. Books, dishes, furniture, and knickknacks are all organized and properly arranged for display. Dirt, dust, stench, noise, although possible, just do not belong here in this staged world. Such scenes set up this world in order to establish its normalcy, its relationship to the Orientalist audience, and its contrast to the just witnessed, evil character of the Middle East. They also give the audience a sense of comfort that heightens the ensuing shock, discomfort, and fear in the audience when the comfort is taken away by an Arab villain.

Here, as in the Iraq prologue, we encounter characters through whom we will experience the story. The story line introduces Chris MacNeil (Ellen Burstyn), mother, divorcée, and actress. Secondly, we meet Father Damien Karras, priest, expert psychologist, and son. Once again, neither character is the strong, superior protagonist with whom we wish to vicariously associate ourselves. We come to pity them, rather than admire them. Both of them remind us of our own character flaws, uncertainties, weaknesses, and repressions. They become easy pickings for a strong assailant. Chris becomes a victim of attack as the demon takes away her daughter's personality and possesses her body. We watch Chris become confused, helpless, frustrated, and desperate as she searches for answers and for someone to help drive out the phenomena occurring in her home. Father Karras is a man with conflicts that disturb the serenity of his character: he is a priest with the responsibility to uphold religious faith, to counsel those in need, and to provide moral guidance; he is also a psychiatrist with the highest credentials and thinks scientifically. This dual role misleads him in his diagnosis of the events to follow. He continually searches for a clinical answer to what we know is really the Arab demon's possession of Regan. His faith is in question, and he is distracted from his job. Moreover, he feels a sense of failure as a son because he cannot provide for his aging, lonely, and impoverished mother.

The Orientalist fantasy should promote our self-esteem and provide us security in the moral uprightness of our civilization. The aforementioned world is the fantasy world that we share with Chris MacNeil, although she is about to lose her grip on this world. Father Karras, a character representing American repression, strains the certainty of our self-image. We know that America is not just an upper-middle-class world. Karras's return home to visit his mother in a ghetto apartment in New York is a journey into this socioeconomic underside of fantasized American life. The screeching wheels of an underground train, the steam escaping from the dark labyrinth of the subway, the bum lying in his own filth, the littered streets, the graffiti-covered walls, the dilapidated buildings of the neighborhood, the dark and musty apartment home, the old and lonely Mrs. Karras, and the sounds of the ethnic radio broadcasts that keep her company and help her pass time are the repressed images of an America that we know exists, but that we would rather not consider in our Orientalist fantasies. The scene showing Karras's walk down his neighborhood street symbolizes well the conflict of fantasy and reality. The magnificent structures of rich Manhattan are seen towering in the distance and yet are removed from this corner of America. Karras's walk is a replay of the scenes in the Middle East where the colossal ruins of a past civilization tower over the labyrinths of the archaeological dig and the Arab village. Father Karras's face, as he ventures through this American ghetto, shows discomfort similar to the expression of Father Merrin's face during his walk in the Middle East. At the same time, both are so dissimilar to Chris's experiences and expression during her walk in Georgetown.

The arrival of the Arab demon in America ushers Karras and Chris into their own hellish worlds. Karras proceeds further into his Hell when he walks through the mental ward of a New York hospital. Like the Hell of Enlightenment Europe, what Camporesi calls "the hospital syndrome,"[27] this Hell is the hospital filled with mental illnesses that take over the mind, leaving its inhabitants, patients as we choose to call them, listless, distant, repetitive, and unaware of their actions. These inhabitants are separated from the rest of humanity, behind glass and bars, and locked away with a key because their condition may infect the healthy. Karras must visit his mother here in the mental ward after she is overcome by hysteria. A shaken Karras, a man whose scientific training allows him to distinguish people based upon their mental fitness, finds his own parent committed and bound to a bed. His uncle accuses Karras of shirking his responsibilities as a son: if he had chosen a more lucrative career path, his mother would not be in this Hell, but in the posh and heavenly world of Park Avenue. In this awful place, Karras tries to explain to her that he is not responsible for her committal, but she rebuffs him in the final moments of her life. His dream sequence replays his guilt and the hellish reality in which he finds himself. The Arab demon encroaches upon him. It takes advantage of his weakness as it penetrates his dream and appears in the symbolized form of the black dog and the white-faced spirit. The white-faced spirit, momentarily piercing through the blackened screen, is reminiscent of the Arab woman in the carriage, whose face can be glimpsed through her black veil.

The demon brings Chris's comfortable world to a screeching halt. The initial setup of place shows those things that will be under attack. The comfortable Georgetown home is rattled by unexplainable occurrences. Family pictures topple and electrical surges make phones ring erratically and lights flicker. Regan's bedroom becomes a frightening place, distinct from the rest of the home; so much so, that we are conditioned to fear the stairway-path leading up to it and the opening of the door that reveals what is occurring inside. This bedroom is freezing cold, distinguishing it as a world apart from the warmth of the home. Inside there are whirlwinds of fury that toss the personal objects of the little girl into disarray. Heavy pieces of furniture move about as if of their own volition and are wielded as weapons against those people who enter the room. Eventually, objects like the bubbling fish tank, which brought a sense of natural serenity and recognition to the room, and the pictures on the wall must be removed to save them from destruction. The bedroom, too, becomes as bleak as a hospital's rubber room and takes on the padded bed and restraining straps of a psychiatric ward. By the time of the exorcism, the bedroom is virtually empty, a zone of extreme cold temperature, monochrome in color, and abnormal in atmosphere. It lacks the accoutrements of civilization. Recalling its origin in the Middle East, the Arab demon has converted it into a chamber of Hell.

The Arab demon denies our gaze here as well. We hear it, we see the characters react to its smell, we witness the cold it produces from the breaths and shivers of the characters, we see its horrific effects on Regan's face and its reflection in the faces of other characters, but we do not see the demon itself. Its strength in terrorizing us is inherent in its invisible presence. We can hear it in the attic and can identify it by its rumbling and tumbling sounds that are similar to those made by the Arabs in the Middle East. It shows the same eyes as that of the Arab blacksmith. The cold wind gusts streaming through the open window into the warm home mark the trail of its alien penetration into our world. The deep green vomit and phlegm discharged from the depth of the girl's body manifest the pollution characteristic of an alien presence in our community. The Arab demon pushes the planchette across the Ouija board before our eyes, but only when it wants to do so. It moves furniture, opens drawers, and tosses the girl about with its invisible hands. Its ghostly presence is obvious in the fiery flare-up of Chris's candle in the attic and in the sudden appearance of vandalism upon a Catholic statue. As noted earlier, it infiltrates Karras's dreams as the black dog and the white face; but since this is shown in lightning-quick flashes, we are not sure of what exactly we have seen. The Arab demon appears as a shadow that floats across the draped window. During the exorcism scenes, it can be seen as a silhouetted figure in tattered clothing as it reaches for its alternate form of the Pazuzu statue.

The gaze, our Orientalist strength, is further taken away through the Arab demon's ambivalence. The Orientalist prefers to work within the paradigms of clear absolutes, pushing the Oriental away from the Occidental Self and into visualized and ideological categories of fixed Otherness. Homi Bhabha shows in his theory of ambivalence that the colonizer is disrupted in assigning the colonized as Other. When the colonized is brought into the realm of the knowable, the colonized is humanized, distinction from the colonizing Self blurs, and the colonized no longer remains wholly Other. As a result, the colonizer must continually use stereotypes to build images that differentiate the Oriental from the Occidental Self. The Arab demon's possession of Regan disrupts our disciplinary gaze, our ability to visually see, define, and subjugate its Otherness, in a similar way. As we assemble knowledge about the Arab demon, we continually assign it descriptions that are human and yet nonhuman. We try to fix it as Other, as male, as inimical, as strong enough to murder and wrench the necks of its victims, but we have difficulty doing so since we cannot lay our eyes on it. Although it has all these characteristics, it manifests itself to us through the form of a little girl previously seen as cute and innocent. Each time we encounter it, it changes appearance, personality, and sound.

We believe there is one demon inside her, and yet the tape recording reveals many voices. Sometimes Regan speaks in her own voice, or sends messages through her body, thereby showing that her person is still there. At the same time the entity growls, wheezes, bellows, snores, and groans in a fashion midway between man and beast. It cries in pain and moans in sexual pleasure. It moves like a human being, flicks its tongue like a reptile, and spins its head like a mannequin. The demon will not stay fixed for us. It remains in slippery motion. Even the screenplay refers to it as "Regan/Demon."[28] Tying it down to the bed not only provides physical safety for the protagonists, but it also allows a bit of disciplinary comfort for the Orientalist viewers.

The Arab demon frustrates our gaze and assaults our sense of security by remaining unseen even when we apply our best sources of Western knowledge. Our finest medical institutions; expensive medical machinery; scientific testing with impressive names like EEG, arteriogram, and pneumoencephalogram; and our power to see into the depths of the brain with X-rays are all shown to be impotent at detecting the Arab demon. The array of drugs, like Ritalin, Thorazine, and lithium, cannot keep it fully under control. The diagnoses of brain lesions, pathological states, and accelerated motor performance become lame and empty evasions for highly paid professionals who cannot determine the cause of Regan's "disease." The audience knows the cause and where it came from because of the Iraq prologue, but the eighty-eight consulted doctors are weak and dumbfounded. Eventually, the stymied medical profession has to resort to the prescription of an exorcist, a ritual from "primitive cultures" or sixteenth-century Catholicism, to try to cure Regan. The Arab demon seems to take us to an antiquated period similar to the place of its origins.

Meanwhile, police detective Lieutenant Kinderman (Lee J. Cobb), with his cool cunning, unwavering tenacity, and amiable disposition, cannot explain what is occurring in the home. He is keen enough to find the material clue of the child's arts-and-crafts sculpture at the site where Burke Dennings's (Jack MacGowran) dead body was found. Yet, he cannot solve the case of a man being brutally murdered in a child's room with only the child at home. The demon evades his search, as well.

The inability to diagnose or identify the cause of Regan's transformation is a breakdown of our language in *The Exorcist*. The characters continually search for words to describe the Regan/demon character. They refer to it as the "devil," "it," "that thing upstairs," "your daughter," and "my little girl." It assails the characters and the audience with gratuitous

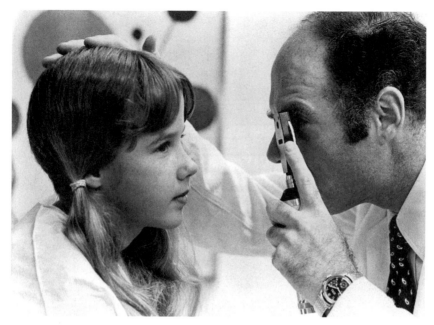

The Exorcist (1973). An innocent-looking Regan (Linda Blair) is examined by one of eighty-eight doctors in order to determine the cause of her "disease." The Arab demon that possesses her eludes our gaze and assaults our sense of security even when we apply our best sources of Western knowledge: the finest medical institutions, expensive medical machinery, scientific testing, and impressive nomenclature, all of which fail to detect the Arab demon. The stymied medical profession reluctantly suggests an exorcist: practitioner of a primitive, medieval, and unscientific treatment. Photo courtesy of the Academy of Motion Picture Arts and Sciences.

swearing and blasphemous language that shocked an early 1970s American Orientalist audience.[29] Its use of language toward characters of authority, doctors, priests, the mother, violates proper protocol demanded by these institutional roles of Western civilization. It speaks in an array of languages: English, Latin, French, and Greek. The recorded wailing, "indistinct gibberish," turns out to be English backward. The audience searches for a meaning to this particular loss of language in a previous experience. It relates this "language" back to the initial perceptions of Arabic in the Iraq prologue: the similar cadence of the muezzin's call, the verbal sounds of the Arab workers, and the backwards direction of language written by the Arab curator. This misuse of Arabic, a determination of Arabic as "deviant" in relation to Western standards of language, further associates the demon with the Arab civilization shown earlier.

The Exorcist (1973). Chris MacNeil (Ellen Burstyn) insists that "that thing upstairs isn't my daughter." She pleads with Father Karras (Jason Miller) to perform an exorcism—her last hope of curing her daughter, Regan. Photo courtesy of the Academy of Motion Picture Arts and Sciences.

The demon also breaks down language in its role as a mimic. Homi Bhabha describes how the colonized upsets the Orientalist category of Other through mimicry in his famous essay "Of Mimicry and Man." Central to British imperialist policy of the eighteenth and nineteenth centuries, as Bhabha notes, was the civilizing of the colonized through an education of English art, literature, language, and habits. The Anglicized intellectual class thus created could then be enlisted to help the British govern over the millions of colonized. But the refraction of British culture through the colonized Other's mind, tongue, and skin color created "mimicry," where what was repeated by the colonized Other was never purely British—it retained native accents. As a resemblance, it was "almost the same but not quite . . . almost the same but not white."[30] Mimicry seemed to parody whatever it mimicked, it was never far from mockery of the colonizer's self-image, and as such it became a site of resistance. Moreover, mimicry became a menace to the colonizer because it created ambivalence of the Other (i.e., the Oriental may act British, but does not look or sound British), which stereotype anxiously tried to conceal, and it located a crack in the certainty and authority of colonial dominance over the behavior of the colonized.

The demon's mimicry is evident not only in its antagonizing of us through the use of English, but also in its sophisticated switching between languages. It does this at will, thereby controlling the topics of discussion. Despite Karras's insistence on continuing a conversation in Latin so that he may gain knowledge of the demon's presence, the demon refuses and mockingly moves to French. Moreover, the demon mimics the voices of other characters that have been introduced and whose voices are distinct in our minds. It speaks with the British accent of Dennings, the murdered director friend of Chris, and in the voice of the bum that Karras encountered in the New York subway. It speaks in the same pleading voice as Karras's mother and even appears in the hospital clothes she wore when he left her in her dying moments — acts that the audience perceives as insensitive audacities. It even laughs like a mischievous child when it triumphs over Merrin. The use of its ambivalence and mimicry is, as Bart Moore-Gilbert observes, referring to Bhabha's postcolonial theory, "psychological guerrilla warfare"[31] that upsets our symbolic order, our imperial prerogative, and our own superior identity.

Shohat notes that in the Orientalist fantasy, the white woman is always at the center of struggle between male protagonists and antagonists. The sexual interaction of the Third World male, who is prone to hypersexuality and the enslavement of women, and the white, Western female, who could not possibly desire such a man, can only involve rape.[32] The white hero will eventually save her from the clutches of the Third World aggressor, therefore giving the white hero the apologia of domination over the Other. Whereas films of Orientalist fantasies will often allude to such interracial rape, *The Exorcist* comes ever closer to actually showing it. It is the inability of the white protagonists to prevent such a rape of an innocent white girl from actually happening before our eyes that further turns this film toward Orientalist fear.

The victimization of the female household fits this ploy perfectly. The demon entices Regan much like the Big Bad Wolf does Little Red Riding Hood in the picture hanging in the basement. With the innocence of a lonely girl, she invites the demon in through the games of the Ouija board played with the avuncular Captain Howdy. She refers to the demon as male-gendered. Even so, as noted by Said, Orientalist tradition knows the Arab for his "bad" sexuality.[33] Faegheh Shirazi elaborates this Orientalist tradition for us further in her discussion of Western representations of Oriental libidinousness. The Western translations of the tales of *The Thousand and One Nights* like E. W. Lane's, Sir Richard Burton's translation of *The Perfumed Garden of the Shaykh Nefzawi*, Bernhard Stern's *Medicine, Superstition, and Sex Life in Turkey* and *The Scented Garden: Anthropology of the Sex Life in the Levant,* and Western interpretations of the Koran like Dante's provided images of the Middle East as "a world revolving around debauchery, perversion, and sexual illicitness . . . in which every sexual behavior known to humankind is allowed and enjoyed" and of Islam "as a licentious way of life" as opposed to a legitimate religion.[34] Sometimes descriptions of Oriental sexuality were considered to be so shocking and repulsive for Western audiences that they had to be expurgated from the Western translations. Shirazi also points out that when the United States and Middle Eastern countries are at odds politically, American society frequently asserts and accepts sexual cruelty as a typical trait of Oriental character.[35] The 1970s, as we have seen earlier, was such a time. True to such form, the Arab demon will eventually turn against Regan in violence. It shakes her bed, sadistically tosses her about the mattress, and, as she complains, is trying to kill her. She begs for it to be made to stop, but the doctors, whom the critic Stephen Bowles accuses of previously raping her under the guise of Western medicine,[36] and her mother are helpless. Its penetration into her body distorts her face, engorges her throat, and rolls back her eyes to make it look as if she is taking on the strange appearance of the Arab blacksmith. It seems to lift Regan out of the bed and then slaps her across the face, leaving a handprint on her cheek, in the scene where it takes possession of her body. If we accept the rape thesis, then we should reconsider what is commonly referred to as the "crucifix masturbation" scene. This notable scene may be masturbation of the demon, but it is also a shocking rape of a little girl with a holy object doubling as a dildo. We must remember that Regan's voice is heard refusing the act, while the Arab demon's male voice demands it to be performed. It is the demonic voice that cries out, "Let Jesus fuck you!" as the holy object is forcibly driven into her vagina. And yet, this confusion over masturbation and rape is the tactic of the Arab demon. It is another strategy of ambivalence.

The film's denouement comes in the scenes of the exorcism. The prior scenes have threatened the Orientalist fantasy and left the audience in a state of submission. Therefore, the film must bring about a resolution in which the Arab demon is expelled and Western civilization triumphs once

The Exorcist (1973). Father Merrin (Max von Sydow) arrives at the MacNeil home. He is the exorcist. His stance is caught in the stream of light emanating from Regan's bedroom. Merrin represents the mythic cowboy who comes to town to defeat the villain that terrorizes it. This scene became a signature of *The Exorcist* and one of the many icons of Hollywood film and 1970s popular culture in America. Photo courtesy of the Academy of Motion Picture Arts and Sciences.

again. It seems appropriate that this American film would need to call in its most revered and assuaging self-narrative of the classical cowboy Western to set things right again. At this point, *The Exorcist* features a sequence that follows the paradigm of what Wright calls the "classical plot" of the American cowboy film. Simply speaking, this plot, as Wright explains, is most known as involving "the lone stranger who rides into a troubled town and cleans it up, winning the respect of the townsfolk and the love of the schoolmarm."[37]

In Proppian fashion, Wright specifies his preference for a morphological approach to the classical plot and supplies sixteen functions: (1) the hero enters a social group; (2) the hero is unknown to the society; (3) the hero is revealed to have an exceptional ability; (4) the society's members recognize a difference between themselves and the hero; the hero is given a special status; (5) the society does not completely accept the hero; (6) there is a conflict of interests between the villains and the society; (7) the villains are stronger than the society; the society is weak; (8) there is a strong friendship or respect between the hero and a villain; (9) the villains threaten the society; (10) the hero avoids involvement in the conflict; (11) the villains endanger a friend of the hero; (12) the hero fights the villains; (13) the hero defeats the villains; (14) the society is safe; (15) the society accepts the hero; and (16) the hero loses or gives up his special status. Within the plot, dramatis personae exist in oppositions between inside/outside of society, bad/good, strong/weak, and wilderness/civilization.[38]

In the narrative of *The Exorcist*, the demon has proven to be a formidable foe of American society. It has displayed a conflict of interests with the society, and its strength overpowers and weakens this society. The protagonists inside the society have not been able to save Regan. The Catholic hierarchy gives permission to perform an exorcism, but not to be conducted by Karras alone. Karras has conveniently played the "fallen cowboy," what Lee Clark Mitchell refers to as an important figure that enhances the hero's masculine character.[39] Here, Mitchell describes a man of education or expertise who has lost self-control, and his characteristics thereby heighten the narrative stakes and the stature of the hero's arrival. Father Merrin, whom the audience has met earlier outside of the society and in the wilderness of the Middle East, but also whom the society has not yet met, is named as having special experience and wisdom in performing the exorcism. He takes on the role of the cowboy hero. Described as a prolific author and as someone who has spent time in foreign missions, he is expected to have the necessary scholarly knowledge about the Oriental. The hero is seen alone again, but this time in the autumn woodland, and is summoned by messenger to proceed to Georgetown. The setup makes it look as if he must come in from the wilderness. The film's most famous narrative image of the silhouetted hero in a brimmed hat, armed with a black bag, facing off against a powerful light coming from Regan's bedroom is another staging of the Western duel. The source of this downward-beaming light, i.e., the Arab demon, arrests him in a metaphoric gaze. Merrin was seen in a similar duelist staging in the scenes of the Middle East. When Merrin is introduced to the members of the household, the demon screams out Merrin's name in recognition. The voice bears down from the bedroom upon Merrin and the other protagonists in the foyer. They must look up under the power of its voice and gaze. The hero has had this kind of confrontation with the villain before.

The cowboy, according to Lee Clark Mitchell, exudes heroism with his

The Exorcist (1973). In Regan's bedroom, now devoid of the trappings associated with an upper-middle-class American child, Father Karras (Jason Miller) acts as deputy to the experienced exorcist Father Merrin (Max von Sydow). In the film's climactic scenes, they work together to expel the Arab demon that possesses Regan (Linda Blair). Photo courtesy of the Academy of Motion Picture Arts and Sciences.

masculinity. He remains high over his enemy, gazing down at him from his mount. He practices restraint and self-control. He is a wordsmith, in that he uses language adeptly and only as necessary.[40] Michael Coyne describes the cowboy as a glib, individualistic, white American knight who banishes evil from the land and brings about the opportunity for renewal.[41] We expect Merrin, in this image, to triumph over the Arab demon in gaze, knowledge, language, and masculine stature. We expect him to right the narrative structure that this Oriental has disrupted. We expect him to rescue the protagonists and ourselves by reestablishing Western order. In an expeditious and determined manner, Merrin wishes to start the exorcism right away. Karras, the fallen cowboy, is to play his deputy. In an important dialogue, Merrin instructs Karras, and us in the audience, on how to fight the Arab demon. Basically, and foreshadowing the coming events, he instructs us that we must carefully exercise our language and our gaze because the demon will try to confuse us. Moreover, he sternly corrects Karras's and our vulnerability to ambivalence. He focuses on the evil singularity of the demon: "There is only one." The litany of the "Rite of Exorcism" is used to reestablish dominance over the demon's current control of language. Unlike in the Iraq prologue, Merrin establishes his authority over language from the outset with the resounding command of "Be silent!" as he stands over the foul-mouthed demon. Armed with holy water, a crucifix, the appropriate religious attire, and the English text, Merrin begins the ritual. The demon tries to overpower our hearing of the litany as it unrestrainedly pours forth invectives, cries, growls, and screams. When it cannot do so, it resorts to seizing and controlling our sight with spitting, bizarre movements, levitations, and head turnings. It violently throws and moves furniture, cracks plaster, and creates whirlwinds that frenetically open and close doors and cabinets. Merrin keeps his self-control by continuing, without respite, the ritual language. Karras's stupefied and emotional reactions highlight Merrin's experienced restraint. In contrast, Karras's actions verge on the ineffective, and he risks defeat by the Arab demon. Eventually, Merrin must dismiss him for faltering in gaze and exercise of language.

Mitchell also postulates that the cowboy hero is a man with a strong, taut physique. When he gets knocked down, he gets back up to defeat his assailant. This is where, once again, Merrin fails us as the hero we would want to have. Merrin is old, gray, wrinkled, and physically weak. His complexion is anemic. His cassock, surplice, and purple stole are the very antitheses of the sexually appealing tight chaps, fringed jacket, and neckerchief. The Arab demon shakes the room and knocks Merrin to the floor. Merrin seems an impotent hero, as he struggles to pull himself up again, although doing a better job of it than Karras. When Merrin's self-control is weakened due to his failing health, the demon laughs maniacally as it begins to triumph. Also visibly shaken, Merrin resorts again to strong, loud commands. Later, but once again, we see him fumble for his medicine in order to stabilize his weak and failing heart. Finally, we come upon him in a scene of the duel just finished. Our hero lies dead on the floor. His weapon of holy water no longer shoots out its contents but rather drips it onto the floor. He is like a dead duelist with his gun no longer controlled in his hand and shooting, but rather with it smoking on the ground and out of his reach. And the demon is on the bed, above him, and exudes the ambivalence of being dumbfounded and giddy from its victory.

This leaves us again without resolution. If we follow the morphology

The Exorcist (1973). As part of the exorcism, Father Merrin (Max von Sydow) and Father Karras (Jason Miller) call out, "The power of Christ compels you . . ." Meanwhile, the Arab demon levitates Regan's body (Linda Blair). The Arab demon steals the power of gaze and language through bizarre physical movements, ambiguity, mimicry, and shocking verbiage. Photo courtesy of the Academy of Motion Picture Arts and Sciences.

of Wright, we have made it up to the twelfth function, but the closure functions of thirteen through sixteen are foiled. This is unacceptable in the classical plot. "If the hero lost the fight in [the plot]," states Wright, "it would be a loss in principle, and society would have to be seen as helpless before the attack of evil."[42] To resolve this dilemma, Karras resorts to the ultimate acceptable Western weapon: the punch. As Thomas Sutcliffe points out, the punch is the ultimate weapon for a protagonist when he is finally at a loss for a sword. To punch with the bare fist is a moral act of good over evil or a manifestation of moral determination. "It argues that winning is the ultimate good and that compromise is for losers."[43] With Karras's punch, we finally take our fearful frustration out on the demon. Broken down to our basest state, wherein gaze, knowledge, and language have been taken from us, our hero defeated, and our society pushed to the point of total surrender, we find redress in Karras's punch. Through the violence of the punch Karras regains the self-control and masculinity he needs for redemption. Karras has given Chris his word that her child would not die. Like a hero, he demands that the demon take him, and then sacrifices himself for the girl and society. He throws himself out of the window and takes the demon with him.

The viewers' consternation at the film's closure surrounds the issue of gaze and the inability of *The Exorcist* to fulfill the Orientalist fantasy and the promise of cowboy narratives. The audience never witnesses the Arab demon being actually vanquished. The religious ritual is aborted. Mitchell points out that when a man is physically beaten, he is seen to reemerge into a self that he already is: masculine.[44] In a bizarre twist, Merrin as our hero does not reemerge as masculine but stays as he already was in the Iraq prologue: feminine. Our hero dies. Karras, as deputy hero, is seen dying in his own pool of blood. Although we see the demon receiving a few punches, we never see it defeated. The film robs us of witnessing justice handed out to a villain who penetrated our land, attempted to destroy our society and to turn it into Hell, raped a white American girl, killed our hero, and contemptuously displayed Otherness, ambivalence, and mimicry. We do not see it banished back to its origin in the Middle East. Instead, the demon just disappears out among the Georgetown crowd in a mysterious way similar to that in which it arrived. It is left free to commit these acts again. Furthermore, though the American household is restored to its peaceful comfort, Chris and Regan abandon the house for a life elsewhere. Despite Chris's belief that Regan does not remember the possession, Regan shows otherwise in her grateful recognition of Karras's friend, Father Dyer (Rev. William O'Malley). Chris does not rediscover religious faith as a result of this experience. Renewal and the masculinity of society are left in doubt. The narrative paradigms of the Orientalist fantasy and the classical Western plot do not provide the security and comfort that the audience desires.

The Exorcist brilliantly crafts a lasting horrific emotion in its Orientalist audience because it is an assault on the Western narrative myths of the Orientalist fantasy and the classical cowboy myth. The paradigmatic structure is, as Kermode rightly makes us aware, rich with symbolic reverberations that are seen throughout the film. Many of the reverberations are established within the important Iraq prologue. In turn, the syntagmatic structure is cleverly iconoclastic. Recall Wright's simile of narrative as language pointed out earlier in this chapter. The demon's aggression is represented as so effective that it pervades the dimension of normative narrative language as well. The source of the paradigmatic "words" is established within the demon's origins, within the heredity of the Arab, and the "words" are dictated by the demon's presence. Moreover, the demon seems to control the syntagmatic "grammar." It commandeers the conceptual orders and modes of action of our culture to which we have become so inclined and accustomed. *The Exorcist* presents the alien Arab demon as culpable for the annihilation of the language embedded in two of our important cultural myths.

Indeed, *The Exorcist* is a disturbing film. However, the emotional discomfort should not be seen to emanate from *only* the graphic assaults on the girl's body, the cinematic special effects, the makeup techniques, the film's dialogue, the mistreatment of sacred institutions, or, even, as argued here, the narrative structure. Another dimension of discomfort should come from the use of the Arab as evil villain, or more directly, from the misuse of the Arab for our Orientalist fear and virtual entertainment. The story about an Arab demon who possesses a little girl, turns our world violently upside down, commits murder twice and is the cause of a third death, and evades all scientific knowledge is a tale far too fantastic, almost ridiculous. It is as fantastic as a tale from *The Thousand and One Nights,* an Orientalist source of imagery and cultural practices in the Middle East. And yet it seemed to work at scaring American audiences in the 1970s and does even today. An explanation of this paradox can be found in Walt Disney's animation theory of the plausible impossible.[45] Disney describes on one of his television programs how animation scenarios work: impossible things can happen if they are prepared as plausible. For example, if Mickey Mouse can create enough velocity in his running approach, he can easily defy gravity and can quickly scale the perpendicular façade of a multistory building. If a cow and a horse are animated with enough anthropomorphic features, they can be seen to converse in English over tea and cakes. Contextual framing then is important here. Similarly, if a proper demonic origin and an apparent demonic race with an aggressive heredity are effectively constructed first, then it is possible that all that happens in *The Exorcist*'s Georgetown scenes can really happen. Those first 10 minutes of the Iraq prologue create enough plausibility that 102 minutes later we have been frightfully entertained rather than disappointed that we wasted the price of our tickets on a film with a story line so preposterous that we walk away with the question "What was the point of that?"

Although Disney speaks of animation, his theory is applicable here as well. After all, the scenes in the Iraq prologue are the staging and editing together, an animation of sorts, of assorted and disjunctive Orientalist caricatures of Arab people. The Iraq prologue is an entextualization of the Arab landscape, Arab bodies and faces, Arabic language, Islamic practices, and slices of Arab life. Since all of the entextualized elements work within the traditions and parameters of Orientalism, a perceived reality in our Western minds, they become the plausible. And, of course, the cinematic assault of the Arab fits within the American political and social concerns of the early 1970s. This was the period of the Egyptian and Syrian surprise attack on Israel, the rise of Palestinian international terrorism striking in Western Europe, a bellicose Libyan leader calling for Pan-Arabism and an Islamic revival, and Middle East oil embargoes against the West. Magazines and newspapers were replete with stories and images of conspiring and plotting Arab leaders; masked Palestinian guerrillas attacking Western institutions like airliners, airports, and the Olympics; fantastically rich Arabs draining the treasuries of oil-consuming nations and unable to spend the proceeds fast enough; frustrated American motorists at the pumps; prototypes of American gas ration coupons; and Midwestern children dressed in winter coats, hats, and gloves studying in their cold classrooms. The American public had been primed to believe that the Arabs were rising up from their "dusty and dingy" capitals, infiltrating the security of American lives, and demanding to be treated with "deadly seriousness."[46] As powerful threats different and distant from us, they could be easily made into Hollywood monsters or the demon character William Peter Blatty wanted to make: real, powerful, evil, legion, and aligned with whatever is opposed to love.[47] The entextualized images of those things Arab are then recontextualized into a string of scenes to create an origin, an Orientalist Hell, that will support the narrative of a horror story that really is impossible. Likewise, the Arab images preestablish the physical characteristics and evil agency of the demon. Adding further insult, William Friedkin gives no acknowledgment to these Arabs as actors or performers in the film's ending text, unlike the American film crew that is given credit under the title "Iraq Sequence." Those people who appeared in the Iraq prologue remain as invisible as the demon and as those Arabs wreaking havoc on our 1970s lives from afar.[48] It leaves these Arab people looking as if their representation is purely documentary, adding to the achievement of realism that Friedkin and Blatty reportedly had wanted to create.[49] Hiding behind the popular ethnographic alibi of Orientalism, the film stimulates our fears at the expense of the Arab culture.

An article in *USA Today,* September 21, 2000, heralded the reissue of the film with eleven minutes of reinstated scenes. Susan Wloszczyna quoted Friedkin as stating that the climate of political correctness today would create controversy in making the same film that was made in the 1970s. The odd thing is that foul language, assault on religious symbols, and the depiction of faltering faith are some of the problems that she highlights as politically incorrect during a presidential race that demonized the media as purveyors of sex and violence. Once again, criticism of the film centers upon those familiar middle-class surroundings with the most dialogue. Nowhere does she address the misrepresentation of Arabs in the Iraq prologue that is carried into the rest of the film.[50] The past oversights and continued blindness of critics to the practice of representing Arabs as evil and inimical to our culture are among the most disturbing aspects surrounding the reputation of American cinema's most frightening horror film.

2 | *Rollover*
ASSAULT ON THE AMERICAN ECONOMY (1981)

*A*LAN J. Pakula's doomsday thriller, *Rollover,* is another American film that taps the fount of Orientalist fear by threatening an American ideology and myth and toppling the myth's carefully constructed heroes.[1] In an important scene at a gala upper-class event held at New York's Museum of Natural History, *Rollover* introduces the Orientalist audience to its heroic characters, Lee Winters (Jane Fonda) and Hub Smith (Kris Kristofferson). Lee Winters is the wealthy heiress to the controlling stock position in the Winterchem petrochemical firm and is the hostess of the black-tie affair. Hub Smith is one of the maverick businessmen in attendance. At the party, Winters is informed that her tycoon husband, Charlie, has been murdered. The audience watches from Smith's distanced viewpoint as she learns the news. "What is it, Hub?" asks senior banker Maxwell Emery (Hume Cronin) as Smith looks on in sympathy. "Nothing," replies Smith. "I was just thinking about the illusion of safety." The audience then watches Winters wrench in painful grief about the news of her husband's death.

"The illusion of safety," particularly economic safety, is a key theme in *Rollover* and in our discussion of Orientalist fear. It is a fear that Americans experienced during the oil-embargo period of the early 1970s and that would remain with them throughout the decade. *Rollover* develops Orientalist fear by focusing on a sense of American security, fostered by a belief in the triumphs of self-reliance, which is found in the success myth of the American entrepreneur. In the progression of the film's formulaic unfolding, which poises the audience for an expected and desired outcome, safety and security are destroyed by the infiltration of Oriental Arab treachery. *Rollover* lauds the American entrepreneur's passion for the art of the deal, the struggle to achieve, the acquisition of power, and the right to claim glamour and wealth as rewards of success. The American is the right kind of capitalist, a hero who is to be celebrated and admired. On the other hand, the Arabs are the wrong kind of capitalists, the villains that should be disdained and feared. The film depicts Arabs as members

of a treacherous race of people who have acquired a colossal and unfathomable wealth, without working hard. Therefore, they do not use their
wealth responsibly, nor do they have the civilized understanding of how
to appreciate it. They are secretive, cold, plotting, distant, and selfishly
destructive. *Rollover* puts forward the fearful fantasy of what could happen if American businessmen lost domestic economic control and their
international hegemony over capitalism to undeserving, destructive, and
business-immature Arabs. *Rollover,* like *The Exorcist,* develops Orientalist
fear through a threatening mythic narrative.

The success myth of the American entrepreneur depicts the entrepreneur as worthy enough to be among the pantheon of American heroes.
Although the unfettered American capitalist has had detractors, such as
Matthew Josephson, author of *The Robber Barons,*[2] the success myth of
the entrepreneur works to show him to be one of the most patriotic of all
Americans. Thomas DiBacco's history of American business, for example,
works to convince its readers that capitalism and entrepreneurship reach
deep into America's past, and, therefore, are part of the national character. DiBacco recasts the Founding Fathers of our nation as entrepreneurs,
implying that the history of America is the history of American business.
Through them, America became the world's first and most successful capitalistic nation, what he calls "a mature business civilization."[3] DiBacco begins with the Pilgrims at Plymouth, who, he claims, became entrepreneurs
when they made arrangements to pay off their debts to their English financial backer in 1627. In committing themselves to this goal, the Plymouth
colonists became the first American business civilization that was dependent on no outside individual for its economic direction. He then dubs
Benjamin Franklin the model of "America's first business success story"
and finds in Franklin some of the quintessential entrepreneurial characteristics, such as ambition; creativity; self-education; and a devotion to research and invention, community service, and philanthropy.[4] The entrepreneurs of the early nineteenth century came up with new inventions
and investments that reached into the fabric of society, and soon no in-
stitution was immune from their influence.[5] By World War II, American
businesses were providing needed supplies and firepower overseas, introduced advances in new products and inventions taken for granted today,
and utilized scarce resources and imaginative ideas that kept the home
folk contented. American businessmen helped win this war and establish
America's dominance as a world superpower. Caught up in his enthusiastic rooting for American business, DiBacco overlooks the human carnage

and suffering of the war and makes the peculiar claim that "World War II was not only a major war but one of those rarities, a relatively good one, devoid of significant conflicts, thanks to the efforts of enterprise."[6]

Burton W. Folsom, Jr., and George Gilder have also written about the American entrepreneur. While Folsom's work exonerates the great American capitalists from Josephson's indictments, Gilder honors the newest American entrepreneurs of the 1980s.[7] From their writings we can identify the syntagmatic and paradigmatic aspects in the success myth of the entrepreneur.[8] In Proppian fashion, it is possible to enumerate the myth's syntagmatic functions. Thus, the morphology of the entrepreneur's story may read like this: (1) at a young age, he demonstrates a promise and desire to succeed; (2) he ventures out to seek his fortune; (3) he proves himself in each task given; (4) he has an idea, a dream, or a vision that he can produce a product or provide a service to the public better and cheaper than anyone else; (5) others ridicule him for his idea, dream, or vision; (6) his first foray into the marketplace is usually met with failure; (7) he impresses other investors with his idea so that he may continue his venture; (8) he becomes so leveraged that he risks losing everything; (9) he meets his enemies, who want to protect the status quo of the marketplace and their own positions; (10) these enemies vindictively try to thwart his efforts; (11) he soon finds his niche in the market; (12) as he expected, he captures the market by fulfilling needs and demands better and cheaper than the established competition; (13) he changes and improves the way we live, where we live, and how we do business in America; (14) he is rewarded with fame, success, material prosperity, and the good things in life; and, of course, (15) he shares his wealth by giving back to the community through philanthropic endowments.

While the syntagmatic structure provides the progress of the entrepreneur's story, the paradigmatic structure provides the archetypic and enviable characteristics and virtues of this American hero. The entrepreneur is an ambitious, hardworking, and determined visionary. Where others see only mountains and deserts, he sees farms and cities. He can espy waste, incompetence, and laziness. When he comes in, he cleans the inefficient operation up, whipping everything and everybody into shape. He thinks about the future, and follows his hunch. He has faith in his cause, does not fear failure, and abounds in perseverance. He is a survivor, and thus he finds more opportunity in a pink slip than in a promotion. He watches carefully, learns, and deals with a poker face. He has an encyclopedic knowledge, and he can be exacting to a fraction and methodically attentive to details. He can be a wordsmith with pithy formulas for success and the ability to persuade others. He understands markets, prices, and human nature. He assesses the strengths and weaknesses of his opponents and pits them against each other, but he always remains fair. As a result, he ceases to fear his rivals. He has excellent judgment about people and ideas and picks the right people for the job. He remains calm and disciplined, does business with a mental toughness that commands respect, rarely loses his temper, and attacks problems and competitors with efficiency. He is a problem solver who focuses on quality and building a better product for a cheaper price. He is more concerned with market issues than politics. He refrains from human vices such as extravagant living beyond his means, gambling, and adultery.

The entrepreneur is celebrated as America's hero and as paragon of the nation's economic life. He is the prize possession of America because he creates the nation's wealth. He gives American youths a notion of the sources of affluence and possibilities their lives hold. He shows the younger Americans that civilization is not routine or natural and that it swiftly declines and decays on the limitations of the forty-hour work week. He teaches youths the process of investment: forgoing present candy for future bags of lollipops, and then forgoing these lollipops as well. He is willing to try anything, and, as a result, he makes what has been accepted as the impossible actually possible. He helps his nation shape its own destiny by producing goods cheaply. America does not claim markets by drawing on natural resources. Markets have to be won in international competition, and the entrepreneur is the visionary knight who claims these markets for the nation by improving products bit by bit. He fights the juggernauts, the behemoths, the titans, and the leviathans. His risk-taking advances the nation into new eras of technologies and markets. He is the embodiment of democratic ideals. Although his wealth can be transferred to his progeny, his talent and vision may not be hereditary traits. He proves that success must be won by hard work. And since his success is not guaranteed to be hereditary, but is woven into our national spirit, everyone in America has a chance to be successful. Above all, he relieves us of the humiliation of expensive dependence on foreigners and keeps America independent so it may shape its own destiny. He looks for an American hold on the market, makes certain that foreign producers cannot do better, and is the source of growth and the American edge. He creates jobs and raises the standard of living for humanity. And yet, while working hard to sustain society, he always takes less than what he contributes. He follows what George Gilder calls the "moral core of capitalism," according to which he knows that higher profits come from giving, through low prices and high wages, rather than from gouging for what the traffic will bear.[9] Society is always deep in debt to him. The more he earns, the more he gives, and the more he gives, the more he earns. His absence would deplete and demoralize the culture of capitalism. Natural resources are meaningless without him and only gain value through his ingenuity and working of the land. Without him, wealth and natural resources would dissolve into scrap, ruined concrete, snarled wire, and wilderness. To shackle him with rules and laws would be a disservice to him, to ourselves, and to the democratic principles he embodies. Instead, he should be encouraged by religion, culture, law, and policy to do his work well. Taking such moral uprightness into consideration, it is no wonder that Gilder asserts that the key to the United States's future is to abound in entrepreneurs.[10]

The myth describes the entrepreneur in terms that depict him in a masculine role replete with sexual prowess and phallic power. He *captures* and *seizes* opportunities, *puts pressure* on the competition, *breaks through* price fixing and the status quo, *spearheads* technologies, *opens* and *penetrates* markets, *makes* markets, *frees* markets from others and *dominates* them himself, and *creates* something out of nothing. His effect is far-reaching, he *drives* the markets, he *fulfills* demands, he *outperforms* others, and he *unleashes* dynamic growth.[11]

Rollover draws from the success myth, maybe even "fantasy," of American entrepreneurialism on both the syntagmatic and paradigmatic levels. First let us consider the syntagmatic approach. In identifying the myth's functions above, we have borrowed from Propp's morphological approach. However, Propp believed that the telling of the folktale must follow the exact order of the functions. Wright, who also uses Proppianism-inspired morphology as an approach to understanding the American cowboy film, has shown that when reading film narrative Proppian rigidity may be too extreme. Wright points out that in film, order can be liberalized and still follow the myth, "for it is easy to recognize a set of essentially similar stories with slightly differing orders of events."[12] Therefore, Pakula may have condensed or altered the order of some functions (for example, functions 1, 2, and 3 are condensed; and function 6 is delayed until after function 10 occurs), but overall the myth is identifiable in *Rollover*.

Rollover's hero is Hub Smith. Smith's entrance onto the cinematic stage is preceded by the financial troubles of Boro National, a small but once successful banking firm in New York City. The audience watches as Boro National frenziedly dumps a $100 million on the international currency market in order to cover its debt exposure, which in turn causes a fall in the international value of the U.S. dollar. Maxwell Emery, president of First New York Bank, an American leviathan bank, steps in to rescue Boro National and the plummeting U.S. dollar. It is in conjunction with this financial drama and a murder to be discussed below that the hero comes onto the stage. As Smith is seen at the gala event, he walks across the screen while the orchestra announces his special status and the life he espouses by playing Gershwin's upbeat and romantic melody, "'S Wonderful." Emery and a distinguished colleague also acknowledge Smith's commanding presence when they discuss him, and the possibility of whether or not he will agree to take over the management of the ailing Boro National firm. Basically, their words mark Smith as the man who is able to come in and clean up the operation. A condensation of the myth's syntagmatic functions occurs here. The subsequent conversation between Emery and Smith locates the initial functions of the myth (functions 1, 2, and 3) as already in the past. The colleague of Emery has announced that Smith is a "glamour boy" who would not be interested in taking on the problems of Boro National. He is thus presented as young, unique among his peers, and someone who has already moved up the ranks, proving himself in each task given. It turns out that Smith has already put in his time working in the trenches for Emery. In his initial rejection of the offer, Smith states that he has had enough of "crash and burn" experiences from the problem loans he previously managed for Emery. Therefore, he suggests that he has already matured in the workplace. With these facts in mind, the viewers assume that the early years of Smith's entrepreneurial story have already been completed prior to the narrative present. The narrative present then begins with the introduction of an idea, dream, or vision (function 4).

Emery is himself introduced as a senior businessman who has successfully experienced the functions of the myth earlier in his life. He is already in the midst of functions 14 and 15 in the entrepreneurial success myth: the acquisition of good fortune and the philanthropic donations to others. He is called a hero for riding in on his "white horse and sav[ing] Boro National," and acknowledged as "the Lion of American banking." His age and knowledge also key the audience to his paternal authority. However, Emery also plays the role of the Proppian dispatcher, present-

Rollover (1981). The trading floor of Boro National is busy with high-stakes transactions in the world's financial markets. The cryptic and quickly changing price boards provide the traders with important information that requires special knowledge and business-literate skills to interpret. The suave and handsome entrepreneur Hub Smith (Kris Kristofferson) enters the scene on his first day of work at Boro National. Smith has been hired to apply his entrepreneurial acumen, knowledge, and skills in order to save this ailing American company from bankruptcy. Photo courtesy of the British Film Institute.

ing Smith with the challenge so that Smith can advance through the myth to entrepreneurial hero status. He lets Smith know that he will only continue bailing out Boro National if Smith, "his boy," takes over the firm's management. Smith is reluctant at first to work with "those turkeys at Boro National" that need a miracle to save them. He is enticed by Emery's appeal to his entrepreneurial spirit: would it not be challenging and rewarding to rescue a failing business and get a chance to become "hero of the week"? Emery is, in fact, promising Smith a quick track to function 14, one of the end results of the success myth. And so Smith, our entrepreneurial hero, takes the job.

After some research into the firm's business records, Smith finds that Boro National is in deep trouble. Roy Lefcourt (Josef Sommer), the failing firm's founder, is wary of Smith taking over his firm and questions his abilities by using a medical metaphor, namely, asking the doctor if the patient is going to live. Smith replies, "The patient has been dead for six months and doesn't know it." Lefcourt, annoyed with Smith's response, is ready to close the firm, but Smith gets an entrepreneurial vision, and he even sees it as a game to be played. In a slight alteration of function 4, Smith does not create a new product but rather provides a service that will save an American firm. If he can earn the firm $3 or 4 million in profit to cover the next dividend payment, this profit would buy the firm time to bring itself back into solvency. Lefcourt balks at the idea (function 5), but Smith pushes forward in revealing his plan. What Boro National needs, according to Smith, is to broker a substantial loan, a couple hundred million dollars, for a customer who is "even more in the shithouse than we are." Boro National can then collect the commission on the loan. Smith's sights become set on Winters's Winterchem Petrochemical.

The heroic role in this film is not exclusively Smith's, but is shared, although not equally, with Lee Winters. She, too, partakes in her own experiences of functions 4 and 5. Winterchem is also on the brink of failure, and Winters has an entrepreneurial vision for her firm. She sees that Winterchem can return to profitability only if it spends more money, rather than scales back, to grow through new product research and development. At a luncheon with Smith and Lefcourt, Winters tells her fellow executives that Winterchem can purchase a small petrochemical firm in Spain that is a real "cash flow machine." The executives ridicule her vision because there is no capital for such a move. Winterchem is already leveraged to the legal limit at Boro National. These board members even patronize her, insinuating that her feminine place is limited to the public relations functions of the firm and that her emotions are too caught up with the murder of her husband.

Although Winters takes on the role of heroine, she needs the encouragement, and probably the paradigmatic character backing, of Smith. Smith sees Winters as the key to getting the necessary loan commission for Boro National. He pushes her into thinking harder about some of the details of her idea, which she does with entrepreneurial fervor. They both push forward and disregard either firm's detractors and problems. After she comes up with the necessary answers about the purchase of the Spanish petrochemical plant, he continues to encourage her and coaches her on how to persuade the other executives to consider her idea. Together they feign her interest in selling her shares to a Japanese firm, which would lead to a foreign takeover and put the other board members out on their "collective ass." Taken in by the ruse, the executives give her the green light to go ahead with a financing deal for the Spanish firm. They also ask that Smith watch over Winters in the deal so that she does not "sell the family jewels" to get the money (function 7). The hero and heroine are united in their quest so that each one's success is dependent upon that of the other. They become so deeply united in their partnership that they also fall into a romantic relationship with each other, a built-in subplot.

But the vast amount of money needed for the loan, $500 million, must come from a powerful and fertile source. Smith's idea is to turn to the Arabs and their oil superwealth. He works out a deal with Sal Naftari (Bob Gunton), an agent who sets up financing deals with the Arabs. His commission is high, 8 percent plus contingencies as opposed to Smith's offered 2 percent, but Smith is willing to borrow every dollar he can. Winters, too, is willing to borrow every dollar that she can as she hesitantly puts up her entire stock holdings in Winterchem as collateral to the Arabs. When the Arabs announce their agreement to the deal (function 7 again), function 8 of the myth is also realized as the entrepreneurs borrow every dollar they can and risk losing everything.

The myth calls for a set of villains, or enemies, that the hero meets along the way (functions 9 and 10). In *Rollover,* the Arabs become these villains. On the next day, the Arabs put a hold on the money that is to cover the Winterchem loan, leaving Boro National dangerously exposed. This seems to be the film's delayed use of function 6, which involves the initial failure of the entrepreneur's idea. Smith reacts with the statement "Shit!" as he realizes that the deal is in trouble and may even be close to falling apart. Meanwhile, Winters, being unaware of the problem and prematurely pushing for the successful completion of the myth, celebrates her new appointment as chairperson of the Winterchem board. The audience learns that Emery, Naftari, and the Arab lender, Prince Khalid (Paul Hecht), are involved in some kind of plot that moves assets, later revealed as gold, outside the United States. The money Smith needs and awaits is part of this plot. Emery sees the Arab hold on the huge Winterchem loan as a rash move, too quick, and highly reckless. He points out to Prince Khalid, "You are playing with the end of the world." In the early morning hours of the following day, the Arabs finally roll over the initial amount of money, thereby giving a reprieve to the uneasy Smith. The rollover is $95 million, minus $5 million that is to be mysteriously deposited into First New York Account #21214.

First New York Account #21214 is introduced early in the film before the audience meets Smith and Winters. Charlie Winters, founder of Winterchem, had been looking into the details of the account in his office late on the night of the gala event at the New York museum. His discovery of the account's details led to his murder by an unidentified assassin with whom Naftari is acquainted. Jerry Fewster (Macon McCalmon), the federal bank examiner, also knows about the account and has received a bribe to keep quiet. In revealing this shady account early on, the film foreshadows function 10, where enemies are involved in thwarting entrepreneurial activity.

Both Smith and Winters stumble upon the account, although separately. Smith finds out that #21214 is an account used to purchase gold, which is then moved out of the United States and into Saudi Arabia. Emery had set Smith up for the fall all along just to help siphon off U.S. gold. The senior banker is portrayed as cavorting with the Arabs to thwart Smith's efforts. Boro National is only the tip of the iceberg, one of a group including fifteen other banks used to move billions of dollars into gold for the Arabs. Smith approaches Emery about his findings, and Emery tells him that managing #21214 for the Arabs is the most responsible thing to do to keep the world's economies afloat, to keep the world from panicking, to keep the dollar from collapsing, and to keep the world from a depression that would make the 1930s "look like a kindergarten." It is only a transfer of capital power, a normal ebb and flow of capital, and the system will be fine provided no one panics.

Meanwhile, Winters has listened to recorded conversations between her husband and Fewster, and she confronts Fewster. Fewster pleads with her to overlook the account and then takes his own life rather than be subject to a possible jail sentence when the cover is blown. Winters feels equally betrayed by Smith, who in the beginning was using her as a patsy of sorts. The audience, however, is encouraged by the narrative to forgive Smith because of his heroic stature and adherence to the myth. Additionally, the constructed villainy of the Arabs drives the audience to him. Winters approaches Naftari, demanding that the loan be renegotiated, lest the Arabs risk exposure. This makes Winters a target for assassination, which is foiled by Smith's timely rescue of her from a kidnapping attempt. The Arabs, consequently, pull out of all their American investments, causing the entire U.S. and world financial positions, institutions, and economies to collapse. Boro National is lost, First New York is lost. Winterchem is lost, Emery commits suicide. The world falls into the throes of a great depression, as Emery had predicted. However, the villainous Arabs are left standing, more financially sound than before and in total capitalistic control.

This Arab plot usurps the syntagmatic structure of the success myth of the entrepreneur. As the film progresses, the myth advances through the functions to the point at which the entrepreneurs leverage themselves to the hilt and risk a total loss (function 8). The audience is then introduced to the enemies, who want to protect their own status quo and their positions (function 9). Interruption of the syntagmatic structure occurs as these enemies, the Arabs, win out over the entrepreneurs (function 10). Although poised for the desired progression, the audience is kept from experiencing functions 11–15. The entrepreneurs' niches are never found (function 11). Capturing the market never occurs for Smith or Winters (function 12). The entrepreneurial team of Smith and Winters is unable to change and improve the way Americans live, where Americans live, and how Americans do business (function 13). In fact, America is left weakened and vulnerable to Arab whims that are beyond its control. The heroes cannot reap the rewards of success (function 14) or share it with the rest of us (function 15). Instead, *Rollover* ends in an unmitigated disaster brought on by the Arabs as America is plunged into total loss: national poverty and the loss of capitalistic control.

An analysis of the narrative through the syntagmatic structure of the film is only a portion of detecting the production of Orientalist fear in *Rollover*. Orientalist fear is also induced through threats to the paradigmatic structure of the success myth of the entrepreneur. *Rollover* spends much of its time and many scenes concentrating on the presentation of the heroes' adherence to the paradigmatic elements of the myth. Thus, the virtues of the heroic entrepreneurs should assure us of the righteousness of their characters, their activities, and their ultimate and inevitable victories. In the process the American Orientalist audience is sutured into the lives of the hero and heroine because of the ideological principles it shares with them. Meanwhile, the other characters of the film are open to a scrutiny and evaluation that are limited to establishing their capabilities to meet or support the paradigmatic elements of the mythic heroes. For example, very little of the film, approximately ten minutes, is devoted to depiction and development of the Arab characters, their world, and their lives. What we learn and see of the villains is mostly through the lens of their antipodal position relative to the paradigmatic structure of the heroes. Thus, Smith's and Winters's characters, worlds, and lifestyles are presented as enviable at first. Before long, however, continued exposure to them makes them so familiar to the audience that anyone else is perceived as alien and even inimical. Contrasts of good and evil develop, in which the possibility of the victory of evil will create feelings of discomfort, insecurity, and even fear in the viewers.

Ironically, this contrast not only relegates the Arab villains to the sphere of evil, but also excludes middle-class America from the sphere of good. Scenes of upper-class lifestyles become the norm for the audience. *Rollover* encourages its viewers to become what Paul Fussell calls "fantasist class climbers," whose movement up in class status is acquired through viewing. Meanwhile, the possibility of falling to a lower class now becomes a source of anxiety and embarrassment in light of their newly acquired ideal egos.[13] Thus, viewers learn to eschew and dislike Jerry Fewster, the federal bank examiner, with his pedestrian and bureaucratic life. His home has kitschy decorations; he has the burdens of a family man, driving a drab and low-priced automobile and dressing in off-the-rack suits and raincoats. His mundane life is reflected in his workplace, where he works at a desk in a pool of unimpressive coworkers. Fewster's physical and mental characteristics are far removed from those of the entrepreneurial heroes. He is nervous and guilt-ridden, and breaks down in tears because of his involvement in account #21214. When the going gets tough, he panics too easily. Likewise, the college professor at Columbia University is another middle-class character. He hosts Emery's lecture to the students and pales in comparison to Emery and Smith when the three are seen together. He is small in stature, presents a bookworm appearance, and wears a tweed sports coat that looks rough and ordinary in comparison to the well-tailored, expensive suits of Emery and Smith. He does not have a great soliloquy to add to the narrative and exits from the film when Emery dismisses him. Middle-class America falls victim to *Rollover*'s antipodal strategy in building heroic characters.

The mythic character of Smith is classically entrepreneurial, and this is summarily established at the beginning of the film. At the gala event, Emery's appeal to Smith to take the job at Boro National includes a recalling of Smith's entrepreneurial characteristics to Smith himself. Emery taunts Smith about Smith's interest in the position at Boro National. In reply to Smith's question, "What makes you so sure?", Emery tells him he must take the job because "you're restless, ambitious . . . and a sucker for a challenge at a star play." Smith cannot disagree. He acknowledges the characterization and identifies himself as the entrepreneurial patriot with the quote "That's the spirit that won the West," a reference to the nineteenth-century American business expansion that made the United States a leading industrial and financial world power. Interestingly enough, money, i.e., Smith's salary increase, is not mentioned as a motivating factor. The hero is amiably motivated by the entrepreneurial challenge and the qualitative reward, not the crudeness of cash.

Smith's visionary strength is demonstrated on his first day at Boro National: Boro National's employees feel the pressure of his powerful presence and gaze as they try to continue to work but know they are to be evaluated by the new boss who has come in to clean the place up. Not only do the employees on the floor notice him, but others outside the firm have called in to ask about him. When Lefcourt, Boro National's founder, asks what information Smith needs to gain an introductory knowledge of the firm, Smith suggests that he will look at a number of financial records "for a start." The request makes Lefcourt nervous. Smith is actually asking for an enormous number of financial documents. The next scene shows piles of documents being brought to Smith. He methodically reads the reports and is undaunted by the voluminous files that are placed in front of him. It is a scene that demonstrates his calm and controlled demeanor and that makes him look as if he is always making little effort at all. But Smith is probing deep into the firm's history and absorbing and learning its secrets. Smith's visionary power and business acumen reveal to Lefcourt what he, the founder, refused to see: "the patient" has been dead for six months.

Although Lefcourt is the founder of Boro National, he is a defeatist, and this characteristic may be the reason why the firm is in trouble. Lefcourt's negative character amplifies the message that Boro National needs Smith's entrepreneurial character. Lefcourt, an incompetent paternal role model, is ready to throw in the towel on his own invention. Smith, the competent model, offers a visionary plan of how to save the firm. He advises Lefcourt with the pithy statement "You can't beat the system, but you can win a game." During a period of the firm's despair, Smith as entrepreneur sees opportunity and is ready to act upon his hunch. Smith is able to master the documents and records that are piled high on his desk, and he detects an opportunity that no one else has. His sight zeroes in on the details of Winterchem Petrochemical. When the pessimistic Lefcourt tries to defeat "glamour boy" Smith with the information that Winterchem is off-limits because it already has borrowed the legal limit from Boro, Smith is not deterred. He has just spent the day learning Boro's financial position and now is ready to use the rules of the game to his benefit. Smith is a classical entrepreneur and has the foresight to see an opportunity in a simple luncheon with Winterchem's executives despite the present constraint.

Winters displays her own visionary strength at the luncheon. She can see that the Winterchem executives are making a mistake in not expanding the firm. She not only tells the executives that the firm must expand, but also presents them with a plan of purchasing a small Spanish firm to give Winterchem needed cash flow. While the board executives' vision is limited to the conversation at the table, Winters's entrepreneurial vision is global: her vision expands as far as Spain. Although Winters's vision is exceptional in comparison to her fellow executives, it remains less acute than Smith's. Throughout the film, she remains Smith's apprentice. This is in accordance with the prevailing American vision of male-dominated and paternalistic entrepreneurship. Although Winters possesses entrepreneurial characteristics, Smith is always in a dominant position over her and puts things into perspective for her or gives her guidance. Smith, playing her capitalist sage, must prod Winters to see further and asks her three provocative questions on the feasibility of the Spanish deal. If she can come up with the answers to these questions, she indeed has a mature entrepreneurial idea. And, as someone who understands human nature, he pushes her further to set her sight, along with his, on something bigger: that being her appointment as chairman of the board of Winterchem. The title of "chairman" gives her, a woman, the right to drive the destiny of her husband's firm in the right direction, to acquire the power of masculine capitalism, to emasculate those men who scoffed at her ideas, and to achieve the goals of male-dominated, entrepreneurial heroism.

Smith's cunning and strategic characteristics are played out in the ruse of the takeover luncheon. When Winters finds out that she is being squeezed out of the firm, the strategizing hero sees an opportunity for devising a ruse that will put pressure on Winters's fellow executives. Smith instructs Winters to make a luncheon date with a Japanese investor who has shown interest in buying Winterchem shares. This luncheon date is to be held at the same restaurant at which Smith will entertain the Winterchem executives. Just as Smith had foreseen, the ruse works: the Winterchem executives think that she will sell her shares to the Japanese investor, and they offer to give Winters the approval for the Spanish deal. Smith, being the fair-minded entrepreneur, offers his help to the losing side, "Would it make you any happier if I kept an eye on her for you?" The disturbed Winterchem executives, approving of Smith's entrepreneurial skills, express their eternal gratitude to Smith if he would use his paternalistic powers over the female Winters, who the executives fear will act irrationally just to get the deal to work. And Smith coyly acknowledges the

Rollover (1981). As the quintessential entrepreneur, Hub Smith (Kris Kristofferson) is a cool dealer, patient, disciplined, calm, and poker-faced. However, the Arabs' peculiar conduct of business baffles and frustrates him. Rather than being up-front and dealing face-to-face, the Arabs control with an invisible hand and often manifest themselves through short messages on the Teletype. Photo courtesy of the Academy of Motion Picture Arts and Sciences.

new loyalty and gratitude of those conquered: "Just your friendly neighborhood banker."

As the quintessential entrepreneur, Smith is a cool dealer, patient, disciplined, calm, and poker-faced. He deals with a mental toughness, rarely loses his temper, and attacks problems with efficiency. Others around him are always more nervous, less confident, and ready to panic. His request for the financial records is matter-of-fact, while Lefcourt finds it overzealous, cocky, and maybe even overwhelming. Despite the mounting pressure from the growing pile of files, he keeps focused, works methodically through them, and accepts more of them with nods of appreciation. While Lefcourt nervously watches Smith discover the secrets of the firm, Smith returns his look through the panels of the glass office with a cool smile. At the luncheon with the Winterchem executives, he keeps his emotions in check when he hears that Winterchem will not need to borrow another penny. Lefcourt, in contrast, immediately reacts to the news by breaking his gaze from the Winterchem executives and replying, "Well, I don't know what to say." All along Smith gazes expressionlessly at the executives. He is sizing up the Winterchem board members, looking for their weaknesses, and admiring the entrepreneurial spunk of Winters. His excellent judgment of character, an entrepreneurial instinct, picks Winters out of the group of board members. After excusing himself to leave, he secretly calls Winters at the table, asking, but actually instructing her, "How good are you at keeping a straight face?" Winters does a pretty good job of parrying his statements as she pretends to be speaking to her secretary. But she is not as skillful at keeping a poker face as Smith. She is somewhat hesitant and a little shaken by the charade. Smith's phone calls never betray his real thoughts and intentions to those whom he calls. Even when the Arabs hold out on the money, his phone call to Naftari is controlled, perpetuating the illusion that everything is according to plan.

When the Winterchem executives begin to panic, thinking that Winters is selling out her shares to the Japanese investor, Smith ignores Winters's performance with the statement, "Well, I'm starved. How about you guys?" And while Smith and Winters reconvene in his office to see if they took the bait, Smith must remind an anxious Winters to be patient. He knows that they must wait as long as it takes for the executives to give in. And his knowledge of human nature tells him that they will.

We witness the extent of Smith's loss of temper during Lefcourt's panic attack about the firm's inability to cover the loans as they await the rollover of funds from the Arabs. Lefcourt is beginning to crack under the pressure and picks up the phone to call the Federal Reserve Board for an emergency loan. Smith is cool, gives a firm and direct command to Lefcourt to hang up the phone, and then threatens him that he will tear the phone out of the wall and even break his arm. When Smith gets angry, his language changes to a more spontaneous use of profanity. The volume of his voice, however, remains relatively constant. When he confronts Emery about being used as a pawn in the #21214 deal, he warns Emery that he is trying to keep his temper. It is here that his voice cracks with emotion, mainly because of Emery's transgression against America. Overall, no matter how angry he gets on the inside, he is always outwardly poised and controlled.

Smith's entrepreneurial masculinity and sexual prowess are apparent in the quality of his voice and his good looks. He has a velvety deep voice that is punctuated with a cowboylike accent. He is full of pithy statements and down-home metaphors. His clever introduction of sexual innuendos into business conversations shows his sexual prowess as entrepreneur and adds to his sex appeal. When Winters asks his opinion about how to handle the presentation to Naftari in order to get the meeting with the Arab lenders, he tells her to be straightforward. At the same time he penetrates her with his gaze, almost undressing her. He coyly adds, "We have nothing to hide, do we?" Winters becomes so nervous because of her captivation with Smith during this moment and the double entendre of his statement that she averts her eyes and fumbles to collect herself for an exit. In another instance, when Lefcourt panics that the loans may not be covered, Smith sticks to his plan and demands, "Come on, Roy. Where's your balls?"

Smith is also a very attractive man. He is young, athletic, at times sweaty, tall, and has a full head of brunette hair that is still not fully grayed, much unlike other characters such as the Winterchem executives and Fewster, the bank examiner. A scar above his left eyebrow gives him the rugged look of a fighter who took a good blow, but remained strong enough to walk away. He seems to pierce objects with his grayish blue eyes. When he smiles, he displays deep dimples. When Smith enters a scene, he coolly swaggers across the floor, where others are seen to notice him. His masculine ability to penetrate is seen when he digs deep into the records of Boro National and Winterchem. Despite being initially denied access to First New York's account #21214, he penetrates Emery's office at night, finds Emery's little black book filled with computer pass codes, breaks the code, and makes off with the details of the account.

At intervals during the deal, he has sex with Winters. On the evening after the Winterchem executives agree to the deal, Smith takes Winters to bed and makes them late for Emery's dinner party. In that romantic scene, he passionately kisses and caresses her body, leads her partway up the rich staircase, and finally sweeps her off her feet and carries her up the rest of the way toward her bedroom. Although in this case we do not witness his performance, we are led to assume that their lovemaking was heated because she had to change gowns, from the virgin white gown she had been wearing to a black gown that she arrives in at the dinner. On the way home from Saudi Arabia after signing the loan, he passionately kisses her in the private jet's cabin. Here he announces his intentions to take her on as a close partner rather than use her as part of a business deal for Boro's gain. After sweating out the rollover of the first $100 million, he strides up Winters's staircase, open-collared, with champagne and two glasses in his hand. He swiftly kicks the door of her bedroom open, enters upon a startled Winters, yanks back her bed covers to expose her reclining body, and mounts her. And after he has had sex with her, she declares over the

Rollover (1981). In *Rollover,* Lee Winters (Jane Fonda) and Hub Smith (Kris Kristofferson) are business partners who become lovers. In this camera shot, cut from the final print of the film, sexual passion is shown to result from the business triumph over the Winterchem board of directors. The elegant marble and iron staircase of Winters's home are indicative of American wealth, but are paltry in comparison to the breathtaking beauty and size of the staircase, a sign of Arab "superwealth," seen later in the Saudi Arabian palace. Photo courtesy of the Academy of Motion Picture Arts and Sciences.

audience's view of clothes strewn about the floor, "I feel like the sack of Carthage." Her statement makes it obvious that his sexual performance was a powerful and energy-zapping experience. Then he initiates intercourse again. Even with his successful discovery of #21214 and obtaining the associated records, he celebrates by having sex with Winters, although this time he is preoccupied and worried — indicating to the audience that although he remains strong, the world around him may not be all right.

Smith's paternalism is obvious when he deals with Winters. But the role model he is intended to eventually be is that originally portrayed by Emery prior to our learning of the details of #21214. Emery is the senior businessman. He is much older than Smith. He has a sallow complexion and thinned-out hair, and is smaller in physical stature. From his office high above the ground, he can look down upon capitalist activity in the world's financial capital, New York City. It is from here, early in the film, as a photographer takes his picture for portraits and he poses in a fatherly stance, that he gives orders to an awaiting staff and instructs his employees that the run on the dollar started just a few blocks away at Boro National.

Emery is publicly sought after for his veteran business knowledge and wisdom. When he speaks, he commands respect, and people listen to him and follow his orders. This "Lion of American banking" is interviewed on television for his insight regarding the future of the American dollar, "our money," and the dangers of Arab financial power. His creed is that the world's economies are intertwined and that every nation must have each other's financial interests in mind. He is always in control and warns others to stay calm and not to panic. His knowledge is so extensive that he even knows who is responsible when Charlie Winters is killed. In another scene the audience witnesses him presiding over the college classroom lecture at Columbia University. He pontificates to the eager college students from a gilded high-back throne, as if he were a sage or king. He is quite certain of his paternal power as a capitalist and arrogantly declares, "I can't speak for the president of the United States. He runs his shop, I run mine." When Smith enters the room, Emery tells them Smith is "a most distinguished banker" who once sat in their place listening to Emery's wisdom twenty years earlier. Here, then, the audience witnesses generations of entrepreneurs: Emery is the paternal figure of the nation's economic life well into functions 14 and 15; Smith is the son, midway through the myth's functions, being readied to take over from Emery; and the students are the young brood starting out on the myth's syntagmatic path, as they are now in the process of developing in functions 1, 2, and 3.

The relationship between Emery and our entrepreneurial hero, Smith, is extremely paternalistic. At the gala event, Emery calls Smith "my boy." Emery knows the entrepreneurial character of Smith much as a father knows the character of his son. At the dinner party to which Smith brings Winters as his date, Emery dines at the head of the table with an approving smile of a father, but one who has detected the budding romance of his son. When Smith and Winters play football in his yard with other young

Rollover (1981). Maxwell Emery (Hume Cronin) is the "Lion of American banking" and sits on a regal throne while lecturing to a group of business college students. His paternal role in capitalist society indicates that he has reached the pinnacle, function 15 of the entrepreneurial myth, and now mentors America's next generation of entrepreneurs. However, his involvement in account #21214 and his secret dealings with the "evil" Arabs mean that he is actually putting at risk the future of American capitalism, wealth, and power in the world. Photo courtesy of the British Film Institute.

people, Emery stands on the patio like a father proudly overlooking his brood of youngsters at play. Even when Smith sneaks into Emery's office late at night, Smith is reminiscent of the son who enters his father's bedroom or study and looks through his dresser or desk drawers to find his masculine secrets. However, here it is not pornography that the son finds but the dirty secrets of the black book of pass codes to #21214 and the account's details.

Nevertheless, Emery's paternalism falters as the film unfolds. Emery is, as noted above, accustomed to others following his orders, given with paternal authority. In one instance, his paternal advice is dismissed, and that is by the Arabs. He warns the Arab prince that the Arabs are wrong in accelerating their plan to siphon off American gold and that it is unwise and dangerous to pull $95 million in one chunk out of an American bank the size of Boro National. He insists that they revert to the schedule of the original plan and not panic about a discovery of #21214. The Arab prince ignores him, patronizes him, and all but dismisses him. "All right, Max. We'll think about it. But I am not sure what our answer will be." And when Emery warns the Arab lender that the Arabs are "playing with the end of the world," the Arab prince returns with the dismissive and disparaging comment "The end of the world . . . as you know it." With this comment, the Arab prince forewarns Emery that his paternal reign is coming to an end.

A crucial display of Emery's loss of paternal authority, his steward-ship over the American economy, and his American heroism is played out when he tells Smith about the Arab scheme and his part in it. But it is Smith who displays true American patriotism when he tells Emery what he has learned about Emery's antipatriotic business deal with the Arabs. Smith, who has shown the poker face of the entrepreneur all along, begins to show a fissure in his façade, as indicated by his cracking voice. His entrepreneurial patriotism manifests itself when he chokes up over the American economy's loss of capitalist hegemony. Near tears, he says, "You're moving the Arabs into gold. You're taking them out of the dollar." He points out that in a case like this Emery should have let the government know about the Arabs' underhanded assault on the American economy. Emery's involvement in the Arab scheme has undermined the imagined democratic principle of the success myth, in which every entrepreneur has the chance to succeed from his own independent efforts.

Emery's defense is that he is no less concerned for American interests despite his actions. He points out that the best anyone can do against the overwhelming Arab wealth and its threat against American financial power is to keep American paternal stewardship over the system. This can at the same time, he assures Smith, preserve the American entrepreneurial spirit. He guarantees Smith this job can only be handled by the businessman; not even the U.S. president has the paternal ability to fore-stall this kind of danger. The fear that Emery instills in the audience is that the Arab threat is a movement that cannot be stopped. To try and stop the Arabs would create an Arab panic, provoking their rash nature, and then a worldwide depression would occur, the dollar would collapse, and money would not flow in and out of America. "In two months," he states, "you'll have breadlines in Detroit, riots in Pittsburgh. In six months, you'll see grass right over Rodeo Drive, and Michigan Boulevard, and Fifth Avenue."

While most of *Rollover* devotes its time to developing the rectitude of the heroes, their activities, and their world, very little time is devoted to developing the character of Arab enemies. Out of the 116 minutes of film, approximately 10 minutes shows the Arab in what is supposed to be his environment: in the desert, the tent, the palace, the bazaar; and on the yacht. But during the time in which the audience learns of its heroes and is encouraged to identify with them, the audience is at the same time learning, albeit subtextually, those characteristics that are Other. As Stuart Hall notes, identity of Self is a dialogic relationship to the Other, where one *is* as much as one *is not* and *vice versa.*[14] What is painstakingly developed as heroic gives the audience points from which to measure villainy. From the syntagmatic functions of the myth to the paradigmatic characteristics of the venerable hero, we can measure the Arab as enemy from his antipodal distance, his visibility, and his business maturity in relation to the heroes.

The difference between the Arabs and the heroes is measured in distance of place, culture, and wealth. Geographical place is set forth early in the film. The film's opening scene unveils place through the texts and financial statistics projected upon the walls of what becomes a large New York office at the beginning of a workday. The titles of these currency and financial securities quotation tables initially give the audience an ambiguous sense of place. It is an international sense of place that develops with the titles of Deutsch Mark, British Sterling, Swiss Francs, Dutch Guilders, Eurodollars, Fed Fund, and U.S. Bank CD's. At the same time, the audience is at a loss as it tries to make sense out of numbers so vast, quickly panned, and prefixed with an array of abbreviations and connections of dashes, slashes, and parentheses. This disorientation is important, because it inspires a sense of awe for those who know how to use these codes with ease. The audience defers to these literate businessmen and -women who staff the various work stations in the room. Place is ultimately reestablished for the viewers with the final illumination of the wall containing the map of the world, with the United States at its center. Jeremy Black points out that a map is designed to establish certain points and relationships and also illustrates themes of power in the minds of its users.[15] Here, then, the audience is assured by being shown that the United States is a financial center with relations to modern Western economies and is a place where business is a most important science. Meanwhile, the Arab Middle East is relegated to the geographic margins, denying its economic importance at this point.

Place in *Rollover* also involves a sense of class and privilege in the world of American wealth. The audience is introduced to the world of America's upper echelon of capitalist society. The film includes scenes in and the accoutrements of skyscraper offices and boardrooms that provide downward gazes upon the world; sleek and stately homes with domestic staffs; fine collectible artworks and overflowing floral decorations; lush green and landscaped acres of estates; power luncheons, formal dinners, and gala events; champagne flutes, cut-crystal tumblers; private jets and limousines equipped with private telephones; furs and jewelry, formal gowns and tuxedos, and designer outfits and classic suits. The audience is not only brought into this world, but it also becomes accustomed to it and even comfortable in it. It is in comparison to these narratively established American standards that the Arabs' world looks ever so exotic.

The Middle East is portrayed as a schizophrenic place. By this I mean that the things we think "fit" into the heroes' world, like symbolic icons of wealth and advanced civilization, are present but do not seem to belong in the Arab world. Symbolic opposites reside close together here. The Arabian landscape is depicted as a vast desert terrain with a single ribbon of road, which is used by camels, with their lumbering gait, and Rolls-Royces, with their luxuriously smooth performance. Out in the midst of this sublime isolation is a pay telephone. Moreover, an open-air tent is erected between the dunes and is decked out with enormous and elaborate Oriental carpets laid upon the sand. Before stepping inside this dwelling without walls, which makes it seem as if one is still outside, visitors must remove their shoes. It seems bizarre to have five Rolls-Royce automobiles surround this tent. The Arab patriarch, a man of enormous wealth, is a feeble man who must be helped up to greet his guests, Smith and Winters. There is no furniture in the tent. The attendees sit on the expensive rugs and have a business luncheon from large trays heaped with steaming rice and meat still clinging to the animals' carcasses. Nobody talks during this lunch. Smith and Winters are only given penetrating stares from the Arabs and are expected to share from the communal plate and to eat with their hands. Assuredly, this is an expensive and high-powered luncheon, but one so culturally distant from those seen minutes earlier in scenes in New York City or at the Emery estate. Moreover, the Arab patriarch is shown not to be a masculine match for or a business-savvy competitor to the American patriarch, Emery. Surprisingly, Smith and Winters adapt to this "alien" environment.

The Middle East is portrayed as a place disagreeable to the Westerner, an object of jealousy, an atmosphere of disempowerment, and a region isolated from the modern nations, as the Rolls-Royce carries Smith and Winters past the Arab bazaar. The Oriental sounds of a flute, the abutting tents of the market, and the types of commodities for sale make economic life in Arabia seem makeshift, ancient, chaotic, unsophisticated, and simplistic. There are no scenes of the sophisticated and capital-intensive oil drilling stations, refineries, and shipping ports that generate the wealth Smith and Winters are wishing to tap. The seemingly simple and immature Arab economy makes the power of Arab wealth appear unfair. The film pictures the Arabs as having done little work or made little effort to deserve such power. Winters states her disdain in a voiceover against this scene, "I feel like a beggar asking them for alms, and I hate it." Smith's reply affirms her thoughts as proper, objective, and realistic. He excludes the Arabs from humanity by stating, "You and the rest of the world."

Even the business office in the Middle East is a place of irrational business conduct. Smith and Winters find themselves in an immense room of a palace that makes no distinction between office and waiting room. Here, there are no windows overlooking a financial district, but only a series of skylights. Peter Burke has noted the importance of the staircase at Versailles as a symbolic presentation of French royalty's power, wealth, and triumph to its attendees at court.[16] *Rollover*'s Arabian palace also has an impressive staircase, captured by the camera only with the help of a wide-angled shot. It is made of marble and is so gigantic that it shrinks Smith's and Winters's bodies, as well as the dramatic staircases of Winters's rich home in New York and those of the endowed American institutions she attends. Ornate furniture is pushed to the sides rather than being placed in the center of the room, as the Western audience would expect. A number of visitors are present, but Prince Khalid sits at a distance from them and conducts the "family" business in a whispering voice, as if he had something to hide. His mention of the "family" implies a Mafia-style organization and a world where the democratic ideals of equal opportunity to succeed are overruled by hereditary autocratic power. As always, Smith remains patient during their long wait, while Winters begins to lose her composure. They are not treated with any special consideration, although they are the film's heroes, with a high-stakes deal in the balance. With the sound of the muezzin's call, business is stopped during the workday, and all the men in the room remove their shoes to congregate in the room's center to pray. In this place business practices are subordinated to the demands of praying at the appropriate time. Winters, the die-hard capitalist, reacts in shock to the "blasphemous" disregard of

Rollover (1981). Hub Smith (Kris Kristofferson) and Lee Winters (Jane Fonda), two American entrepreneurs, approach the Saudi Prince Khalid (Paul Hecht) for an enormous loan to fund their business ambitions. Styles of appropriate business attire seem to clash. The Arab prince is presented as wielding an overwhelming and arrogant financial power over the two successful Americans and making Winters feel "like a beggar asking for alms." Photo courtesy of the British Film Institute.

business. "I thought we had an appointment," she indignantly tells Smith. Smith cleverly answers, "This [meaning prayer to God] is an appointment." Winters's smirk not only acknowledges Smith's clever pun, but it also signals the Arabs' "business-immature" way of conducting business appointments. The activities of the Arab become laughable and are the subject of comic relief for the audience.

The style of dress in the Middle East is also shown as being different from that of the Western protagonists. Stella Bruzzi's study of costumes in film makes us aware that costumes are noteworthy. For Bruzzi, costumes must be considered in film studies, as they can be read as impositions of meaning upon character development and can actually create a discourse of their own.[17] While viewers become accustomed to the glitzy garments of Winters and the classic conservative styles of Smith in the American scenes, they are unaware that the costumes are in actuality priming them for the character differences of the Arab Others. In turn, the Arab garb becomes one of the few noteworthy symbols of character in a narrative that curtails Arab character development. Upon arrival at the luncheon tent, Smith's suit, tie, and clean-shaven good looks and Winters's long white dress and high heels contrast with the long, flowing white robes, red-checked kaffiyehs, mustaches and goatees, and sandaled feet of the Arabs. While the attire of Smith and Winters seems appropriate for stepping out of an expensive vehicle to attend a business luncheon in New York, it is out of place when the world of high finance is transplanted to the desert. At the same time, in Western eyes, the Arabs, in robes, look underdressed and anachronistic for the discussion at such a high-powered luncheon. The length, white color, and wind-fluttered movements of the robes in the wind match the feminine style of Winters's dress. Meanwhile, Smith, the masculine hero, stands out against them in his dark suit. The viewers feel uneasy in accepting the robe, with all its perceived informal, anachronistic, and feminine qualities, which has come to reflect the new attire of financial power.

Attention to costume provides more opportunity to determine the development of Orientalist fear in *Rollover*. The attire Prince Khalid wears on his yacht can be read as a discourse of mimicry. Prince Khalid is first introduced to the audience in the Arabian scenes. The audience does not see him as a part of his own mythical trajectory, which would give him positive character attributes, including proper and clear enunciation of his name. He blends in with the other Arabs, wearing a robe and mustache and goatee in the tent scene. In the palace, he comes more to the audience's attention because he makes the deal. Being portrayed without a human character, he becomes for the audience a body in royal robes that wields the power of the purse strings over Smith and Winters. In this costume, he dictates the terms of the loan with a poker face and reminds Winters that she is considered a "risk" by the family business and can go elsewhere if she can find a better deal. But, not unlike a loan shark, he also taunts her that he knows that she has nowhere else to go, otherwise she never would have come all the way to Arabia. The Arab costume, or "Arab kit" as noted by Jack Shaheen,[18] characterizes the man inside the clothes and becomes a stereotype of foreign, dictatorial financial power.

When seen on his yacht in Monte Carlo, Prince Khalid wears a black suit and tie. This attire not only meets the audience's expectation of appropriate attire for business discussion, something that has been witnessed in all the previous scenes of *Rollover*, but also matches the business attire of Emery, the Western paternal role model of capitalism. Emery stands in his suit and firmly tells the prince, "You cannot pull $95 million in one chunk from a bank the size of Boro National. . . . There will be no collapse in the foreseeable future unless you panic and start it with some damn fool move like this." Prince Khalid, now Emery's sartorial mirror image, responds, depicting a doomsday scenario, "And if you are wrong, what then? We wake up one morning, our oil is gone; we find that we have sold all we have for paper money that is worthless." This reprimand makes Emery break his gaze. Prince Khalid's choice of dress and use of capitalist thought are acts of mimicry flying in the face of the paternal capitalist and create a sense of ambivalence and menace for the Westerner. Prince Khalid is now seen to have adeptly adopted the cultural habits of the colonizing West, for which he should be commended. But, just as Bill Ashcroft, Gareth Griffiths, and Helen Tiffin point out in their description of "mimicry," Prince Khalid is a "blurred copy" that can be quite threatening because he is never very far from mockery.[19] In fact, he smirks at Smith's comments that the prince does not have both oars in the water, and he talks down to Emery. Now dressed in Western business costume, on an equal sartorial level, he tells Emery that the world, as Emery knows it, is coming to an end. In this scene, there is a crack in the certainty of Western dominance over the behavior of the East. Prince Khalid shows Emery that he is to become Emery's replacement in looks as well as in financial power. Fear is heightened for the audience: if out of fear the audience pushes the Arab threat back into the Otherness of the robe, it must also realize that the financial power of Prince Khalid in the robe may not be far away. Rather than conforming to Western stereotypes of the Middle East, the Arab has arrogantly infiltrated the capitalist ideology and the American economy.

These scenes are, however, very short and take little time to play out. Orientalist fear in *Rollover* also emanates from paranoia that the Arab presence lurks somewhere "out there" in the margin, with a watchful eye on our every move and a controlling hand in our every affair. Invisible as they may be, the Arabs have crept into American life and command a power over it from afar. Although we see very little of Arabs in the film, we hear of them often, mostly as a homogeneous collective whose motivation and interests are always in some relation to our own. After the initial fall of "our money . . . the dollar," a newscaster tells us of the historically unprecedented danger that the American economy faces because so much wealth is concentrated in the hands of one group: "the Arabs." Although Emery tells the newscaster that Americans are "an anxiety-prone people," she reminds him that the Arabs are a substantial "reason behind" American anxiety.

Rollover (1981). The Arabs are slow in rolling over funds to Boro National. As rumor quickly spreads that the Arabs may actually be pulling funds out of Boro National, other players begin to panic. The values of the dollar, mark, yen, pound sterling, and gilder on the international markets plummet and put the company into deeper trouble. Hub Smith (Kris Kristofferson) must make rapid decisions to hedge against the looming disaster. His answer: buy dollars to give the outward impression that there is nothing wrong. Photo courtesy of the Academy of Motion Picture Arts and Sciences.

In the scene of the gala event, the film cleverly symbolizes this invisible Arab presence and the scrutinizing power of the Arabs. In this scene, the American business elites enjoy their success by gathering together and offering their upper-class wealth in charitable contributions to the public museum. It is a display of functions 14 and 15. W. J. T. Mitchell points out in his visual studies book about dinosaurs that the dinosaur skeleton given to the natural history museum is an ideal object of capitalist philanthropy. According to his description of Andrew Carnegie's *Diplodocus carnegii,* the gift of the dinosaur to the natural history museum is a symbol of Carnegie's patriotic gift of national pride, a conspicuous display of American wealth, bigness, and modernity, and a personal display to the public of his own power.[20] In this scene of *Rollover* we see the wealthy capitalists following a similar ritual. Although there are no dinosaurs here, the late-twentieth-century capitalists stand in front of the once great strength and beauty of stuffed wild animals in dioramas most probably financed by their contributions. They range from corals and fish to larger predators such as polar bears, walruses, sharks, and giant squid. In a certain respect, the animals portray an evolutionary chart of the natural world from simple organic soup to ferocious meat-eating predators to the capitalists who are the pinnacle of the food chain. It is a certain sense of security that these guests enjoy in their giving, in their civility, and in their natural and financial class positions. But, just as Smith points out, security is an illusion. Above the partying crowd lurks a leviathan, a much larger mammal that is too big to fit within the purview of the camera lens: the stuffed whale. If the animals on the floor contextualize the strength, ferocity, and power of the American capitalists, then the whale above, in the margins and out of sight, symbolizes an unnoticed opponent for sovereignty over the natural world and the evolutionary chart: the Arab superwealthy. The mammoth creature, size being indicative of wealth, dwarfs them. And the camera zeroes in on its surveying eye, the symbolic Arab gaze that looks down upon the unnoticing, seemingly safe, crowd.

The Arab controls with an invisible hand, which can reach into American lives and can even murder. As Charlie Winters works late in his office discovering the details of account #21214, he feels the presence and gaze of someone behind the curtains. The leather-gloved assassin, who is hired by the Arabs to protect Arab secrecy and is suggestive of Mafia-like business tactics, lurches out to murder him just in time. His leather-gloved hand indicates that, although a Caucasian-American commits the act, it is a darker-skinned being that is guilty. The leather-gloved hand absconds with the blood-soaked information. As if by proxy, the assassin keeps the nervous and guilt-ridden Fewster under a watchful eye so that he will not crack. And the assassin murders Winters's driver during the attempt to kidnap and murder Winters after she dares to blackmail the Arabs.

The Arabs are difficult to reach in their far-off lands, so the heroes must use their intermediaries, such as Naftari. The Arabs are able to convince others, like Emery and the assassin, to do their work for them. Little information is given about the Arabs apart from what Naftari tells Smith: "These people are unpredictable. They make up their own minds." When Smith is stymied over the delay of the first $100 million to be rolled over, a whopping loss in interest that he declares not even the Arabs can afford, he must obtain news from Naftari. Furthermore, it is Naftari who informs Emery of the Arab decision to pull all assets, not the Arabs themselves. And although Naftari is well connected with them, he plays as if he, too, is distant from them.

Moreover, the Arabs are those who give the heroes impersonal directives that seem irrational, inconsiderate, and nonchalant. They manifest themselves through short messages and noises of the Teletype. Their appearances through the Teletype come when they choose, and not as quickly as the heroes would like them. Smith must wait at the office until the early morning hours for them to announce the rollover of the funds. The Arabs have no regard for Smith's concern for the deal, for his fatigue, or for Lefcourt's fears of federal prosecution should they whimsically choose to back out of the deal. Even their final decision to withdraw all the funds from American investments is announced in the same way, via cold, bold-faced Teletype message, to Naftari. All the crucial decisions, other than the loan to Winters, are made from afar, offscreen, without display of logical reasoning, and without direct contact. The sweeping decision, "immediate withdrawal all U.S. banks," comes out of the Teletype. It taps the emotions of suspense as the Arabs reveal themselves and control our heroes' fate slowly, letter by letter, forcing the reading viewers to anticipate the next word and the meaning of the message. The message from a distant dictator that is awaited by the human being at the receiving end gives the invisible Arabs a dominant power over the receivers, including the audience. The Arabs' presence is apparent in, and yet immune from, the perils of chaos that occur throughout the world once the decision to pull their money out of American banks has been announced. Their actions have caused the global chaos, but they do not suffer from it.

Rollover uses classic mythic scenes of the 1929 Wall Street crash to develop the fear of financial ruin in the contemporary imagination fifty years later. At Boro National, a silent trading floor is given its orders from the floor manager. The audience hears the words "The Arabs yanked every penny they had with us. They hit all the other outfits too, so it's across the board. That means every bank in the country out there is going to be struggling for liquidity trying to cover those cash withdrawals." The floor manager announces, "We're dumping everything." He gives the selling directives that will zero out all the numbers that were seen projected on the walls in the beginning of the film and were associated with American dominance. The trading fury starts with his words "All right, let's hit it. And pray." It is as if the world has come to the final struggle of good and evil that only God can right, and of course this "right" must be in favor of the Americans. Lefcourt tries to give Smith ideas of how to save themselves, but the defeated and distraught hero dismisses him with the words "It's over, Roy." The scene of frenzied selling is intended to symbolize the economic maelstrom of a failing capitalist structure and a battle to minimize losses. A tearful worker gives the manager the financial casualty reports: "Stock market's off 75 points, the dollar's depreciated 10 percent and moving down. They even yanked the Eurodollar deposits that weren't due. First New York is practically down the tubes and gold just went over [$]2,000." To which the manager replies, "By tonight that will be cheap." The scene sounds much like William K. Klingaman's description of October 24, 1929, "Black Thursday":

> A furious wave of selling engulfed the exchange. Good stocks, bad stocks, all were tossed indiscriminately into the maelstrom. Blocks of ten to thirty thousand shares of stock were unloaded wholesale upon the sinking market by frantic brokers who watched helplessly as prices dropped five or ten points *between each sale* of high-priced issues such as RCA, AT&T, and U.S. Steel. Mob psychology reigned unchecked. Minute by minute, the violence of the selling movement kept increasing until the market broke under the strain and became completely demoralized.[21]

Even the floor manager loses faith in the dollar and secretly calls his wife to take a suitcase to the bank and withdraw all their money. Scenes of bank runs, frenzied selling, falling prices, lost life savings, civil chaos, organized prayers, American dollars burning, disbelief, and despair are shown from a CNN report that includes the words "The growing paralysis of the industrial world has left millions without jobs, without money, and without hope." The CNN logo with real-life documentary narrator George Page as newscaster endows *Rollover*, a fictive narrative, with a sense of documentary realism and possibility. Entextualized footage of actual mass congregations or protests of people in famous cities around the world is recontextualized to produce a sense of global panic in relation to *Rollover*'s Arab treachery. Images of peaceful prayer at the Vatican, demonstrations in Washington, fire in front of the White House, protests in Rome, fighting in Seoul, confrontations with police in London, chanting crowds in Cairo, Madrid, and Paris are enlisted and juxtaposed to one another to create a unified bankrupt world, which "seems to be teetering on the very edge of anarchy." The scenes are meant to show that the rash Arab decision is far-reaching and too much for humanity to bear. Maxwell Emery, with a suicidal bullet in his head, stares nonseeing at the television report.

On the one hand, we are satisfied that he has received just punishment for aiding the foreigner in creating this debacle. On the other hand, we are discouraged because even the paternal figure of capitalism has lost faith.

To show that not only the West suffers the effects of the treacherous Arabs, the Communist bloc also appears in the newscasts to be affected by the Arab-induced depression. The Arabs are thus marked as a menace to the entire human race. They have defeated capitalism at its own game and at the same time destroyed the Communist system. The Arabs' effect is as destructive as a nuclear bomb. Kim Newman's study of "end of the world" movies points out that evil totalitarians, global war, alien invasions, capitals in flames and turmoil, and nuclear winter are the icons of an imagined world ravaged by nuclear holocaust. Aliens, mirroring the worst forms of mankind, and colossal giants are the icons that emerge from the nuclear fallout.[22] *Rollover* borrows from this film genre by creating an atmosphere of world war started by a far-off enemy and a defensive reaction emanating from an order to the front line from a centralized office. However, *Rollover* replaces the Cold War scenario of United States versus USSR with the United States versus the Arabs. Boro National's office is left in total darkness and depleted of its people. Human activity has halted and a dead silence reigns. Computers and business machines are covered with tan tarps, turning the once animated, productive office and discernible place into a desert wasteland. We have seen in *The Exorcist* this same ploy: the Arab destroys the Western world and makes it as desolate as his own. *Rollover* ends with the Arabs reigning over the world with their unfathomable wealth as a colossal giant—a popular American fear in the 1970s. And even in the film's end the Arabs, though unseen, are symbolically present as the shadow that darkens Boro National's world map like a black cloud blocking out the sun. In the nuclear war films, the bomb has fallen into the wrong hands. In *Rollover,* it is not the bomb per se. The world can be destroyed almost as soundly if capitalist power falls into the wrong hands. Capitalism has been taken over by a race that is crafty, myopic, rash, uncivilized, evil, business-immature, and definitely not entrepreneurial. The world is doomed, with the exception of one light that shines upon the heroes in the desolate Boro National office. The entrepreneur has been unable to secure America's primary position in world economic advancement. The work of the Founding Fathers, as described by DiBacco, has been overturned and the prideful course of American history has ended. America is no longer economically independent, but relies upon a foreign power for its economic direction. Despite the entrepreneur's virtues, evil has triumphed and changed the course of history. Smith, the entrepreneur, has lost capitalism to an invading force.

Nevertheless, there is some room for hope, words to succor the American Orientalist audience, and a reprieve from complete and final devastation. We must remember that the entrepreneur is a survivor who finds more opportunity in a pink slip than in a promotion. *Rollover* confirms the belief that America will win another day as long as entrepreneurialism remains a part of our national character. And so, Smith announces that he is trying to "look for a way to begin again," and Winters offers to join him as his partner. *Rollover* ends with the American entrepreneurial spirit still raising its head.

*U*NLIKE *Rollover,* with its entrepreneurial heroes, John Frankenheimer's *Black Sunday* has no American heroes.[1] It is their very absence
that proves to be important in revealing a sense of anxiety for the American Orientalist audience. In their place is the Israeli hero, Major David
Kabakov (Robert Shaw), a leader of an antiterrorist commando unit, who
has come to America to foil an Arab terrorist plot against the United
States. This plot entails an attack on Americans where they feel most at
home and where it will hurt them the most: at the Super Bowl game. However, Kabakov's Israeli methods seem rather extreme to and are definitely
not appreciated by American law enforcement despite his attempt to protect Americans. FBI agent Sam Corley (Fritz Weaver) sternly points this
out to Kabakov and his partner, Robert Moshevsky (Steven Keats), "Yes,
well, I'm going to have to give you a warning. In your own operational
circle in Israel, I understand behind your back they call you 'The Final
Solution'—a man that takes things to their ultimate conclusion and beyond. . . . Yes, well you're not going to do it here. Whatever you may think
of our methods, you'll play by our rules or leave. In fact, you'll be lucky
to be allowed to leave. I mean it. It applies to both of you." The American
Corley, as Moshevsky later states, needs a bit of "Israeli advice."

Neither Corley nor any of the other American characters in the film
display any heroic characteristics. In fact, they can be considered as characters that disappoint an audience versed in the ideology of American
exceptionalism and the American frontier myth. To make matters worse,
one of the villains and engineers of the attack is a disenfranchised and
deranged American Vietnam veteran who has painstakingly planned and
designed the assault on his own country. Frighteningly so, *Black Sunday*'s
cinematic America is on its path to a mood of "malaise," a term President
Jimmy Carter would later use in diagnosing the real America. Orientalist
fear develops when Arab terrorists creep into the country, take advantage
of this situation, and victimize the American people. This ailing cinematic
America is, in essence, subject to its own incompetence, Arab infiltration,

and surprise attack while shackled and weighted down by demoralization and dysfunction.

Black Sunday appeared in American theaters at a time when, as described by Richard Slotkin, the "American frontier myth" no longer defined crises and provided scenarios of resolution for the nation. The myth had been shattered after such experiences as Vietnam, Watergate, the Arab oil embargo, and stagflation.[2] Furthermore, Melani McAlister points out that by 1976, "the public image of the U.S. military was quite low, and the assessment of Vietnam as a misguided intervention and an unwinnable war was commonplace."[3] However, she adds that with the Israeli victories over the Arabs in 1967 and 1973, the Israeli will to fight Arab terrorism, and the successful raid on Entebbe in 1976, American culture became enthusiastic about and vicariously riveted to the young, small, but victorious Jewish nation. McAlister notes, "After Entebbe, and after Saigon, Israel became a prosthetic for Americans; the 'long arm' of Israeli vengeance extended the body of an American nation no longer sure of its own reach."[4] Similarly, the Israeli Kabakov in *Black Sunday* becomes a protagonist who has to take on the role of the frontier hero for the Americans in order to save America from itself and from the opportunistic treachery of the Arabs. The "Israeli advice" that Moshevsky is talking about is an act of reminding America of its need to recapture its lost frontier spirit.

Slotkin's work is important in understanding the American sense of frontier and the concomitant use of violence, and it provides an interesting paradigm useful in reading the actions and motivations of characters and the cinematography in *Black Sunday*. The American frontier myth, according to Slotkin, centers on the conquest of the wilderness and the subjugation or displacement of the native peoples who originally inhabited it so that "we" Americans might achieve "national identity, a democratic polity, an ever-expanding economy, and a phenomenally dynamic and 'progressive' civilization."[5] The myth deals with the redemption of the American spirit as something to be achieved through a scenario of separation from civilized life, temporary regression to a more primitive or "natural" state, and regeneration through violence. Central features of the myth, then, are conflict and violence, which often deal with the struggle against nature and nonwhite natives. Instruments of violence such as the rifle, as Slotkin states, become symbols of civilization and progress as much as the axe or plow.[6] Episodes of "savage war" characterize each phase of the westward expansion.

The concept of "savage war" is based on the belief that the enemies are "savages" who, by the combination of their "blood" and culture, are inherently incapable of and opposed to progress and civilization. This makes white European-American coexistence with the savages impossible on any basis other than subjugation. Struggle against the savages is a struggle to defend civilization from them. The struggle is inevitable and considered a just and righteous cause that can only end when the savages are rooted out and exterminated. The savages are bloodthirsty and are capable of committing heinous acts, i.e., "savage acts," when in conflict. These savage acts are so extreme that they defy the laws of nature. The savages massacre, torture, terrorize, rape, and sexually mutilate members of the civilized race. Therefore, progressive and civilized people must meet these enemies on the savages' own ground and fight on the very terms with which the savages fight. The civilized race learns to respond in kind, partly from outrage, and partly from recognition that imitation and mastery of the savages' methods are the best way to defeat them. This means that the normal restraints of civilized custom and morality must be suspended in order to achieve victory. The American principles of "fair play," "democracy," and "government by the consent of the governed" must be abandoned in defense of progress and civilization until the savages are annihilated. There are no compromises. Once the savages are eliminated, the Americans can return to a better life without consideration of guilt or moral decay.[7]

In the "savage war" scenario there is a particular heroic style embodied in the American. The heroic style is modeled on the progressive frontier hunter and has been extended to such figures as the cowboy, corporate manager, and military man.[8] This hero is part of civilization and a paragon of virility. His use of violence proves that he is truly red-blooded and aristocratic. The American frontier hero is an agent of civilization, of progress, and of the white race. He must, therefore, be recognized, revered, and encouraged by the civilized society. He must be licensed to shoot first and ask questions later in order to exterminate the savages if that is what the preservation of civilization requires. He has an intimate knowledge of the enemies' thought processes, and he can destroy the enemies with the enemies' own weapons and tactics. He is, as Slotkin calls him, "a man who knows Indians" and can even be so extreme as to be called an "Indian-hater."[9] He can mirror the enemies in professional skill, ruthlessness, terror, and action. He believes in taking the shortest way possible with the savages and never fails to embrace an opportunity to kill them. In his historical past, he may have had an experience of horror committed by the savages, and he may suffer from an atrocious loss caused by the savages. There are two possible outcomes for this type of hero: he exterminates the savages and returns to civilization to participate in its progress; or he is carried so far into the "dark" side of the savage war that he becomes dependent on perpetual engagement with the objects of his hatred and can never return to civilization.

Savage war in *Black Sunday* is the war against the Arab savages, in this case, the Palestinian Arabs. The film portrays Palestinian Arabs as ruthless, vengeful, and indiscriminate killers. On the other hand, the Israeli Kabakov plays the heroic "man who knows Arabs," who can and will defeat the savages in the mythic frontier so that civilized society can flourish. In an odd twist on the American frontier myth, the mythic frontier and the battle scene of the savage war do not lie somewhere "out there" in a landscape waiting to be civilized. It is, in fact, in the United States itself where the spirit of progressive civilization has somehow been lost.

Black Sunday's Americans have lost their sense of the American frontier myth. As a result, America has become impotent, mundane, irrational, and powerless. America has turned inward from the tragic experiences of the 1960s and 1970s, in particular the defeat of the Vietnam War. The Vietnam experience, according to Slotkin, was a recasting of the frontier ideology taken overseas by the Kennedy and Johnson administrations. But after defeat, America, just as it is represented here in *Black Sunday*, no longer had the "progressive" visionary power it once had.[10]

Michael Lander (Bruce Dern), a U.S. Navy pilot, is introduced to the audience via a propaganda film produced by the North Vietnamese and now viewed by the members of an Arab terrorist cell: Black September. In this film, Lander walks slowly to the microphone, bows to his captors, and speaks while other demoralized American POWs sit in the room without objecting to his speech, as if they are in tacit agreement. Lander squints under the bright lights, under the close-up shot of the Communists' camera, and under the scrutinizing gaze of the Arabs watching the film. Moreover, his image in the black-and-white film embodies, for the audience, a dreamlike flashback to the Vietnam experience buried deep within the American psyche. Lander, no longer a righteous frontier hero, admits that his military actions were atrocities that were unnecessarily savage and deserve to be punished as war crimes. He shows himself to be repentant about his destructive actions, which sought to eliminate his enemies, and about the suffering he has caused. He calls for America to end the war. The defeated frontier hero admits his guilt and shame, whether he be-

Black Sunday (1976). In their hideout somewhere near Beirut, Black September members view an older film clip of U.S. Navy pilot Captain Michael Lander (Bruce Dern) as a POW in the Vietnam War. Lander squints under the bright lights of the Communists' camera recording the event and the gaze of the Arab viewers watching the film. Lander, as seen here, is no longer a righteous frontier hero and admits that his military actions were atrocities that were unnecessarily savage and that he deserves to be punished for war crimes. Photo courtesy of the Academy of Motion Picture Arts and Sciences.

lieves his words or is forced to say them. And the American audience that has acquired a cultural anxiety of defeat and shame from the experiences of the war is interpellated by Lander's humiliation.

When Lander returns home as a four-times-decorated hero, he is no longer in control of his mental faculties. He now suffers bouts of severe depression and paranoia, a result, the film suggests, of the Vietnam experience. The film spends much time constructing his mental instability.

Lander moves quickly between being a man with a calm and collected demeanor and being a raving, sobbing, and dangerous lunatic. Lander is always on the edge of snapping. He no longer flies those fast, sleek, and penetrating jets over the Vietnam frontier, bombing and shooting the enemy. Now he flies the plump and lumbering Goodyear blimp over crowded football stadiums, taking photographic shots for television stations. After a difficult and stressful day of flying the blimp in which he was unable to meet the photographic requirements of the news media he laughs at his failure, carefully buttons his handsome uniform, and walks away with a confident saunter. Yet later that night, he hides in his darkened and messy home. Wild-eyed and disheveled, he aims a loaded shotgun at Dahlia (Marthe Keller), the Black September commando who has become his girlfriend, because of her seemingly small transgression of not calling him for three days. Dahlia calms him down, but the next day he is ready to snap again when she encourages him to keep his appointment at the Veterans Administration for ongoing psychiatric counseling. She hopes to keep others from seeing Lander's mental instability and thereby becoming suspicious of the impending attack that they plan on the Super Bowl crowd. While awaiting his turn in the VA waiting room, he trembles and sweats from anxiety, and then puts on the demeanor of a collected man in front of his counselor, Mr. Pugh (William Daniels). Lander can whistle his way through police and FBI agents on an impounded vessel while disguised as a telephone repairman, and at the same time engineer a murderous telephone bomb that will rip the head off the one who answers the fatal call. He can calmly and extemporaneously play the role of a real estate scout for a conglomerate purchasing a tract of isolated land and, moments later, can marvel at the beauty of death and destruction he can cause. In essence, Lander falls victim to the mental anguish developed during his frontier experience in Vietnam. For Lander, the frontier experience proved devastating. He has not been able to return to civilization to lead a "normal," let alone a better, life. Although he may be lost on the "dark side" of the savage war in Vietnam, he does not continue his war against the Vietnamese enemy. Instead, he is so twisted that he has turned against his own nation and has mistaken his American compatriots as the objects of his savage war.

However, Lander is not the only one suffering from mental dysfunction. American civil society as a whole is showing signs of disturbance. America has become rude and sluggishly bogged down with bureaucracy. When Lander reluctantly goes to the VA, dressed in his handsome pilot's uniform in an effort to perform normally, the surly receptionist is un-impressed. Her plump physique and fingernail-filing while at work are symbolic of an America that has become languid, passive, and too bureau-cratic. Although Lander arrives on time for his 10:30 A.M. appointment, he is coldly and boorishly told to take a number, which turns out to be num-ber 52; and the next to be called is 23. Lander must wait in a room crowded with handicapped, older, and less physically striking veterans who must be attended to before his number is called from the loudspeaker. The re-ceptionist's humiliating demeanor is exemplified when she announces his number via the PA system despite the fact that he is only one of two people left in the room. His seat is close enough to her that a personal address would have been more polite, but such a gesture would be alien to this new national character. The use of the PA system even symbolizes an American culture's desire to distance itself from the war experience and the soldiers who may be blamed for having lost it. Once Lander is inside the coun-selor's office, it becomes apparent that Mr. Pugh is not at all acquainted with his case, making his wait, in retrospect, seem even more frustrat-ing. Even with Lander's large file in front of him, Pugh exhibits glaring gaps in his knowledge of Lander's case. For example, Pugh is unaware that Lander's wife left him one month after his POW release and that she refuses to let his young children see him. Pugh does not blame his own incompetence or laziness for his lack of preparation, but rather the bad note-keeping of an absent predecessor.

The American government is also depicted as becoming dysfunctional. Despite his mistreatment as a returning Vietnam hero in the care of the government, Lander sardonically points out to Pugh, "Don't be dismayed, sir. The government did everything that they could." He goes on to de-scribe how a U.S. naval officer was dispatched to his wife to counsel her during Lander's captivity. Instead of helping Lander, the government en-voy undermined him by telling her that it was likely Lander would be less of a man upon his release due to the high rates of impotency and homo-sexuality among former POWs. Also, Lander suggests that the govern-ment envoy was giving her "a little dick on the side." But it is the govern-ment itself that has become impotent, and it is Lander's intent to make this obvious. In one example, he uses his wits and physical skills to prove this as he prepares for the terrorist assault. When Lander and Dahlia are caught by the U.S. Coast Guard smuggling crates of plastic explosives into the United States, Lander takes the Coast Guard on a high-speed boat chase. He is able to outrun the government boats, outmaneuver them, and hide from them despite their sophisticated and high-powered equipment. He outruns two Coast Guard vessels and escapes with perfect timing, something he had planned in advance. He slips his boat under a railroad bridge that cannot be raised to accommodate the Coast Guard boats' pursuit, a metaphor of American impotency. The bridge is already committed to an oncoming and scheduled freight train. Instead, the U.S. Coast Guard must give up and admit defeat.

Other American law agencies are also powerless, but it is Corley who represents the epitome of the American government's impotence. Corley is the FBI agent who is slow in action, sluggish in processing information, and soft when confronting the enemy. When arriving at the impounded ship that supplied Lander and Dahlia with the plastic explosives, Moshevsky, the Israeli agent, must prod Corley to dispense with simple introductions of law enforcement agents to each other. Moshevsky rushes Corley on board the ship so they can get on with the investigation. Corley boards the ship as Washington's law enforcement representative just as the officials of the Customs Department and Coast Guard are willing to surrender custody of this detained Japanese ship, under Libyan charter. Although the audience has witnessed that the Japanese captain is definitely involved in the smuggling, he denies it and the government officials on board the ship are happy to accept his story and let his ship go. In turn, Corley unknowingly passes by Lander, who is disguised as a telephone installation man. Lander is installing a telephone bomb on board to silence the Japanese captain so that he will not endanger the terrorist plot. Lander, the perpetrator, is right in front of Corley but passes unnoticed by Corley. The government officials are also willing to accommodate the Turkish shipper who is involved in the smuggling scheme by letting the other cargo in the hold go without further investigation. They are perfectly satisfied that everything is in order after a routine search, although the Israeli Moshevsky demands more information from the now indignant Japanese captain. Moshevsky notices and mentions the impotence of the U.S. government to Corley as they both witness the government officials' acquiescence in the clearance of the ship. Corley does not enter into the discussion but remains passively standing by as the others discuss and decide the fate of the ship and then exit before he can speak. Moshevsky jabs at Corley with the sarcastic statement "It's wonderful to see the FBI step in, Mr. Corley." Later in the film, Corley cannot get the president of the United States to cancel an appearance at the Super Bowl even though Corley knows that the president's life is in danger. The political needs of boosting presidential popularity ratings, an expected outcome of the public appearance, override the FBI's warnings of national risk.

Black Sunday's America has become what Susan Jeffords calls in her book of Vietnam War narratives a "feminized" America. Jeffords shows us how more recent post-Vietnam representations work to remasculinize America in response to the infiltration of feminine characteristics, much like those shown in *Black Sunday,* resulting from the loss of the war and the enactment of civil rights legislation. Feminized characteristics include weakness, passivity, nonaggression, and an inclination to negotiate—traits that are shown to be responsible for losing the Vietnam War and for the diminishing power of the white American male. An America such as this has strayed from the patriarchal culture where masculine characteristics, male-male bonding, assertiveness, and decisiveness, dominate. In her analysis, Jeffords chooses films according to the presence of remasculinizing narratives in them. However, this discussion of *Black Sunday* confirms how, as she asserts, the Vietnam experience has feminized America, and in the process created an environment of vulnerability that makes the nation an easy target for an aggressive outsider. Yet the conclusions, whether analyzing the Vietnam narratives or *Black Sunday,* are the same. Jeffords concludes from her investigations that the female gender is the real aggressor against American masculinity. Indeed, what happens in *Black Sunday* also confirms Jeffords's deduction. Here, too, the enemy of America is on one level the Palestinian Arab, but it is also the female gender.[11] Her name is Dahlia.

Dahlia is introduced early in the film as she takes us into the film's narrative, beginning with the establishment of place: the Arab land. *Black Sunday* opens with the presentation of pre–civil war Beirut. Unlike the ancient vistas of the Middle East in *The Exorcist* or the depictions of mega-wealth in the desolate and backward land in *Rollover,* this Middle Eastern land is portrayed as a labyrinth full of the symbols and events of political instability, violent gunfights, and deadly explosions. For the audience, it represents an exotic frontier that is indeed somewhere out there. Borrowing from Martin Rubin's study on the construction of Hollywood thrillers, we can say that the presence of the labyrinth is important to establishing the thriller aspect of the Arab environment in *Black Sunday.*[12] The labyrinth creates a chaotic Arab place where one can easily get lost. The film opens with the audience viewing the city from its oceanfront. This oceanfront is chaotically filled with nondescript, low-level buildings and seaport docks. Subtitles tell the audience that this is Beirut on November 12[, 1976].

Then, suddenly, the film cuts to the Beirut airport. Frankenheimer uses a handheld camera to enhance the experience of the labyrinth. This cinematographic method creates a sense of unsteadiness and disorientation inside the labyrinth for the audience. The cinematic gaze fixes on the back of a woman who has just arrived. Her long brown hair is pulled back in a ponytail, and she wears a Western-style skirt and blazer. The film creates an exercise for the audience's cinematic gaze, as it must be trained to recognize and follow her as she travels and leads us into the heart of this Arab land. She becomes a fixed object that we must rely upon as a guidepost in this strange land. This woman seems to entrap viewers from the start, making them dependent on her and aware of their weaknesses as Americans in a foreign land. First, the woman enters into a crowd of kaffiyeh-covered heads, symbolizing the entry into the Arab world. The camera then cuts to a line of soldiers standing behind a row of barbed wire outside a building. To the audience, this land seems so unstable that it requires a military constantly on the defense and on alert. While it seems that she has been lost in the crowd, or maybe has given the audience the slip, the cinematic gaze can pick her up again in the distance as it glimpses her getting into a taxicab. The cinematic gaze follows her taxicab past marching soldiers and Arabic marching commands. Upon arrival at the dark portal of an Arab bazaar, she exits the taxicab and enters the labyrinth of the marketplace. She pulls the audience deeper into this mysterious Arab frontier. She makes her way through the labyrinth-like marketplace in a sequence filled with quick contrast-of-view camera shots of twists and turns, staircases, spices, colorful cloths, trinkets, a funeral procession, crowds, running children, covered women, shuffling old men, and loitering young men. In *Black Sunday*, there is no grand introductory background music—so typical in many other thriller films. We only hear the sounds of the Arab frontier–like boat whistles, car horns, traffic, indiscriminate voices, strange language, chanting crowds, and Arabic music. Dahlia's seemingly Western form, then, becomes a very important crutch to lean on in this world. We finally get a chance to see her face during her quick meeting with a swarthy Arab man who whispers to her, but the audience is not allowed to hear his message over the street noises. Once she gets the message, she takes off again into the labyrinth. The cinematic gaze at times follows her and at other times gets lost again, and the audience must pick her out from among the crowds. Her Western-style appearance, different from the rest of the inhabitants, makes this less difficult. She, too, seems uneasy in this place. She constantly looks over her shoulder and about for direction and in fear of being watched. Finally, on the other side of the bazaar, she quickly and quietly gets into another taxicab and is driven to a gated compound, guarded by bodies with kaffiyeh-covered heads and automatic rifles. Kaffiyeh-covered peasants pass by with their goats and donkeys.

In the next scenes, the audience learns that Dahlia is a member of a Black September cell housed inside the compound. Moreover, the audience comes to understand in these scenes, and throughout the film, that Dahlia is a woman with the ability to assert power over men. She makes forceful demands on men, persuades them and controls their actions, and takes on disguises that fool them. She portrays the classic profile of a modern terrorist of the 1970s: young, well educated, militant, and willing to die for her cause. But most of all, she is dangerous because she is a cold-blooded killer of men. She enters into the compound welcomed, not stopped, by the lethal guards. Inside, she stands in a room otherwise filled with male terrorists and watches the film of Lander's POW confession. Showing signs of her characteristic impatience, she struts in front of the screen and shouts in Arabic for the Lander film to be turned off. The male projectionist complies with her demand. Her knowledge of the Arabic language differentiates her from the English-speaking audience. Her heavy accent when speaking English will keep her at a cognitive distance from the audience at all times. She storms about the room, complaining about the others' lack of trust in her work; and she insists that the film be destroyed because it is dangerous proof that they are preparing an attack involving Lander. While the rest of these Black September terrorists are concerned that Lander may be too weak for the plot, Dahlia is insistent and convinces them that she knows this man and that she can control him "like a child." When the Japanese member of the cell asks what is to stop this American from surrendering as he did in the film, Dahlia brags about her complete control over him, "Me. I'm there to stop him. He depends on me completely." She also makes demands on the others in the room and even emasculates them. She insists that in the next few days she will make the taped announcement that will be played to the American public after the attack. She states sardonically, "I shall give the American people the state of their nation." Then, she belittles her Arab boyfriend, Nageeb (Victor Compos), when she coyly reveals her in-depth knowledge of Lander. "He reminds me of you," she tells Nageeb, referring to her carnal relations with Lander and Nageeb's sexual intimacy with her.

That night Dahlia's impatience gets the best of her, and she makes the tape before getting into bed with Nageeb. The making of the tape provides the audience with its first insight into these terrorists' savagery. Nageeb lies naked in his bed and watches Dahlia, draped in a robe but naked underneath, as she seductively speaks into the tape recorder. The making of the tape, on which she speaks of attack, murders, and revenge on Americans, sexually arouses both of them. Her talk of attack, murder, and revenge constitutes their foreplay. After finishing the recording, she lies in Nageeb's arms and bites at him like a lioness biting at her mate during copulation.

Dahlia's female body also makes her dangerous. Her body exudes sexual seductiveness and femininity that mask the seriousness of her threat. The audience falls for this trap early in the film. Her appealing feminine beauty in the Arab bazaar is a welcome and reassuring sight for the audience when compared to the Orientalized, veiled Arab women. When Kabakov and his commando unit storm the Black September compound, he shoots everybody that moves. He kicks in Nageeb's bedroom door and without hesitation pumps Nageeb full of bullets. Dahlia is in the shower, and when Kabakov rips open the curtain, revealing Dahlia's naked body, he hesitates. As her wet and naked feminine body cowers in fear and submission to the only male who has the power to ultimately defeat her, Kabakov keeps her under his masculine gaze and the horizontally poised barrel of his assault rifle. Kabakov somehow determines that this woman with the beautiful body can be of no harm. So he returns to his mission of killing men. Later, after listening to the tape and hearing the feminine voice, Kabakov realizes that he made a potentially deadly mistake: This woman is far more dangerous than many of the men he killed that night in Beirut. He spends the rest of the movie searching for more information about her, for another glimpse of her, and for a chance to kill her when they meet again.

The danger of Dahlia masked by her female body continues throughout *Black Sunday*. On her return to Lander's home, where he awaits her in darkness and with the rifle, Dahlia is able to use the sexual appeal of her body to entice Lander out of his psychotic rage, into a continued compliance with the plan, and into bed with her. She convinces him that nothing went wrong in Beirut, leaving out the fact that the Israelis raided the compound and took the tape recording. She strips down to her undergar-

Black Sunday (1976). Dahlia (Marthe Keller) is a Palestinian terrorist on the loose in America. Her seductive and feminine body is a distraction from her terrorist activities. She easily disguises herself as harmless and slips into secure areas unquestioned on numerous occasions. Although Israeli agent Robert Moshevsky (Steven Keats) has the instinct to challenge her identity, he turns his back on her in an elevator, thereby allowing her to stab him in the neck with a syringe filled with potassium chloride. Dahlia then steps over his dead body and disappears into the night. Photo courtesy of the Academy of Motion Picture Arts and Sciences.

ments and seductively invites him into bed. Further on, as she attempts to murder Kabakov, injured in an explosion, in his hospital room, she dons the outfit of a sister nurse, blends in with the other nurses, and is able to walk right past the unaware Corley. She makes her way into back areas of the hospital, finds the necessary potassium chloride and syringe to murder Kabakov, walks down the corridors of the hospital, and locates Kabakov in his room. Although Moshevsky, more vigilant than the American Corley, stops her from entering Kabakov's room and demands that she accompany him first to security for proper clearance before she administers Kabakov's "medicine," her female body dupes Moshevsky as well. He saves Kabakov, but he ultimately lets his guard down around her and allows her to stand behind his back in the elevator. When the audience next sees the elevator open, Moshevsky is seen lying on the floor of the elevator with a hypodermic needle sticking in his carotid artery. Dahlia triumphantly steps over his collapsed body. She coldly leaves him lying dead on the floor.

Her body allows her to move freely into other secure areas and remain elusive within the United States, whereas a male body would likely prove to be too obvious and too threatening. During the heightened security of the Super Bowl, Dahlia, claiming to be from room service, gains access to the room of the pilot who has been scheduled to replace Lander. The pilot is in his bathrobe, reclining on the hotel bed and bragging about his upcoming piloting of the blimp. The female body's entry during his heady mood leads him to make sexual advances to Dahlia. Upon seeing her attractive figure, he makes the lascivious masculine statement "I have something for you, darling." She declines his offer and shoots him with the pistol hidden underneath the room service tray instead. Wounded in the shoulder, the pilot lies on the floor bewilderedly looking up at the female standing over him and reaching for her help. But mercilessly, she finishes him off from her towering position. When Lander returns the blimp to its landing field in order to pick up the deadly contraption that will rain the darts upon the football stadium, Dahlia is able to make it through the security point, staffed by two male officers, with the deadly weaponry.

Furthermore, Dahlia's body may be seen as dangerous because she is an Arab woman who is conceptually uncontrollable. Dahlia does not conform to American-imaged stereotypes of the Arab woman. Faegheh Shirazi's book *The Veil Unveiled* shows that Westerners have learned to culturally accommodate and exploit the image of the Middle Eastern Muslim women as women in veils. Veiled Middle Eastern women are used in Western advertising, erotica, and film to support stereotypical beliefs that these women are exotic, backward, romantic, seductive, and/or oppressed. But in *Black Sunday*, Dahlia is not veiled and cannot be conceptually disciplined into such stereotypical categories of the Middle Eastern woman. Dahlia wears Western-style clothing, a sign of mimicry, and shows her disrobed body in a number of scenes. In some cases the veil has been incorporated into American popular culture to inspire the audience's aversion to things Islamic or as a symbol to be feared, as it later was incorporated during the Iranian crisis of the late 1970s and has been today in the crisis of Afghanistan. However, Dahlia's unveiled countenance may be an example of when the Arab woman without the veil is also disconcerting because she cannot be stereotypically confined. In this case, it is not the veil that creates fear, but the absence of it from her body that makes us fear her.

While Dahlia remains elusive by blending easily into the American population, Arab males cannot do so as easily. Kabakov knows where to find the Egyptian diplomat in Washington and secretly meets him in the open National Mall. Kabakov forces the Egyptian to submit to his heroic wit and a political maneuver that really amounts to blackmail. But this highhandedness seems acceptable for Kabakov's character because it seems to be the only way to deal with Arabs. The Egyptian diplomat later makes Kabakov aware of Dahlia's name, face, and background. Speaking of her as if she were a monster, the Egyptian states, "Take a good look. After all, *you* made her." Finally, Kabakov can see Dahlia's face in a photograph. The audience, too, sees her in a new light. Her photographic image has a stereotypically threatening Arab nature, as it shows her dressed in a black-and-white Palestinian kaffiyeh and holding an assault rifle. Moreover, she is shown to be an audacious female holding the masculine symbol of the rifle.

Now that Kabakov can tell the FBI who she is, the FBI is able to locate her whereabouts in Miami; but the FBI agents are too incompetent to actually find her. Mohammad Fasil (Bekim Fehmiu), a superior officer in Black September, does, however, find her. He has come to Miami to warn her that the American authorities know her identity and to get her out of the country because the plot has been called off. However, Dahlia, having savage instincts, is zealous to massacre Americans. She adamantly refuses to call off the plot. Although Fasil reminds her that he is her superior in the organization and that she therefore must follow his orders, she refuses to obey. Dahlia again slips away from the FBI and Kabakov, but her male superior is not that lucky. Despite his attempts to blend into American life, the FBI's camera catches him in a snapshot, and Kabakov is able to identify him as the leader of the murderers of the Israeli athletes in the Munich Olympics. When returning to his Miami hotel, wearing a hat pulled down low and carrying a bag of groceries, he is unaware that Kabakov can see him through an FBI scope, and that numerous FBI agents are watching him from undercover positions on the street, rooftops, and hotel lobby. Once he becomes aware that he is about to be captured, he goes on a murderous shooting spree, and Kabakov and Corley chase him through the streets of Miami. Kabakov's pursuit eventually leads Fasil to the beach and into the water, where Kabakov shoots and kills him. While the dead male terrorist is pushed off American soil and back out beyond the shores, the female terrorist remains at large, threatening America.

Once back in California, Dahlia hears from Lander that another pilot has been chosen to replace him in the blimp on the day of the Super Bowl. Dahlia refuses to accept defeat. However, she momentarily panics over the mission being lost, and she begins to rebuff Lander. Her rejection is too much to bear for Lander, who blocks her escape and has an emotional breakdown. After having been rejected by his wife, this American male military hero cannot bear another snub by a woman. Realizing his total submission to her, Dahlia then assures Lander that he will fly, and the two begin to plan the murder of his relief pilot and Lander's commandeering of the blimp.

The image of the blimp itself is another example of the female-gendered enemy in *Black Sunday*. Unlike the fast-moving, penetrating fighter jets Lander flew in Vietnam and in defense of America, the blimp is at first seen as a slow-moving, voluptuous vessel incapable of destruction. The blimp cannot speed into all-seeing positions against strong winds, despite the television directors' desires. Later, when Lander and Dahlia turn it into a murderous machine, the blimp cannot even outfly a helicopter. The blimp's feminine symbolism relates to Dahlia's, as it seemingly maintains the same speed as Dahlia's car when it is seen traveling overhead. The benign blimp, contradicting its singular maleficence at the Super Bowl, usually communicates messages such as "Merry Christmas" and "Buy Goodyear Tires" to those on the ground. Its size is enormous, and it takes an all-male staff of mechanics and attendants to control it and see to its well-being. These men "tame" it and keep it under control by tying it down with many ropes and cables. But when Lander and Dahlia take control of the blimp, the blimp is unleashed as a femme fatale.

The feminine character of the blimp becomes evident in the way in which it is expected to kill. Unlike a fighter jet, which carries and skillfully fires phallic missiles of death, the blimp does not display its payload, nor does it contain this male-like, penetrating shooting force. The deadly payload is designed as a smooth and concealed attachment to the blimp's underbelly and will explode while remaining attached to the blimp. The underbelly is filled with six hundred kilos of plastic explosives, forged from iconic statues of the ultimate symbol of virginity, maternity, and femininity: the Madonna. The explosive compound is more powerful than that used by the Americans in Vietnam, but this foreign explosive is also less stable. A subtle comparison of masculine shooting and feminine

Black Sunday (1976). The Goodyear blimp, under the control of the Palestinian and deranged Vietnam veteran, makes its way toward the Super Bowl. The blimp's mammoth feminine appearance reduces the height and strength of the phallic lighting stanchions, making their skeletal construction look weak and vulnerable. The masculine football player looks on as if in bewilderment. Photo courtesy of the British Film Institute.

pushing is intimated. Instead of precision shooting to deliver bullets, the blimp will indiscriminately push out, almost birthlike, the 180,000 darts needed to kill the American spectators.[13]

The stadium wall allows only a partial view of the blimp as it enters the stadium. This half-view makes the blimp appear similar to an enormous female breast crashing into the crowd. The breastlike appearance is further highlighted by the nipple-like tip, or nose, of the blimp. Its bright red color, as opposed to a soft pink or flesh color, makes it look inflamed, sore, and angry. As it crashes into the stadium, the out-of-control "breast" first assaults, in Godzilla-like fashion, the erect lamp stanchions. Whereas the breast is normally hailed as the part of the female body that nourishes the infant and also as an object of lust and beauty, this colossal symbolic breast renders the crowd helpless. People are seen scrambling in fear of this unleashed monstrosity that has gone awry.

While the Americans are part of the problem in *Black Sunday*'s narrative, Kabakov is the masculine hero who possesses the proper frontier spirit that can defeat the "feminine" Arab plot. Kabakov is the epitome of Slotkin's "man who knows Indians." He is the "man who knows Arabs" and is able to defeat them on their own savage level. This identification of the Israeli as pioneer is an American ideal that Lawrence Davidson claims reaches back to American popular opinion of the 1920s. The Zionist, he points out, was seen by Americans as a "reincarnation of the American pioneer," living the American experience on the Eastern frontier.[14] Michael Suleiman's study of American images of Arabs supports Davidson's claims and says that Arabs were likened to the American Indians. He adds that the "ideology of Savagism and the basic orientation toward Indians were then applied to the Arabs, especially Palestinian Arabs, in their conflict with Zionism and Israel."[15] In the 1970s, Israel was deeply engaged in settling the newly acquired territories, won from battle with the Arabs, and in fighting Arab terrorism at home and abroad.

Kabakov watches, imagines, makes decisions, and acts in ways that deal with the savage mind of the Arabs. He and his commando team, which he stealthily leads, make their way into Beirut, as shown at the beginning of the film. First by raft, and then through the streets by automobile, he and his commando team make their way toward the Black September compound. Just like Dahlia's experience, his experience in the Arab land is portrayed as a trip into the labyrinth. His trip is recorded with the use of quick contrasting camera shots, many of which were taken with a handheld camera. Kabakov has a knack for making his way through the habitat of the Arabs. The Israeli commandos have already infiltrated the Arab land, as can be gleaned when the audience sees kaffiyeh-covered men cut open chained gateways from the inside. Once in sight of the compound, Kabakov leads his team by firing the first shot and hitting his first target: an Arab.

Silently making his way into the compound, Kabakov navigates with ease through the twisting corridors and directly into the very center of the terrorists. Along the way, one of the Israeli commandos plants bombs with which he will blow up the compound once the mission is completed. First, Kabakov bursts into the communications room, kills the operator, and riddles the equipment with bullet holes. Then he makes his way to Nageeb's room, kicks open the door, and, without asking any questions, pumps Nageeb full of bullets. Continuing on, he finds Dahlia nude in the shower. Although his instincts fail him with regard to Dahlia, whose life he spares, he instinctively grabs papers that might contain important in-

Black Sunday (1976). This publicity still of *Black Sunday* reveals much about the Israeli agent Major David Kabakov's (Robert Shaw) character. Kabakov is a "man who knows Arabs" and is endowed with the frontier spirit, a spirit that Americans have lost. He carries the civilizing tool of the wilderness, the gun, and, unlike the Arab savages, he knows when and how to use it with high accuracy. To his left, the photo shows the amazing act of courage and strength that he performs when he harnesses the Goodyear blimp and pulls it back out to sea before it explodes, thereby saving thousands of American lives. Photo courtesy of the Academy of Motion Picture Arts and Sciences.

formation and the tape recording that, as he later finds out, holds the "smoking gun" to the terrorist plot. All of this killing is done without a word from Kabakov or his commandos, and this silence depicts their cool and disciplined advance toward achievement of the mission. Once the center has been wiped out, he makes his way back through the labyrinth of corridors. When the Israeli bombs explode, he is forced to change course but still knows how to find his way out of the compound and back to the getaway vehicle. The commando who accompanied him deep into the compound is shot and killed just before the two escape the compound, which highlights Kabakov's knowledge, his masculinity, and his special status compared to all others. Moshevsky breaks the silence of these commandos at this point, and his choice of language conveys to the American audience that he and his comrades are most likely on the "good" side. Moshevsky does not give orders in his national language, Hebrew, in contrast to Dahlia's debut, in which she spoke in her native Arabic with English subtitles provided for the American audience. Instead, he orders his fighting men into the getaway van in English. The use of English bestows a "like us" character on the commandos for the audience. Once inside the getaway van, Moshevsky pants like a man after sexual intercourse, saying, "It was good, Major." Kabakov remains silent but seems satisfied.

Kabakov's position as the "man who knows Arabs" becomes evident when he is matched against the Americans, who seem to have lost this certain frontier instinct of detecting savage danger. Kabakov and Moshevsky go to Washington, D.C., to inform the American government of the upcoming Arab assault. On November 17, inside the Israeli embassy, Kabakov plays Dahlia's tape-recorded announcement. The feminine voice threatens and blackmails the Americans. It is interesting to note that while other males cannot keep Dahlia in control, the heroic Kabakov is able to control her voice with his finger upon the tape recorder. The message says:

> The American people have remained deaf to all the cries of the Palestinian nation. But if a foreign people took all of the states of Virginia, Georgia, and New Jersey and forced the people of those states to leave their homes and lands, would they not feel bitter and betrayed? Therefore, understand how we feel. People of America, this situation is unbearable for us. Until you understand that, and stop helping the Israelis with arms and money, we of the Black September movement will make it unbearable for you. From now on you will share our suffering. Today's horror is nothing to what will happen unless your government acts now. We have begun the year for you with bloodshed. I shall not rejoice over my part in this action. And we hope it will not have to continue. We want to be your brothers. The choice is yours. *Salām ʿalaykum.*

Kabakov tells the two American officials, Corley of the FBI being one of them, that the tape is important because it is not just a threat. He reads from his notes showing that he has studied the implications of the tape. It is, as he points out, an announcement that is to be played after a specific assault. While the type of assault is still unknown to those in the room, the assault itself is inevitable unless it can be stopped. The posture, positions, and movements of the Israelis in the room display a sense of seriousness about this threat to America. Moshevsky stands and often bites his fingernails, the ambassador sits on the arm of the couch stroking his face with worry, and Kabakov leans forward, hunched over the recorder, holding his face in his hands. The Americans, on the other hand, take in the information of the recording, but show less immediate concern for the threat and are less understanding of its meaning. Corley and the other government official (the film's narrative does not specify his name or title in this scene) listen to the tape, but unlike the Israelis, they sit back comfortably and glance at each other from time to time. The anonymous American official wonders if Kabakov's raid had not already aborted the plot. When Kabakov tells him that Dahlia is still alive, and that therefore the threat is still there, the American official overconfidently states, "Presumably scared as hell." Moshevsky, Kabakov's partner, who is far less diplomatic or patient with American miscalculation and inaction than Kabakov, corrects the American for his ignorant statement: "Black September does not scare. You either kill or get killed." Kabakov laments his mistake in not killing Dahlia when he had the chance. He projects the image of a man who constantly applies his knowledge and learns from his actions.

Moshevsky gives the Americans a rundown of Israeli intelligence information about the female voice they have just heard. This the American official shrugs off with a flip of his hand, a tilt of the head, and a passing of responsibility. "Well, we'll put our Lebanon people on it tonight," he says. "You know, Sam [Corley], I really think that the ball is more in your court than in mine." The Israeli ambassador puts the Israeli hero, Kabakov, on the side of the Americans by stating that Israel will assist in any way possible. And Corley, a man who works within the legal limitations when fighting the "savage," points out that he can only issue a general alert to certain governmental departments with the scarce information they have. Kabakov, however, intimates that although the information is inadequate for now, a more aggressive investigation must be made and alert issued.

Kabakov knows that one cannot work within limitations when it comes to dealing with the Arabs. Many of his actions in finding and capturing Dahlia involve confrontations with others. These confrontations are notably violent and threatening when they involve characters of foreign nationality in the United States. Interestingly enough, he, too, is a foreigner. But his frontier spirit aligns him so well with ideals of American heroism that American viewers accept him as one of their own. While Corley acquiesces to lifting the impounding order against the Japanese captain and his ship, Kabakov and Moshevsky choose to take matters into their own hands. Late at night, they quietly await the captain's return to his cabin. When the captain does return, Moshevsky holds a knife to the captain's nostrils and then threatens his throat, creating a squeamish discomfort in the audience. Kabakov, playing the "good cop," assures the captain that he does not want to have him killed as long as the captain cooperates. The captain, shown earlier to be arrogant and indignant at the questions of the American authorities, is now frightened and submissive to Kabakov and Moshevsky as he confesses to what he knows. When Kabakov follows the captain's information leading to the Turkish importer's office, he shoots the lock on the door, kicks in the door, and without questions fires warning shots just above the head of the Turkish importer. Then Kabakov forces the barrel of his pistol, a denotative phallic symbol and a connotative symbol of Kabakov's overpowering masculinity, into the man's mouth. This scene symbolizes a male/male rape, with Kabakov on top and the Turk on the bottom. Kabakov forces the man to break into tears. Although the audience reels back in discomfort, it accepts the action as being necessary when dealing with terrorists. Kabakov barks commands at the man and questions him about Dahlia — questions that he can barely answer with Kabakov's pistol member forced against his teeth and tongue. When Kabakov confronts the Egyptian diplomat in the National Mall, he blackmails the diplomat into providing the information about Dahlia. The secret meeting and deal are accomplished in the shadows of the distant American Lincoln Memorial and Washington Monument. The fact that the safety of Americans is being assured through the accented voices of foreigners and that the monuments remain silent and distant further underlines Americans' lack of power over their own safety. Luckily, Kabakov, the good-accented man, knows how to deal with the Arab for them.

In contrast, Kabakov does not treat white Americans in the same way as he does other foreigners. Rather, he treats them with reason, courtesy, and respect, although he does not get the same treatment from the Americans whom he is trying to save. Kabakov admonishes Moshevsky for the rude comments Moshevsky makes to Corley in reference to Corley's impotence on the Japanese ship. When Kabakov is in the hospital after being wounded by an explosion on the Japanese ship, the admitting nurse asks him a series of informational questions. Corley finds such questioning too bureaucratic, and asks if it is necessary. Kabakov, on the other hand, answers with patience, respect, and politeness. He is certain to thank her when she finishes. During his fact-finding interview about the security of the Miami stadium and the Super Bowl event, he politely and patiently questions the American NFL manager. Kabakov does not remove his gun to coerce information from the NFL manager, as he did with the Turk, even though the NFL manager does not agree with Kabakov that the Super Bowl should be canceled. Even after realizing that the blimp is to be used in the attack on the Super Bowl, Kabakov acts differently to the white Americans. His breaking into the communications office in the Arab compound and his breaking into the communications trailer of the television directors are shown to be quite different. Despite the urgency of the moment, Kabakov enters the trailer to find out about the location of the blimp. Although he must yell at the technicians to get their attention and answers, he does not choose to shoot here. Instead, he questions and uses expressions like "Excuse me" and "Can any of you gentlemen please tell me what happened to the blimp?" Meanwhile, the camera technicians shout back at him to keep quiet and to get out. These Americans rebuff Kabakov even though he is trying to save them. At the same time, Kabakov treats them differently than he would have treated other foreigners when barging in on them in matters of emergency.

Kabakov falls within the extreme realm of Slotkin's "man who knows Indians": He is carried so far into the "dark" side of the savage war that he becomes dependent on perpetual engagement with the objects of his hatred and can never reintegrate into civilization. Kabakov's admittance into the hospital after being wounded by Lander's telephone bomb on the Japanese ship is an informative scene that builds his heroic character. Here, we learn that his history includes atrocious loss. The admitting nurse's questions and Kabakov's answers reveal that most of his family is dead. The reach of death in this middle-aged man's family includes his father, mother, wife, and two sons. He lies in bed with his hands behind his head, and the audience can see a six-digit number tattooed on his left underarm, suggesting that he is a Holocaust survivor. Although he does not reveal how his family members died, his subdued tone suggests murder. His approximate age in 1976 (let us say early forties) allows us to deduce that his parents' deaths could have been as victims of the Holocaust (the tattoo giving us a clue) or that they, his wife, and his sons could have been killed by Arabs in the early years of the Israeli state (since he has had a long career in Israeli intelligence). Regardless of the exact identity of the perpetrators, the deaths are experiences of horrific loss, due to anti-Jewish treachery, for this frontier hero. Only his daughter is alive, and the fact that she lives in "Jerusalem, Israel" implies that she remains alive because there is a Jewish national place for her to live. Additionally, he realizes in the hospital that he and Moshevsky are men that cannot emerge from the dimension of savage war. They are men who are removed from civilized life, or their lives as civilians in Israel. Similar to Roy Harvey Pearce's Indian haters, they are stuck in the stranglehold, becoming so savage themselves that they are forever incapable of returning to civilization.[16] Kabakov states that he has killed and murdered people for thirty years (i.e., since the end of World War II and the establishment of Israel). He and Moshevsky will have to be put down like "old dogs" if peace ever comes to Israel because they will not know how to live or what to do. While doubt about his unfettered commitment to savage war has, at this moment, entered into his mind, Dahlia's murder of Moshevsky reaffirms his commitment to savage war. The news of Moshevsky's murder awakens him from a morphine-drip high, and he rips off his hospital bracelet and seeks revenge against the savage Arabs. Moshevsky's body is loaded onto an international jetliner, and Kabakov watches in silence as the coffin enters the cargo hold. The death of his friend and fighting partner makes Kabakov realize that he himself is now alone and can never return to civilization unless it is as a corpse. With this in mind, Kabakov embarks on a more intent pursuit, a deeper journey into savage war, and the total annihilation of Dahlia.

While the Americans do not know how to deal with the Palestinian found in Miami, Kabakov proves his role as the "man who knows Arabs." With a glance at the photograph of the man in question, taken by the FBI, Kabakov can identify him by name (Mohammad Fasil), by context (the leader of the Munich Olympics murders), and by danger index (very dangerous). Kabakov knows that Fasil should be taken alive, because his information would help foil the terrorist plot. The significance of arresting Fasil alive is something that the Americans just do not understand. Throughout the chase scene, the American FBI agents move to shoot, and Kabakov must constantly yell at them to hold their fire. Fasil, the Arab, is so alien to America that he actually turns the American streets into a labyrinth. Like the demon in *The Exorcist* and the Arab villains in *Rollover*, he is transforming American space into the "degenerate" place of the Middle East. Since Kabakov knows and understands this terrorist, he can follow him — something the American police and Corley have difficulty doing. Kabakov must shout commands to the Americans, indicating which directions to go within this labyrinth, even though he has only arrived in Miami a short time ago. And when Corley tries to approach this cornered terrorist with reasoning, Kabakov knows that the American is too naïve to control this situation. Kabakov chooses to shoot Fasil dead just at the moment in which Fasil turns to shoot the unarmed Corley. Annoyed with the American's naïve approach toward the Arab and with losing the opportunity to capture the Arab alive, Kabakov admonishes Corley by saying, "I told you about that man, Mr. Corley. I should have let him shoot you." Kabakov's superior knowledge and his ability to know just what the Arab intended to do have saved an American life.

Shooting is a highly important issue in *Black Sunday*. It is a characteristic action that plays an important part in displaying heroic and villainous, civilized and savage, and masculine and feminine roles. Kabakov is a precision shootist; he has been shooting for thirty years in the name of upholding civilization. His shots are staged as clean, well calculated, effective, and efficient. In the terrorist compound, he and Moshevsky shoot and kill the Arabs they confront in order to penetrate the terrorist cell and to escape with the necessary intelligence. But he is shown to be responsible with his gun, and he never fires indiscriminately. His shots kill the masked bad guys, or known participants in the terrorist plots. He never shoots innocent people. When he bursts in on Dahlia, he shows the signs of thinking before he shoots and lets her live. He later realizes that too much consideration in savage combat has become a mistake, though, because now she is the major threat to civilization. When he chases Fasil through the streets, he never fires his pistol until it is absolutely necessary in order to save Corley. And when he does finally shoot at Fasil, his bullets are deservedly and decisively fatal. Kabakov knows just how to use the gun effectively. When he forces his gun barrel into the Turkish importer's mouth, he never pulls the trigger. He uses the gun to coerce a needed confession from the man. Cocked and ready to fire, the gun is eventually withdrawn when Kabakov gets the necessary information. "I don't know why," he tells the Turk, "I think I am going to let you live." And true to his word, he leaves the man alive. Kabakov's and Moshevsky's shots are the only ones that are lethal for the Arab terrorists. As for the Americans, they never shoot except for one missed shot aimed at the Goodyear blimp made by Corley. Americans are portrayed as a people who have lost their pioneering characteristics, which include the expert handling of the gun, and have therefore become completely impotent in savage warfare. In the scene chasing Fasil through the Miami streets, they often aim their guns at the terrorist but never shoot. Maybe this is because Kabakov gives the orders not to shoot. But in these instances, Kabakov knows the proper use of the gun, and so the Americans follow his instructions. Corley, unarmed, eventually faces a cornered and armed Fasil on the beach. It seems ludicrous that the FBI, America's ultimate police organization, is trying to reason with Fasil in spite of his savage murder spree just moments earlier. Rather than shooting, Americans get shot. In pursuit of the Goodyear blimp at the Super Bowl, an overly emotional Corley holds an automatic rifle and shouts, "All right. We're going to shoot the goddamned thing down." He has had enough, but he does not understand when or how to shoot. The helicopter pilot must remind him that it would be a mistake because the dirigible is filled with helium. The cool and discriminating Israeli Kabakov must step in and carefully clarify the objective for Corley, the helicopter pilot, and the audience, "We are going to kill the pilot."

Lander is a better shot than the other Americans. However, his participation in the plot forfeits his citizenship and his stance as a hero. He is one of the villains. His past heroism may give him better marksmanship with the gun now, but he lacks the moral control needed to shoot with heroic justification. He is able to kill two with his gun, including a victim whom he shoots in the back. But his present and overpowering villainy makes his attempts at murder more indiscriminate and savage than those of Kabakov. His character is centered less on killing with a gun than on killing using more barbaric means. He is calculating enough to pinpoint the exact moment when the Japanese captain will answer the phone, but the explosion that severs the captain's head is a gruesome method of murdering. During his test firing of the darts in a remote barn, he murders, in ghastly fashion, an innocent and simple man who gets in the way of his test. His plan with Dahlia to kill the sports audience is designed to indiscriminately massacre tens of thousands of innocent people.

The Arabs do shoot. However, their handling of this tool of civilization is shown to be less skillful in order to highlight their uncivilized character. They often miss, are less calculating, and shoot indiscriminately. They are too slow to kill the Israeli commandos who invade their compound. Only one Arab makes a lucky enough shot to kill an Israeli. Fasil's

Black Sunday (1976). Israeli agent Kabakov and American law enforcement officers pursue Fasil (Bekim Fehmiu), an officer in Black September, on the streets of Miami. Fasil tries to escape by taking a young American girl hostage and going on an indiscriminate and excessive shooting spree through the American city's streets. Only half of his shots hit their target: but in *Black Sunday* having control over one's gun translates into having a civilized nature and moral righteousness. Photo courtesy of the British Film Institute.

shooting spree is fairly well aimed but totally indiscriminate and excessive. He kills innocent people that have nothing to do with the fight. He kills them because they happen to be in the way. He shoots six Americans dead, choosing them at random as he comes across them on the streets. But he is only accurate enough to hit his targets about half the time. He has just as many misses, six total, one of which sends a group of innocent American children running in fear. These other missed shots are made at Kabakov. Kabakov not only shoots well but also is able to dodge the

Black Sunday (1976). Dahlia (Marthe Keller), the Palestinian terrorist, and Lander (Bruce Dern), the deranged Vietnam veteran, commandeer the Goodyear blimp for their treacherous attack on the American Super Bowl. Dahlia's gun threatens those who wish to stop her, but, when it comes to using this tool of Western civilization, her shooting accuracy is deficient. Photo courtesy of the British Film Institute.

Arab bullets better than the Americans. Even when there is nothing for Kabakov to hide behind while on the open beach, Fasil misses Kabakov and hits the sand instead. Fasil's violent killing spree includes grabbing indiscriminately an American girl and holding a gun to her head to make his getaway.

Dahlia, too, kills with the gun, but her aim is less efficient. When she shoots the pilot who is scheduled to relieve Lander in the blimp, her first shot at him wounds him in the shoulder even though she shoots him at point-blank range. She has to finish him off with more shots once he is lying on the floor and reaching for her. She later kills seven more people, including those inside the helicopter that she shoots down, during the blimp's progression toward the stadium. Yet she sprays the bullets from her automatic rifle rather than making clean and accurate shots. The "feminine" nature of Dahlia's shots with the rifle are further highlighted by scenes that show a male football quarterback passing the ball with pinpoint accuracy to his teammates. Her shooting is portrayed as a feminine-indiscriminate "pushing out," or "spray"—as opposed to a masculine-aimed "thrust," or "pump" — that causes her to miss often and casts doubt on whether she is really an efficient killer or just a lucky one. One of her bullet sprays wounds Corley, but does not kill him, and puts him out of action and control for the climax of the film. Although Kabakov kills her in the end with an automatic rifle, he shows that there is a masculine technique in delivering the rounds from this weapon. His bullets fire rapidly, but do not spray in a haphazard manner. They stream outward and pinpoint Dahlia's body, Lander's torso, and the electronic box that is the power source of the explosives. Kabakov's masculine shooting hits the blimp's engine accurately enough so as not to damage the skin of the helium-filled dirigible.

Kabakov's intuitive knowledge of the Arabs tells him just where to look for clues and for the dangers that the Arabs exude. Kabakov knows how to ask the right questions. While Corley makes telephone calls in the background of the FBI office to see if any suspect shipments have come into the country, Kabakov and Moshevsky work in the foreground searching through photographs that might give a clue to the woman behind the tape-recorded voice. When Corley reports his findings to Kabakov, the two Israelis dismiss Corley and his information as trite and work harder at their own task, which they know will reveal a more concrete answer. During a search of Fasil's Miami hotel room, Corley and his men can only find a few weapons and some fake passports. It is Kabakov, with his great instincts, who focuses on the Super Bowl brochure found among Fasil's belongings. It is Kabakov and his questioning of the Americans he meets that bring about the revelation that the Arabs are going to attack the big game. Prior to the sporting event, it is his gaze that surveys the stadium for possible ways of attack. While Corley asks a security official about security procedures to be followed at the game, Kabakov stays away from such elementary inquiries. He knows that the only answer is to cancel the Super Bowl, and he tells Joseph Robbie, owner of the Miami Dolphins, this outright. The American Robbie can only answer with astonishment, "It is the most ridiculous suggestion I have ever heard. That's like canceling Christmas." Corley agrees that the Super Bowl cannot be canceled, even though Kabakov estimates that eighty thousand people might die. While tens of thousands of Americans, including Corley, stand in the stadium on January 8 unaware of and unable to fathom the danger they are in, the alert and wary Kabakov stands in opposition to them. The Americans, including the FBI's Corley, get lost in their world of patriotism and look up at the United States flag during the playing of the national anthem just before the game begins. Meanwhile, Kabakov remains vigilant and looks in the opposite direction for signs of danger. When Kabakov points out to Corley that the power of the stadium lights can be used as a power source to set off an explosion, Corley says that the lights must stay on because they are needed for television.

Kabakov's heroism comes to its ultimate climax when he tames the enormous and murderous blimp single-handedly with his bare hands. His performance is superhuman, and definitely unrealistic. But his superhero capabilities are perceived as plausible because of the careful construction and performances of his heroic character developed throughout the film. The audience has been directed to rely upon him as the only capable savior for the nation. While others have succumbed to the feminine, terrorist Arab, Kabakov is the only one who is masculine and civilized enough to save the day. Although Kabakov's shooting has been able to kill Dahlia and to take Lander out of commission as a pilot, the blimp is still on its deadly descent into the stadium. Moreover, Lander is able to light a fuse that will cause the explosion of darts to occur without the electric power source that Kabakov has destroyed. Kabakov attempts a death-defying move, lowering himself onto the blimp via the helicopter's cable. This he does without any second thought, fear, or suffering of vertigo. He intends to hook the cable into an eyelet on top of the blimp and then have the helicopter pull the blimp away from the American crowd and out to sea. But the blimp crashes into the stadium, sending people fleeing, falling, and trampling each other in chaotic fear. However, just when the blimp is a few feet from the field, and just before the fuse burns to the top of the explosive material, Kabakov gets the hook into the eyelet and motions to the helicopter to pull upward. The blimp is unrealistically pulled back out of the stadium. It is extracted more quickly and easily than it moved in. The blimp is toted off to sea and unhooked, and its deadly payload explodes over the water. The spraying darts hitting the water show the vast devastation that had been planned for the innocent American public. The helicopter flies to shore with Kabakov, our hero, swinging from the dangling cable just before the credits roll.

Frankenheimer's *Black Sunday* creates Orientalist fear by showing the savagery of Palestinian Arabs infiltrating a weakened and feminized America. The film is an interesting twist on the American frontier myth in which only the Israeli, a man who knows the savagery of the Arabs, can help the Americans. The film's use of real events (Vietnam, Munich, the Super Bowl), specific dates, real people (Terry Bradshaw, Tom Brookshier,

Joseph Robbie, Pat Summerall, and a Jimmy Carter look-alike), real commercial labels (Goodyear, CBS, Dallas Cowboys, and Pittsburgh Steelers) blends fiction and fantasy with the real world in order to create the fear that this just might happen in real life. But the masculine, civilized Western world conquers over the feminine, savage, infiltrating Arabs at the end of *Black Sunday,* although not to the credit of America. What remains to be resolved at the end of *Black Sunday* is finding a remedy for the ailing America that still suffers from the Vietnam experience and is still vulnerable to Arab villainy.

4 | *Three Kings*
ASSAULT ON VICTORY CULTURE (1999)

U.s. Army Major Archie Gates (George Clooney) is distraught in the beginning scenes of *Three Kings*.[1] Despite the surrounding triumphant revelry of Desert Storm's coalition forces, Gates cannot muster the same celebratory fervor in the Iraqi desert as his comrades.[2] It is March 1991, and the war, we are told from the opening titles, is just over. Gates, a Delta Force GI and once doing important work behind enemy lines in Iraq, is now assigned the more tedious and less valorous job of media escort. He tries to partake in the jubilation by pounding away in sexual intercourse with one of the female reporters, but this only gets him into trouble with his colonel, who walks in on them flagrante delicto. The colonel berates Gates for shirking his responsibilities in this "media war." He is supposed to be acting more professionally and escorting a different reporter, Adriana Cruz (Nora Dunn), to whom he has actually been assigned and to whom he feels no attraction, mentally or sexually. For Major Gates, something about this war and this victory is just not right.

In the scene to follow, he is called on the carpet by his commanding officer. "I don't even know what we did here," Gates yells back at his CO while pointing to the Iraqi surroundings. "Just tell me what we did here, Ron." The colonel shoots back quickly, "What do you want to do, occupy Iraq and do Vietnam all over again? Is that what you want? Is that your brilliant idea?"[3] Unable to come to terms with the military "chickenshit,"[4] Gates replies, "Fuck it, I am retiring anyway." Responding to which the colonel puts him straight, "Until you do, you're an army officer. You're still taking care of that reporter. So, do it right." The colonel walks away from him and boards an awaiting helicopter, an icon that brings back to the American audience memories of the frustrating war in Vietnam. As the chopper flies off, Gates is left in the whisking sands, where he shakes his head in bewilderment.

Like the films that I have analyzed so far, *Three Kings* taps the fount of Orientalist fear. However, *Three Kings* has some unique and interesting aspects. The previous films deal with the Arab assault on a weakened America and take place in America. In contrast, this film shows a strong masculine America that has already defeated the Arabs at the beginning of the story. Moreover, this film suggests a struggle against the Arabs that Americans have undertaken outside their own homeland, a struggle located in the Middle East. But the Arabs still are portrayed as threatening to America, even here under these circumstances. Orientalist fear, as I have asserted earlier, develops in part from the Arabs' power to threaten American ideology and myth. While it seems that the first Gulf War has "exorcised the ghost of Vietnam" and put the United States back on the path to glorious military triumphs, the Arab villains in *Three Kings* keep the American heroes from reclaiming their rightful destiny, or what Tom Engelhardt calls America's "victory culture."[5] From these early scenes of the film, the audience has been cued to the hero's frustration with the present state of affairs. Gates must seek a way to reconcile the Gulf War experience within the American myth of war, the role of the heroic and masculine warrior, and the meaning of military victory in the next one hundred minutes of the film. He will draw upon his classic Special Forces character, reminiscent of Robin Moore's fearless, cunning, compassionate, and sometimes disobedient character of the Green Beret.[6] The hero's struggle to set the myth right again and the struggle against the efforts of the Arab villains to keep the myth unbalanced are the verbal and visual narrative premises of the film.

Engelhardt's victory culture is the ideal American view of a national destiny that is victorious in the struggle against aggression. Such "triumphalism," as noted by Engelhardt, is so much a part of American culture that it is "in the American grain."[7] The path to victory is deemed certain, and victory culture assures Americans that even the setback of a lost battle, like the Alamo or Custer's Last Stand, is only a "springboard to victory"[8] and that ultimately defeat will be redeemed with total triumph. American victory emanates from the righteousness of the nation's historical being, what John Hellmann calls "the American errand."[9] America has always considered itself a nation that is a light of freedom, democracy, and enterprise in the world. Traditionally, America's errand is to go forth and spread such light into the world's expanses, i.e., the frontier wilderness, and to fight against the dark forces of oppression, tyranny, and stagnation associated with the torpidly civilized (traditional Europeans) and the ignorantly savage (the native Indians). Victory, in the execution of this errand, is the outcome of the American war story, a 250-year-old narrative formula through which Americans often define their ideals, practices, performances, and themselves.

The war story begins with the white American male clearing the frontier for civilized settlement. During this endeavor, he encounters a horde of Others: savages, nonwhites, classically depicted as "Injuns." These Indians oppose his civilizing efforts and ambush him and his American community in the most "heinous" of all styles: the sneak attack, a surprise assault on a peaceful, unsuspecting people.[10] The Indians commit savage atrocities against the Americans. They capture and hold the white women or the American frontiersman himself. While in captivity, the suffering Americans are tortured, humiliated, and forced to partake in barbaric acts, the most appalling being cannibalism. The war story, therefore, portrays the savages as aggressors emerging from the land, and the American man as having the right to react and set out deep into the wilderness on a vengeful, yet defensive and civilizing, campaign against them. The frontiersman is known to set out alone or in a small band of brothers. The difference in numbers between the Americans and the savages is important to the narrative because it casts the American role as defensive. Moreover, the comparison of how many of *them* and how few of *us* are killed establishes the justness of the American cause, proves the Americans' innate superiority, and demonstrates America's foreordained destiny of power in relation to Others. The American slaughter of the savages in retaliation for their atrocities has become a spectacle of pleasure and celebration in American culture.

This war story, as Engelhardt shows, reached the apex of its mythical application during the Japanese invasion of Pearl Harbor and through World War II. War stories, in this context, encompassed the idealized transgressions of ambush and the heroism of the last stand and contextualized them as events that proved the murderous intent of the Axis enemies. The victories in North Africa, Europe, and the South Pacific became idealized examples and lessons of the myth that were replayed as ideological dramas of just cause and moral righteousness on the Hollywood screen and even in children's games. However, the day that the Americans dropped the first atomic bomb on Japan, the American war story began to slip away from the national grasp. Victory became questionable when such catastrophic costs as tens of thousands of civilian dead within seconds and nuclear fallout were weighed in the balance. The beginning of the nuclear age meant that nations would be defenseless when nuclear bombs were used as weapons. If the enemy chose to strike first with its atomic arsenal, there would be no chance for retaliation. America would have to adopt the strategy of becoming a "first strike" nation, which would place it in the role of aggressor and in conflict with its self-image as defensive combatant. Furthermore, if America became the first-striker, it placed America in conflict with its civilizing self-image, because nuclear bombs would inflict such vast devastation that there would be nothing left over which to be triumphant. The nuclear age began to jeopardize the concepts of ambush and last stand in America's postwar imagination. Nuclear annihilation of the enemy was not a celebratory spectacle to be joyously watched, but rather a potential American shame. As a result, post-1945 America fell into "triumphalist despair" — in which triumph came with grave consequences of conscience. Nuclear might, an enormous military power advantage, could not be turned into a weapon of victory. The loss of the victory culture deepened with the experiences of Korea (considered a draw), Vietnam (considered a loss), and the Iran hostage situation (considered a humiliation), to name but a few. America entered a period in which it had to restrict its victories to "struggles [in] areas where [it] could strive for a victory that would be largely symbolic of what could not now be done with abandon [i.e., nuclear strikes]."[11] Victory culture in America ended after 1975, according to Engelhardt.[12] By the early 1990s, America could no longer assuredly and without restraint apply the myth of the war story to explain its current disputes and altercations with, and its military actions against, its enemies.

But Gates, the hero of *Three Kings,* finds himself at a new juncture in American history, or so the audience is at first led to believe. As previously noted, the first Gulf War has just ended: the Americans and their allies are the victors and the Iraqi army, the world's fourth-largest army, is the beleaguered and defeated. America had championed the fight and led the liberation of Kuwait from Saddam Hussein's captivity. America had accomplished the task in this foreign land in a very short amount of time, and the war was won without resorting to nuclear weapons. As noted by Cruz, the journalist in the film, America's armed forces had "exorcised the ghost of Vietnam with a clear moral imperative." America, so it seems in this film, is back on the path of victory culture.

The partying, carousing, and sophomoric skylarking army men in the beginning scenes of *Three Kings* celebrate a perceived renewal of victory culture. The troops dance, jump for joy, participate in water fights, and hoot and holler. However, the celebrations are true masculine ostentations in which a remasculinized army displays its male-to-male bonds. Unlike the emasculated army, as interpreted by Susan Jeffords, this American army proudly displays the masculinity it derived from victory.[13] The men dance with each other flamboyantly; some wear just their briefs. They sunbathe together in the Iraqi sun and toss around balls. Images of masculine bodies pumping iron, of hairy chests puffing outward, and of muscular arms flexing flash across the screen. Wholesome, white-toothed male smiles are flashed, as well. Man-to-man shoulder holding and tumbling ensue. Soldiers give each other clipper haircuts and comment on how handsome the recipients look. Alcohol drinking and sprays are part of the carousing. Nerf footballs are tossed about, and there are rough tackles that include breaking furniture. And if that is not explicit enough to convince the audience of the remasculinized, male-bonded American army, then the image of soldiers pissing into communal outdoor tubes takes the idea further. These urinal tubes protrude into the Iraqi ground and extend the American males' penile length, hardness, and penetration while the pissing soldiers coolly pose for the panning journalists' cameras and flash "V" for victory signs.

As depicted in these scenes, the victory in the Gulf War is not only a military victory that reestablishes the victory culture, but a regeneration of American masculinity. The victory, as revealed here, accomplishes more than just driving out the "ghost of Vietnam" and making the boast of "Hey, we liberated Kuwait" possible. Rather, it expels the female and the feminine and leads to "the remasculinization of America."[14] First, remasculinization means a restriction of the role of women in the society, and this is symbolized in the film when the female soldiers within the group are more limited in their movement than the men. Oftentimes, the women soldiers are difficult to discern. Dressed in their fatigues, they blend into the thicket of male bodies and make appearances in the blink of an eye. Due to this blurring effect, the audience is unable to look at the women soldiers. Some of them are shown as so physically unattractive that the viewers in the audience are not expected to find pleasure in gazing at them. They dance with inhibition and rigidity in comparison to the men, who do not ask the women to dance with them. The women do not partake in the jumping contests, football play, or furniture-busting tackles. They stand in the background and let the men enjoy the homosocial horseplay spawned by war victory.

Second, remasculinization means that feminine roles are controlled, kept in check, and pushed out of the masculinizing culture. Journalism, as depicted in this film, is feminized and controlled. In the real Gulf War, journalists were viewed as inimical to a total and unquestioned victory. This perception was a carryover from the Vietnam War, when journalists were blamed for sowing the seeds of indecision and dissent on the home front, for fettering combat, and thereby for keeping American soldiers from victory and subsequent celebration. Herbert Schiller reports that the Gulf War was actually two wars: one of the Allies against Iraq and the other of the military against the press.[15] *Three Kings* tries to reflect this negative opinion of journalism and analogize journalism with the feminine. As part of redisciplining journalism in this new war, the film's male military officials rename the profession as "the media," and they are aware that it must be tightly controlled and directed to protect victory culture. Moreover, two female characters represent journalism. Although they are given some identity, these female journalists are degraded to sex objects for male pleasure or as cat-fighting females over whose bitching voices the colonel must shout when he tells Gates, "I really don't need this shit, Major."

Third, remasculinization encompasses the reestablishment of what Antony Easthope calls the "masculine myth," the dominant myth of masculinity.[16] This myth posits masculinity as natural, normal, and universal. It claims that masculinity is pure and of one substance through and through: a man must be male and masculine and nothing else. Sexual desire is heterosexual only. Anything that threatens this self-identity is repelled or repressed, much as a castle wall repels outsiders and the interior Panopticon represses insiders, and this includes masculinity's opposite: the feminine. Freud believed in the constitutional bisexuality of each individual, carried over from the infantile stage. At infancy, the human is a mixture of masculine and feminine, seeking pleasure without shame regarding its source to satisfy the erotic impulses, and the potential is never lost as the human ages. Freud's theory about sexual orientation is that it is no more than a preference, a predilection. This is quite contrary to popular culture's acceptance of the masculine myth, which insists on a man's determined sexuality, and Easthope reminds us that the masculine myth is actually the man's struggle to manage and cope with his own femininity and his desire for other men.[17]

The masculine myth feigns invisibility, and when it is called to attention or into question, its power is challenged. In *Three Kings*, however, masculinity, overly glorified by communal singing of "God Bless the U.S.A." and bicep flexing in front of the American flag, calls itself

Three Kings (1999). Major Archie Gates (George Clooney) suffers from triumphalist despair. He does not feel connected with the revelry of the victorious Allied Coalition Forces in the first Gulf War and is frustrated with his role in this "media war." He is a Special Forces officer, but now he has been assigned the less valorous job of escorting the temperamental, demanding, and female journalist Adriana Cruz (Nora Dunn) to her news stories. Photo courtesy of the British Film Institute.

into question. The audience may wince in vicarious embarrassment when viewing this rediscovered masculine/victory culture. Even the journalists are tiring of the victory as a story. Cruz herself is having difficulty presenting yet another story about celebrating troops, deeming its newsworthiness as "evaporating." Furthermore, too much masculine fraternizing, idolizing, celebration, and segregation risk bringing questions and accusations of homoeroticism and homosexuality to the fore and undermine the masculine myth. The celebratory scenes of male soldiers dancing and in horseplay are excellent examples of homoerotic suggestion. As for Gates, who furiously applies his masculine strength in intercourse with a female reporter and clumsily knocks over expensive media equipment in the process, he seems to know that victory, remasculinization, and the masculine myth are in question.

Gates is under a cloud of triumphalist despair. The declared military victory in the war should be the denouement of the war story and this film, but it is shown at the film's beginning. The war story is concluded before it begins, and so his statement "I don't even know what we did here" should not be seen as unusual. Gates's situation recalls Judith Roof's discussion of narrative ends, middles, and beginnings. The end, according to Roof, cannot come too soon or be too terminal to the narrative. The end, to be successful, must provide the belief and hope of a new beginning—it must be narratively reproductive. Roof likens the narrative end, sexually speaking, to orgasm achieved after the excitation, delay, and discharge of the narrative middle, and the end must move toward the path of more sexual activity and reproduction of new narrative beginnings.[18]

There has been no display of bravery and heroism to justifiably lead to this triumphant ending in *Three Kings*. Thus, this masculine partying and carousing in the name of victory seems to him as undeserved, premature, and, therefore, shallow. Without the heroic plot of a war story unfolding first and showing scenes in which masculinity is developed and tested, the celebratory scenes of victory seem overindulgent, arrogant, and likely to lose historical significance. To borrow from Roof, the celebratory scenes come just to cum without the foreplay, and this may be why Gates's performance on the female journalist is seen as so tactless and maladroit. The scenes of victory at the film's beginning rob the audience of the accoutrements of a victorious war: life in the frontier, the ambush, the enemies' capture of the white women and men, the sortie into the wilderness to track down the enemies, the tests of strength and cunning, wholesale slaughter, rescue, and the triumphant return home. Thus, the film denies Gates the justification to revel in the glorious victory. He is also weighed down with the feminine when he is forced to submit to the desires and whims of the media war and Cruz's nagging. He knows that to enjoy the fruits of victory and to achieve a sense of masculine self will require more than just the ostentatious display of manhood in celebration of victory. He must reenact a hero's journey to victory. Susan Mackey-Kallis describes the idea of the heroic journey very well:

> Such a quest does not involve simply the hero's discovery of some boon or Holy Grail, however; it also involves finding him- or herself, which ultimately means finding a home in the universe. Home is often the literal home from which the hero sets out, but more significantly, it is a state of mind or a way of seeing not possible before the hero departs. The hero's journey, in Joseph Campbell's words, "is a labor not of attainment but of reattainment, not discovery but rediscovery. The godly powers sought and dangerously won are revealed to have been within the heart of the hero all the

time." The hero's quest is a double quest that often requires a journey home not only to the place from whence the hero departed but to a state of being or consciousness that was within the hero's heart all along. To put it simply, the hero's journey outward into the world of action and events eventually requires a journey inward—if the hero is to grow—and ultimately necessitates a journey homeward—if the hero is to understand his or her grail or boon and is to share it with the culture at large.[19]

Although victory culture is deeply ingrained in Gates's mentality, he has yet to go out and find it, make it part of his awareness, and return home to share it with his culture. If victory culture peaked during World War II and ultimately failed in Vietnam, then Gates would have to draw the following conclusions: he has to reinstate masculine, heroic deeds and experiences similar to those of the 1940s and eliminate any action or experience similar to those embarrassing legacies of the 1960s and 1970s. Take, for example, Tom Brokaw's descriptions of World War II's American soldiers that left Brokaw no choice but to dub them "The Greatest Generation." Brokaw's victors had experienced face-to-face combat situations with ideological enemies that had tested their strength and bravery, provided opportunities of national service and sacrifice, and allowed them to return home to loved ones and to ordinary lives with stories of achievement and heroism. They had swept across continents and oceans, conquered vast territories while on their open-ended tours of duty, participated in one historic battle after the next, given life and limb patriotically, and liberated peoples who poured forth to greet them and to exuberantly display their gratitude for the American victors. Experiences like these provided that sense of greatness, certainty, and manliness that Brokaw highlights with a letter from veteran Howard Schultz:

> And it was my moment, and I'll remember it as the one time I was the complete man. I was standing up for something, and that was the thing, sort of justifying my place in history and on this planet Earth. And the cause was a just one. All the yet unborn kids would benefit.[20]

Unlike war stories of World War II, Vietnam stories seem unable to bestow masculinity and pride through victory. Myra MacPherson, for example, describes Vietnam War soldiers and their civilian contemporaries as "The

Haunted Generation."[21] Her "losers" were wounded and died in combat with an enemy who was seldom seen and whose identity was often in question. The war in Southeast Asia exposed the frailty of the human body and mind in warfare. American soldiers returned home rejected by their society and learned that the war they were fighting had divided American society at home. They went into the unknown jungle where lines of combat were blurred. They struggled to take territory that would be abandoned days later, reported their success based upon destruction and body count, fought a war that Washington politicians would not allow them to win, divided internally among themselves along racial lines, experimented with drugs, and, toward the end, began avoiding combat while on patrol to save their own lives. South Vietnamese citizens were often indifferent or hostile to American help. When *Life* magazine ran the photographic proof of the My Lai massacre on December 5, 1969, approximately a year after the event itself, America saw itself as the aggressor in this war. As MacPherson notes, "No matter what the enemy did to our soldiers, My Lai punctured the pristine myth of American 'goodness' in war; GIs were not handing out bubble gum, they were slaughtering babies. Color photos confirm the undisputable horror."[22] In contrast to Brokaw quoting the veteran about his sense of gain, achievement, and optimism from World War II, MacPherson quotes veteran Paul Regan, revealing his sense of loss, uncertain possibilities, and defeatist pessimism from Vietnam:

> I lost a lot of youth; I would have had a *girlfriend* for the three years I was in service. . . . I was better off, because I probably would have ended up knockin' someone up and bein' married with fifteen kids.[23]

Caught between the historical experiences of these two extremes, clearly, Gates must choose the mythic path of the former, the more glorious of the two, and the one for which the American audience will cheer him forward if he is to be the hero. Indeed, occupying Iraq and reliving Vietnam all over again, as the colonel suggests would be the result of Gates's restless desire, is not the acceptable path that Gates will want to take. And whatever this journey is going to entail, the journey must be what Jeffords calls "a man without woman trip."[24] This trip will require ditching Cruz while he goes on his journey, because as a female she will adversely infect the masculine experience in the wilderness. This point is proven in the film when Cruz is out in the Iraqi wilderness looking for Gates. She and a male military escort find dying oil-soaked pelicans in an oil-contaminated marsh, and she breaks down in tears. This environmental disaster, along with the burning of oil wells in the prior scene, is meant to show an example of Arab savagery in the wilderness. In an attempt to be humorous at the same time, the film shows her femininity as infectious when her emotions break down the male military escort. He begins to cry for the birds, as well.

Gates sees his opportunity when he hears the rumor, ironically told to him by a woman, about a treasure map that locates stolen Kuwaiti gold hidden in Saddam's bunkers, outside of the coalition base area and in the wilderness of Iraq. With a bit of sleuthing, he learns that a group of grunts, Troy Barlow (Mark Wahlberg), Conrad Vig (Spike Jonze), Walter Wogaman (Jamie Kennedy), and Chief Elgin (Ice Cube), found this map hidden between the ass cheeks of a surrendering Iraqi soldier. Cupidity induces him to stray from the heroic journey that would have been for the sake of inner, personal growth and for the sake of his society. Instead, in defiance of Mackey-Kallis's narrative formula of the hero quest, he puts the quest for boon or grail above all else. After all, he is still the product of a post-Vietnam America that, as H. Bruce Franklin notes, is often represented as a nation run by bureaucrats who revile the warrior hero and his virility and martial prowess. He is part of a weak and "decadent America subjugated by materialism, hedonism, and feminism."[25] Society is expected to provide him little support, and therefore Gates must place his material comforts first, his sense of inner self second, and the concern for all others much further down the priority scale. In a later scene, he reminds the men that personal necessity overrules love, respect, and God as the most important thing in life. With a pull of rank, he takes control of the "ass map" from the men and formulates a plan similar to the strategy, swift execution, and popular conception of the Gulf War itself: ditch the female Cruz, find the gold in the wilderness, retrieve it, keep the treasure to ensure financial superiority at a later date, and return to base—all in a short period of time. The plan is based on the naïve assumptions that Cruz can be duped and that the gold can be found, taken, and shipped home. Gates assumes that there will be no shooting, and his superiors will not notice the absence of the men. When the other men balk at the plan, Gates only has to remind them of their humdrum, working-class lives at home. As each man momentarily considers his life in flashback, their civilian lives are shown to be stressful, routine, frustrating, and even boring. As a result, they quickly agree to Gates's plan. The plan draws on the ideology that a warrior does not go to war without bringing something back; but rather than having the objective of returning with something that will benefit the whole of society, the plan is self-centeredly motivated to make life better for these men only. With such selfishness and short-sightedness, Vig dreams of purchasing a house outside of Garland, Texas, and Chief Elgin fantasizes about obtaining a Lexus convertible.

Further proof of the lack of accomplishments warranting boasts of victory is the battle-immaturity of the Gulf War soldiers that Gates takes on as his associates. Much of it is displayed through Vig's and Wogaman's stereotypical half-witted, Gomer Pyle characteristics of innocence, Southern-style twangy locution, behavior, and ignorance that are intended to be humorous to the audience. However, battle-immaturity is also displayed in the early scenes of the film when the audience is given a point-of-view shot from Barlow's combat experience. The camera simulates Barlow's viewpoint as the point soldier running through the open desert toward an Iraqi position. He encounters an Iraqi soldier in the distance and questions his platoon as to whether or not there is to be any shooting of people. This platoon, out on patrol, is not only unconcerned about these frontier occurrences, but it also does not have the discipline, knowledge, or battle-maturity to deal with them. In fact, these soldiers have not yet learned to respect the concept of wartime. Instead of staying in formation, poised for the possibility of attack, they linger, distracted: some soldiers argue over a piece of gum; and Wogaman helps Vig locate the grain of sand, a nuisance of the Arab landscape, that is irritating Vig's eye. Once Barlow announces that the Iraqi has a weapon and then shoots him, the platoon rushes to Barlow to see the prized kill and to congratulate him. "Dag. I didn't think I'd get to see anybody get shot in this war," states Vig while we hear the click and zip of another soldier's Polaroid camera taking a souvenir picture of a dead Iraqi—obviously an oddity to them rather than the norm. In another example, Wogaman complains about not getting a chance to use night-vision goggles and then wears them during the day. He refuses to take them off even when given orders to do so, when talking to his immediate superiors, or when pulling temporary sentry duty. Further into the film's narrative, Vig gets the opportunity to launch a grenade deep into an Iraqi bunker, but before he does so he complains about getting a splinter in his finger.

The scene that most brings the battle-immaturity of these men to light is seen when they set out into the Iraqi wilderness with Gates. These American soldiers' disrespect for wartime is symbolized by a doll of Bart Simpson, an American cartoon character known for his disregard of rules and order and for his unfettered acts of narcissistic pleasure. The doll and the American flag are attached to the military vehicle as hood ornaments that lead the way into the wilderness. Gates drives the vehicle with a pensive expression on his face. Barlow, Vig, and Elgin sit in the back of the Humvee playing an improvised game of skeet, using Nerf footballs as the targets and shooting with powerful semiautomatic rifles. So overmatched is the fired round to the target that the plastic adolescent toy is pulverized when hit, providing some comic relief. The game playing is accompanied by childish bickering over fair throws, football trivia, and competency of shots. The game comes to a halt when Vig overindulgently attaches a grenade to a football for maximum destruction. An annoyed Gates stops the Humvee like a parent stopping a car of children partaking in backseat mischief. The chastised soldiers respectfully explain their behavior as an outlet from having no opportunity to see battle action other than on CNN or when Barlow shot the one Iraqi. Vig's flashback of Barlow's shooting of the Iraqi is an embellished recollection that falsely depicts the Iraqi's head popping off and blood spurting high in the air.

Vig's statement and flashback demonstrate Jean Baudrillard's observation that "the Gulf War did not take place," but rather was a war of hyperreality.[26] Hyperreality means *more than real* and occurs when the distinctions between representation of the real and the real itself become so blurred that the distinctions dissolve. We are left with simulacra in which events lose their identity and the original meanings of such events are destroyed. In the case of the first Gulf War, Baudrillard sees the events as overpowered and dominated by the Hollywood-like language and scripted statements of the American politicians, commanding officers, and soldiers. The events were further limited by the journalists' inability to witness and report the war beyond what was officially given to them as reportable. And while military cameras took us closer to the events of smart bombs impacting with the targets, the silent and grainy pictures, the awe of technology, and the accompanying narration of "experts" removed the hellish nightmare of war's pain, destruction, and carnage. This new way of seeing real combat became a model with which the viewing public was indoctrinated, structuring the experience of the war. Vig's statement and flashback point out a quandary for the audience that mirrors the historical dilemma surrounding Gulf War narrative: the reconciliation between what was seen (Vig's recollection) and what actually happened (Barlow's experience). The popping head is retold as reality refracted through Vig's understanding of war, gathered from media simulation of American victory (his statement regarding CNN; media reporting made and censored to protect American masculinity in the war), and his deep desire for remasculinized killing of the enemy (his statement, "Fuckin' badass"). Although the audience has seen Barlow's original killing of the Iraqi, this second telling, with visual evidence provided, Vig's statement "I was there," his statistical details of the story not derived from the original occurrence (a single shot from four hundred yards away and the head popping three feet in the air), and an overall entertaining aesthetic, intertwines with what was previously documented as real. Vig becomes a momentary pundit analyzing and spinning the original occurrence. Distinctions between the original experience and the new version implode, the new version of the shooting becomes more than real, and we are left with the hyperreal. The audience suffers some discomfort about the discrepancy between what it saw up-close and through Barlow's experience and what it sees now, now being claimed as truth. Without the power of rewind to substantiate the truth, as is the case in the theater, the audience is not allowed to verify the actual occurrence and is expected to acquiesce to the new telling and to accept the new visual as true. The result of this second viewing is that the Iraqi's painful death, as witnessed in the first version, is trivialized and the meanings of human pain, destruction, and carnage (a lesson of Barlow's experience) are destroyed.

Gates, in an effort to educate these soldiers into the reality of war, takes them off the road to see some half-buried corpses and enemy bodies dismembered earlier by American aerial bombs. Like a teacher's lecture to a high school biology class with a mannequin and its plastic organs as a classroom aid, Gates's explanation is illustrated with an animated simulation of a bullet entering Barlow's gut. Here, too, hyperreality is part of the explanation, with models and simulation standing in for the real. Gates elaborates that if a bullet does not kill the victim, sepsis will. Elgin knows this information already, Barlow just now grasps the concept, and Vig acts as if he will never understand.

Gates also realizes that he must rehearse the mission with these "green" soldiers. After staking out a steer, several yards away, as an imagined Iraqi guard, the men simulate rushing the castrated beast/emasculated Iraqi as they plan to do later. The steer moves away and is blown apart by a submerged cluster bomb. The men have been given their first experience of the danger of war and the Iraqi wilderness. They stand stunned and amazed at what just happened and are showered with bloody animal parts. It is a baptism of gore. Their battle-immaturity reveals itself in the character and words of Vig, who declares, "Ka-boom! Y'all see that cow's head shoot up? Like a cartoon. It's fucking crazy." Even reality, for Vig, is reconciled to a model, i.e., a cartoon, and war remains hyperreal.

The heroic journey is proven to be skewed from the start because of the men's motivation and lack of maturity. However, this war story remains ever more incomplete, and its success is more questionable, because it lacks a savage enemy. These American soldiers need enemies—heinous in their deeds, strong in their might and numbers, deeply motivated by their hatred against the American and civilization—so that justness of cause can validate victory culture. Gulf War narrative, often overdetermined in this aspect, assures Americans that Saddam Hussein is the epitome of evil, another Hitler, and that his Iraqi army is a formidable fighting machine with overwhelming numbers. The narrative depicts the dark and swarthy Saddam as having acted unilaterally in his violation of international law: he took Kuwait for his own. He is portrayed as a tyrannical killer who used chemical weapons on his own people and ordered the arson of oil wells, destroying valuable natural resources and unleashing an environmental catastrophe. He ordered wild SCUD attacks on Israeli residential areas. His brutal, but well-disciplined, armed troops did his bidding, raped Kuwait, and even pulled at least three hundred premature babies from their incubators—an accusation later found to have no foundation but well suited to the narrative. Saddam's Iraq, in the name of civilization, reason, and humanity, had to be disciplined and defeated.[27]

However, the Iraqis in *Three Kings* do not seem, at first, to meet the qualifications for inimical savages. Their actual behavior does not match with the model that the soldiers anticipate or with the expectations of an American Orientalist audience. Therefore, these Iraqi soldiers frustrate the myths of the Gulf War narrative and the traditional war story narrative that are so needed to bring back victory culture. The Arabs, lacking explicit savagery, upset the myths. This is well established in the opening scene of the film. When Barlow comes upon the Iraqi position in the desert, he is faced with an enemy standing far away. The Iraqi in the distance confuses him, and Barlow is uncertain as to how he is to react. The enemy waves a white handkerchief in his left hand, but at the same time holds his rifle in his right hand. After Barlow ascertains that the Iraqi has a rifle and it appears that the gun is pointing in his direction, Barlow shoots the Iraqi. Barlow rushes to the hill and sees the Iraqi choking on his own blood and looking at Barlow, baffled as to the necessity of the shot. Barlow is overcome with nausea at the sight and shame at the possibility of having made a mistake. The immature and racist reaction of his platoon, noted once again in Vig's statement of "Congratulations. You just shot yourself a rag-head," renders the spectacle of savage killing an embarrassment. The Iraqi's ambiguous status between a surrendering soldier and imminent threat frustrates any relief, revelry, and sense of justice served that might attend the American killing of the enemy.

The Arabs further frustrate the celebratory scenes of a remasculinized American army during the subsequent scene of Iraqi surrender. The celebrations and alcohol consumption are halted with the captain's shouted orders that more Iraqis have to be taken prisoner the following day. This undertaking is made to sound, catering to the expectations of the war story, difficult and militarily challenging. However, the scene shows broken and pitiful Iraqi troops surrendering en masse and without resistance. They come out willingly and without American troops needing to exert much military effort in the struggle. In fact, some American soldiers just stand around with their weapons at ease. Most of the Iraqis are dressed in ragged clothing, show bewilderment and fatigue on their faces, and beg for mercy. In their hands they carry a peculiar paper that contains the orders to surrender in English and Arabic on its verso, and in cartoon pictures on its front. The pictures are important because they offer another instance of Baudrillard's point of Gulf War hyperreality. But there is disappointment in the fact that the model (a cartoon) and reality (the actual scene of the Iraqis surrendering) cannot be reconciled here into such a perfect order. Unlike what the pictures portray as the model, there is no clean and erect Iraqi soldier meeting with an American, and, after the Iraqi surrenders his weapon, there is no sitting down to a communal feast in the real experience. Reality, as seen before the eyes of the American soldiers, does not conform to either the cartoon or to the savage punishment dictated by the war story. The Iraqis, in their total submission, are making things difficult for the army's self-proclaimed remasculinization.

This conundrum is most frustrating to Vig. Barlow tries to follow the instructions and attempts to replicate the image of the model printed on the paper, and he chooses to politely ask the Iraqis to remove their "turbans." Vig, contrarily, is less patient and has to instigate some sort of resistance from the Iraqi soldiers to fulfill the war story's narrative. The eagerly submitting Iraqis keep Vig from maintaining the quality of victory needed for his remasculinization. To provoke the Iraqis into the role of savage enemy, Vig taunts them by swinging at them, swearing at them, and calling them racist names. He waves his pistol in their faces, as if the pistol is a symbolic penis that validates his masculine dominance over them. Barlow orders Vig to stop, since polite bigotry is the more efficient way to get the Iraqis to cooperate—a better adherence to the cartoon picture. And he politely asks one Iraqi soldier to disrobe, "like all the other towel-heads." When the Iraqi does not cooperate, again frustrating the GIs, they disrobe him forcibly. This seems to suit Vig just fine, because the ripping off of the Iraqi's clothes resembles a gang rape, and, with a little help from the struggling Iraqi, reestablishes Vig's masculine strength and supremacy over the Iraqi. To Barlow's, Vig's, and Wogaman's surprise, the coercive disrobing is suddenly halted when they see that the Iraqi has a document inserted into his anus.

Vig's frustration with the Arabs' indeterminacy as savage enemies is further underscored by this war's unclassifiability. Unlike previous wars, this war exists in a period of tolerance and multiculturalism, antithetical to the "good" wartime of the Greatest Generation. According to Paul Fussell's discussion of World War II, "Looking out upon the wartime world, soldiers and civilians alike reduce it to a simplified sketch featuring a limited series of classifications into which people, in the process dehumanized and deprived of individuality or eccentricity, are fitted."[28] Once again, the Arabs do not fit into the typecast model, or submit to the hyperreality, of enemies. Vig must take on the task of determining the Arabs to be savage enemies by himself in order to make sense of the war, and he finds that his superiors deride him for it, even if only half-heartedly. To distance himself from the Iraqis, he must totally reject their humanity. Vig dons a rubber glove before coming into physical contact with the Iraqi's rectum and complains when he does not have a second glove while unrolling the piece of paper. Then, he decontaminates himself from the Iraqi by compulsively washing his hands. He also uses antilocution (derogatory verbiage) to force the Iraqi back into the classificatory model. His statement, "Lord knows what sort of vermin live in the butt of a dune coon," brings this to the fore.

His use of "coon" brings chastisement from Chief Elgin, who, partly due to his African American roots, also objects to any future use of "sand nigger." But Elgin's identity complies with American victory culture and the masculine ego. He is not only susceptible to strategies of compartmentalization and absolute truths during wartime, but also vulnerable to the desire of having mastery over the feminine and eschewing his own feminine role. Therefore, when Barlow confers with Vig and tells him that "towel-head" and "camel jockey" are perfectly good substitutes, Elgin gives his approval. These terms seem to no longer threaten Elgin's own ethnic and masculine identity, but rather are pushed onto someone else. Vig apologizes and explains that he is confused "with all this pro-Saudi, anti-Iraqi-type language and all that." To Vig, they are all Arabs and should all be the enemies. And later, Elgin finds it easy to overlook the fact that a video replaying the Rodney King beatings might correlate with his own violence toward an already surrendered Iraqi army or his exploitation of Iraqi soldiers to labor for his monetary benefit as they lift and tote bags of gold for him.

The discovery of the "ass map" is probably the best example of the Arabs' threat to the war story, and to understand this requires consideration of psychoanalysis and the concept of anality. Antony Easthope provides a clear discussion of how feces are central to the issue of control and mastery, and ultimately play an important part in the masculine ego.[29] Easthope follows Freud's thoughts on childhood toilet training. When the child surrenders his/her feces to the supervising adult, the feces act as a gift; when the child retains them, feces act as a narcissistic pleasure, like money, something to be kept for him/herself. The ass map of *Three Kings* symbolizes the human struggle with feces. Unwilling to give it up outright to the American soldiers, the Iraqi struggles against the disrobing. Vig's discovery of the protruding map brings the film's key characters together through states of shock (Vig: "Whoa! Whoa! Whoa!"), curiosity (Wogaman: "Do you think he ate it?" and Vig: "What is it?"), fascination (Barlow: "It's important enough to squeeze your cheeks for."), desire (Cruz: "I want the story this time."), and possessiveness (Barlow: ". . . my Iraqi ass map;" and Gates when he and Barlow struggle for it: "Don't get grabby, Sergeant."). There are often scatological references to the ass map, as when Cruz is trying to get a French Special Forces soldier to give her information about it, but he acts like he does not know. "This guy doesn't know shit," she states. Gates refers to the tent where Barlow has the map as the "proctology tent," and when he smells his fingers after he touches the map he states, "You're on the path to truth when you smell shit." Also, Gates tells of how it is the path to millions in gold bullion formed into bricks, a possible play on the phrase "shitting bricks."

The men sit around the map (the symbolic feces), analyze it, put it under iridescent light, and discuss its value. The map remains a narcissistic pleasure rather than a gift. While the Iraqi was unwilling to give it up, the soldiers are unwilling to give it up as well, and they see the monetary value of keeping it for themselves. The greater stash of "feces," i.e., the gold, is to be kept secretly for themselves, and it is not intended to be returned to its rightful owners. But when such a scenario is played against the war story, which means that the frontiersman goes into the wilderness for the benefit of his society, Gates's journey is destined to be devoid of real success. Without returning with the boon as a gift to his society when he comes home, the journey inward will never be fulfilled. And so, the Iraqi's "feces" is keeping victory culture in abeyance.

Comically, then, the Humvee journey into the wilderness is not so much the hunt for Saddam Hussein's bunker, but rather a gangland act of searching for Saddam's anus. Anally penetrating Saddam, thereby feminizing the enemy, taking a masculine stance over him, and stealing his feces from him are the goals of the journey. The Iraqi soldier only contained a simple ass map, but if one can penetrate deep into the Arab ass of the big man, the man who holds all of the Iraqi riches and the former Kuwaiti wealth, i.e., the type of obscene wealth Linda Blandford stereotypes as Arab "super-wealth,"[30] then one can find the most undreamed of riches that Saddam holds for himself. The journey in *Three Kings* is an act of "Saddamy,"[31] and its homoeroticism heightens the need to keep Cruz, the female, out.

When the small band of American soldiers enters the Iraqi village outside of Karbala, its ambitions for remasculinization are thwarted again by the Iraqis' too easy submission. The American soldiers force their entry into a corridor that they believe will lead to the bunker. The Americans are given no resistance from the Iraqi soldiers as they wave their guns, symbolic of their penises and thus their masculinity, and a document that they claim states their rightful entry, according to orders of President Bush. Many of the Iraqis are dazed by the sudden appearance of American soldiers in the village and lay their weapons down in submission. Some are frightened by the soldiers' frontiersman demeanor—flashing their guns and covered with cow blood mistaken by the Iraqis for human blood from a recent massacre—and scurry out of the small band's way. Others are so prone to sycophancy that they cooperate freely without information as to why the Americans have come. Posters showing a smiling Saddam seem to oversee the sudden American presence. Barlow later complains of other villagers and soldiers alike, "They were ignoring us like we weren't even there."

Additionally, the soldiers' blinding narcissism and overly cherished masculinity have misled them in their journey to a successful war story. The Iraqi villagers come out to welcome the soldiers as if they are being

Three Kings (1999). Gates (George Clooney), Barlow (Mark Wahlberg), Elgin (Ice Cube), and Vig (Spike Jonze) drive into an Iraqi village after the Allied Coalition Force's victory in the first Gulf War. They are searching for stolen Kuwaiti gold. Unlike the American soldiers in World War II who liberated civilians from tyranny, these American soldiers are battle-immature. The Arab crowd begging for their help bewilders them, and they lack a clear understanding of war and the purpose of the hero's journey. The soldiers' motivation for this journey into the Iraqi wilderness is to greedily enrich themselves. Photo courtesy of the Academy of Motion Picture Arts and Sciences.

liberated, just as in the classic scenarios of a just war like World War II. These men, however, are not prepared to accept the honor or the responsibility of liberating the villagers from the clutches of Saddam's soldiers despite Vig's words that "We are here to protect you." The motivation of the journey is to gain selfishly, not for the benefit of the villagers or even the American soldiers' own society. They look in bewilderment when people beg for milk, food, and protection. When they cannot find the bunker in the village, they leave the begging crowd behind. And unlike any model soldier from the Greatest Generation, who might have offered gum, chocolate, or pantyhose to the liberated villagers of Europe, Gates and his men throw a begging man off the back of their moving Humvee, leaving him rolling in the dust. Their persistent avoidance of the feminine blinds them as well. Strangely, Iraqi soldiers choose to attack a milk truck that tries to enter the village rather than this small band of American men.

The truck careens out of control and bursts, pouring milk everywhere and dowsing the Americans. The feminine tries to wake them from their overdetermined masculine adrenaline in this act of milk dowsing, so that they may see that they are losing their way in the war story, but just yet they cannot see beyond their narcissistic and homoerotic goal.

They return to the village when Gates becomes aware that the Iraqi soldiers have duped them into believing there was no gold there. He realizes that some soldiers, posing as villagers, were congregated around the village well. They were protecting the actual opening for which these Americans are searching. This must be Saddam's inner sanctum, because its discovery by the American men makes him and his evil ways more transparent. They find here not only stolen property from Kuwait, but a new painting of Saddam lovingly kissing a small child, with another to the side. It implies Saddam's sexual deviance as a child molester. After easily subduing the guards, because they do not fight, Gates, Barlow, and Elgin make their way into the opening found next to the well. As they break down doors, they enter into a first chamber that contains medium-priced electronic equipment and household appliances. These items the Iraqis offer to the Americans freely in a manner reminiscent of the stereotypical sycophancy of Arab bazaar merchants. When Gates is offered a food processor, he refuses it. The persistent Iraqi soldier encourages him to take it for his wife. This raises the ire of the antifeminine Gates, who slaps the item to the ground and barks back, "I'm divorced." Meanwhile, Barlow's temper also rises when he tells another Iraqi, who tries to entice him with the stereo equipment, that the music playing is bad music. The music is Eddie Murphy's "My Girl Wants to Party All the Time," and, as the lyrics reveal, it also deals with the feminine. The male sings about being spurned by his female.

Another chamber reveals civilians being tortured, whom the Iraqis refuse to give up and in whom the American soldiers have less interest than in the electronic equipment. The final door opens to a downward cylindrical stairway, outlined with piping, which takes the men deep into the ground. The passageway symbolizes an anal canal, complete with veins, arteries, and the inner workings of the colon. At the very end is a door that opens to a stark white room filled with light. The light provides the room with a purity and sanctity, unlike all other places in the Iraqi landscape, and connotes the symbolic penetration into the center of Saddam's corpus. Here, packed in plain black suitcases that are lined up in a row in the middle of the room and thereby simulating the coveted Freudian feces,

Three Kings (1999). The Iraqi "ass map" leads the American soldiers (George Clooney, Ice Cube, and Mark Wahlberg) to Saddam's bunker, which they deeply penetrate through the cylindrical tunnel (symbolic of Saddam's anal passageway). At the end of the tunnel, the soldiers find a column of black suitcases filled with stolen Kuwaiti gold (symbolic of Freudian feces) that they will claim and keep for themselves. Photo courtesy of the Academy of Motion Picture Arts and Sciences.

are silver place settings and tea services, Rolex watches, jewelry, and wallets. And while Barlow and Elgin begin to pocket some of the treasure in a childish frenzy, Gates orders them to put everything back. He reminds them that they are not petty thieves and that they must stick to the plan of getting the big prize: the bricks of gold. Deeper in the room, in more black suitcases, they finally find the desired gold bricks. It is too obvious what they are meant to symbolize when Barlow yells out "Shit!" as the bricks rip through the bag and fall on his foot. When Barlow commandeers a truck to take the gold, a magazine in the truck can be seen, which now shows, in contrast with all previous pictures, a stern and possibly angry Saddam face.

The extraction of the gold is only slightly contested by the Iraqi soldiers. However, when a jeep full of Iraqi reinforcements arrives, the audience expects typical enemy resistance, especially when the reinforcements threaten the Iraqi civilians, order seems to break down, and everyone ignores Vig when he barks, "The United States military's in charge here." Vig's declaration is challenged by the arriving Iraqi commander, whose threatening stare is hidden behind dark sunglasses. But surprisingly, the stern-looking Iraqi CO turns out to be quite courteous and accommodating, and the apparent threat evaporates. In fact, he strangely offers the labor of his men to help the Americans take the gold out of the bunker in Louis Vuitton bags. The entire deal is brokered between the Americans and the Iraqi commander while in the background Iraqi Shiite civilians are herded away and beaten, a child is threatened with a police club, and a woman is wrestled to the ground. The masculine narcissism keeps the American soldiers from seeing the human tragedy around them. While it would seem that this background activity of Iraqi violence is proof that the Arabs are animalistic, it actually highlights American inhumanity and narcissism, because the Americans are distancing themselves from the war story narrative. In fact, the scene implies an Arab mockery of the very meaning of American frontiersmanship.

Furthermore, the Iraqis have changed the meaning of the gold, which the Americans are too slow to understand. The free and courteous giving of the gold, the Iraqi commander's statement that Saddam has other problems today, and the jealous guarding and control of the prisoners deflate the value of the gold. The gold, by the choice of the Iraqi soldiers, is now only of secondary importance. The Iraqis know that the rebel prisoners represent the real prized possession of Saddam. Gates tells his men that the Bush administration, while encouraging civilian rebellion, is not interested in protecting the civilians or engaging the Iraqis in battle over them. Therefore, the prisoners and their rebellions, not the American soldiers and the gold, are the immediate threat to the Iraqi regime in postwar Iraq. Once Gates arrives again outside the bunker, he sees that Vig and Barlow are bemused by their loss of control in the village courtyard. They look to Gates for further explanation and just stand by while the Iraqi soldiers dominate the outside scene and abuse the villagers. An Iraqi soldier introduces Gates to the Iraqi commander, "This American next to me is without manners [adab]." This is spoken in Arabic without English subtitles and is important because it keeps Gates and the non-Arabic-speaking American audience from communicative control. The commander replies, "No problem," and treats Gates with the very courtesy he seems to lack. The Arab image of ambiguity is highlighted, as the Iraqi commander is courteous and friendly, while, at the same time, he is ruthless and oppressive. The scene is symbolically torn between an Iraqi soldier's hand offered to Gates in help and the same Iraqi's bloodied knuckles caused by striking the civilians. And while Gates thinks he is being cool and masculine in his answers to the commander's accented and grammatically flawed English, the Iraqi commander actually mocks Gates by forcing him to communicate in a sort of baby talk. "You take the Kuwaiti gold, yes? Saddam cannot keep?" asks the Iraqi commander. Gates replies, "We take the Kuwaiti gold, yes. No, Saddam cannot keep." The Iraqis have deflated the value of the gold, reestablished their control in the village, brought Gates to use infantile English, further entrenched him and his men in their narcissistic quest for gold, and therefore put the Americans further off the track of their war story.

Although Gates excludes woman, i.e., the female journalist, from his journey and disdains the Iraqis, it is a woman and some of the Iraqis who put him back onto the proper track of a moral war story. With the gold packed up inside the getaway vehicles, the American soldiers "saddle up" into their driving positions to leave, avoiding further contact with the Iraqis. A woman civilian, held back by an Iraqi soldier, pleads with them in English, "Don't leave. Please. Help. Look. Please." The Iraqi commander orders her to be shot, and the soldier holding her executes her with a shot to the head. The village is consumed by a deafening silence. The American soldiers look away in shame. Gates drops his head on the Humvee's steering wheel.

The scene, the woman's pleas, and the silence are critical to the narrative's trajectory. They offer the American soldiers and the audience a moment to reflect on the status of the journey, heroism, and masculinity—in essence, the achievement of victory culture. While at one point the men and the audience are caught up in the action and excitement of revenge and mastery over Saddam and the Iraqis, now the conduct of the American soldiers and all that has happened are submitted to evaluation. The scene itself is a reimaging of the famous photograph of General Nguyen Ngoc Loan executing a manacled National Liberation Front prisoner in Saigon in 1968. H. Bruce Franklin describes the originally photographed Vietnam experience thus:

In a perfectly framed sequence, the notorious General Nguyen Ngoc Loan unholsters a snub-nosed revolver and places its muzzle to the prisoner's right temple. The prisoner's head jolts, a sudden burst of blood gushes straight out of his right temple, and he collapses in death.[32]

Franklin notes the image as one of the most shocking, influential, and enduring images of the Vietnam War. It invaded the consciousness of millions of Americans as they sat watching it on their television sets in the comfort of their own homes.[33] In replaying the image in the Iraqi context, the film brings about a historical shame for the American characters and audience. While Gates and the American audience desire to distance themselves from the Vietnam experience and move toward a more World War II–type experience of victory culture, it becomes clear that they have failed thus far. They are truly on the Vietnam end of the spectrum, following MacPherson's rather than Brokaw's model. The Iraqis and the woman prisoner of *Three Kings* have placed us at a critical juncture, or maybe they have forced us Americans to realize that we have thrown ourselves into this corner of the world in pursuit of our own agenda. To continue on this way, in spite of what has just happened, would be to accept, or to foster, another Vietnam experience — a misguided journey into the quagmire. In dropping his head against the steering wheel, Gates realizes this and is forced to change the course of the journey.

The silence is broken by the woman's daughter pleading for her mother's return to life and then by her pain as an Iraqi soldier drags her away by the hair from the dead woman's corpse. Gates walks out of the Humvee and is torn between the Iraqi commander's request for him to leave, Barlow's plea to stick to the plan of taking the gold and leaving, and Elgin's suggestion to help the people and then go on their way. Under the protective guns of the three other soldiers and held in check by the many Iraqi soldiers poised to counterattack, he walks coolly to an Iraqi soldier who holds the father at knifepoint and thrashes the soldier with his martial arts training. He then decides to take the civilians back to camp with them. Gates is in the process of snapping out of his narcissism, which has blinded him up to now, and realizes the beginnings of the moral war story for which he has been searching. Gates's narcissism is further broken as he struggles with the Iraqi commander over a rifle, and a slow-motion shootout in the village square ensues, with Iraqis being shot. Gates is wounded in the arm. Barlow gets shot, too, but he is saved by his bulletproof vest. The violent premise for the war story, which Gates frustratingly could not find before, is now apparent. The world suddenly seems changed. Above his head, the clouds in the sky rush past as if his head has suddenly cleared. Elgin experiences the same symbolic awakening. Vig's overhead sky is clear, but, true to his character, he remains uncertain. Only Barlow is denied this overhead sky shot, and he contests

Gates's decision, asking, "What happened to necessity?" Gates announces that it has just changed.

Appearing on the scene is an Iraqi tank, whose firepower could overwhelm the small band of American men and their guns. At the same time, the men load up the Iraqi civilians and hit the trail back to camp, much to Barlow's dismay. The Iraqi tank kills a small boy, who was sniping at the Iraqi soldiers, and then the Iraqis pursue the retreating Americans and the civilians into the desert. The theme of Saddam's anus is repeated here again. From the village square that holds the opening to Saddam's bunker and symbolic anus, the Iraqi soldiers shoot mortars of poisonous gas (i.e., symbolic flatus) that eventually overcomes the fleeing men and civilians. Gas was one of the most feared weapons of Saddam Hussein and was considered one of the most uncivilized, cruel, and even uncouth forms of warfare for an American military privileged with high-tech weaponry that is considered much more efficient, precise, and gentlemanly in exterminating humanity. The vehicles careen off the path and into a minefield. The Humvee explodes and Barlow's truck overturns, stopping just short of hitting a land mine. The thick gas, like tear gas but ten times its power, is unleashed with deafening explosions as if the crude Oriental despot were forcefully breaking wind. The gas, strong enough to eventually make Gates vomit, blinds him.

The anal theme is also made apparent in the following abduction of the men. Each of the men performs actions of heroism worthy of the mythic roles of World War II soldiers saving the lives of civilians. Gates and Elgin help each other and gather the civilians. Each offers his gas mask to a civilian, and Gates leads the civilians away from land mines and inquires about the children's whereabouts. Gates and Elgin have become aware of the moral path of the war story and consciously make this effort. Barlow gives up his gold in favor of the war story, but does so unconsciously. He has not embraced the new "necessity." As two children run by him in panic, he chases them in rescue while still clinging to a bag of gold. When he cannot keep both children from running further into the minefield and still hold the gold, he drops the gold and chooses instead to save the children. The effort toward conscious acceptance of the moral path of the war story defines how the Americans are abducted in the following scenes. Barlow is captured by the Iraqi soldiers and taken back to another one of Saddam's anal chambers: Oasis Bunker, a strongly fortified bunker and a nest full of Saddam's Republican Guard. Underground rebels rescue Gates, Elgin, Vig, and the civilians, and they take them all into an earthly opening somewhere out in the desert. This opening is smaller, made of cracked and dried stone, and appears as if it has been neglected. This cavity is more womblike, softly lit by candles, and is a place where these three Americans will be nursed and nurtured back to health.

In both cavities the men will be spiritually transformed so that they can bring the war story back on track. However, experiences in the two cavities differ. In Saddam's symbolic rectum, Barlow undergoes interrogation and torture at the hands of the Iraqi soldiers, a fitting sentence for Barlow since he is the furthest away from understanding and accepting the war story. Meanwhile, in the rebels' cave, symbolic of the female vagina, Gates, Elgin, and Vig are nurtured and reasoned back from the errors of their ways. Their treatment comprises a more benevolent education, since they were already on the way to accepting a more virtuous role in the war story. In both cases, the bunker and the cave, the Iraqis remind the GIs of the paradoxes of American policies concerning race and ethnicity, democratic and capitalistic principles, family values, and commitment to Third World development.

The Iraqi interrogator chastises Barlow for a racist culture that creates self-hate in Michael Jackson, thereby forcing Jackson to submit to a surgical assault on his African features. "Your sick fucking country make the black man hate hisself, just like you hate the Arab and the children you bomb over here." Interestingly, Barlow denies hating children but does not protest to hating the Arab. The interrogator reminds Barlow that his selfish quest for gold has broken a ceasefire. He questions whether the American army will come back to help the people and children of Iraq. He tells Barlow that American bombs wounded his wife and killed his son while the boy was asleep in his bed. Confronted with flashbacks and hypothetical scenes, Barlow and the audience are forced to see the effect of American bombs on the Iraqi's son. Barlow and the audience see Barlow's wife and daughter safe in an American suburb. They also see how the two would die if bombed at home. The Iraqi tells Barlow how he joined the army to make a better living, and Barlow begins to see that the two of them are very similar in economic motivations and their love and commitment to their families. His interrogator declares that he received training from the Americans during the Iran-Iraq War, including training on how to interrogate prisoners. This American science of interrogation is now being applied to Barlow. Barlow explains that the Americans are in the Arab land to save Kuwait because aggressive invasions of countries, like Iraq's invading Kuwait, create instability in the world. However, the Iraqi questions the validity of his statement. To teach Barlow the real reason America is concerned about stability in the Middle East, the Iraqi forces Barlow to drink motor oil and states, "This is your fucking stability, my main man." While the Iraqi provides rational insight into American duplicity, he upsets the American self-image, and the audience finds his lesson disconcerting. His characteristically Oriental proclivity for violence dominates the scene and diminishes the opportunity for American self-examination. The scene depicts the Iraqi as perpetrator because he brutally assaults the American. Even the Iraqi turning on the electrical shock winces at his own sadism. And so, I believe, the opportunity offered by the film for the American audience to be introspective and critical about its culture and foreign policy is lost. It is followed too soon with the film's overplay of the inimical Arab characters and their assault on the American in the act of torture. The important opportunity is displaced by the audience's reaction of shock, fear, and anger at the stereotypical Arabs and their behavior.

In contrast, the men in the more feminine cavity learn the errors of their ways with less violent means and without traumatic flashbacks and flights of imagination. In the confusion of the gas attack, Vig blames Elgin and Gates for Barlow's separation from the rest of the group. In this place of recuperation, the three reconcile and reaffirm their male bond, which is no longer based on the materialism that has taken them this far, but on loyalty, brotherhood, and their determination to find their lost friend. While they still are concerned with their gold, how much they still have left ($23 million), and how they can save themselves from a court-martial, the rebel leader schools them in their American paradoxes. He had studied business in Kentucky and had come back to Iraq to open a number of hotels, but the Americans had bombed his upstart cafés, thus ruining him financially. And now, he states accusingly, the Americans will leave the Iraqi people in the clutches of Saddam. He condemns the American soldiers for being a band of thieves, while they, the civilians, are the ones actually fighting Saddam and dying. Gates denies the allegations and offers a portion of the gold in return for their help in rescuing Barlow. But the rebel leader asks if it really is the Americans' gold, since it was the rebels who saved it from the wrecked truck. The rebels want Gates to provide American protection to them as they make their way to safety in Iran, but Gates knows this would bring attention to his being AWOL. When Gates and his men refuse to escort the rebels to the Iranian border, part of the deal to help rescue Barlow, the rebel leader states, "The big army of democracy beats the ugly dictator and saves the rich Kuwaitis. But you go to jail if you help us escape the same dictator?" Once again, it is the remembrance of the death of the man's wife and child that changes Gates's mind. The war story will progress further on track, away from the narcissistic goal of capturing gold for selfish pleasures and toward the rescue of a comrade and the safe escort of the fifty-five civilians to Iran, which suddenly, and quite ironically, becomes a destination of freedom in this American myth.

The Americans and the rebels concoct a plan to retrieve Barlow. Finding a group of refugees and Iraqi army deserters in the desert, the men are welcomed and congratulated on their victory in the Gulf War. Still, Gates is uncomfortable with the idea of victory without the completion of the war story. The Iraqi army deserters control a bunker that contains a fleet of luxury vehicles that were once part of Saddam's loot taken from Kuwait. While Gates and Elgin try to get the vehicles for free by patronizingly appealing to all of the parties present to unite their efforts with George Bush's move to defeat Saddam, or in Elgin's masculine tone "Kick Saddam's ass," the Iraqis want money. At first it may seem that the Iraqis are retarded in their understanding of the war story, because they are concerned about monetary gain — a preoccupation the Americans have moved beyond now — and not moral principles. However, this time money is wanted as a means to get food for the people, not for the selfish consumption of the luxury items on which the Americans originally planned to spend their newfound wealth. The Iraqis can see through the American men's sudden moral rebirth and transparent promises of overthrowing Saddam. Their request for money is actually highlighting the Americans' ignorance in understanding the civilians' needs, and the initial refusal to pay exposes the Americans' doubtful commitment to these people. While the men are on the path of the war story, they really are quite immature as of yet. Their boisterous cheering for taking on Saddam indicates this, and is reminiscent of their immaturity in the earliest scenes of masculine celebration, a style that does not work out here in the wilderness.

Since there are many Republican Guard soldiers in the bunker, and the assembled team of three Americans and some Iraqi rebels is small in comparison, the rescue plan must be devised with American ingenuity and be based on outwitting the enemy. This will require the use of a ruse, an understanding of courage, and some reliance upon the American versus Arab gunfighter knowledge that has been touched on in the discussion of *Black Sunday*. Gates learns that the one thing the Iraqis fear most is their

Three Kings (1999). Gates (George Clooney) and Elgin (Ice Cube) try to bargain with an Iraqi rebel for a fleet of cars to use in their attempt to rescue Barlow, now a prisoner of the Iraqi Republican Guard. An Iraqi civilian (Cliff Curtis) tries to help them. The two Americans appeal to the Iraqi's hatred of Saddam, but this Iraqi wants money, not for the selfish desire of wealth and luxury, but to provide food and clothing for his people. He highlights the American soldiers' failure to understand the civilians' needs. The Americans' initial refusal to pay illustrates their disingenuous commitment to these native people. Photo courtesy of the Academy of Motion Picture Arts and Sciences.

despotic leader, Saddam himself. So Gates insists on an impersonation of Saddam to frighten them. When the Republican Guard soldiers see a cortege of expensive automobiles driving through the wilderness desert, they believe the rumor that Saddam is angry with them and has come personally to kill them. It is a ruse that shows not only the cunning of the American soldier, but also the craven character of the Iraqis. While Vig questions his own courage to meet the objective that faces them, Gates, the elite American soldier, tells him a secret of American heroism: act first; the courage is obtained after the deed is done, not before. The Iraqis, in contrast, do not and, by virtue of not being American, cannot hold the key to this secret, and we see them scramble out of the bunker, drop their guns and Slim Jim beef jerky, and run away at the sight of the white limousine and its tinted windows. Gates and Elgin, the American heroes, emerge from the limousine as if the battle to come is a gala event, a moment the audience has been waiting to see. When some Iraqis figure out that they have been duped, they begin to shoot, but once they are fired on, they flee, too.

The Iraqi aim is rarely clean. Iraqis often shoot and miss, spray bullets from their guns and from helicopter fire, kill wildly and without precision and skill, and often use firepower that is overmatched to their target. For example, a tank shell is used against a child sniper, a rocket launcher is used to destroy an Infiniti convertible, and machine gun sprays from a helicopter indiscriminately mow down civilian bodies without consideration of their threat level. Even the Iraqi rebels, although fighting on the side of the Americans against Saddam's soldiers, shoot many bullets in order to make a kill. At the end of the film, they no longer will be allowed to carry guns. As the civilians face the Iraqi border police, who have cocked their guns for potential fire, Gates insists that the Iraqi refugees be disarmed and that "Only American soldiers will carry guns."

Americans, however, are superior when it comes to killing with guns. As seen in the opening scenes of the film, Barlow killed with an effort of rationality and with a single shot from a distance. His shot was targeted and fatal, although it may have been immature because it produced a painful and messy death. Decisive, rapid, deadly, clean, smart, and distanced are all characteristics of the virtuous and virtual American killing in the Gulf War, according to Asu Aksoy and Kevin Robins. Such characteristics are opposite those of the Vietnam experience.[34] Gates's earlier educational lecture about the ramifications of shooting, explaining that sepsis is often the cause of death from a bullet wound, is intended to teach not only respect for wartime, but also how to commit a clean and appropriate kill—American-style. Part of that lecture is to remind the men that patience and tolerance are needed when handling a gun. The shootout in the village, presented in slow motion, complies with the etiquette of gunfire because the Americans remain cool and controlled, and are able to exchange fire, as the enemy attacks first and the Americans shoot back in retaliation and with greater effectiveness. Note, too, that as Gates and Elgin make their way through the underground bunker to save Barlow, they are careful of their gunfire. Elgin's staid trigger finger prevents him from killing more civilians held in captivity behind a locked door, freeing them rather than murdering them. Meanwhile, Gates chooses not to kill an Iraqi soldier who is more worried about saving himself and a stack of Levi's blue jeans than about fighting the Americans. The Levi's-carrying Iraqi now represents a shadow image of Gates's earlier narcissistic self. Trigger fingers are saved for more decisive shots at those who have taken

Barlow captive and have tortured him. Gates kills two of the torturers and only wounds the Iraqi interrogator, giving Barlow the opportunity to kill him in order to take revenge on him. When Gates hands him the gun to kill off the interrogator, Barlow, now more battle-matured, chooses to spare the Iraqi's life but scares him by firing into the wall just above his head. These are calculated misses intended to frighten the interrogator and to demonstrate Barlow's superior American nature, which does not succumb to anger with a firearm as the nature of the Iraqi does. Fear reduces the Iraqi to tears, in contrast to Barlow, who even under the pain of torture, fought his fear and never broke down. The event shows that Barlow has matured in captivity and that his progression is now on track with the war story.

Meanwhile, Elgin is fully on track with the war story. Elgin single-handedly brings down the murderous Iraqi helicopter with his quarter-back throw of a Nerf football loaded with explosives. Whereas before the Nerf football was part of a skylarking game of skeet shooting played by lost and selfish soldiers, now it is a decisive and brilliant weapon in the hand of a mature American soldier. One targeted and determined throw of the football at the enemy helicopter by the male and muscled arm of the American soldier ends the deadly Iraqi spray of bullets. American masculinity based on precision shooting is reestablished over the feminized push of Arab destruction. Following a clear moral objective of the war story, the American no longer blunders but becomes capable of heroic and superstrength deeds.

The Iraqi soldiers get in two targeted shots that are relatively good in relation to their previous shooting record. However, the fact that they strike Vig and Barlow unawares during a happy reunion only highlights the Iraqis' evil character. Vig has been hiding underneath a dead body from the helicopter's shooting spree. When he sees that Barlow has been rescued from the Iraqis, he crawls out from under the body, excitedly calls for Barlow, and runs to meet him. However, a pair of hidden Iraqi soldiers shoots at them, fatally wounding Vig and then injuring Barlow severely. The possibility of sepsis becomes very real in Barlow's body. But even here the Iraqis are not skillful with the gun: neither instant death nor sepsis occurs in Barlow. Barlow's lung begins to collapse, and he cannot breathe. Gates skillfully administers first aid by inserting an air valve into his chest and saves him. Barlow must turn the key on the valve every fifteen minutes to keep the lung from collapsing again until they can get him better medical attention. The two Iraqi snipers are not so lucky, as Gates soundly executes them, masculinely pumping many bullets into their bodies with his rifle. The American overuse of bullets seems justified in this case because the Iraqis have devilishly executed a sneak attack.

While it seems that the Iraqis have once again attempted to overturn the war story with the shooting of Vig and Barlow, the Iraqi action, in a certain sense, may have been necessary for the proper progression of the war story's masculine narrative. The masculine myth, recalling Easthope's definition, requires resistance to homosexual tendencies in the male. Whereas Easthope acknowledges the male reliance on and fetishization of the male social bond and body, the masculine ego desexualizes and represses outright desire that is equated with homosexuality.[35] Vig and Barlow have, throughout the film, transgressed the boundaries of this desire. Vig, we are told in the very beginning, "wants to be Barlow," and he seeks to be close to him. He dances in a sexually suggestive way with Barlow and mounts Barlow during a tackle, showing a revolver — a phallic symbol — to him, and both scream in psychic unison during their masculine rush. During the celebrations, the two find time alone to groom each other with hair clippers and comment on how handsome the other looks. While Barlow may bicker with and demean Vig, Vig cannot deal well with their separation after their vehicle crashes in the Iraqi wilderness. He cries out for Barlow, fights Elgin, who attempts to take him into the safety of the cave and away from Barlow, and blames Gates for Barlow's separation from him and Barlow's abduction by the Iraqi soldiers. The two do meet again after Gates saves Barlow from the torturous hands of the Iraqi interrogator. The first words from Barlow's mouth after the rescue are "Where's Conrad?" — Vig's first name — and he goes out to search for him. When they see each other, they romantically run to each other, open-armed, as if into a lover's embrace.

If the journey is to be successful, however, the two men must deny their homosexual desires and return to their former heterosexual lives and to society, bringing benefit to both. As Judith Roof enlightens us, homosexuality is a nonreproductive barrier to the heterosexuality of reproductive narrative.[36] Barlow has to adopt again the roles of husband and father to provide for a new narrative beginning when the war story is over. During his separation from Vig and unbeknownst to Vig, Barlow reunites with his wife, calling her on a cellular telephone that he finds among the many hundreds that the Iraqis have stolen from Kuwait. He reaffirms his love for his wife, the baby, and the heterosexual life he has left behind at home. His wife makes the necessary calls to headquarters so that a rescue team can save the men U.S. Cavalry–style in the desert. Vig, who seems to have no heterosexual future and cannot return from the journey without claiming Barlow for himself, dies. While Vig dies fearing death, he also dies sad about having to let Barlow go. His only solace is that he will be taken into the wilderness to be buried in a martyr's shrine, which will also absolve him of his prior ignorance and prejudices. Barlow holds him, comforts him, and sobs for him. He never lets Vig's hand go, even while his own life is at stake. Later, he grieves in tears over the loss, and he makes the final decisions over his companion's funeral arrangements: he is to be buried in the wilderness, wrapped mummylike in white muslin cloth, at the shrine just as he had wished. Out of respect for the intimacy between the two, Elgin and Gates do not argue against Barlow's wishes to do with the body just as Vig had asked. As the rebels take Vig's corpse to the border, a still concerned Barlow tells Elgin, "Make sure they take care of Conrad, all right?" Although it hurts Barlow deeply, the end of their relationship is necessary in preparation for a triumphant return home. For the audience, Vig's death is ameliorated by the knowledge that many more Iraqis died in relation to this single American loss. And this one loss is satisfactory for the war story and victory culture because it is far less than the 58,209 American lives lost in Vietnam.[37]

With their spiritual realignment and emergence from their respective abductions, the liberation of the civilian rebels and even more civilians found in captivity at Oasis Bunker, the rescue of Barlow, the proven evil of the Iraqi soldiers, the battle against and victory over the enemy, and the death of Vig, the men have realized that the gold is no longer important. Barlow, however, fears the prospects of going to jail for being AWOL. His concern is warranted because, up to this point, the soldiers' actions and adventures have yielded very little in terms of victory culture. In fact, if we accept the experiences of World War II as being close to the achievement of full victory culture and Vietnam as being on the opposite end of the spectrum, then the men have fared no better than the soldiers of MacPherson's Vietnam: the soldiers in *Three Kings* have so far broken the ceasefire, caused death and destruction, been wounded or killed, and stolen gold. Although they are on the path to victory culture, i.e., they have the necessary spiritual means, they have yet to commit the ultimate actions of victory culture: saving civilians and the world from tyranny. Gates is certain that the liberation of civilians and their safe passage into Iran will right all wrongs in the eyes of those back home and at base, giving their actions the moral standing of an American military campaign. The welfare of the innocent and weak must become their priority. And so the American rousting of the Iraqi soldiers brings forth the emotionally charged scenes not only of the civilians being freed from torture and saved from death but also of children reuniting with their families. The American soldiers give some of the gold to the civilian women and their families. They secretly offer some gold to those soldiers back at base who are willing to break the rules and drive a convoy of trucks to transport the civilians safely to the border. To symbolize his move away from narcissism and materialism, Gates is shown taking one of the designer bags that once held the gold and slamming it into a barrel of fire. Once the trucks arrive, Gates puts medical attention for his men and the civilians first, demonstrating concern for their welfare. He shrugs off immediate attention to his own gunshot wound, which the audience viewing his heroic strength and determination may have forgotten. Cruz, the journalist, also arrives with the convoy, along with her escort Wogaman, and is mostly interested in the story of the gold. The men have changed because they have been regenerated through their violent experiences out in the wilderness. But the woman continues to judge them and holds them to the feminine standards that reigned over American victory culture in the post-Vietnam era. While Gates outwardly denies the seizure of the gold, he humbles the female journalist when he offers her the right kind of war story for reportage: the liberation of desperate civilians and their subsequent deliverance to safety.

The civilians are loaded on the trucks for transport to safety. To highlight the difference between the American soldiers previously in the village outside of Karbala and those they have now become, the men show a new concern and politeness toward Iraqis. Gates stops one of the Iraqi army deserters who has fought the Republican Guard with them and now personally and politely invites him to come along with them to the border. When the man declines and says, "No. I will stay here and fight Saddam," Gates offers him his hand and his wishes of "Good luck." Barlow, too, shows this new concern and politeness. Following his subterranean ordeal and rescue, he hugs the leading rebel after ascertaining that the Iraqi man is indeed on their side. At first, however, he pointed a pistol at him because he assumed the man, being Arab, is the enemy. He now asks about the emotional and physical welfare of the man's daughter, cheerfully inquires, "How can we help you?", and insists that the new objective be the safe escort of civilians. When they begin the trucking of the civilians to the Iranian border, Barlow is no longer willing to throw the people from the moving vehicle as he did before in the village. Now, we can hear him telling a little girl, "Sit down, honey. We're going to pull out fast, okay?" Chief Elgin and Adriana Cruz also participate in this more polite treatment of the Iraqi civilians. Elgin, too, is concerned for the passengers' safety during the quick start of the trucks, and Cruz, who now understands and yields to the virtuousness of the heroes, helps load children onto the trucks. Further evidence of this new consideration for civilians comes when Barlow becomes concerned that Wogaman has not properly met everybody. He and Elgin begin introducing Wogaman to individuals.

But the contrast between where the men once were and where they now are becomes more evident at the Iraq/Iran border. As the men are about to safely deliver the people into Iran, American army helicopters arrive much like the American Cavalry. From the helicopter loudspeaker, the colonel boldly pronounces upon the people and the foreign terrain below that the men are under arrest for being AWOL and in violation of American policy. He orders them to move away from the refugees and to surrender. The army, refracted through Richard Slotkin's mythology of the American frontier, is part of the base left behind, the "Metropolis," or "old Europe." These army soldiers are unlike the heroes who have ventured into the wilderness, now regenerated through violence in the frontier, and risen to a new life for "new Americans."[38] The interruption of the arriving army sends the civilians into a frenzied dash toward the border. Once on the ground, the American army pulls the civilians from the rescuing hands of Gates and Elgin, handcuffs the heroes, causes the temporary arrest and physical abuse of the people at the hands of Iraqi border soldiers, refuses to listen to reason, taunts the heroes, and shouts over their pleas to help the refugees. These intruding soldiers almost let Barlow die because they will not free his hands so that he may open his air valve. Moreover, they interrupt Cruz's reportage, assault her camera, and tell her that she is out of the journalist pool for her participation in this event. The American army has brought into the wilderness chaotic actions, frenzied shouting, and now confused fighting that is common back at the base. The army brings with it its chickenshit mentality as the captain barks at the pleading and suffocating Barlow: "Hey, you fucked me. Now you're fucked! So shut your mouth!" Like the American army of Vietnam, this army has blundered in its attempt "to win the hearts and minds of the people" whom it is supposed to protect and liberate. This American army has, once again, thwarted victory culture.

At this point the American heroes become fully aligned with the war story and victory culture. With the civilians imprisoned and roughly handled less than a hundred feet from the Iraq/Iran border, the heroes facing court-martial, and Cruz removed from the journalist pool as a result of the colonel's anger, the men tacitly agree to announce their recovery of the gold. They ultimately give up their narcissistic prize and thereby renounce their selfish materialism in favor of the lives of the civilians. They agree to show one brick of gold to the colonel but refuse to tell the location of the rest of the gold unless the people are allowed over the border. After all, the people helped them recover the gold, the heroes in turn made a deal with the people to get them across, and keeping a promise is "a soldier's honor." When Gates pleads with the colonel, he appeals to the colonel's narcissism. Gates, now free of this selfish burden, entices the colonel with the opportunity to return the Kuwaiti gold, to save some refugees, and to ultimately earn that gold star for which he has been working and waiting. The colonel's acceptance of this type of reasoning, the kind that carries a reward of self-interest, finally makes the colonel tell the Iraqi border soldiers to allow civilians and rebels to cross over to Iran safely. The colonel, despite his compromise with Gates, shows his shortsightedness regarding the achievement of the war story and victory culture, and he ungratefully assures the men that they will still be court-martialed.

Nevertheless, the mythic structure of the heroes' adventures requires that the men return to magnanimously offer their society the lessons of their journey. Therefore, the audience is told via the ending subtitles that the men were honorably discharged. The court-martial must not have been upheld and rightfully could not have been, since they heroically provided the narrative with triumphalism. Their honorable discharges, the audience is also told, were due to Adriana Cruz, who finally got her chance to provide exemplary reporting with an original story. The GIs return to their civilian lives, which are now better than they were before they went to war. Their journey has provided them with revelations, and they accordingly deserve to be rewarded. Elgin triumphantly leaves his airline job to work for Gates, who is now, just as he hoped he would be one day, a military consultant in Hollywood, and is seen to be working with other men. In other words, Gates and Elgin teach others how to act out victory culture for their society. Barlow is shown happily living a heterosexual life with his wife and two children. He is also on the track of a successful entrepreneurial career in carpet retail. Unlike veterans of the Vietnam War, these Gulf War veterans do not endure drug addiction, unemployment, homelessness, guilt, debilitating physical handicap, broken marriages, offspring with birth defects resulting from chemical poisoning, or posttraumatic stress disorder. These happy endings act as proof of the successful achievements of the war story and victory culture. The heroes are better off and their worlds more meaningful than what was depicted in the celebrations of Gulf War victory at the beginning of the film, the narcissistic quest for gold, and the dead-end futures awaiting them at home. The fact that the colonel's postadventure life is not shown or celebrated exemplifies his lack of contribution to victory culture. We are not even told if he got his gold star. Elsewhere in the world, things are assumed to be better, as well, because of American victory culture. The closing title informs us that Iraq returned the gold to the Kuwaitis, obviously after being forced to do so by the Americans. After receiving the gold, the Kuwaitis are said to have announced that some of it is still missing. This last statement is highlighted with the sound of a tin bell that whimsically hints that the refugees made it to Iran with the rest of the gold that the Kuwaitis are missing. While they may be living and establishing prosperous lives financed by this gold, the audience cannot be certain because they are not afforded the same biographical footnotes as the Americans. The Iraqi civilians and rebels just disappeared into the landscape as easily as they appeared in the first place.

Jack Shaheen rates this film as one of the best depictions of Arabs in Hollywood film today. He bases his rating mainly on the film's distinction between good Arab rebels aligned with America and bad soldiers of Saddam that fight the American soldiers. He believes that this film depicts Arabs as "regular folks," and he is relieved to report that many offensive scenes, like an Iraqi woman exposing her breast and Iraqi soldiers eating dead animals, had not been included in the final script. He too easily brushes off the removal of the map from the Iraqi soldier's rectum as "a cheap laugh."[39] Although I understand his relief in seeing instances of what he claims is representational progress, I believe that my methodology and analysis show otherwise, and I find *Three Kings* to be a film that continues to denigrate the Arab character. Moreover, I question Shaheen's assertion that *Three Kings* is an antiwar film. Arabs are still totalized into an exploitable Otherness. They are appropriated as pawns in the narrative to jeopardize the American myth so that the Americans can defend and reassert the myth for themselves. Later, other Arabs are used as shields and excuses to avoid the audience's outright condemnation of the heroes' narcissism and materialism, which take the audience into a vicariously entertaining experience of a sometimes comic action-adventure. Furthermore, Arabs are employed to ameliorate an American audience's triumphalist despair, often reflected in the Vietnam War film genre. The Arabs in *Three Kings* are used to help the audience legitimate and feel better about regenerating its militaristic national self through the classic war story genre. If I may borrow a quote from President George H. W. Bush, "By God, we've kicked the Vietnam syndrome once and for all"[40] — on the back of the Arab caricature. Although *Three Kings* does show the shortcomings and immaturity of the American soldiers in their quest for the war story and the heroic journey, it gives them the chance to redeem themselves and thus bring about a successful rite of passage, a happy ending, and a vindication of the righteous American spirit. The American soldier is no longer the bad guy in the war story. The Arabs, sadly enough, are not as lucky.

*I*N the introductory scenes of *Rules of Engagement,* director William Friedkin, also the director of *The Exorcist,* presents his two heroes as honorable American military men.[1] Terry Childers (Samuel L. Jackson) and Hayes Hodges (Tommy Lee Jones) are tough career marines and devoted comrades. As we see in the initial scenes that act as flashbacks to the year 1968, these men once served their country in the quagmire of the Vietnam War. While there, they commanded American troops in a hostile environment and placed themselves in harm's way. They fired upon a difficult-to-see enemy and took fire in return. Under these difficult circumstances, these men were resolute in their command, mission, responsibilities, and, above all, their loyalty to their unit, the corps, and their nation. Hodges gets wounded, returns home, serves his country as a military lawyer, and then retires with the honors of his distinguished service. On the other hand, Childers rescues this wounded friend without demur, continues to serve his country in the battlefields of later American combats, and gets promoted through the ranks of military battle command. Despite their military experiences and the wisdom they have acquired throughout their careers, in the America of the narrative present they are shown to be uncertain about their identities as colonels. Twenty-eight years after their service together in Vietnam, the two warrior friends are reunited at Hodges's retirement celebration. In the narrative present, they walk together in an autumnal wood at Camp Lejeune, North Carolina. This wood of their later-aged years foreshadows a period of their lives that proves to be more dangerous than the green Vietnamese jungles of their youth. Vietnamese jungles were burgeoning, verdant, and thick with undergrowth that provided cover in which to hide. In this North American wood the vegetation has gone dormant, the ground is covered with dead and dry leaves, and the barren trees provide no hiding place for these men. Childers consoles his friend Hodges, who never came to terms with serving his country in a desk job. Childers points out to his friend, "You ain't missin' nothin', Hodge. It's a whole new ballgame—no friends, no enemies; no front, no rear; no victories, no defeats; no mama, no papa. We're orphans out there." Childers is describing a discontent with the "isms" of the Clintonian era, such as multiculturalism, postmodernism, deconstructionism, and relativism. The "evil" Arabs in *Rules of Engagement* are depicted as using this discontent, in a period which many perceive as one of cultural upheaval in America, as a vulnerability opening America to attack.

Childers's "a whole new ballgame" represents his nostalgic lament for the "old ballgame"—a time, we may assume, that hails from a pre-1968 period that the two men knew together in combat. From his description of the "new" we can deduce that the "old" was a period of certainty and clarity of conceptual boundaries rather than of questioning and blurred cultural vision. Childers's "old ballgame" refers to the type of world that today's American conservative movement wants to protect and reassert — a post–World War II America, built upon a selective historical memory of events and sweeping time periods, purged of many of the American experiences of the 1960s and 1970s. According to the conservative movement's narratives, America is a nation on a historical trajectory toward greatness and under divine guidance. The nation was founded more than two hundred years ago when European settlers came to a wilderness and virgin land to build a new civilization with a new political system that improved upon the broken one that was left behind in the Old World. The nation was founded upon clear principles set forth in texts that are considered to have taught, regulated, and protected men: the Bible, the Ten Commandments, the Declaration of Independence, the Constitution, and the Bill of Rights. Together these texts are seen as having designed an ethical system that outlines the values of the citizens' duty to a Judeo-Christian God, commitment to moral conduct, and devotion to life, liberty, and the pursuit of happiness. The texts were employed in the framework of a political system that stresses the ideals of fairness, equality, justice, limitations on government, and the rights of the individual in society. Therefore, these texts are referred to as the foundations of the ideologies of Western democracy and capitalism. In this context, conservative narrators state that these American founders, who preserved and/or wrote these texts, were great, courageous men with visionary power and perseverance, and today's Americans must be proud to call them "our Founding Fathers."

Into this nation, as we are told, the world's populations came, settling and civilizing the land. America became the "great melting pot" that took people with diverse experiences, nationalities, religions, and languages and united them into a devoted, English-speaking, democratic people. This "good" nation of the conservative myth courageously confronted evil when necessary. It challenged, since its foundation, the barbarism of the red savage, the tyranny of European colonialism, the horrors of slavery, the bloody threat of secession, the devastation of economic depressions, and the brutality of fascism. And in all the battles against evil, America ultimately won. Despite Nikita Khrushchev's bellicose threat "We will bury you," this America buried him and the menace of Soviet Communism. This nation, we are reminded, made some of the greatest discoveries in world history, invented tools that enhanced productivity and standards of living, produced some of the world's greatest literature and universities, and found cures for debilitating and deadly diseases. It unlocked and unleashed the power of the atom, set out on the awesome quest of going to the moon, and is now sending unmanned missions to Mars.

Indeed, according to the myth, America has had its problems, setbacks, and scandals along the way. But the myth explains away these events as momentary experiences that America has overcome. America is said to have learned and benefited from these events. The success of this mythic nation is used as proof of God's approval of the nation. While other great nations and civilizations have weakened or perished, America is seen as still standing strong. The myth asserts that America, compared to its contemporaries, is the freest, richest, and mightiest nation of all. America is the most advanced, enviable, and compassionate nation in the history of the world. Its devotion to peace, justice, and liberty is unsurpassed. Americans are the healthiest, happiest, proudest, and most patriotic people in the world. And as for those critics who want to question such narratives of America's exceptionalism, the myth's supporters often silence them with the rhetorical question "If America is not so great, why would people risk their lives daily at the border just to get in and become one of us?"

This mythic America is the "old ballgame," and the new one is its antithesis. The "new ballgame," in asserting another America, attacks the very principles upon which the "old ballgame" is based and turns long-established truths and traditions on their heads. Conservative writers characterize this alternative view of America as having originated in the liberal enclaves of the 1960s college campuses and in the context of the Vietnam War. No year was more decisive than 1968, *Rules of Engagement*'s chronological dividing line as well, when America was deeply involved in Southeast Asia. Nineteen sixty-eight became the watershed year that rocked American self-confidence and led the American culture to a new period of critical self-assessment. Until then, America's leaders assured its citizens of the righteousness of their cause in Vietnam: Asian nations could fall to the evil of Communism like dominoes if South Vietnam succumbed to such a fate. America, as the nation was told by its leaders, was defeating the enemy in Vietnam, and the cessation of fighting was imminent. However, in the early months of that year, the enemy attacked Khe Sanh, launched the Tet Offensive, and attacked the American embassy in Saigon. The Communist enemy overran American forces at Lang Vei and assaulted Hue, and large losses of life on both sides occurred. As these events were seen daily on television, the American people began to perceive that the war in Vietnam could not be won. And yet, 206,000 more troops were being requested to fight the war. In turn, President Lyndon B. Johnson and General William Westmoreland had lost credibility, and the antiwar movement had gained momentum. Larry H. Addington's history of the Vietnam War states that there was "growing public hostility to the war, or at least to the way the war was being waged."[2] Johnson abandoned his reelection plans when Democratic candidates gained strong support for their antiwar platforms and his unofficial presidential advisors, known as the Wise Men, repudiated his war policy after formerly supporting it.[3]

And as if the war were not enough, other events tore apart the social fabric of America at home. Martin Luther King was assassinated on April 4. The assassination sparked the worst riots in American history throughout the nation's cities and towns, resulting in civilian deaths and the deployment of some fifty-five thousand federal and state troops in the nation's streets to restore order. The racial divide in America widened. Two months later on June 5, Robert F. Kennedy was shot and killed while on the campaign trail for the presidency. While Richard M. Nixon and the Republican Party promoted an election platform with a secret plan to end the war, the Democratic Party fell into disarray. Its Chicago convention in August was threatened by an enormous rally of protesters. With further threats of the Yippies (Youth International Party) poisoning the Chicago water supply with LSD, Chicago's Mayor Richard J. Daley assembled a large police force to confront the protesters and to protect the city. Americans watched on television as their own police beat and arrested many of the five thousand protestors, as well as bystanders.

The years that followed may have been no better than 1968, marked as they were by similar disturbing events. On December 5, 1969, *Life* magazine shocked the American public with stories and images of My Lai showing American soldiers as perpetrators of atrocities rather than protectors. The war and the bombing continued despite Nixon's promised secret peace plan. As the new American president, Nixon had actually widened the war into Cambodia on April 29, 1970. The protests for peace grew and took hold on American college campuses. The National Guard's confrontation with protestors at Kent State on May 4, resulting in the death of four students and the wounding of more, became known as the "Kent State Massacre." In mid-1971, the Pentagon Papers revealed that American presidents, extending as far back as Harry Truman, had exaggerated American stakes in Indochina. Critics argued that the arrogance of those in power, and not national security, was at the root of the problem. The Papers showed that Vietnam policy was misguided foreign policy. Thousands of American lives were lost in the defense of doubtful theories about Communist expansion and American victory. A year later, on June 17, 1972, the president of the United States authorized the burglary of the Democratic National Committee headquarters at the Watergate Hotel. Americans later witnessed impeachment proceedings against Nixon over the issue, the pressure of which caused his ultimate resignation in August 1974.

This tumultuous period shook the faith of many Americans in their country's leaders and fundamental principles. Postmodernist and deconstructionist thought gained credence, and such theories took root in a culture that questioned the certainty of its institutionalized beliefs. A movement developed that reassessed the proclaimed righteousness of American politics, history, and society. The literary canon and the great narratives of tradition and accepted truth that informed Americans about Western civilization and the America of "the old ballgame" were weakened and even belittled as propaganda of white Western superiority.

The 1960s youth culture, as conservatives often describe it, was made up of many antiestablishment, radical, peacenik liberals who were susceptible to and welcoming of such destructive thought. Today, they are replacing their parents' generation (hailed by some as "The Greatest Generation") and are now inheriting America's leadership roles. They are assumed to harbor their 1960s radical ideals even today and to be attempting to put them into practice. Since the university had been their fertile ground, many remained to complete graduate studies and became academics. They now have infiltrated the upper echelons of America's universities, and have redesigned curriculums to advocate their views. Others are accused of making headway into our elementary schools and having a toehold in our corporations. And when William Jefferson Clinton — "the avid promoter of multiculturalism," in the words of Alvin J. Schmidt — was elected president of the United States in 1992, these liberals took the ultimate prize of the White House and have continued to infect the offices of the nation.[4] The "new ballgame" is *Rules of Engagement*'s reference to the era of multiculturalism and all its theoretical and ideological cousins: postmodernism, deconstructionism, and relativism.[5]

The "new ballgame" declares an end to theories of absolutism, claims of objectivity, and beliefs in ultimate truths that have in the past silenced and oppressed humanity. Instead, it promotes a plurality of interpretations for events. It declares a "new" America that promises to eradicate racism, celebrate diversity and tolerance, incorporate previously excluded voices, value all cultures and practices equally, and protect the rights of the underprivileged and minorities.

However, those in opposition to the "new" maintain that the "new" arrives with violence and destruction in mind. They fear this change of culture and often contextualize the arrival of the "new" in paranoid terms of revolution, dictatorship, extremism, and war. Those who protect the "old" complain that the "new" is, in actuality, the opposite of what it claims to be. The conservative professor David Thibodaux views the "new" as a movement of those who are alienated from and discontented with traditional values. He asserts that they self-righteously pick apart meaning, distort facts, even to the point of lying, and break down morality to a moral relativism in order to meet the goals of their personal political agendas. "If history does not serve the purposes of displaced, oppressed minorities," he states, "it is simply changed."[6] Lynne Cheney sees the "new" as a way of promoting the importance of race over the quality of individual character. The "new" is an ideology, she insists, that works against the principles for which Martin Luther King, Jr., and the civil rights movement fought. She further points out that it is a destruction of standards of truth and accepted reality, which breaks down the idea of accountability, responsibility, fairness, justice, and honor in our society.[7] Keith Windschuttle sees the "new" as a rejection of the scientific method of the Enlightenment that is based on observation and inductive argument. Truth and knowledge become relative, and reality is questionable. History becomes fiction, the past is inaccessible, and intellectual disciplines break down.[8] Richard Bernstein likens the "new" to a late-twentieth-century *dérapage,* the kind of sociopolitical backward skid that the French experienced under Robes-pierre: What was "aimed supposedly at a greater inclusiveness of all of the country's diverse component parts, . . . has somehow slipped from its moorings and turned into a new petrified opinion of the sort it was supposed to transcend."[9]

These critics depict the "new" as violent, oppressive, persecuting, and backward in its quest. They consider it a Trojan horse in America and call its adherents "warriors" who wish to conquer the nation. They allege that the "new" is a transmutation of Marxism, Stalinism, Nazism, Saddam-like despotism, terrorism, and McCarthyism that seeks to devalue Western civilization from within. They also believe the "new" does the following: it reacts in totalitarian mob fashion, looks to clone American intellect, persecutes the individual, and threatens civil liberties; it invents language and speaks in secret code; it threatens free speech and polices thought; it insists that America is inherently racist, and, as a result, the "new" lashes out and victimizes white Christian males through reverse discrimination and affirmative action; while it seeks to reward minorities (including feminists, homosexuals, blacks, indigenes, ethnics, the disabled, the insane, prisoners, drug addicts) with special assistance and privileges, in reality it lies to them, gives them false hopes, and ultimately debilitates them; it invents new histories, heroines, and heroes; it demonizes the "old's" narratives and texts and defames the Founding Fathers; it threatens unity, promotes balkanization, and de-values America; it seeks to destroy God and reason; it eradicates the belief in truth, and since truth is the foundation of justice, it annihilates justice in turn. The "new" is dangerous, inimical, and deadly. It must be confronted with force and destroyed because American existence and Western civilization as a whole may cease to exist if it wins. This, the conservative movement assures us, is a cultural war.[10]

Rules of Engagement is a film that deals with this struggle between the "old" and the "new." Most importantly, it deals with the struggle over the issues of objective truth, cultural relativism, racism, and justice. While this film induces Orientalist fear as a threat to the conservatives' remembered or imagined America, *Rules of Engagement* is also a sleight-of-hand example of producing such fear by actually supporting a different myth. This other myth is a conservative narrative designed to confront the "new," in particular, what John K. Wilson calls "the myth of political correctness (PC)." According to Wilson, conservatives invoke this myth as defense against multiculturalism, but it really is meant to be played offensively. The PC myth is used in *Rules of Engagement* to counteract those who support the "new," or those who are PC. Wilson maintains that the myth of PC is full of distorted anecdotes recycled over and over again, peppered with imagined and invented incidents that are designed to create excitement and false impressions. This myth continually repeats these anecdotes so that they appear to be the pattern rather than the exception. Wilson shows that the PC myth relies upon mixing fact and fable, truth and error, report and fantasy all on the same plane of credibility. Additionally, he claims that it relies upon sowing fears of the endangerment of Americans.

The PC myth depends not only on the villainy of a minority mob that is filled with deep-rooted anger, but also on the gullibility of the myth's audience, which unquestioningly condemns the mob with united outrage. The myth trumps up the power of those who wave the flag of political correctness and who, by the way, are always considered as unqualified for and undeserving of such power. The myth depicts a besieged citizenry that quickly falls in line with PC demands out of fear, and it pities the inevitable victim role of the white male, who is denied his rightful inheritance and stands alone in resistance. The myth has made multiculturalism into a frightening movement, making use of the loudest accusing yell of "Political correctness!" in order to place guilt upon others (those accused of PC) and to escape one's own responsibility (those who oppose PC). This myth denies that those who oppose PC have any responsibility for racism, because prejudices are things of the past, "as if no one believes [in] them anymore[,]" and debris "created by hypersensitive minorities who 'look for insult.' "[11] In fact, the myth completely dismisses racism. It ignores those who use racial epithets to abuse other people, and condemns derisively those "extremists" who may criticize others for their racism as creators of division. The myth of PC calls for a struggle for the American soul between politically correct liberals and non–politically correct conservatives, and so one cannot reason with the former but must defeat them totally. Moreover, the myth distracts its audience from discussing real questions about equality, freedom, intellectual excellence, and justice.

The narrative of *Rules of Engagement* is similar to the PC myth. While it overtly acts as if in defense of Childers and Hodges, their heroism, and their American loyalties, it is actually an attack on the society that supports multiculturalism and its ideological cousins (the "new ballgame"). This attack relies upon the most outrageous and extreme Orientalist stereotypes of Arabs and uses culturally accepted institutions of truth to prove that these stereotypes are objective realities. In fact, this film recycles some camera shot themes that Friedkin used in *The Exor-*

cist, twenty-seven years earlier. In its attempt to show that it is nonracist, the film cunningly overdetermines racial harmony in America. Furthermore, anyone choosing to accuse the film of being "racist" is deflected not only because the narrative shows that the Arabs themselves prove the fact that they are guilty, but also because one of the heroes—Childers—is African American. The narrative forces those in the audience who would cry "racism" to choose the sacrifice of one minority character over that of the other. The film's white hero—Hodges—tries to sort things out in an effort to help, but in the end he must step to the side. The narrative screeches out accusations of PC conspiracy, and, as a result, it creates the audience's paranoia. The narrative's loudly accusing cry of the PC myth encourages the audience, ultimately, to embrace the indiscriminate gunning down of the Arabs as the lesser of two evils and to dismiss the narrative's culpability for designing such a fate for the Arabs in the first place. The film provides visual evidence that implicates Arab guilt and shows the efforts of the politically correct characters to thwart what has been shown as truth. And since the culturally accepted values of truth, freedom, equality, right, good, and justice are designed to prevail at the end of the film, then it is blasphemous to question such evidence and scenes as lies, oppression, inequalities, wrongs, destruction, and injustices dealt out to Arab people or to suggest that the scenes reinforce the images that Arabs are typically assigned. Any inquiry, including this film analysis, is in due course dismissed as just the irrationality of politically correct individuals.

In the first chapter of this book, we saw that paying attention to Friedkin's Iraq prologue is important to understanding *The Exorcist.* In that film, Friedkin invokes characteristics of evil that are later used to enhance the evil of the demon in Regan's bedroom. This knowledge linked the demon to the nefarious Arab. In *Rules of Engagement,* too, the beginning scenes of the film are essential to understanding the later events. Friedkin uses these initial scenes as touchstones of knowledge that help make sense of those scenes deeper into the narrative. The scenes of the "old ballgame," the good old times, help us assess and judge the "new ballgame." Therefore, it is important first to contemplate the implications set forth in the initial scenes.

The 1968 flashbacks to the Battle of Ca Lu provide the audience with the didactic view that when American soldiers have a job to do, as they did in Vietnam, they execute their tasks as required. American interests must, and can, be protected objectively without all the political bickering of race bias or preference. This contradicts the theories of critics, such as Myra MacPherson, who claim that racism, from the draft programs to the training camps and into Southeast Asia, was a part of American immorality in the Vietnam War.[12] In Ca Lu, Hodges and Childers lead a platoon of men on a search-and-destroy mission. The platoon's composition shows no signs of racial bias. Black, white, and Asian men fight together as Americans, equally armed, facing the same danger, and ready to do the same job. In fact, there are more white men than blacks and Asians in the platoon. Childers offers a plan for attack on the enemy position at Ca Lu, but Hodges overrules it. The overruling of the plan is not based on who makes it but on the merit of what seems to be a better idea, and Childers readily agrees. They decide that while one of them will lead half the platoon over the hill, the other one will lead the remaining half through the swamp. The decision about who takes which route does not require the use of affirmative action's bureaucratic debates and decisions, since either choice is equally dangerous. Therefore, it is determined as quickly and objectively as possible and as the situation of battle requires: by a flip of the coin. The flip sends Childers over the hill and Hodges into the swamp, and neither balks at the determination of who goes where.

In this "old ballgame," the power of gaze is a most important asset. In this world there is an objective reality, a distinct and single narrative of what occurs. To establish one's gaze over this reality and those in it gives the gazer a decisive advantage of knowledge and power: the chance to kill first and the rights over the narrative. The lesson of gaze is played out in the Battle of Ca Lu. Childers happens to see the enemy before the enemy can see him. On the other hand, Hodges does not see the enemy, but the enemy sees him. The result is two separate and bloody firefights. In the jungle, Childers is able to kill North Vietnamese soldiers, force them to their hands and knees, and capture their commander, apparently without any American casualties. In the swamp, Hodges and his men, whose steps symbolize America's slow, blind step into the quagmire of the Vietnam War, cannot lay eyes on the enemy. They become confused and fall victims to a sneak attack, the most heinous type of attack on Americans, according to Tom Engelhardt.[13] They are surrounded and pinned down from enemy fire. In this last-stand battle, all men in this group are killed except Hodges.

Childers can hear the gunfire in the distance. While, at this point, he cannot see what is going on and is thereby rendered powerless to help Hodges, he must reestablish a sense of gaze in order to stop what is happening to Hodges and the American troops. Childers does so by ordering the enemy commander *several* times to use his radio and call his forces off Hodges's position. With time running out, Childers must resort to naked violence in order to regain control. In the style of General Nguyen Ngoc Loan's famous execution of an NLF (National Liberation Front of South Vietnam) prisoner in 1968, Childers threatens to shoot the Vietnamese radio operator in the head if the commander does not cooperate. The commander silently refuses, and, now regarding himself as forced to act, Childers executes the radio operator. However, this execution comes with an offer directed at the commander and the interpreter. Childers yells out, "Call your men off Hodges now! [to the interpreter] If he does, he can go. He's got my word on that. [to the commander, and now pointing the gun to his head] If you don't, I'll kill you where you stand." The tactic works. The enemies attacking Hodges's position are called off, and they retreat into the wilderness. Hodges sets off a flare, he is saved, and Childers honorably keeps his word and lets the commander go.

The incident in Vietnam is not over: in order to silence those who would condemn Childers's execution of the man as racially motivated, cold-blooded murder, the camera forces the audience to survey the barbaric deeds afflicted on the American, although not the Vietnamese, soldiers. Throughout the swamp, American soldiers lie bedraggled, bloodied, and dead. To heighten their horrific deaths in the Third World and to make the audience's skin crawl, the sound track is laced with the high-pitched, buzzing sound of mosquitoes surrounding their corpses and probably feeding off their blood. It was clearly a bloodbath and a depressing loss of American life. The Vietnamese were undoubtedly enemies because only enemies could conduct such a sneak attack, and therefore they are not worthy of visual contemplation. Only Hodges is lucky enough to survive, albeit severely wounded. The witnessed terror of the battle, the loss of men, and the horror of dying in this miserable place relegate to the background any alternative narrative like the condemnation of racism in this American war. The Vietnamese radio operator was executed because Americans were dying, not because he was of another race. The original 1968 photograph of General Loan's execution of his prisoner, to which the aforementioned scene intertextually alludes, shocked Americans and became a symbol of barbaric violence, excessive loss of life, and questionable objectives in the Vietnam conflict. However, in this film, with so many Americans killed in action, executing one Vietnamese cannot be deemed excessive, and in a peculiar way the infamous killing of 1968 is seemingly exonerated as well. Moreover, the commander was given the choice, even though it was a choice of no choice, and *he* ultimately chose to sacrifice the man's life. His action of inaction thereby relieves Childers of responsibility.

When racism does raise its ugly head more overtly, as it does when Childers calls the Vietnamese soldiers "slopes," it is unique and excusable in light of the tension of battle and the 1960s historical context. The attitude evident in the utterance cannot be discerned in Childers's following actions. "Slopes" is used, but it is said only once. Childers replaces it with the more generic, non-race-specific appellations "motherfuckers" and "son of a bitch." Although the names are gender-specific, they become acceptable, even polite, terms in masculine combat to designate any enemy "Other," particularly those enemies who are seen to attack Americans (recall Vig's struggle with racist remarks in *Three Kings*). Furthermore, the 1960s was a period of heightened awareness of racism. The racist slur was a way of talk in America prior to a civil-rights-conscious culture. The use of these flashbacks of violence so early in the film poises the audience for rhetorical self-examination to be carried into the film's following scenes. The film encourages viewers to ask themselves, could not anyone of us see him/herself losing momentary control of speech and action in such a situation? And would not he or she sacrifice the enemy to save Americans? As Childers states in a later dilemma in the film, "You think that there is a script for fighting a war without pissing somebody off? Follow the rules, and nobody gets hurt? Yes, innocent people probably died. Innocent people always die." To succor the audience's agreement with Childers's action, the Vietnamese commander himself admits later in the film that he would have done the very same thing if he had been in Childers's place. In one of the last scenes, he even salutes Childers as a fellow warrior.

The flashbacks of the "old ballgame" give way to present-day America and Hodges's retirement party. Here again, there are scenes where there is no problem whatsoever with racism. The marines gather in a bar to pay tribute to this popular colonel and his thirty-two years of service to his country. The camera shows the audience that today's armed forces are more diverse than ever. These uniformed soldiers include women and men of all ages and races. This large group laughs, drinks, and huddles together in the happy harmony of honoring one of their own warriors. Race relations in the 1990s seem to be better than they ever have been. Childers, who has traveled halfway around the world to attend the event, is reunited with his friend, and Hodges accepts him with a big smile and

Rules of Engagement (2000). Hayes Hodges (Tommy Lee Jones) served his country in the jungles of the Vietnam quagmire. *Rules of Engagement* shows that the power of gaze over the enemy was important in 1968, and seeing the enemy first could mean the difference between life and death. Hodges and his men do not see the enemy and fall victim to the enemy's gunfire. Although Hodges is seriously wounded, he is the sole survivor of his team. Photo courtesy of the Academy of Motion Picture Arts and Sciences.

open arms. Friendship and their sense of duty override their race differences. This scene shows that old prejudices between races no longer exist.

Furthermore, Childers presents Hodges with a gift and offers some remarks that are very important for the narrative. Childers's presentation and speech point out that there are some redoubtable truths on which American culture is based. Hodges's service medals and a scimitar have been framed for wall display and to memorialize his career and service to his nation. The scimitar is symbolic, as Childers explains, of the early

Rules of Engagement (2000). Colonel Childers (Samuel L. Jackson) is sent on a mission to Yemen when the American embassy there is threatened by protesting Yemenis. The mission is expected to be a "babysitting," since the enemy is easily seen and assessed with the latest high-tech American tools of representation and gaze. However, in their villainy, the Arabs have eluded the American gaze and prove to be more dangerous than expected. Photo courtesy of the Academy of Motion Picture Arts and Sciences.

American victory over the Barbary pirates on the shores of Tripoli in 1805. The Pasha gave Marine Lieutenant Presley N. O'Bannon the Mamluk sword as a symbol of gratitude to the American nation. Marine officers have carried one ever since as a further symbol of the warrior. The story is important here because it echoes the point made earlier that when American soldiers are sent into action to protect American interests, they do what they must to do it right. The story is an account of a moral early American military campaign and subsequent victory outside of America's borders. Even non-Americans, exemplified here by the Pasha, are seen to acknowledge and validate the deeds of American marines and the righteousness of the American cause. There is no change in this historical principle. Moreover, Childers makes the statement "You know the story," as if the American narrative of the battle is a commonly accepted metanarrative, key knowledge of identity, and, as such, of unquestionable veracity.[14] The reception of the sword and the story is a stalwart ritual that testifies to the meaningfulness of Hodges's thirty-two years of distinguished service and a progression of history in which the present is shaped by and is an improvement of the past. This event places Hodges into the pantheon of American warriors, even though Hodges has never come to terms with his administrative post.

The principles set forth in this "old ballgame" should continue to hold as true. Although Childers has stated that the "new ballgame" is no longer the same, just how different the "new ballgame" is comes to be tested and revealed in a notorious setting of American myth destabilization: the Middle East. Childers is later shown on board the *USS Wake Island* being briefed on his new orders to go to Yemen, where there are some demonstrations around the American embassy.[15] The Yemeni government has pulled out its own security forces out of fear, thus shirking its responsibility, even though, we are told, there is no hostility in the crowd. While the Yemenis and their forces are now noted for being craven and irresponsible, the American forces are depicted as intrepid because they must go in and do the job for the Yemenis. The marine presence in the Arab country will be "babysitting," as the ship's commander patronizingly calls it.

The American gaze over the Arab land is depicted as so powerful that the Americans can virtually see the Arab city before they even get there. The American ship's technology flashes computerized maps of the country and the embassy area on screens so that plans can be better assessed and made. Colored squares and lines mark off areas of concern, planned approaches, and positions to oversee the demonstrators. Yellow dots mark off the Yemeni demonstrators into numbers and density of concentration, in the process dehumanizing them. The American technological advances in the ability to gaze show the unquestioned might and sophistication of the United States over other nations. This gaze symbolizes the control and supremacy Americans believe they have acquired over knowledge and objectivity in the present period. So far, the "new ballgame" looks to be a historical improvement over the "old ballgame." Unlike in Ca Lu, where antiquated observation technology brought about inconsistent plans of attack and heavy American losses, this technologically advanced gaze makes military action look like a simple task with a clear-cut plan. Childers is able to quickly assess the situation and prepare a narrative on how to go into the Yemeni land and how to accomplish the mission. He plans to take one platoon and a Tactical Recovery of Aircraft and Personnel (TRAP) team in there quietly, "babysit," and, if the situation gets "hot," evacuate the ambassador and his family. Unlike Hodges at Ca Lu, the captain agrees "exactly" with Childers's plan. Within seconds, the American forces fly off with orchestrated fanfare to do their duty. The camera shots of the American helicopters flying over the Yemeni land present the flyover as easily navigated, gracefully executed, and symbolically conquering. The Americans not only are on the way to save the day, but seem to have control over the ensuing narrative.

But the situation on the ground is not as it seemed when looking at the computer screen onboard the ship. In fact, the Yemenis, complying with narratives of Orientalist fear, defy the American gaze. Since the Yemenis are more hostile than originally diagnosed, Childers revises the situation from being a "babysitting" job to being an "ugly" mission. The initial aerial view of San'a shows little life in the city. The city seems to be at a standstill. Karim H. Karim discusses the use of visual signifiers of Muslim threat in the mass media. We can extend his discussion to include aural signifiers of Arab threat in Friedkin's films.[16] Friedkin's introduction to the Middle East in *The Exorcist* evokes, with the voice of the muezzin, a sense of alienation and unease in the American Orientalist audience. In *Rules of Engagement,* Friedkin introduces the Middle East with another common aural trope of representing the landscape. This trope became popular during the Iranian Revolution and still remains popular for producing fear in Americans about the Middle East. The peacefully quiet Yemeni landscape gives way to the sounds of an angry mob chanting anti-American slogans, and the sound is then accompanied with Yemenis holding protest banners in Arabic script. This chanting and the images of the protest seem to be the only human noise and activity in the Arab city, implying that the city's inhabitants have no other voice or role. From the American helicopters and the windows of the embassy, American soldiers observe more people continually joining the crowd, and the mob constantly grows. Yemenis in *Rules of Engagement* are shown as a belligerent and hostile people, who resort to mob violence without any apparent reason. All Yemenis are shown to be aggressive, as men, women, and children participate in this demonstration of hate. Dark faces, some toothless, others veiled, and still others far too young by American standards for such hatred, are distorted in anger. This angry, amorphous mob chants in Arabic, "America! America! Withdraw from Yemen!" Clenched fists are raised and waved in accord with the chant's cadence. The film shows even a Yemeni policeman, one of their own ilk, feeling uneasy about this Arab fury.

Since the Middle East is supposed to be a place where little makes sense, no explanation about Yemeni grievances is provided for the audience. Yemenis exhibit this behavior without reason or provocation, as if such behavior, and the hatred that inspires it, are innate traits of Arabs. Their taking exception to the American presence in Yemen, from the possibly complicated commercial, political, and anti-imperialist reasons suggested by Ziauddin Sardar and Merryl Wyn Davies for why non-Americans object to the American presence in their lands, is downplayed.[17] Indeed, the narrative omits any reason. The film only offers the scene of the frightened ambassador's wife (Anne Archer) explaining the Yemeni behavior to her confused and scared child. Her explanation also acts as a clarification for the similarly bewildered audience, "The people are upset about some things, darling. . . . No they're not mad at your daddy. . . . They want attention. They're trying to get attention so that people will listen to them." The explanation for Yemeni anger is oversimplified. Contextualized in such a way, this explanation dismisses intellectual inquiry and discussion about American neocolonialism as unnecessary and childish, and Third World frustration and protest as bad behavior on the part of the Yemenis.

The Yemeni convergence on this American embassy relies on the American audience's ability to intertextually relate its cultural memory and fear of legendary Indian attacks on American outposts and the real-life siege of the American embassy in Tehran of 1979. Similarly, Childers's helicopter arrival relies on the audience's cultural memory and relief at the legendary arrival of the U.S. Cavalry to save the outpost and a this-time successful, although not as it happened in real-life, Operation Eagle Claw.[18] This American embassy is in disarray. Embassy personnel frenetically dash around with boxes containing important American information that must be saved or destroyed. Ambassador Mourain (Ben Kingsley) himself is depicted as a cowardly diplomat who stands as outpost deputy for President Bill Clinton, Vice President Al Gore, and their smiling portraits on the wall. Although he does not exhibit any overt multiculturalist tendencies, he exemplifies the type of citizen who easily buckles under pressure and cowers down in the face of mob tyranny. He is quick to cede ground to those who question America's rightful presence in the world. Unnerved by the growing Yemeni mob and its angry shouts, Mourain hurriedly crams papers into his briefcase and insists upon, even yells for, an immediate evacuation of himself and his family. He is eager to retreat and disown his confidence in the American civilizing effort and American righteousness. There is no attempt on his part to give an objective assessment of the situation to state security analysts; nor does he wish to lead a courageous stand against this mob. The ambassador is scared. He just wants out of there, and that is all the assessment he finds necessary or is willing to make.

However, before Childers and his men arrive on the scene, the mob's mood moves to frenzied aggression, which forces the American diplomat into hiding. The Yemenis, seemingly without reason, scurry for stones and throw them at the embassy. Women ululate excitedly. The hostility escalates to gunfire from snipers on a rooftop across from the embassy. Since the film's camera lens looks down at the Yemeni mob or across to the opposing rooftops, the illusion develops that the stones and gunfire are being aimed directly at the film's audience. These camera shots delineate positions of viewing experience for an American audience as oppositions of a defensive "us Americans" versus an offensive "them Yemenis." Soon Molotov cocktails are thrown at the building. And to show that Yemeni aggression is wild rather than controlled and directed, the mob is seen attacking parked vehicles surrounding the building as if only to exact maximum destruction. When a surveillance camera is shot, a tool of American gaze has been attacked. At the same time, this action is an attempt to erase historical evidence and to silence truth. As the American helicopters that bring in Childers and his men approach the city, the Yemeni gunmen begin to fire upon them as well. In essence, then, the Yemenis are portrayed as aggressors, firing the first shots without provocation. The gunmen are accompanied by black-shrouded women who hold frightened babies in one arm, proving themselves irresponsible mothers because they put their children in grave danger, and with the other arm wave their fist in anger. The mob then uses a battering ram to breach the security of the embassy fortress, knocking it against the fortress gate.

Childers and his men seem to arrive just in time. The American audience's toleration is taxed further when the shooting from the snipers becomes more intense. As the marines move in and take their positions on the rooftop, the snipers pin them down, as very little cover is provided by the low walls surrounding the rooftops. After much firing with no hits

Rules of Engagement (2000). The expected babysitting operation in Yemen turns "hot" for the Americans when the protesting crowd of Arabs grows in volume and turns to violence. The Arabs chant for American withdrawal from Yemen, begin to shoot and kill marines, and try to breach the embassy walls. The craven American ambassador demands that he and his family be evacuated immediately. As seen above, U.S. Marine Colonel Terry Childers (Samuel L. Jackson) and his men provide protection and a hurried escort for the ambassadorial family to the awaiting helicopter. Photo courtesy of the Academy of Motion Picture Arts and Sciences.

(as shown in prior films, Arabs are poor shots), the Yemenis finally shoot three marines, killing one of them. In comparison, the marines maintain their discipline and self-control by holding their fire. Childers finds the craven ambassador hiding under his desk, from where he complains about the marines' sluggish response to his request for help. Childers helps the wife and child of the ambassador to the awaiting helicopter amidst whizzing bullets, reassuring the panicked child that he is safe. The ambassador, himself, runs to the awaiting helicopter without staying close to his family, and he even tries to board the helicopter before his wife and child. When Childers realizes that the ambassador has not completed his official duty of taking the American flag with him, Childers risks his own life to perform this duty. He reenters the dangerous area, crawls to the flagpole, and begins to lower the flag. The Yemeni snipers, with their total disrespect for America, shoot at the flag even when the lowering of the flag signals to them that they have won the battle. The bullets penetrate and rip at the flag. It would seem that since the Americans are withdrawing in compliance with the desire of the Yemeni mob, there would be no need to continue the shooting. Nevertheless, the continued fire shows a certain immaturity in the Yemenis, who actually look for all-out destruction rather than the achievement of a military objective. Despite the danger, Childers delivers the flag, hurriedly folded triangularly, to the ambassador with the style, collectedness, and confidence of an "old ballgamer." In response, the ambassador, the deputy of the "new ballgame," now expresses gratitude, "Thank you, Colonel. I'll never forget this."

Upon Childers's return to the rooftop of the embassy, the gunfire intensifies and the crowd acts more frenzied. The situation on the rooftop turns into a struggle for the American marines. Childers pants and grunts as he crawls on his elbows and stomach past two white marines covered in blood and under medic care and one black marine who is dead. He passes two more dead marines along his way, and another dead and bloodied marine actually falls on top of him from above. And then a bullet hits Childers himself. Childers observes that hostile fire is coming from within the crowd on the ground, although the audience cannot see this at this time in the film, and he orders his marines to engage hostile fire in the crowd. While his orders are questioned by Captain Lee (Blair Underwood), he insists, "Waste the motherfuckers!"

The use of "motherfuckers" to describe the non-American enemy must be justified and proved to be a nonracist appellation. Just as in Vietnam, it is uttered by a man in combat who has been pushed beyond his limits of tolerance and leniency. The narrative acknowledges that in the 1960s racism was a problem, and so the term "slopes" was used. But now, over thirty years later, according to the myth of political correctness, racism no longer exists. The Arabs are being condemned for evil behavior, not for being another race or ethnicity. The film builds tension with the continuous chanting, stone throwing, fiery explosions, shooting, and killing, and all of this has moved the audience to impatience equaling that

Rules of Engagement (2000). Colonel Childers (Samuel L. Jackson) is pinned down by Arab gunfire and sees American marines being killed. Looking down into the Arab mob, he gives the order to his men to "waste the motherfuckers!" Courtesy of the British Film Institute.

of these brutal Yemenis. Therefore, when the Americans open fire on the "motherfuckers" below and the American bullets rip open the bodies of the rioting people, it would not be unexpected for a release of tension to result for the American audience. In a hail of American fire, Yemeni men, women, and children seem to get just what they earned, or actually what they have been so calculatedly set up to deserve. As they are decisively mowed down with American weaponry, they also intertextually pay for those who have attacked Americans similarly before them in the Wild West, Vietnam, and the American embassy in Iran. The event intimates a historical progress, producing a favored protectorate for the "old," where mistakes of the past have become learning experiences and are improved upon—here with ultimate retaliation when Americans will take no more. However, Childers, as a seasoned American warrior, knows the limits of decency, and he calls a ceasefire soon enough. While the camera sweeps over the carnage below, the audience can see and hear flies feasting off the dead and bloodied Third Worlders, not Americans this time. Bodies are strewn about, and Yemeni women wail in despair. Childers gazes down upon the carnage and confidently announces, "Mission complete."

Under the "old ballgame," Childers's announcement is correct and objective. The "babysitting" turned "hot," the ambassadorial family was evacuated, the American flag was removed, the marines secured the building with tolerance and honor, and they were now ready to leave. By these accounts, the mission has been completed, albeit with collateral damage left behind. But, as the multiculturalists would question: Is the fate of the

Yemenis fair? Is it deserved? Did Childers, a man who knows and can cite the rules of engagement by heart, follow those rules to help save the innocent? Despite the momentary pleasure of witnessing a strike at the Yemenis, an American audience of the multicultural 1990s experiences a sense of uneasiness about what has just occurred. This is shown in the face of Captain Lee, whose disapproving look at Childers reminds the audience that a "new ballgame" exists. And soon the audience is whisked away to the Washington, D.C., traffic (much like in *The Exorcist*) and back into the world of Western civilization, or actually to the present world of the "new ballgame."

In the Washington office of Mr. Bill Sokal (Bruce Greenwood), the film's fictional national security advisor to President Clinton, Sokal flips through the headlines of the major American and world newspapers. The newspapers picture and headline the eighty-three dead and over one hundred critically wounded Yemeni men, women, and children. The headlines ask questions about responsibility and condemn Childers forthrightly, particularly in the foreign press. To Sokal, who applies the rules of the "new ballgame," the truth of what actually occurred in Yemen is not of concern. In compliance with multiculturalism and its theoretical and ideological cousins, the issue of truth is not essential because truth is considered unknowable. Truth is subjugated to tolerance, to ways of seeing, and to the politics of how Others view and think about American actions. What may have been true, the facts of bullet trajectories from the snipers and intelligence reports of possible terrorist plots, is of no concern to Sokal. He argues with Marine General Perry (Dale Dye), who has been called into his office to account for Childers. Perry, who is used to working under the "old ballgame" rules, says that Childers's action was the only possible response to the loss of American lives. On the other hand, Sokal, who upholds the rules of the "new ballgame," relativizes the American deaths against the eighty-three Third World men, women, and children killed. Sokal rants at his own aide and at Perry about the possible reactions of Arab nations in retaliation for this American action. At one point he cries out, "Didn't he [Childers] know where he was? The Middle East!" The Middle East is subsequently marked as a "through-the-looking-glass" place where America cannot do what is necessary or right, but rather must be exceedingly cautious in its every action. It is a place where America must be overly tolerant of anti-American sentiment, where Arab and Muslim states are highly critical of any such American action, and where America must be submissive to the political whims of Arab and Islamic rulers.

Sokal is among those Americans who quickly believe in American culpability whenever something goes wrong. As a Clintonian, he is a 1960s generation intellectual who has now made his way into the echelons of power and who clings to multiculturalist concerns. He seems to be afflicted with what Alvin J. Schmidt diagnoses as the malady of multiculturalists: "white man's guilt."[19] As a man who probably has never been in combat, since those of his ilk protested the Vietnam War, Sokal easily looks for a number of more peaceful actions that Childers could have taken, rather than accepting that combat demands clear-cut actions to which there are limited alternatives. However, as one of the typical multiculturalists of the PC myth, he contradicts himself as a matter of course without seeing his fall into *dérapage*. While he looks for American responsibility, he does not want his administration to take the blame. While he insists that there can be no cover-up, he does not want to consider that others above Childers gave him the mission and the authority. While he demands proof, he ignores the crucial evidence of a videotape from the embassy's surveillance camera that will eventually show that the Yemeni men, women, and even children did indeed have weapons and shot first. He is willing to ignore historical fact and to wield his political power to remove proof in order to obtain his desired outcome. In his attempt to do what is right, he does what is wrong. In consideration of the greater in number, he sacrifices the rights of the individual. Therefore, Sokal sets out to see that Childers is court-martialed for the murder of eighty-three people. He sets forth the accusation that Childers ignored the U.S. armed forces' rules of engagement. Childers could even get the death penalty. Meanwhile, Sokal hides, then destroys, the videotaped evidence that proves Childers acted in accordance with the rules of engagement in Yemen. In so doing, he destroys the American gaze and its inherent benefits.

The lines are drawn further between the "old ballgame" and the "new ballgame" as Childers and Sokal obtain their lawyers for the trial to take place in a quick eight days. Childers refuses the Clintonian counsel of "Bob Bennett or one of those guys" up in Washington and asks Hodges to represent him. Childers wants an "old ballgamer," not one of those disdained "Starbucks drinkers who's never seen combat." Hodges is reluctant at first because he knows that this Clintonian government is going to come after Childers with everything it has and because he feels him-self unable to meet the demands of stellar lawyering. Nevertheless, he realizes that what is at stake is more than just a favor owed to Childers for saving his life in 1968. He sees that the "new" has gone too far. His university-attending son, who earlier is described as "Smart Hodges," the one who studies too much, and who is part of the "new ballgame," derides Hodges for accepting a case in which he has to defend a man accused of killing "innocent women and children." In the tradition of multicultur-alists, Smart Hodges reiterates the "new ballgame's" basic beliefs and is quick to accept the innocence of Third Worlders and the culpability of Americans. Hodges scolds him and reminds him that the American legal system's presumption of innocence until proof of guilt is at stake here—a point that his son further belittles with a joke about the idealism of Abra-ham Lincoln. Hodges's father, retired General H. Lawrence Hodges, also warns Hodges not to take the case because he believes that Childers has disgraced the corps. But Hodges reminds him that if this government can rewrite the history of one man's distinguished service to his country, then it can deconstruct the history of every man. This government, employ-ing such revisionist practices, can change his father's distinguished career into a service of dishonor. Actually, this government's new history could jeopardize the Hodges family's white, upper-class lifestyle built on ca-nonical standards of achievement, success, and progress. Childers himself will remind the audience that the institutional history of American mili-tary action is at stake. The prosecution calls him "the warrior's warrior," and now the character of all of America's warriors is in question. "If I'm guilty of this," Childers points out after looking at a photograph of the statue at the American Vietnam Memorial, "I'm guilty of everything I've done in combat for the last thirty years."

Sokal has chosen Major Mark Biggs (Guy Pearce) to prosecute Childers. In a staff meeting of racially diverse generals and the secretary of defense, Sokal introduces Biggs to this group, which is ready to crucify Childers. His introduction designates Biggs as a "new ballgamer," one who is a dis-ciple of academia, a Stanford Law graduate, and one who is just repaying his tuition to the military before he will take on the world as a career law-yer. In comparison to Hodges, he is young, strikingly handsome, sharp, confident, and even cocky. He is admirable and yet hardly likable. He is the type of soldier that Hodges refers to as a "beachboy," who may have never spent time in combat. He may be one of those who "might've spent one day in Grenada, maybe two days in Kuwait," according to Hodges.

Yet he has the power to prosecute Childers and quite possibly to affect Childers's and America's fate. He cannot be expected to honor the value system of a warrior like Childers. He does not even respect Childers's conduct at Ca Lu, which he will later use to insensitively chide Hodges and condemn Childers. He is not the kind who can understand the Childers-type soldier who volunteered to go to Vietnam or what service in Vietnam was like. He is unable to accurately describe the life expectancy of a man dropped into combat in Vietnam in 1968, although he convincingly feigns an answer.

Sokal seems secretly pleased to hear the duplicitous talk of Biggs. Outwardly, Biggs states that he is not interested in being "a hired gun" pursuing a vendetta against Childers. He has taken the job because of the case's merits and will only try Childers on good evidence. However, we see that in private he and his young staff are the "new McCarthyites" who concoct new versions of events that sound plausible, but are downright false. They are willing to dig up every incriminating piece of evidence on Childers and Hodges within their power to muster but overlook possible evidence that holds the truth, like the videotape in Sokal's possession. While Hodges must plan his defense with the few resources available at the base, these "beachboys" strategize from the well-equipped boardrooms of the government. These prosecutors are even willing to deny the truth and alter historical fact to get the desired outcome — Childers's conviction. Biggs, like the new multiculturalist theorists whom Keith Windschuttle derides, will alter history by steering away from Childers's patriotic service as context.[20] Biggs has constructed a "new" narrative that stretches and ultimately ignores truth: Childers went out to Yemen with the intent to kill; he was sent to Yemen, where there was no violence prior to his arrival at the embassy; Ambassador Mourain did not feel that the situation warranted evacuation, but Childers ignored him; sniper fire came from across the street; and Childers shot "the wrong people." Almost all of this "new" narrative, the audience knows from prior viewing, is a lie. And while this story is knowingly concocted, slides of wounded Yemeni children are featured in the background to show their innocence and victimization by American violence. Multiculturalists, who often deride others for colonizing the bodies of the "Other," are themselves shown as guilty of assaulting the Yemenis with a misuse of their images to promote their own agenda.

The pressure of this multiculturalist assault, in which the just cause of American action is questioned and derided, takes its toll on the two "old ballgamers." Childers becomes agitated with Hodges's young assistant, who views the case as a losing cause. A crowd of mainly young and angry civilians attacks Childers's truck and calls him "guilty," "disgusting," and a "butcher." Like a stereotypical Vietnam protester, a youth calls him a "fucking baby killer" and spits on Childers's marine uniform. Childers physically batters him for his assault on this American symbol of service, honor, and patriotism. Hodges also loses his cool with Biggs when Biggs pressures him to take a plea bargain. Hodges pleads with General Perry for an extension of the court-martial hearing so that he may gather missing evidence, which the audience knows from an earlier scene may be locked away in Sokal's desk. Perry, an "old ballgamer" who has now obviously buckled to the power of the "new," flatly and cowardly denies Hodges's request, and Hodges is inclined to take the plea bargain offer. Before heading on a whirlwind fact-finding mission to Yemen, Hodges finds Childers with an almost emptied bottle of scotch, a scribbled out suicide note, and a revolver on the table. Childers is looking at a picture of his parents and is in tears. The "new ballgame" is hard-heartedly sacrificing the best of the "old ballgamers," and the "old ballgamers" are losing spirit.

Hodges's fact-finding mission to the Middle East distresses him rather than empowering him with information that would clear Childers. This portion of the film depicts an Arab culture that is not only continually undeserving of the type of adulations multiculturalism promotes, but also demonstrating its true desire to overpower the West without, were the balance of power reversed, extending the same type of tolerance — a point, according to conservative critics, that multiculturalism naïvely refuses to see.[21] Much like the Middle East depicted in *The Exorcist*, this Middle East is an environment capable of weakening and enervating the Westerner. Hodges, echoing Father Merrin in Iraq, takes himself, and the viewing audience, on a meandering walk through the neighborhoods of San'a, and both experience its innate dangers. As a through-the-looking-glass land, Yemen zaps the innate confidence of the Westerner, given to him by his exceptional culture, and leaves him powerless. The film immediately establishes the dangerous atmosphere in the Arab realm: a Yemeni cult of violence precedes Hodges's formal entry into the urban life of the city. Just before he enters the land from the airport terminal, the audience sees the flash and clash of Oriental daggers that Yemeni men use in a cultural dance. Other men cross Hodges's pathway, carrying rifles slung over their shoulders, and uniformed Yemeni police stand with their rifles at the airport doorway, the portal of Hodges's entry into the scene. A young American soldier greets Hodges with a jeep. He is not in uniform and does not salute the arriving colonel because, as he tells Hodges, to show Americanism would incite the snipers who lurk here. Such verbal orientation to the land, along with visible examples of dangerous Arabs in the crowd, makes all Yemenis to be encountered suspect. Therefore, the two Americans must hide their cultural behaviors and protect themselves with bulletproof vests. "We're not the most popular team in town right now, sir," he tells Hodges. Even the new American embassy, the audience is later told, had to be removed from the urban center and into a bunker that is behind a mile of protective barbed wire. America must surrender its outward pride and righteousness in this wilderness.

Hodges's every move is watched by the Yemenis, and he continually struggles to recapture his power of gaze in this land. While he looks about and notices the foreign flavor of the people, their clothing, and their language, the camera and the audio tracks work together to prove that he and the audience are engulfed by the Yemenis' gaze. Wherever Hodges goes, and from whatever angle he looks upon the land, Yemenis have already laid eyes on Hodges and the audience's point of view. While Yemenis gaze upward or downward at him within the screen's field, sounds of Arabic bombard him from beyond the visual perimeters. When he arrives at the hotel, a woman looks down upon him standing in the street. When he looks down on the street from the hotel room, an old man turns around and, with a powerful eeriness, glares back at him (recall Merrin's being captured in the Arab gaze). The din of Arabic music, prayers, and talk, occasionally punctuated with shouts, fills in the visual background. Moreover, the pestering Third World buzz of flies reminds Hodges and the audience of the environment's anticipation of dead flesh.

He uses his digital camera, cheap and tinny in comparison to the sophisticated technology of the USS Wake Island and symbolic of his presently weakened gaze, to recapture and fix his American power of gaze upon the old embassy. His first snapshot of the embassy captures the broken lens of the surveillance camera on top of the embassy, a symbol of the Western gaze upon and knowledge of the Yemenis that has since been usurped. Then he photographs the bullet holes in the embassy walls. Later he takes pictures of a surveillance camera that never was damaged and that is the same camera that provided the videotape with proof of Yemeni violence originating in the crowd. When Hodges feels a presence behind him, he turns to look and sees that a black-veiled woman stares down upon him from the rooftop where the snipers once stood.

When Hodges enters the corridors of the embassy, it is like he is entering a haunted house. He is surrounded by Arabic graffiti, written on the walls in dripping red paint that looks like blood, calling for Yemeni control of Yemen. A man's shout in Arabic alarms him into thinking that someone is behind him, but there is no one there to be seen. The destruction around the embassy and inside the rooms, which were once neat, organized, well appointed, and civilized in the American fashion, shows the type of havoc the Arabs bring when they gain control. Broken glass lies upon the floor, papers and overturned furniture are littered about. The picture of Clinton has been smashed to the floor, and Vice President Al Gore's picture hangs askew. The pictures show how much consideration these Yemenis have for the liberal principles of American multiculturalism that are touted as providing a place at the global table for Third World cultures. Hodges quickly picks out an American flag ripped to shreds and thrown on the floor. The abused flag is evidence of the Yemenis' unmitigated hatred and disrespect for America. In the internal courtyard, burned and overturned vehicles and office equipment are scattered on the ground. On the roof Hodges finds an area stained with the dried blood of an American soldier. His walk through the ransacked embassy serves to prove the Arabs' inclination to trash civilization if they are left to their own devices.

The rooftop surveillance camera that was not shot out by the Yemenis reveals a remnant of American power. The camera's angle in relation to the courtyard makes the audience think that there may be proof of what really occurred there. This momentary hope for truth empowers Hodges to scan the courtyard and to freely reenact Childers's movements that day. Hodges uses the cadence of the group prayer below to imagine the rioting Yemenis of that fateful day. He dodges behind the rooftop cornices, makes his way along the platform, as if hiding from the power of the Islamic prayer below, and finally falls into the same corner from which Childers looked down upon the crowd and, having been wounded, gave the fatal order. But his sudden burst of vicarious understanding of Childers's military mind-set and strategy is commandeered by a little Yemeni girl, barely ten years old, with an amputated leg. She has been watching his moves and stares up at him. With her urchin appearance and unsteadied pose upon her crutches, she stands inside a courtyard with dried blood on the ground.

While the little girl's gaze seizes Hodges from afar, the Yemeni gaze finally accosts him in close proximity during his walk in the labyrinth of the city streets. His path leads him to an area where he seems to have lost his direction. While other Yemenis stare at him, one Yemeni and his friends approach him and shout at him in Arabic, "Hey, haven't you done enough to my country? Murderer!" Quickly a furious crowd descends upon him. Hodges tries to reason with the people, but they do not respond in kind. They ignore his English pleas and angrily shout and push him. The camera takes on his point of view, thus placing the American audience in the midst of these angry and threatening Arab faces and shouts once again. The camera lens spins about the hate-filled Yemeni people in order to evoke a sense of confusion for the viewing audience. An overhead camera shot shows the size of this abusive crowd united against Hodges. Finally, he breaks away and runs from the crowd back to his hotel room, where he splashes cold water on his face to regain his composure.

At one point he controls the gaze over the Yemenis when he sees the little one-legged girl again. He follows her, without her apparent knowledge, to a children's hospital, where he is confronted with the sight of wounded and dying Yemeni men, women, and children. The dead and mutilated Yemenis seize the power of gaze back from him. The place is like a chamber of horrors or a charnel house, where the doctor, Dr. Ahmar (Amidou), appears to be more like a butcher wearing a bloodstained apron than a doctor in a lab coat. The children and women look at Hodges listlessly with their open wounds and blood-soaked bandages. Again, the flies whisk about, coming to feast and spawn upon their flesh.

This final scene in Yemen, in which Hodges can no longer stand up to the Yemenis' gazing onslaught, shows a defeated Hodges. As he walks out, bewildered and shaken, a Yemeni boy takes a final gazing "shot" at him. The boy stands in front of Hodges and shapes his small hand to resemble a pistol. With Hodges in the sight of his make-believe gun, he silently fires at the broken-spirited American. In Vietnam, Hodges became wounded because he was devoid of gaze. Here in Yemen, he is devoid of gaze again, and he walks away as if he is spiritually wounded. Hodges walks into the shaded labyrinth dejected, watched from behind by the little girl and haunted by the eerie cries of dying babies. In a dream on an airplane home, he jumbles the images he has just seen in Yemen with images of death at the Battle of Ca Lu. He recollects the sounds of the muezzin's prayer, which add to the uncontrollable flow of the images in his subconscious. He is haunted to the point that he breaks down.

The pressures of the case could not force him to lose control back home in America. Even when Biggs turned the screws on Hodges in his office with the offer of a plea bargain, Hodges did not accept Biggs's offer of an alcoholic drink. When Hodges found Childers on the verge of committing suicide, he took the bottle away from Childers and hid it away so neither could consume it. Hodges is a recovering alcoholic who has strongly avoided temptations under pressure. However, the Arab land can bewilder the Westerner, and for Hodges it has distorted what actually happened to his friend Childers. Hodges himself has become confused and becomes lost in a multicultural paradigm that blames Childers, the Westerner, for the anger, suffering, and appalling conditions of these Yemenis. He begins to believe that Childers's actions were indeed the result of racism. Multiculturalism has taken a grip upon him, and the Yemenis have attacked him while he is in this state of weakness. He has lost confidence in "the old ballgame," and, symbolic of his loss of self-assuredness, he turns to the bottle, gets drunk, and once back home physically thrashes Childers and accuses his close friend of outright racism.

In between scenes in the Arab land that are discussed above are scenes of Yemeni lies and deceit about that fateful day. In an interview with a Yemeni man, Hodges is told that the Americans fired upon the crowd that was only trying to defend itself. When Hodges asks if the Americans fired first, an accusation that the audience knows is not true, the man nods affirmatively. In another interview, a Yemeni soldier defiantly defends his position that this was a peaceful demonstration that did not need the Yemeni security forces, let alone American forces. He sneers, emphatically thrusts his finger at Hodges, and says that the Yemeni army never found any weapons in the civilian crowd. The videotape from the unbroken camera reveals otherwise in a later scene back in Washington. The tape, which Sokal refused to acknowledge earlier, does show the audience that men, women, and children removed an array of firearms from their bodies and shot at the American soldiers.

Hodges's many experiences in Yemen are linked together through the appearances of identical black audiocassette tapes with Arabic writing. As he walks through the destroyed embassy, he sees the audiocassette tape on the floor. When he opens the ambassador's desk drawer in his plundered office, he finds a copy of the tape. In the interview with the belligerent Yemeni soldier who insists there were no weapons found on the dead bodies, Hodges glimpses the tape lying on the soldier's desk. Finally, he notices the tape underneath a dead man's bed at the children's hospital. Although the contents of the tape are not at first revealed, its black color, the eerie background music heard when it is seen, the camera's fix upon its appearance in places of destruction, anger, lies, and death lead the audience to believe that it is sinister. While the Arabic script states "Islamic Jihad's Call against the United States of America," its title and content are not readily known to the non-Arabic-literate American audience. However, the fact that the audiocassette's label is written in the foreign script that appears in protests of anger and as graffiti in an atmosphere of destruction leads such viewers to believe that the tape is made to terrify them. Moreover, the audience gets the impression that all Yemenis have listened to the audiocassette and that the tape is deeply embedded in the Yemeni culture. In fact, Hodges later states that audiocassette tapes are a method of disseminating information in a highly illiterate society. Hodges collects some tapes as he goes along in Yemen, using these later as evidence in Childers's trial to prove that Childers and his marines faced a hostile enemy.

The trial becomes a final showdown of the "new" versus the "old." To a jury whose gender and racial diversity restate the point that there is no such bias in American justice even though the minority jurors sit separately from the white male jurors, Biggs opens his argument by presenting an enlarged photograph of the massacred Yemenis and states that it is "a day of sadness, a day when America has to accept responsibility for its failures and its mistakes as well as its glories." Hodges, on the other hand, states in his opening arguments that Childers saved the lives he was supposed to save that day, he did what his country asked him to do, and Hodges himself would have done the same if he had been in Childers's position. He claims that now Childers is being unfairly treated because the mission went awry. The unfair treatment of Childers and his own lack of self-confidence as a lawyer going up against the "new" establishment, according to Hodges, were enough to make Hodges violently sick to his stomach just minutes before the trial began.

The prosecuting "new" attorney provides a number of witnesses who testify to the events of that day in Yemen. These witnesses aggravate the audience because they evade, distort, and deny the true facts, which the audience has already witnessed to be established. For example, Ambassador Mourain's testimony is the first and most egregious of all testimonies. The night before the trial, Sokal summoned Mourain, but just before his arrival Sokal reviewed the videotape that shows the audience that the Yemeni crowd did shoot at the marines. Sokal blackmailed Mourain by stating that unless Childers is held totally accountable for the massacre, Mourain's diplomatic career will be finished because he should have known of and prepared against anti-American sentiment in Yemen.

Rules of Engagement (2000). Colonel Hayes Hodges (Tommy Lee Jones) defends his friend Colonel Terry Childers (Samuel L. Jackson) from the charges of murder in a military courtroom. The courtroom drama is more than just a prosecution of Childers and a defense of his honorable career and righteousness as an American warrior. It represents a battle in a war, as perceived by cultural traditionalists, against the threat of multiculturalists, the assault against truth, and the tyranny of political correctness. Photo courtesy of the Academy of Motion Picture Arts and Sciences.

After Mourain's departure, Sokal destroyed the truth-bearing evidence by throwing it into a roaring fire, and thereby derailing the system of justice. He expected Mourain to lie on the witness stand so that Childers would be convicted, and the next day the craven Mourain does choose to forget that which he promised Childers he would never forget.

Mourain retells the Yemeni events to make Childers look like a raving lunatic, hostile and disrespectful toward the ambassadorial family, intent on keeping the ambassador from performing his duties, and set on teaching the Yemenis an imperial lesson. Childers, according to Mourain's lies, refused a peaceful resolution with the concocted statement "Diplomacy is bullshit at this point. . . . Nobody fucks with the American flag." The entire incident, as it is retold, could have been resolved if Childers had not kept Mourain from addressing and reasoning with the "crowd." Mourain's intent is to show that Childers was in an intolerant, anti-multicultural mood. Mourain's answers to Hodges's cross-examining questions avoid "yes" or "no" statements of fact. In postmodern fashion, he highlights the opportunity for interpretation of events and answers, "as a general principle," "if in fact," "to the extent possible," "I would suppose so," and "it's my understanding." Such phraseology remains noncommittal, blurred, open to subjectivity, and closed to an objective reality. Hodges must press him to make "yes" and "no" statements of fact. Mourain's deceitfulness is not only aggravating to Childers and the audience, but also embarrassing to Mrs. Mourain, who sits in the courtroom witnessing this assault on truth. While she is disturbed with her husband's lies, she, like the ambassador himself, buckles to the "new" ballgame's threat against her upper-class, diplomatic lifestyle, which Childers risked his life to save and protect, and is willing to allow truth, innocence, and American justice to be jeopardized to save her lifestyle. She not only refuses to tell the truth, but she takes the stance that truth cannot be fully known. "I don't know what the truth is. Colonel Childers is on trial for what he did outside of the embassy. I wasn't there; were you?"

Captain Lee, the soldier who originally questioned Childers's orders on the embassy rooftop, is also evasive during testimony. However, his evasiveness is not because he does not want to tell the truth, but rather he does not want to tell a lie. Biggs tries to get him to agree to the prosecution's embellishments of the truth with leading, speculative, and nonevidential questions to which Hodges continually objects and which are all sustained by the judge. When his back is up against the wall, Biggs, in what is considered typical PC manner, resorts to exposing the racist words that Childers used in giving his command to fire. While the audience and Childers sit silently to contemplate the appellation of "motherfuckers," Lee dodges the question (an aggravation to multiculturalists) and does not bring attention to the meaningless words used in combat (a relief for those opposed to political correctness). All that matters to Lee is that he gave the order to fire. However, Biggs will extrapolate from Lee's testimony that the crowd below was not the main threat. The snipers on the opposite rooftop were the main threat at the time. Childers, Biggs declares, is guilty of stereotyping all Arabs as dangerous, as deserving of American fire. Additionally, Hodges's cross-examination of Lee runs into an upheld objection by Biggs. Hodges, in conservative manner, then redirects the questions to Childers's patriotic rescue of the American flag under Yemeni attack.

Dr. Ahmar, the Yemeni doctor whom Hodges has met at the children's hospital in Yemen, testifies that he was among the first to arrive at the scene and found no weapons among the dead and wounded. But the audience knows that he must be lying or unaware of their existence, because the destroyed videotape already has shown the audience that the people did have guns. His disheveled appearance, worried face, and insistent cries of cultural innocence portray a man confused by reconciling a desired reality with a haunting truth. Hodges counters his denial with an alternative to proving the existence of the "smoking guns," submitting the audiocassette tape found around Yemen as evidence. He makes the doctor translate the Arabic audiocassette, and the foreign language puzzles all the Americans in the courtroom and those audience members who do not understand Arabic. Dr. Ahmar reveals the words, with embarrassment, as "We call on every Muslim who believes in God and hopes for reward to obey God's command . . . To kill Americans and plunder their possessions wherever he finds them . . . To kill Americans and their allies, both civil and military, is [the] duty of every Muslim who is able." The contents of the audiocassette make everyone in the courtroom and the American audience feel uncomfortable, threatened, vulnerable, and scared, just as the audiocassette's prior appearances were designed to do. However, Biggs tries to counter this evidence with the multicultural argument that this single tape is in no way representative of the Yemeni people. Dr. Ahmar tries to support Biggs's point by insisting that he is not a member of Islamic Jihad.

Sokal's testimony is absolutely false as to the existence of the surveillance tape from the embassy, and is a denial of America's rightful power of gaze and access to truth over the Yemeni people. He not only lies to Hodges while under oath, but he also lies to his own side. He even has the audacity to become annoyed with Hodges's quest for the truth. Hodges refers to an inventory manifest of embassy property brought back to the United States. The document proves that there was a surveillance videotape taken from the embassy. When pushed as to the whereabouts of the videotape, Sokal is quick to eschew blame and places the custody of all evidence with his own Major Biggs, a strategy that catches Biggs by surprise. Biggs is not aware of any such videotape, unlike the audience, and the evil multiculturalist Sokal shows his willingness to sacrifice his own protégé to save himself. Hodges announces to the jury and the audience that if the crowd was as docile as Biggs professes, the prosecution would be showing the Yemenis to be so, but since the evidence does not bolster the case of the prosecution, the videotape is now missing.

The surveillance camera acted as an American disciplinary tool over the Yemenis. It provided a singular view for those who installed it, and it has become an accepted tool of objectivity and truth in American culture. While it was difficult for the Americans to see the enemy in Vietnam and America was therefore vulnerable to the enemy, American-installed cameras on the embassy make it easy to watch the Arab enemy. When the Yemenis destroyed the first camera, they destroyed this American imperial gaze over them. The images the second camera recorded become, in turn, a metanarrative—a valued and accepted objective description of history, which tells the Americans how the Yemenis of that day behaved and whether they deserved such treatment in kind. Interestingly, the earlier real-time scenes of the crowd do not show the Yemeni crowd shooting at the marines, nor do they show weapons among the dead bodies. However, since the videotape is an accepted source of truth, a purveyor of metanarrative, and the cinematic audience is powerless to rewind the film to affirm what it saw, the videotape overrides what the audience actually saw in the earlier scenes, and the audience is expected to willingly place its faith in the videotaped images. But multiculturalism and its theoretical and ideological cousins defuse the singularity of the Western gaze and narrative. Multiculturalism diffracts such a gaze with the inclusion of various and alternative narratives. While multiculturalism is most often a reasonable intellectual endeavor, the conservative movement contextualizes it as a consistent endeavor of irrationality and violence. Sokal's destruction of the videotape, then, is designed to be a similarly odious violation of truth. The use of fire to destroy the tape shows not only his intent to violently eradicate truth, objectivity, and the metanarrative, but also shows his intent to treasonably weaken the American gaze, the American power over truth, and the American power over the enemy.

Hodges punches holes in Sokal's testimony that there was no prior concern with Yemeni aggression. He provides date-enumerated examples of Yemeni aggression noted in a State Department report. He forces Sokal to read aloud a list of Yemeni acts of aggression, defiance, and inconsideration toward human and even animal life, which include: a grenade thrown at a police car, sixteen Western tourists abducted by fundamentalists, a bomb explosion in a car parked near a school, a stun grenade thrown at a newspaper kiosk near a police station, a military officer seriously wounded by Yemen's "first donkey bomb." The instances of Yemeni violence cited all occurred within less than fifty days. Biggs, using relativism as a tactic, tries to show that acts of violence are equally egregious domestically in the United States. He submits headlines from the day's *Washington Post*, which include: "Agent and Kidnapper Killed in the Rescue of Businessman's Son," "Bomb Threat Evacuates Museum of Natural

History," "Officer Chases Truck Driver and Fires 38 Times," and "Husband Shoots Wife and Himself in Street." Biggs's point is that if military action is necessary in Yemen because Yemenis are violent, then similar military action is deserved in America because Americans are also violent.

Prior to his own testimony, Childers recalls his experience of this day in Yemen for himself and once more for the audience. As he walks past the ceremonial lowering of the flag, he patriotically salutes the flag in the tranquil twilight and in flashbacks he remembers the different reception the Yemenis gave the American flag in Yemen. The images of the flag coming down on the embassy rooftop show the Yemeni gunmen shooting holes in the flag, accompanied by the shouts of the Yemeni mob. His flashbacks replay Mourain's statement of gratitude to him and for his labor under dangerous Yemeni assault. A flashback shows the dying American soldiers, and, for the first time, the audience sees what Childers actually saw and heard through his own eyes and ears: men, women, and children shooting at the American soldiers on the embassy rooftop. It shows Childers's continuing assessment and reassessment of the situation and Childers's steady patience pushed to the ultimate episode by the Yemenis. And while the videotape provided television-framed and silent pictures, these flashbacks are as aurally vivid and as visually wide-screened as the film's narrative present, thereby providing a more assured sense of witnessing and visual truth for the audience — Childers's experience is like ours.

This evidence further bolsters the case for Childers in the eyes of the audience. The continual reestablishment of Yemeni guilt throughout the film with such views corrals the audience, leading away from multicultural leanings that may linger or have developed during the film. While the audience may have felt sorrow and discomfort for the little girl with her amputated leg, it loses this compassion when it sees that she herself fired a gun at the marines. Childers's positive performance under Hodges's questioning, furthermore, shelters him from guilt. However, just as in his questioning of Captain Lee, Biggs returns to the PC crutch of accusations of racism when his back is against the wall. Biggs insists that Childers recollect the exact wording of his orders to shoot. While Childers cannot recall them or does not want to recall them, Biggs and the audience know full well that Childers's words are incriminating, especially to a jury that is unaware of the true occurrences in Yemen, to which the audience is already privy. In an attempt to peg Childers as racist, he gets Childers to lose his cool and to boisterously admit to the order "Waste the motherfuckers!", although Childers insists the appellation was justified because they were killing American marines. Biggs must push further the racist factor in Childers's order to shoot by showing individual pictures of bloodied and dead Yemeni men, women, and children. The audience winces in shame at the visual display and dramatic questioning: "Are these the motherfuckers? These? These? Are these the motherfuckers that you ordered to be wasted?!" While the rules of engagement are meant to protect the lives of innocent people, Childers proclaims that in this case he was not going to follow such "fucking rules" if it meant that American lives were being lost. His announcement echoes the multicultural belief that racism includes adherence to American exceptionalism and Euro-centrism, according to which American and Western lives are of greater value and deserve greater protection over the lives of Orientalized people. This kind of damning statement, in the Clintonian era, even upsets Hodges, who later dresses Childers down not only for making the statement, but for not telling him about it earlier.

The jury's return after deliberation with a verdict of not guilty of the charges of conduct unbecoming to an officer and murder is an immediate victory for Childers and a long-term victory for the "old ballgame." Just before deliberation, the closing arguments summarize the conflict at hand. The "new" wishes to make an issue of the death of Third Worlders and the American proclivity to racism, imperialism, and excessive military force. Biggs places the photographed death scene of the Yemeni people before the jury and the audience for contemplation. The "old" fights to make an issue of the Yemeni attack on America, the need to preserve American sovereign rights, and the protection of honor for those who patriotically defend America and all for which it stands. Hodges places a photograph of the besieged embassy façade over the death scene to show the Yemeni attack on America as the predominating issue. Hodges's closing arguments, which play to the patriotic heartstrings of the courtroom and the audience, even win him the admiration of his multiculturally inclined son and doubting father, who have come to watch his performance. The narrative therefore promotes the persuasiveness of Hodges's soliloquy over that of Biggs. The jury and the audience must choose between the two concerns and their summarizing images.

The narrative designs truth, its institutions, and its possession by "the old" to win out over the multicultural movement, and the Yemeni Arabs are resubordinated to that truth and the system of justice it upholds. Childers's exoneration may be a relief to those who have been privy to certain information, as the narrative ensures the audience is, that proves the multiculturalists are liars, cheats, and enemies of the American way, and that the Yemenis have taken advantage of an American period of cultural weakness. The audience is expected to be satisfied with Childers's exit from the courtroom, his defiance of the screaming American PC mob and liberal media shown to his far left, and his disappearing walk ahead and to his right into the orderly American military landscape. It should be a pleasure to later learn from the postscript that Sokal is jailed for obstruction of justice and Mourain is fired from his ambassadorial position for perjury. It should be satisfying to learn that Childers retires with full honors. The "old," in the end, vanquishes the "new."

However, what is of concern to a discussion of Orientalist fear is how a jury, under such circumstances, comes to this decision. The Arabs in *Rules of Engagement* are guilty of shooting first. The film's narrative guarantees us, time and again, that this is the irrefutable truth. We, the audience, know it because the film provides us with omniscient and privileged visual evidence of the shooting mob, backed by the verification of truth enabled by modern, although frame-restricted, video surveillance, and further supported with Childers's clear and personal flashbacks. It may have been difficult to see in the jungles of Vietnam, but not here in Yemen. And yet the jury, we must remember, did not see any of this evidence. The jury members went with the evidence and testimony at hand. Without access to the videotape, the jury should have been inclined to believe that Childers came to Yemen in hostility and that he murdered scores of civilians. Childers's courtroom behavior portrays him as a man who does snap under pressure; he did not follow the rules of engagement in Yemen or in Vietnam; in fact, he defames them in the courtroom by calling them "fucking rules"; and he is inclined to use appellations that demean Others. Testimony shows that Yemen can be dangerous, that there are those Arabs who wish to destroy the United States, and that Childers may have had a combat excuse for his murder of the radio operator in Vietnam.

The testimonies and evidence, as presented to the jury, seem to incriminate Childers, with a possible exception: Did a missing videotape create enough reasonable doubt in the minds of the jury? The lost videotape might have been a critical factor since Sokal's postscript conviction is a likely outcome of such doubt, but it is not the central theme of Hodges's closing arguments and the narrative leaves the answer unclear.

The jury's return to the courtroom is as swift and decisive as the next film cut. We must assume that the jurors deliberated, but we are not shown the reason or logic by which they digested the information. As a result, questions tend to creep into mind: In reaching its decision, did the jury fall back upon its own belief in the "old" over the "new"? Did it opt for American exceptionalism as an answer to difficult questions of fairness? Was it guided by "old" hatred, fear, and stereotypical beliefs about Arabs as evil enemies? Did it become blind to the deaths of eighty-three men, women, and children? The "old ballgame" may get its victory at the end of *Rules of Engagement,* but these questions may gnaw at our viewing consciences after the credits roll.

CNN's *America Remembers*
THE "REAL" ATTACK (2002)

*T*HIS book has thus far discussed Orientalist fear created in American popular films and examined Hollywood's unreal constructions of the Arab enemy. In these fictions, the characters of the "evil" Arabs are portrayed as threatening to American ideologies and myths. The alleged Arab treachery, equally inherent in all their kind, is, in relation to reality, as illusory as the American ideologies and myths themselves. But how do these fictions hold up in light of the events of September 11, 2001? In view of what occurred on that fateful Tuesday, it seems that the Arabs are "evil" in real life as well as in American fiction. Osama bin Laden and his jihadist followers have since been blamed for actually attacking America on this infamous day. Arab perpetrators hijacked four passenger jetliners, killing approximately three thousand people, and crashed them into the World Trade Center towers and the Pentagon. They also may have planned to attack the White House or the Capitol Building, a contingency that sent the president of the United States and the U.S. government leadership into DefCon bunkers. These sneak attacks have come to be considered the most heinous crimes against America since Pearl Harbor. Undeniably, it would seem, the Arabs had proven themselves to be America's enemies, and Orientalist fear was not only a natural and proper reaction but also a blameless attitude. CNN has compiled news clips and commentaries onto a ninety-minute DVD, entitled *America Remembers,* as an attempt to document September 11, 2001, and the months that followed.[1] At a significant point in the documentary, CNN shows head-and-shoulders photos of the Arab hijackers of the four American airliners. The camera narrows in on the frozen stares on the men's faces, music with a tension-building crescendo plays in the background, and CNN anchorwoman Paula Zahn states, "We finally saw . . . the faces of evil. People who carried out the most mind-boggling attack and assault on America, who had claimed so many innocent lives. Looking into the eyes of these hijackers."

America Remembers is intended to be a documentary of real images and people. The film features many of CNN's reporters and employees speaking about their own experiences of that day, their reports, and their thoughts. It presents pictures and footage of the American government and its leaders reacting to the events of that time. It shows the fear, concerns, and emotions of American citizens under war-provoking attacks. Many of the people in the documentary are well known. They are people we recognize as part of our everyday interaction with television, of our culture, and of the politics of foreign affairs. Some of the people speaking in this documentary are not recognizable, but their anonymity highlights their roles as average people and makes us aware of the tragedy's deep reach into a real American citizenry. These horrendous events led to great loss, pain, and suffering for the American people, and CNN tries to create a "historical record" of these events with a montage of film cuts punctuated with emotive music, decorated with patriotic graphics, and woven together through a narrative of dramatic remembrances. What actually happened on that day in September and in its aftermath is neatly packaged onto a portable, hand-sized disk that seems to legitimize CNN as the most reliable narrator of the event, thereby promoting its own commercial status, and that is ultimately more about CNN than about the events themselves. Copies of the DVD are displayed and sold in many video, electronic, and warehouse stores next to and among Disney, horror, action/adventure, family, and comedy genre films. However, is *America Remembers* a fictional movie having commercial and entertainment qualities rather than a historical record? In this chapter, I shall argue that it is.

To grasp the transformation of the real event into a fictional movie, we may borrow from discussions of representation prevalent in Holocaust studies. Endeavors to represent the Holocaust have often been derided as inherently fictional, condemned as obscene, and shunned as taboo by virtue of their very attempt at portrayal of the real when the real is beyond the imagination. While the traditional contention has been that the Holocaust is confined to the realm of the unimaginable and beyond description in human language and depiction in pictures, it has recently become the subject of a great debate in this present era of collective, manufactured memory. Yosefa Loshitzky has edited a series of provocative articles that deal with the representability of the Holocaust and American popular culture's attempt to do so in Steven Spielberg's *Schindler's List* (1993). Many of the contributors support the traditional contention and question the commercial and emotional claims that the film is a "flawless representation of the Holocaust." Barbie Zelizer, for example, points out that

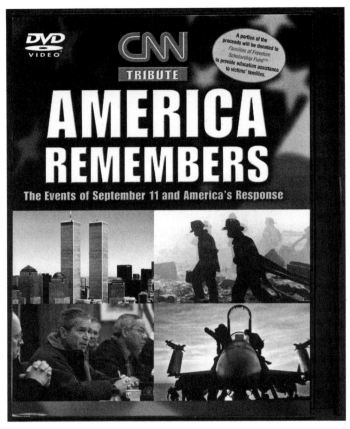

CNN Tribute: America Remembers (2002). *America Remembers* is marketed as a documentary of real images and people of September 11, 2001. What happened on that day and in the following months is neatly packaged on a portable, hand-sized, ninety-minute DVD, which is displayed and sold next to Disney, horror, action/adventure, family, and comedy genre films (DVD cover shown above). Is this a proper way of remembering the historical events of that day and of imparting information about the Arab perpetrators? Or does the presentation prove to be a fictional movie for entertainment, a legitimization of CNN as the most reliable narrator of the events, a testimony to CNN's professionalism? Is the story ultimately about CNN rather than the events themselves?

while popular culture may be the current conduit of historical knowledge, we must recommit ourselves to the distinction between event-as-it-happened and event-as-it-is-retold.[2] Omer Bartov reminds us that survival narratives cannot provide full authenticity because such narratives distort the event. Bartov acknowledges the imperfections of human memory in survival narratives. More importantly, he states that by definition survival narratives exclude the stories of the murdered, who were killed "not because they did not want to be saved but due to a combination of circumstances in which individual will and skills rarely played an important role and chance was paramount." Furthermore, he points out that representation can never be free of bias, distortion, and the limitations of the conventions within which acts of representation operate. This is why he believes that documentaries that rely on a montage of film footage and claim to portray the past "as it really was" (a masquerade of objectivity) can be more pernicious than the fictional films that act out the past with "authenticity." As he notes, the available footage of the Holocaust is problematic because, while the Nazis filmed to prove the myth of the decadent and subhuman Jew, the Allies as liberators filmed to prove Nazi depravity, to create hatred for the Nazis, to legitimize the war effort, and to motivate Allied troops to keep on fighting. Anything that did not fit the objectives of the filmmakers was summarily left out.[3]

Miriam Bratu Hansen informs us that representation in film is a product of the film industry, such as Hollywood in the case of *Schindler's List*. Therefore, the real events must be disciplined to the desires, concerns, and tastes of a certain consumer audience. Representation of real events must rely on the classical narrative of compositional unity, motivation, linearity, equilibrium, and closure — "principles singularly inadequate in the face of an event that by its very nature defies our narrative urge to make sense of, to impose order on[,] the discontinuity and otherness of historical experience."[4] Narratives create subjectivity of experience for the characters inside it, and, in the process, the viewers or readers come to identify with these characters and their experiences. Meanwhile, experiences of others outside the particular narrative are silenced, and the totality of the event is impoverished. Sara R. Horowitz takes this point further when reminding us that film narrative only provides us the alternatives of the hero (to whom we will cling) and the villain (whom we will abhor). The antipodal balance derived from the clarity of hero and villain characters "frees viewers from questioning their own possible collusion with racism or prejudice."[5]

While I do not suggest comparing the events of September 11, 2001, with the Holocaust, I do believe that the theoretical issues of representing the Holocaust can instruct us on how to consider the limitations of film images, narrative, and characters in our representations of historical atrocity. Moreover, the events of September 11, as Sandra Silberstein points out, have become reified, epic-ized, and elevated from atrocity and terror into purposeful war through an American patriotic and political discourse.[6] Accordingly, they have been condensed into the sacred and indexical terms "September 11th," or "9/11," which have taken on a transcendent essence requiring great emotional and patriotic reverence in American society. September 11th is so unique and historically important that it does not even require the year to distinguish it chronologically or historically from any other date. President George W. Bush tells us that: September 11th has become a national tragedy of grief and sorrow; America has suffered great loss and is filled with disbelief and a quiet and unyielding anger; the events of September 11th are unprecedented despicable acts resulting in the mass murder of innocents, perpetrated by an evil force, the very worst of human nature, within a single day, and thereby forcing us into a different world; the folks who committed these cowardly terrorist acts promote a perversion of religion, they follow the path of fascism, Nazism, and totalitarianism, they stand on the wrong side of God, they threaten our way of life in a war that they have chosen and waged against us by stealth, deceit, and murder; and this is not only our war, this is the world's fight, civilization's fight, for freedom and justice against fear and cruelty, which will eventually be buried in history's unmarked grave of discarded lies.[7] September 11th has thus been inducted into the annals of American history to stand along with Gettysburg and Pearl Harbor; September 11th has become *the* American tragedy of our times.

If these tragedies are as the president and many other Americans revere them to be, then theories of Holocaust representation can teach us the flaws of language, pictures, and narrative and can make us aware of our human limitations, despite good intentions, in the representation of atrocities that we claim as our history. These theoretical discussions can make us realize that any attempt to describe, reenact, or revisit September 11, 2001, can only be fictional, particularly when it is condensed into a ninety-minute DVD. CNN is a member of an "interpretive community,"[8] and *America Remembers* must not be considered as representing the event-as-it-happened,[9] but rather as the event-as-it-is-retold, i.e., a fictional movie.

Allow me to take this a step further, then. Barbie Zelizer pushes Holocaust representation to another limit. Among the many important lessons to be learned from her book *Remembering to Forget* is her particular point that representations may have limited ways of seeing the atrocities themselves, as well as ways of representing and seeing recent and future atrocities. This prism of prior experience of the Holocaust becomes *the* interpretive framework, creating an atrocity aesthetic, for Western understanding of genocide in Rwanda and Bosnia. Recent atrocities such as these cannot stand in their own historical context, nor can they generate their own historical meaning. Rather they are continually reconciled in Western media to the atrocities of the Holocaust, and so we see less of the real atrocity at hand.

Zelizer's point is important when contemplating CNN's *America Remembers*. The actual events, now cut and pasted into fictional film and made accessible to popular memory, also have an interpretive framework that has been preestablished, and the events find themselves disciplined and subordinated to this interpretive framework. In essence, the events are further fictionalized in a narrative of retelling through this interpretive framework. Arab villains and their attack on America have already been inculcated into American popular culture in the fictional films of Orientalist fear. *America Remembers* interprets the events of September 11th with some of the very tropes discussed in the previous chapters. Interestingly enough, the narrative contextualization of these events has elements of the previously discussed films that help to induce shock, horror, and awe: the Arab enemy causes American financial ruin, crashes into landmarks, is at war with the Americans, wields our own cultural tools against us, and takes advantage of our move toward multiculturalism. While the Arab enemy is not defeated, the film shows a proper course that taps our inherent frontiersman strength and resolve, and we are assured of an eventual victory, although yet to be achieved.

One of the most notable of all tropes is the confrontation by Arab villains of American ideology and their threat to overturn American myth. *America Remembers* has tapped, as an overarching narrative structure, the popular myths of September 11th adopted in much of 9/11 literature today.[10] A telling example of one such myth is used by Daniel Benjamin and Steven Simon, who refer to a "paradigm lost" as a result of September 11th. According to the paradigm, America believed itself to be tough on terrorism and thus successful at deterring terrorist assault:

[T]errorists would be dealt with decisively because Americans rightly expected their government to protect them, and every effort would be made to ensure that justice would be rendered when harm was done. Terrorism would be combated vigorously to strengthen deterrence, so no one would conclude that the United States could be taken advantage of with impunity. Whenever possible, America worked with other countries to disrupt terrorist operations, and it used its military might against terrorists when doing so made sense. The United States did not make concessions to terrorists, appease them politically, pay them off, or hustle them out of the country when they were accidentally arrested, as Europeans did in the 1970s and 1980s.[11]

This paradigm was predicated upon a perceived empirical science of terrorism. Terrorist attacks were sporadic and limited in scope, and rarely broke double-digit numbers of dead victims. "Americans were more likely to die from lightning strikes, bathtub drownings, or poisoning by plants and venomous animals than at the hands of terrorists."[12] Terrorists had always sought incremental change, not a wholesale revision of the status quo. While they wanted to be taken seriously, they never sought to inflict so much violence as to elicit massive retaliation. Therefore, terrorists never threatened the safety of large numbers of American citizens, let alone American power. However, September 11th shattered our science and our paradigm of terrorism:

On September 10, ordinary Americans had no conception that one of the bloodiest days in the nation's history would be the work of terrorists, not of another nation. They did not identify Islamist radicals as a group intent on killing thousands. If pushed, they might have named skyscrapers in lower Manhattan as a potential target of attack, but mostly because the Twin Towers had been bombed eight years earlier. They had no inkling that a suicide attack on such a scale was a possibility or that anyone on earth had the wherewithal, or, more important, the desire[,] to carry out such a crime. In fact, most Americans, if asked, would have likely said that their nation had never been more secure. More than a decade after the end of the Cold War, it had become a truism that the world had not seen such a dominant power since ancient Rome.[13]

And:

The murderers came out of nowhere—from a milieu that few had any inkling of—and acted in a way that was utterly irrational by the standards we employ. For most, the coordination of the suicide of nineteen young men to achieve such massive killing was unimaginable and therefore could not be defended against.[14]

However, the monstrous degree of atrocity, for which CNN seems to revere September 11th, lies not just in the number of people that perished on the hijacked airplanes and in the buildings below (a number CNN will eventually stop pursuing in the story itself until the ending credits), but in the number of myths, the old paradigm included, that the Arab enemy was able to overturn in a single day and in the subsequent effects on our mythic selves. CNN interprets September 11th in terms of these myths in order to impose horror, to elicit emotion, and to designate the Arabs as "evil," as well as to regenerate an American sense of strength, pride, and heroism. CNN relies on a general belief that the normal, the average, the classic, and the routine comprise the collective American experience. The event-as-it-is-retold becomes a ritualized story that begins with myths shattered, continues with the ensuing chaos, and ends with the just reestablishment of order through the old paradigm, albeit now predicated on an improved science. In this ritual, CNN disciplines September 11th to the story pattern Miriam Bratu Hansen calls the "classical narrative," as noted above. It feigns the creation of a narrative of multiple viewpoints by using eyewitness reports and candid shots. However, this is the story of September 11, 2001, as professed to have been experienced by CNN, and, despite the ruse of pluralism to establish its credentials as a narrator of history, CNN shows no humility in presenting itself in the most admirable, heroic, professional, and magnanimous light possible.

America Remembers begins with the darkened screen that soon displays the orange light of the sun's dawn rays peeking over the earth's circumference. The rising sun is supposed to signify the normalcy of a new day's beginning and the inability of the human being to stop this natural/divine event. The human being must therefore, as all living creatures always have done and will do, acquiesce to the earth's revolution and begin the new day as it is presented and as civilization expects.

CNN makes great efforts to paint September 11, 2001, as another ordinary day in America. The "normalcy" of the day is retold with the montage of narratives of CNN staff who describe the monotony of their morning rituals on September 11 as those of just another day. Staff members recollect getting out of bed, being at home in the kitchen, returning from dropping the kids off at school, just planning a day to get away from it all. These Americans are depicted as living the "normal" American life of home, family, and individuality that all Americans are assumed to have been living that morning. The replay of the morning weather report emphasizes further the importance of monotony in America on that day as part of the overall narrative. Here, the reporter's statement is cut so that it begins "elsewhere, pretty quiet today, beautiful weather, Midwest, Northeast," without any reference to the abnormality this day will bring. Anchorwoman Carol Lin states, "It was the most routine day. There was virtually no news that day." The major news of the day, as it is shown, was the ritual experience of primary elections in this democratic society. The elections are opened with the monotone, packaged, and almost unconvincing expression of New York City mayoral candidate Michael Bloomberg, who tells CNN reporters that "It's going to be a great day." People are shown on their way to work, standing in for the rest of the American populace, and represented by the images of trampling feet on a sidewalk pavement. We see planes take off at an American airport, as they do on any given day. Narrative remembrances further include reports of overlooking a routine news floor during the morning meeting, conducting the assignment of a news beat, driving on the freeway, or just pulling into a parking space at the Pentagon. Habitual as the day was, it meant for some just turning on the television, just flying over an awakening Manhattan, or just contemplating another birthday. Nothing and no one were noteworthy as remarkable or heroic.

CNN talk show host Larry King frames the "normal day" for what seems to be dramatic effect. However, King's framing of the day in reference to the Kennedy assassination is made to set up not only the myth of routine but also the importance of what the day was to become through tragedy. At the same time, this framing heightens the myth of the professional reputation of journalism, CNN's place within the occupation, and its authoritative right to narrate September 11th. Zelizer's book *Covering the Body* discusses the importance of the events of the Kennedy assassination to the profession of journalism and to the media organizations. On another routine day, November 22, 1963, journalists were covering what seemed to be just another presidential campaign trip to an American city, but the "hot moment" of the presidential assassination created an opportunity for the press, particularly the television journalists, to prove their ability to react, their flexibility toward rapidly moving events, and their interpretive ability, enabling them to dominate and establish their authority over the narration of one of the most important dates in

American history. King begins the narrative in *America Remembers* with his statement "You know, there are certain days that will always etch in your memory. The day Kennedy was shot, I remember exactly where I was and what happened. That was certainly the most momentous day . . . until 9/11." With these words, King not only puts September 11th on the level of sacred American dates for the viewers, but also marks the day as another "hot moment" when journalists were able to prove their professional mettle. While, as Zelizer argues, the press corps had to put forth great effort to gain control of the Kennedy assassination because it missed the actual event by never catching the moment of the assassination itself, the media caught the images of September 11th. Moreover, because of new technology and the organization of the twenty-four-hour news channel, the journalists were able to respond quickly and get live pictures that were as historically striking as the moments when Kennedy was pronounced dead and when Jack Ruby shot Lee Harvey Oswald. King's concluding words, "It [September 11] will be etched forever. This day changed all of us," contextually frame this "normal day" into one of the most iconic moments of American life and culture, one of the greatest moments of journalism and CNN in particular, and the compelling narrative that *America Remembers* is about to present to its viewers. Even more importantly for later consideration, they establish CNN's authority over the narrative of September 11th.

Just as the narrative and scenes of the "normal day" are concluded with King's words, the CNN newsroom is shown to be moving into "Breaking News" motion. While the events of September 11th throw American lives into turmoil, as shown in the upcoming images, they put the newsroom staff under pressure but not into a state of breakdown. The narrative of the "normal day" is shattered by an all-of-a-sudden rush of news staff through the newsroom during a scheduled commercial break, spinning and focus-attempting camera action, and some employees looking distraught while others yell like commodity traders. These scenes give the impression that there is an inability to determine what is going on in these fast-changing moments. But the director's command to an anchorwoman to hurry back to the set for the segue into "Breaking News" shows that CNN can respond with immediacy and confidence. CNN's technical ability to immediately bring the awesome scenes from Manhattan to television, just after these moments of confusion, is noted in anchorwoman Carol Lin's statement "And up comes the picture of the World Trade Center tower with a *huge* smoking, gaping hole in it. And I said, 'Holy God.' "

While New York has been shown to be a busy, industrious, and ener-getic city on a "normal day," the site of the burning building has changed that prior impression of America's foremost city. To define this change of daily routine, an average man on the street (unlike the CNN employees, he is not identified with a subtitled name) explains to the camera that he was at one moment looking at his watch, realizing he was late for work, and at the next seeing his place of work on fire in the distance. Where at one point the traffic of the city is punctuated with sirens of emergency ve-hicles headed toward the burning building and honking horns of taxis, the street scenes become silenced by the heart-pumping background music of *America Remembers*. The camera shots no longer show people moving toward their places of work. Now they show people stopping, gathering in the streets, looking upward, and slowly walking toward a location where the spectacle can best be seen. Some stare, others show expressions of be-wilderment and disbelief, and still others show emotion through tears and by embracing each other. And while people were at one time headed in their personal directions away from cameras on the street, the narrator now tells us that some people were seeking out CNN to tell what they have seen: "The other thing that happened was people were coming up to us, who were eyewitnesses to the incident," states Phil Hirschkorn, CNN pro-ducer. ". . . One thing you saw on the street were rows and rows of people. People just standing, sort of hypnotized by the flames in disbelief."

However, this momentary halting of American life, a disorder in the orderly conduct of the "normal day," does not daunt CNN. In a tale of triumph, where journalistic instinct is on display as an admirable profes-sional characteristic, Rose Arce, a CNN producer, follows her "hunch." She points out that while everyone else, the average person on the street, has stopped and is looking up toward the sky, a fact to which many scenes attest, she instinctively hurries toward the building. Her acute journalistic instinct works again when she flashes her CNN identification to a passing vehicle and asks the driver for a ride. The vehicle takes her within blocks of the burning skyscraper, the center of the story, and fortuitously sets her up to be "the first," as she is placed closer to the scene of the next part of the story, where the second plane flies into the south tower.

At this point in the narrative, another myth is shattered: the "normal accident." When the first image of the burning tower is shown, it is not clear to those in the narrative what actually happened. Anchorwoman Lin states that she saw a huge hole in the World Trade Center's north tower. The film uses a replay of the initial announcement by Lin that there are

unconfirmed reports that a plane has hit the tower and CNN is just beginning to work on the story. CNN has to "put together the pieces" to
confirm that a large passenger jet rather than a small airplane has hit the
tower and to determine whether this was by accident or intention. The film
splices the audio of various news radio reporters in with the street scenes
and a view of a handheld radio in order to show that information at the
time was confusing, secondhand bits and pieces. But CNN, the television
news company, is able to make sense of the situation because, as producer
Hirschkorn notes, the hole was many stories high and many stories wide.
It could not have been "a Cessna or a stunt plane at that point in time."
And still it looked like just another fire that was going to be put out, as the
sirens of racing fire engines and rescue crews on the audio track suggest.
In the interim, one eyewitness notes that the plane came into the tower
as if it was in distress, also indicating that this was a "normal" plane crash
with an unlucky, but still coincidental, target.

But producer Arce's proximity to the north tower actually shows that
this is not a "normal accident." While the pictures of the raging fire in the
north tower are shown as a possible accident, they also act as a template
for what is to come next. What is occurring in the north tower is to be repeated in the south tower, thereby confirming that these events are intentional. The number of replays of the incident, eventually five, drives home
the deliberateness of the crashes. Arce tells of a second roar overhead, and
the film produces four, and later a fifth, differently angled sequences of the
second plane flying toward the south tower. The fourth replay ends in im-
pact, explosion, and screams and declarations of disbelief from onlookers.
While Arce declares that her first thoughts were that this was a dream, i.e.,
it could not be happening, the four sequences of the plane barreling toward the south tower and producing an image mirroring that of the north
tower show that these events are not "normal accidents." Arce recalls her
wonderment as to why the plane was flying so low in a big city with tall
buildings. Arce's teary-eyed and voice-breaking quotation of a small girl
who witnessed the second plane hitting makes us poignantly aware that
the myth of the "normal accident" is being shattered. Arce says the girl
innocently and plainly stated to her father, "Daddy. Look, they're doing
it on purpose."

Accordingly, the myth of the routine commercial flight was now shattered as well. Planes in America periodically crash, but they do not inten-
tionally crash into buildings. Commercial flights have their own rituals
of checking in passengers; clearing passengers through security; boarding

passengers; taking off close to prescheduled times; whizzing toward their destinations; providing safe, comfortable, and courteous in-flight service; arriving on time or, even better, earlier than expected; and thanking passengers and encouraging them to fly the airline again. Even when things do not go as planned, narratives of cancellations, delays, lost baggage, and surly employees are routinely told within their own realms of truth and acceptability and have become part of the "normal day" of airline travel. Air travel in America had become a routine part of our day, whether for business, pleasure, or personal need, as was shown in the beginning rituals of the "normal day" in *America Remembers*. American Airlines Flight 11 was a Boeing 767-200 that carried ninety-two people en route from Boston to San Francisco. United Airlines Flight 175, also a Boeing 767-200, carried sixty-five people en route from Boston to Los Angeles. Each airplane carried about ten thousand gallons of jet fuel. While each airplane took off on time, its passengers, crew, and ground support, too, are believed to have gone through the routine rituals of beginning their day and those of typical flights.

Later, the film shows that these "normal" rituals of flight have been interrupted for everyone in the United States of America. A CNN employee shouts out the need for someone in the newsroom to confirm that the Federal Aviation Administration has grounded all flights across the nation. CNN correspondent Miles O'Brien does just that for the audience now in the narrative present. He tells us that once New York City was considered under attack, every nongovernmental flight was canceled, and those that were en route were ordered to land at the closest and most available airports. However, instead of showing the events of canceled flights and those interrupted in progress, what is shown is a reduced presentation of a radar screen of the United States and green blips representing airplanes in flight. As the green blips begin to diminish, the viewing audience is reminded that this is a most stunning and amazing spectacle to see. The audience is told that this was an unprecedented and very dramatic decision. Thanks to CNN, the audience is now seeing the remarkable event via the radar as O'Brien speaks through the replay. Forty-five hundred blips are reduced to zero on the map in just under two hours, although for the audience this event, through a fast time-lapse effect, lasts only seconds. The "normal day" of routine flights has now been reduced to a silence in the sky over America, and the once animated map of the country becomes still and seemingly vacant.

September 11th's relationship to the myth of the "normal day" is exemplified further in the CNN coverage of the most powerful American citizen, the president of the United States. President George W. Bush is shown beginning his "normal day" while on an educational campaign in Florida. As the scene portrays him, he is up at the crack of dawn, beginning his jog at a Sarasota, Florida, resort. "Just warming up," he tells reporters. The voice-over of CNN White House correspondent Major Garrett tells us of the president's "normal day." "This was as ordinary a day as you can possibly imagine," states Garrett. The schedule was clear and straightforward: visiting Emma E. Booker Elementary School and reading a book to a children's class, making some general statements about the importance of education, and then flying back to Washington. Even the president's remarks to the reporters are strictly confined to the intended schedule. While the reporters ask him about tax cuts, he sticks to the already set routine and will not let the media divert him from his planned issues of the day. Garrett remarks about the president's schedule, "It couldn't be simpler."

While the assembly of the children in the classroom looks ordinary, the lesson seems routine, and the conduct of the classroom appears regular, the president's visit itself could not be anything but abnormal. It is not every day that the president of the United States comes to this school. The school grounds are teeming with Secret Service, and news crews, cameras, and lights are crammed into the classroom. And yet the preparations, the excitement, and maybe even the ambivalence toward the presidential visit have no part in this narrative. CNN cuts out this aspect of the day for these American citizens because abnormality would not support the construction of its narrative of September 11th, which as we have seen is so reliant on the myth of the "normal day" in America.

But the president's "normal day" is also disrupted, and it is CNN's obsession with this "normal day" that makes the pinpointing of the disrupted moment so important to cover. While we are told that the president has already been informed of the first airplane hitting the north tower, we see him continue his schedule, seemingly to maintain the day's sense of "normalcy," although his expression is contextualized to be one of preoccupation and distraction. Like the journalists at CNN, he is shown to be professional, and he, too, has a hunch that the event in New York is not an accident. The interruption by his chief of staff, Andrew Card, with the information of the second airplane hitting the south tower creates the defining moment of the shattering of normalcy. It is Card's on-screen whispering of this second piece of information that is of importance here, because CNN was not able to capture the presidential reaction to the initial announcement of the first incident. CNN is able to cover the moment Bush is told that another plane has hit the south tower and therefore makes the event an important issue. Garrett's voice-over tells us that the president now understands, and Bush is shown to shake his head in the affirmative as if agreeing with Garrett's assertion that a war on terrorism has now begun.

Instead of making a few general statements about education, the president now makes general statements about the events in New York City. He makes a statement about a national tragedy that has occurred in America, about the apparent terrorist origin of the attacks, and about America's intolerance for terrorism. He leads the assembled at the school in a prayer and adds, "May God Bless the victims, their families, and America." Instead of flying back to Washington, he, as Garrett informs us, begins "this amazing daylong odyssey across the middle of the country." As the president is whisked back to Air Force One, we are shown armed military men on the streets en route to the airplane.[15] The president of the United States, the most powerful man in the world, is kept away from his home and office in Washington. His location in America must be secret because he is no longer safe. Soon Air Force One is shown in flight, its right wing flanked by two fighter jets for protection. Garrett informs us of what the president's advisors back in Washington tell him: to stay where it is safe on Air Force One until what is at the "bottom of all this" can be determined. They tell the president of the United States, "Don't come back." The president, who follows this advice, is shown, freeze-framed, waving to the press pool on board his jet, as if he is making his departure from public view.

The "normal day" was interrupted in Washington, D.C., as well. At the Pentagon, American Airlines Flight 77, en route from Dulles to Los Angeles International, has crashed into the Pentagon, creating a huge explosion, a great ball of fire, and smoke billows like those we have already seen twice in New York City. Here the "normal" reaction of firefighters arriving on fire engines to put out the fire seemed to have no effect. "It was like a cruise missile with wings," states a witness as he describes how the plane hit the Pentagon. While people were already at work in this bastion of American military might, meaning they had started their "normal day" heading into the building to conduct the business of American power, they are now encouraged to get out by some people inside who have understood that there has been an attack on the building. Instead of conducting work, they are brought to a standstill looking at the spectacle. Finally, they are told by security people to "run, run, run" away from the building. At this time, hundreds of people thought that another plane was heading for the Pentagon. CNN Pentagon correspondent Jamie McIntyre has a professional hunch while others run for their lives, and he risks his life to get the story. He tells how he tried to place a CNN camera from his office into the hallway of the Pentagon. According to his reasoning, if the building were to continue to burn, CNN would have live and exclusive pictures of the burning building from the inside. But, as mishap would have it, he did not have enough cable.

Across the Potomac, the congressional "normal day" was also interrupted. CNN congressional correspondent Kate Snow recalls that although the Senate and the House had gathered in session, the members walked out of their offices and off the floors. Another plane was believed to be headed toward Washington, D.C. Snow tells us that she ran away from her place of work. The film now shows people running away, and we hear a voice yell out to citizens, "Stay away from the Capitol." The speaker of the House and other top leaders of Congress had been quietly evacuated. In the meantime, the White House and its grounds are being evacuated. When sending news crews away, a security guard yells out the statement "No choice! No choice! Right now." Even choice, something that fills "normal days" in the American democracy, has been suspended. One police officer tries to bring "normalcy" back to the White House area by saying, "Go have lunch, do something else. Please." Not only are the usually seen reporters removed from the White House area, but even the often unseen, "downstairs" staff, symbolized by the evacuating cooking staff, is forced to leave its place of work. As people are shown running away, John King, CNN White House correspondent, states that some people ran out of the White House crying, and that, for the first time in five years, he saw Secret Service agents with automatic rifles around the grounds. The White House has always been a place of American power and policy, a place of news and information, and a place of touristic gawking and admiration, but now one Secret Service agent announces to people, "This is not the place to be." The "normal" tone of the town seemed to have changed. "Everything was different. Everything was different," states John King.

The film turns the story and our attention back to the events in New York at this point. The World Trade Center towers were an American architectural marvel. While other cities boasted of their tallest buildings, New York City could boast of *two* awesome towers that were, at the time of their construction, the tallest in the world. These great giants were anchored deep into the ground and housed great business organizations of American capitalism and the global economic order. While they were built not more than twenty-five years earlier, they had been adopted as landmarks of New York. The city skyline could no longer be imagined without them. However, the mythic character of the towers was changed on that day as well.

David D. Gilmore discusses the characteristics of monsters in his book devoted to studying and understanding them. Gilmore points out that depictions of monsters across cultures show that they loom large and tower over human beings, providing a symbol of paternalism over the populace. Monsters have gaping maws known often to emit great roars or to spew fire and smoke, while their sharp teeth rip human flesh apart as they devour mankind in ghoulish meals. Their appearances blend and blur cultural boundaries, and they harbor inimical attitudes toward humankind. Gilmore further notes that monsters may cause feelings of horror and are to be feared; however, they also capture our awe and are revered.[16] *America Remembers* seemingly plays upon this point to create these very feelings of horror, fear, awe, and reverence regarding the World Trade Center towers. It is fair to ask ourselves, "Were WTC 1 (north tower) and 2 (south tower), as they were often referred to, man-made monsters that were highly tamed and designed to serve humankind practically, aesthetically, and egotistically?"

In the beginning scenes supplementing Larry King's memories, pictures of the Twin Towers are shown. The two buildings are shot from the street below. The slow, spinning pan of the camera shows their enormous scale. Their giganticism and the spinning of the camera cause a sense of dizziness for those who dare to size them up. But these were gentle giants, places of work and sites of entertainment. People were struck by their powerful importance; they admired them for their seemingly perfect symmetrical beauty; they were empowered by their architectural triumph over the land and nature; and they were drawn to them. At the end of King's reflections, we see an aerial view of the two colossi distinctively towering over the urban sprawl and penetrating the hazy atmosphere of New York City. While Gilmore may imagine monsters that were grotesque, evil, and retrogressive, these disciplined Frankensteins were intended to be picturesque, benign, safe, and modern, and never, never expected to be otherwise.

But once the two airplanes crashed into the facings of the towers, they became the evil monsters that Gilmore describes. The airplanes opened huge, dark orifices in the buildings that Phil Hirschkorn describes as many floors high and many floors wide, thereby creating deformities. The explosion of jet fuel created an incinerator (Hirschkorn tells us it was a fire of about 2,000 degrees Fahrenheit) that spewed forth thick black smoke and melted steel. Office papers blew out of the jagged holes, and the broken facings of the buildings looked like teeth around these gaping maws. Carol Lin calls their newly acquired look "disturbing." CNN anchorman Aaron Brown is shown overlooking the monsters from afar. What were once shown as sleek towers standing out in the New York City skyline for all to admire, Brown calls now "a grotesque sight." People no longer have pleasured wonderment on their faces when they look up at the towers, instead looking at them with shock, disbelief, and fear. Spinning camera shots peer straight up at the towers and give a new view, a view that is horrific. Masses of people move hurriedly away from them. Meanwhile, people also run away from other American architectural Goliaths. Kate Snow told us earlier in the film that she ran away from the Capitol because she did not want to die. Places of work have become places where one could get killed. More ghastly still, the film captures the moment when people become stuck on the higher floors of the north tower, frantically waving for help. They are trapped inside the raging beasts, and their only choices are to jump to their deaths or be engulfed in flames and smoke. The photographically blurred bodies sadly fall to their horrific deaths. While we are unable to personally experience these final moments of their lives, the shock and screams of those below are replayed and let us feel sympathy for them. The World Trade Center towers are no longer sights of pleasure.

While the New York City rescue teams are shown getting ready to confront the monsters and to save those humans inside them, the south tower begins to tumble down, unleashing clouds of smoke, ash, papers, and debris. The reaction of the people below shows how horrifying this monster has become. Recalling scenes from *Godzilla* and other monster movies of urban destruction, CNN shows the city dwellers and workers running for their lives, away from the destruction that rushes to overcome and consume them. People are heard screaming and children crying. However, unlike the monsters in the archetypal Culture Hero myths that are often destroyed by "good," these monsters have robbed the New York City rescue teams (posthumously designated as "heroes"), far too soon, of their abilities to contain them or to bring them down. As Hirschkorn notes earlier when arriving on the scene, "To us it just looked like a big fire. You never thought the buildings were going to collapse. You thought the fire was going to be put out." The brightness of the sun, Arce tells us, was blocked out, and the day turned to night. What she once noted as the deafening roar of fire engines and police cars arriving at the scene to re-tame the monsters and to reestablish "normalcy," now became deathly silent.

Yet Gilmore says that we stand in awe of monsters because they are our cultural "super-id." We fear them because of their punishing effect on us, but we are fascinated with them because they unleash the raw emo-tions and desires of our ids. The monster says "no" but also says "yes" to our perverse desires to observe no limits, respect no boundaries, and attack and kill without compunction. The monster is a sadomasochistic pleasure of the human conscience. Susan Sontag also describes the horror and pleasure of disaster in the images of science fiction films. According to Sontag, there are certain "aesthetics of destruction, with the peculiar beauties to be found in wreaking havoc, making a mess."[17] She also states, "One can participate in the fantasy of living through one's own death and more, the death of cities, the destruction of humanity itself."[18] She notes that this pleasure soothes us by lifting us out of the unbearable humdrum of life or distracts us from real or anticipated terrors by an escape into exotic dangerous situations, which have last-minute happy endings. But at the same time, terrors neutralize what is psychologically unbearable, thereby inuring us to them. She is particularly concerned with our secret and playful desire for and acceptance of nuclear disaster.

On September 11, 2001, the falling towers were horrific sights. A single viewing was effective enough to cause a turn of the head in disgust and collective depression. CNN, however, replays these sights again and again, and the resale of such images in DVD format allows us to play, back up, and infinitely replay these images. After the monstrous south tower is shown to fall, a section of the wall of the Pentagon falls, and then we are indulged with images of the north tower collapse. The presentations of these collapses are interesting when compared. In the Pentagon case, no commentary accompanies the images of its collapsing wall, nor is there a close-up view of the horrifying effects. The Pentagon incident seems to be added to show the devastation in Washington, D.C., similar to what oc-curred in New York, but, since its scale pales in comparison, it is glimpsed and, without CNN commentary, is forgotten.

In the north tower's collapse, we are shown the twin image of what we saw moments before in the collapse of the south tower. Presentation of the events in this way may indicate strange aesthetic motivations, as if the first incident was shown for its quality of the "incredible," and the latter incident is shown for the qualities of repetition and "fascination." Here, Brown recaps what is happening for us. Images of the destructing south tower are replayed from different angles while Brown announces the appearance of a mushroom cloud (provoking imaginings of nuclear disaster). Different scenes of the streets of New York are shown covered in ash and debris, which Arce calls a "blizzard," implying nuclear winter. Later she explicitly compares the effect to a nuclear disaster. Many people are filmed as they walk around coughing, hobbling, and covered in a monotone color of gray (suggesting the survivors of a nuclear disaster). The desire for the nuclear imaginary, for the "plausible-impossible," is satiated.

What was first described as an accident, then as intentional plane crashes, Brown now calls "attacks" that have put us into the "midst of an extraordinary catastrophe." When the north tower collapses in front of our eyes, Brown recalls how he went silent for a bit to "let people watch it." And while at the time of the original broadcast he believed that it was something that defied words, he now tells us that while he has seen many bad things in his career as a journalist, he has never seen anything like this, "certainly not in my country." But his retrospective description acts as an invitation to the audience to see this again and again, to view it now as an even greater anomaly, to possibly revel in the pleasure of disaster and destruction with more pictures of the buildings' collapse, encroaching mushroom clouds, ash-covered streets, twisted architectural skeletons, and staggering, gray human figures. The play and replay now have made the World Trade Center towers into monsters of breathtaking beauty that have crushed the "humdrum" of the "normalcy" of days. Their astounding falls over and over again make us look to the aesthetics of their destruction and inure us to the terror of those who just jumped out of the windows or those who were buried underneath their collapsing floors. To think of these victims might prove to be too unbearable. Now the whole experience can be seen as a spectacle choreographed to the dubbed-in music on the DVD.

And while CNN does recapture the importance of people as the center of the story, the film concentrates on the stories of the living and again replays the images of the two towers, from the plane crashes to their final collapse. The tales of survivors are told and retold through cut-and-pasted

personal tales of the event. And yet these tales are still impersonal, because the people who relate them are not identified by captioned name
like the CNN employees. But we must remember that these tales are only
part of the story and provide a skewed recollection. Many experiences,
like those of the people who perished, have been excluded, and, to recall Omer Bartov's point, not because they did not want to be saved but
because chance was paramount.[19] Pictures from inside the buildings are
displayed. In an interview "with a guy," as Brown calls him, this "guy" retells his escape from inside, where there was darkness, smoke, screaming,
and fear. Brown tells us how he thought this was an incredibly powerful
story, of which there must be thousands, and to which, he assures us, he
could listen, as each would be as compelling to hear as the first. And while
we watch the mass exodus of people from their city, we are given a final
overview of the city of that day, which is hidden behind a smoking cloud,
with the Statue of Liberty standing almost alone.

Even though the World Trade Center towers may have become sadis-
tic monsters, they, partaking of the duality of monsters that Gilmore describes, are "victims" as well.[20] CNN's reporting reminds us that they are
fatally wounded versions of our friendly giants, and their wounds were
inflicted "on purpose" (Arce). The attacker has been able to avoid our
gaze while doing the evil deed. Sometime in the middle of the story of this
ordeal we are told that the towers fell victim to monstrous human beings:
"hijackers," later known as "terrorists." In the midst of this revelry in the
aesthetics of disaster, another plane, United Airlines Flight 93, en route
from Newark to San Francisco, is announced as being "hijacked." The
events of September 11th are updated and upgraded as information is unfolding, and the screen frames of CNN's reports change as well. The first
images of the north tower are contextualized with on-screen frame captions from "Breaking News: CNN Live" to "Breaking News: World Trade
Center Disaster" to "Breaking News: Reports of Plane Crash into World
Trade Center Tower" or "Breaking News: Voice of . . . ," with a specific witness's name announced. Along with a scene showing a woman in Washington running away, the framing captions show "Breaking News: Capitol, Treasury, White House Evacuated." Not until the hijacking of Flight
93 are we explicitly instructed that these "accidents" are actually attacks:
"Breaking News: Attacks against Targets in New York and Washington"
and "Breaking News: America under Attack: Terrorists Crash Hijacked
Airliners into World Trade Center, Pentagon."

The myth of the "normal flight" is overturned again, along with the myth of the "classic hijacking," but now with an aesthetic of its own. CNN shows us the radar representation of Flight 93's route, with CNN anchor Miles O'Brien reporting. The plane moves across the mapped screen "way out, all the way out toward Ohio, and then took a drastic 180 degree turn, was headed clearly for Washington, D.C., when the crash happened in Pennsylvania. It's, I think safe to say, a prominent target in Washington [that] was the goal." This continual quest to pinpoint critical turning points becomes part of the CNN September 11th narrative: the exact moment when we first heard of the crash into the north tower; the moment and facial expression when the president was informed about the events in New York; the precise frame of the second plane hitting the south tower and the third hitting the Pentagon; and the specific moment when Flight 93 turns, heads back east, and crashes. This effort of pinpointing shows that there is an obsession of isolating critical moments in the disruption of the myth of the "normal day."

The common strategy of dealing with a hijacking included getting the plane to land safely, getting the airplane to an isolated airport location, determining the identity of the hijackers, keeping the airplane on the ground while winning release of the passengers, wearing the hijackers down with negotiations, and, if necessary, using law enforcement action to overcome the hijackers to save the lives of the passengers. Now this strategy had become obsolete. The hijackers no longer played by the rules of the game. They no longer took airplanes to negotiate for a list of demands. They had taken the airplanes, our own American assets, and used them as missiles to attack American landmarks. While hostages were in the past used as bargaining chips, they were now being used to increase the death toll. We are told that the hijackers of the fourth plane are "terrorists" armed only with the simple tools of red bandanas for masks and box cutters to commandeer the craft. Their weapons were not the type that airport security routinely looked for on a "normal day."

The first step to a "happy ending" on a "normal day" would have been to get Flight 93 to land safely. However, CNN cautiously celebrates its deadly and obliterating crash in Pennsylvania and makes it into a moment of relief, gratitude, and commemoration. After having been informed that it is "safe to say" that Washington had been the target of the airplane, we may now admire the destruction of the airplane in the images of a mushroom cloud (estimated by an unnamed witness to rise to at least four to five hundred feet in the air), broken pieces of metal (that collapsed in on themselves), and a smoldering crater. We are even encouraged to marvel at the totality of the destruction because, as we are told, the flight data recorder was buried fifteen feet inside the crater. We may celebrate the destruction of Flight 93 because it never made it to Washington, D.C., to destroy another American landmark and kill innocent people on the ground. We are invited to revel in quiet relief over its destruction in a serene green field in Shanksville, Pennsylvania. While the old myth of the "normal hijacking" would require that passengers sit back and not endanger others by attempting to retake the airplane and commit acts of heroism, passengers on Flight 93 broke the "normal" rules. Due to their resourcefulness in making telephone calls in flight, the passengers were able to identify the real monster: Arab terrorists. But breaking the rules alone is not enough to rejoice over. CNN correspondent David Mattingly tells us that the key here was that, in light of the life-and-death situation making all the usual rules void, the passengers gathered information using the modern technology of their cellular phones, shared the information with authorities and family members on the ground and among themselves, and opted, above all, to take a vote, affirming democracy in the face of death. Their fighting back is celebrated as pure American heroism thrown in the face of these terrorists, because they had armed themselves with democratic principles. The fact that the passengers used the democratic principles as weapons has turned them into heroes of the Classical Hero Myth. They are, to borrow from Gilmore, "braver, more dauntless, and stronger than ordinary men, as well as supremely virtuous."[21] Although they died in the process, they acted in the interests of the American community and democracy. Mattingly tells us that we should honor the site of their destruction as the "first victory of the War on Terrorism." They are a collective and no longer need to be identified by their individual images, experiences, or personalities. They can be imagined, as shown in the film footage, as identical, Americanized wooden angels staked in the ground at Shanksville. Four images, however, are deemed important to reveal. The photographs of four male American passengers, who are believed to have been the leaders of the passengers confronting the hijackers, are shown: we see a man kissing a child, another man posing for a snapshot, another interacting with a loved one, and the last of the four smiling. But without their names, they become a quick set of images displayed more as a contrast to the previous set of four images of the hijackers/terrorists, who are shown in black-and-white snapshots, either suspiciously averting their eyes or unsmilingly staring into the camera.

Now, the buildings can be surveyed as victims of "zealot, terrorist pigs," to quote one eyewitness. America, this eyewitness says, "will persevere." The audience is now galvanized to look at the Arab enemy with anger. While her words may be just the raw and emotional reaction of a survivor, the American president is shown to contextualize this eyewitness's feelings in a more official, diplomatically controlled manner, instructing us to view the enemy with proper patriotic anger. While at Barksdale Air Force Base in Louisiana, the president announces to the world, "Make no mistake. The United States will hunt down and punish those responsible for these cowardly acts. . . . The resolve of our great nation is being tested. But make no mistake. We will show the world that we will pass this test."

As Bush moves about the Midwest in Air Force One and the press pool on board is shown to strive, professionally, for accuracy in taking notes of exact times of historical moments, his moves add to the imagination of disaster. When the president of the United States arrives at Offutt Air Force Base in Nebraska, we get to see him being escorted into an underground DefCon bunker. While Americans have known that these bunkers existed and have been imagined in our science-fiction movies, as *America Remembers*'s audience, we now actually get to see one used in a real crisis. An elite group of people is escorted to an average-looking blockhouse. The high-powered figures in suits go through a door and disappear down a staircase. A soldier closes the door behind them and locks them in, and the sign on the outside panel of the door says, "WARNING: Restricted Area." They have entered what Major Garrett calls "an underground, fortified, concrete-reinforced war command center created for the nightmare of a nuclear attack." Later in the film, John King talks of how unusual it is to have three fighter jets flanking Air Force One. King says that in this case it was "as you see in the movies." These photographs not only exemplify the aesthetics of disaster, but also the aesthetics of the power and elite status of the American presidency, and such aesthetics boost the aura of this American president.

Sandra Silberstein looks at the use of ceremony and rhetoric to establish Bush as president of the United States during the aftermath of September 11th. Silberstein points out that the administration gained from September 11th because the legitimacy of the presidency had been contested after the Florida voting debacle in November 2000.[22] Here, too, in CNN's presentation of three pictures and the use of rhetoric accompanying them, we can see CNN's making of the president through the aesthetics of disaster. While Vice President Dick Cheney and prominent White

House staff and cabinet members are shown huddled together over a telephone in a secured facility in Washington, Bush is shown on Air Force One, talking on the telephone in solitude. The pictures imply that this president is giving directions and orders to waiting administration members. As the pictures are seen, the president's words "I have been in regular contact with the vice president, the secretary of defense, the national security team, and my cabinet" are played to contextualize the visuals. The third picture shows him under protection during, and in command of, a doomsday scenario—the "nightmare of nuclear attack" mode—without the danger of nuclear fallout. While some have questioned the appropriateness of his disappearance from sight on that day, a continuation of the questions about his inadequacies as president, CNN shows Bush as firmly being the commander-in-chief at all times.

The nuclear holocaust theme is played further as CNN shows us the aftermath of the New York City attacks. We are shown the collapse of WTC 7, a forty-seven-story building, which was effected by the collapse of the two giants before it. WTC 7's collapse creates a billowing plume that envelopes the city streets. Fire continues to rage in the surrounding buildings. Arce walks through the streets during these postattack moments and now provides a remembrance narrative of her walk. Her walk through the streets recalls the classic films of nuclear disaster. Arce calls it a "nuclear winter," and it does in part reflect the conventionally imagined image of nuclear winter taken from H. G. Wells's description of the dead Earth in *The Time Machine:*

> The darkness grew apace; a cold wind began to blow in freshening gusts from the east, and the showering white flakes in the air increased in number. From the edge of the sea came a ripple and whisper. Beyond these lifeless sounds the world was silent. Silent? It would be hard to convey the stillness of it. All the sounds of man, the bleating of sheep, the cries of birds, the hum of insects, the stir that makes the background of our lives—all that was over. As the darkness thickened, the eddying flakes grew more abundant, dancing before my eyes; and the cold of the air more intense. At last, one by one, swiftly one after the other, the white peaks of the distant hills vanished into blackness. The breeze rose to a moaning wind. I saw the black central shadow of the eclipse sweeping towards me. In another moment the pale stars alone were visible. All else was rayless obscurity. The sky was absolutely black.[23]

The New York streets at the site (later to be held in popular esteem as "Ground Zero"), which earlier were places of great traffic, have now become still. Human sounds from the buildings have been silenced. Traffic lights no longer signal, a McDonald's restaurant is shattered and empty, and a snowlike substance whirls in the air and on the street. Arce demonstrates how the pulverized building materials, and maybe even incinerated bodies, flurry like nuclear snow as she sifts through the accumulated flakes, almost playfully, for the camera. She describes the real-life scene as a fictional movie scene from the 1983 ABC television film *The Day After*.[24] She finds photographs, parts of desks, papers, and a résumé submitted by an applicant for work in the World Trade Center among the debris, but the humans to whom these items once belonged are missing. Stores, once vibrant with colorful displays of merchandise, are covered in this "snow," so that all color is erased and washed in white and gray, interrupted only by the burning orange fires. "Normal day" commercial products covered by this "snow" appear to be tomblike artifacts from thousands of years ago. The blue skies have turned black. Arce recalls trying, at one point, to estimate the number of dead, but she admits that she finally gave up from being overwhelmed by the thought and just accepted that every single life lost is painful.

Jeff Greenfield, CNN senior analyst, talks about New York Mayor Rudy Giuliani's comment "This is as horrible as you could imagine, and maybe worse." Giuliani is shown announcing the high number of rescue team officers that the city had lost. Paula Zahn's television report from that evening's news is played and tells of some 265 firefighters confirmed dead and 85 police officers missing on the first night. The destruction is, we are told by a witness, "enormous." A policewoman is shown vomiting in reaction to the scene. A lone fireman is photographed, and the camera's focus widens to show his insignificance in relation to the destroyed building's rubble in which he stands. It is a sight that only a deity can fix. And so, an anonymous witness calls for God in this time of despair: "God save our country and what was done to it today."

However, the silence of nuclear winter that Wells speaks about is not actually there in New York City. The perverse desire for a nuclear disaster, which this CNN contextualization seems to promote, dangerously inculcates "a strange apathy concerning the processes of radiation, contamination, and destruction"[25] as it overturns our imaginations of such a disaster with a false simulacrum.[26] There are still the human sounds of rescue teams and people trying to help. The city still seems to be alive, and the mayor even comes with his entourage to view the destruction. Giuliani's scolding of a question-shouting reporter for failing to put his mask on for protection, while the mayor himself does not wear one for his own protection because he is answering media questions, almost becomes the "unintentionally funny" dialogue that Sontag warns against when we desire disaster too much. While the aesthetic may call for nuclear disaster to be there, the real thing thankfully falls short.

The real events have been constrained by the framework of the fictional nuclear movie, to which we have all become inured. At the same time, the lines between this disaster and nuclear disaster have become blurred. Could it be that CNN lets us believe that we can absorb and survive nuclear disaster? Kim Newman, in her study of apocalyptic genre films, says that in these films nuclear disasters are generally presented as being a result of a loss of control and that these catastrophes are caused by politics and politicians or are accidentally triggered by a lone madman or malevolently functioning machines.[27] However, *America Remembers*'s September 11th nuclear-scenario-evoking narrative presents an intentional effort having no just cause, a premeditated and surprise attack made by a group of Arabs, and with no connection to American politicians or politics.

The toppling of the myth of "normalcy" and "invulnerability" foreshadows the next scenes illustrating the American spirit's resolve, which the president discussed earlier. In essence, America's resolve results in either the righting of our myths or the adjustment of our myths to ultimately make us stronger, more courageous, and of greater righteousness. While the nation has been attacked with an almost-nuclear effect, America is depicted as amazingly strong enough to survive the attacks and brave enough to confront them and the enemy.

Once the narrative stage of the attacks has been completed, there is now the need to prepare the path of America's renewal in the September 11th narrative. If the "normal day" changed in America, then this change must be pondered, even grieved, and a new and better "normalcy" must be established. A pre–September 11th period and a post–September 11th period are created, with the latter period not starting later, on September 12, but beginning on the evening of September 11, 2001. In this post–September 11th period, there is the urgent need to create "normalcy" as proof that America will not surrender to the enemy's attacks. The Capitol Building is shown with its flag flying at half-mast to mark the grieving period of the nation. On the evening of September 11, 2001, the members of Congress are shown assembled on its steps singing "God Bless America." The pre–September 11th period was filled with a contentious political atmosphere that drew sharp lines of political enmity between Republicans and Democrats, right and left, conservative and liberal, religious and secular, prolife and prochoice, majorities and minorities, and rich and poor. This post–September 11th assembly of legislators is portrayed as representing a bipartisan desire during "this critical moment in U.S. history" to come together and sing with a unified voice, to unite under patriotic proclamations, to uniformly affirm the existence of God, and to put America and its public servants on the side of righteousness. Best of all, we are told, this was an impromptu circumstance: "I think," says CNN congressional correspondent Kate Snow, "they learned something out of being stuck in the same bunker together for a few hours."

And while a new "normalcy" is being established, a part of the old "normalcy" must be reestablished as well. Congress had to present itself as still in existence. CNN correspondent Wolf Blitzer informs us that routine is reestablished with the arrival of the president back in Washington on the evening of September 11. He informs the audience of the routine procedure of the arrival of presidents in Washington, D.C. Once Air Force One arrives at Andrews Air Force Base, the helicopter known as Marine One flies President Bush to the south lawn of the White House. The audience sees the president arrive on the south lawn just before the sun sets and just as Blitzer noted. Bush, it is announced, plans to address the nation that evening. Furthermore, as the president is shown descending from the helicopter, greeted by military and staff members, and just before walking into the White House, John King tells us that establishing "normalcy" was paramount:

> Their goal at the moment was almost more than what he said, [it] was to show the president was at the White House. And they feel secure enough that the president can be at the White House. Um . . . psychology, if you will, to the country that the government is there. There is stability. There's a crisis, but . . . that they're on top of it. Just the picture of the helicopter landing and the president walking in, then the president on television from the White House, was meant to convey a message of "You know, they tried to knock our government out — they failed."

Since America is still in a stage of shock, the president of the United States makes a speech to the nation that taps sympathetic emotions and also sets the course for the nation. He closes the evening of September 11, 2001, as an abnormal day, a historic day, and a day when a new "normalcy" is established. His speech, therefore, is not about anger, fury, fear, and vengeance, but about spiritual strength, calm, remembrance, the challenges ahead, and positioning us on the right side of God and goodness. The audience hears a small portion of the speech the president gave as it sees nighttime images of the changed New York City skyline and the increased police protection around the United States Capitol Building.

New "normalcies" emerge with the sunrise of September 12, 2001. On September 12, the sun is not shown in the film to rise serenely like it did the day before. Rather, the sun is shown big and bright in the sky. The light rings around its disk shape make the sun look as if it is pulsing and almost as if it is glaring angrily down on the Earth, implying disapproval from the heavens of what has happened. The sky of the new day, however, is shown to be as clear and blue as the day before. And yet, on September 12, we see the smoldering cloud that emanates from New York City. The beautiful skies, the smoldering cloud, and CNN's morning headlines announcing "WAR!"—only twenty-two hours after the first attack on the north tower—remind us that there are new "normalcies" in the American life. As the camera shows Ground Zero, CNN analyst Aaron Brown informs us, "If yesterday was surreal, today is all about reality. Today we can start to get a dimension of all of this." City officials are said to have no idea of what kind of reality they were going to confront. Reality means to face the devastation, to begin rescue and recovery efforts, and to show that America cannot be beaten. This means that Americans have to make great efforts to recapture the routines of the "normal day." As presented by CNN, creating a new "normalcy" involves an effort, sometimes strained, to bring back the routines of the humdrum days that were taken away. At the Pentagon, CNN reports, employees open its daily business at 0800. The Pentagon has to assure Americans and the world that despite the devastation it is still in operation. At the Capitol Building, the dome light burns all night long. It indicates that Congress is still in session. Kate Snow tells the audience that the burning light acted as a symbolic beacon, showing her that "Democracy was still okay." At Ground Zero, rescue workers are on schedules of twenty-four hours on duty, and twenty-four hours off duty. They are not going to give up until they are 100 percent confident that one of their own is not buried alive.

However, reality showed that "normalcy" could not be so easily re-established. While vehicles were always a part of city life, the overabundance of trucks and police cars moving about is different. Streets are closed, and it is difficult to get around. There is no place to get food, and nobody is going to work. The stock exchanges are closed, and the bustle of Wall Street is shown to be absent. All public schools in New York City are closed. "There was no business for anyone to do," says Aaron Brown. Rescue teams approach the devastation as if it is a "normal experience" like the Oklahoma City bombing, where people would be found injured but alive, but this is not the case here: either people are okay, or they are dead. Television broadcast scenes from September 13, 2001, show an evacuation during working hours of the Capitol and a building in New York City being evacuated due to bomb scares. We see people move outside, hold each other, and cry out against the "terrorists." Even CNN's working day is affected, as Paula Zahn and Aaron Brown are caught up in the interruption of their work routine. As Brown states, "We were living, all of us, in this odd cocktail of fear and rumor . . . and vulnerability."

Part of the new reality, or the "abnormality," of the day is, as CNN correspondent Christiane Amanpour states, the newly posed questions of America's citizens: "Why? Who are these people? Why do they hate us?" CNN had tried to answer this question earlier in the film. Between the scenes showing the president giving commands from his bunker on September 11 and Arce describing nuclear-like catastrophe, CNN tried to find out who was at the bottom of these attacks. *America Remembers* shows subtextually that CNN, in its investigative professionalism, was already trying to answer these questions before other Americans were even asking them. CNN correspondent Nic Robertson is shown to have been in Kabul, Afghanistan, at the time of the attacks in America. Kabul seems to stand in direct contrast to New York City. Stereotypically Third World, the city is in the throes of its "normal day" filled with a populace of bearded men and veiled women, open-air markets offering simple commodities such as greens and tomatoes, jumbled traffic, and low-height, monotone buildings. Robertson is one of only a handful of journalists stationed there, proving that CNN was in the right place at the right time. He notes that these other journalists were "instinctively" coming to CNN to get information as to what was happening back in the United States when the news of the attacks was filtering out. Robertson's description of the Taliban as "forcing" the reporters to stay in one area contrasts with the seemingly free rein that reporters enjoy in the United States, illustrated by Arce's stroll in the "nuclear winter." Wakil Ahmed Mutawakel, the Taliban foreign minister, is shown to give his press conference four hours after the attacks, and CNN's textual framing of the event marks CNN's "being there" for this important moment. Mutawakel gives his condolences to the United States, but he still denies Osama bin Laden's culpability, even after the audience has heard John King claim that bin Laden is a suspect. Mutawakel is said to have stated that bin Laden could not have engineered these acts because they were too large for such a simple man. Alternatively, CNN suggests the possibility of bin Laden as the culprit by showing him from prior video footage as he takes aim at a target with a rifle, thus highlighting his "evil" and dangerous Arab proclivities. The film also punctuates Mutawakel's words with prior footage of bin Laden reclining and resting in a cave. The Taliban leadership not only is portrayed to be dishonest but to be going out of its way to be dishonest and mockingly sympathetic to the United States.

Nonetheless, now that Amanpour has posed the American citizenry's questions of "Why? Who are these people? Why do they hate us?" pictures appear of angry Muslims in Asia, gathered in crowds in front of the camera, holding up the Arab bin Laden's picture in support of him. The pictures show bin Laden lecturing his audience with exploding American F16s drawn around him, and the Muslim crowd holding the pictures brandishes its own firearms. Robertson reports to us that bin Laden is someone that certain followers of Islam in this part of the world might behold as a leader. In contrast to the harmonious and soothing picture of the congressional gathering on the Capitol steps or the crowds of New Yorkers and Washingtonians acting in fear, these crowds are hot-tempered, wild, and shouting threateningly in unison. The use of this footage suggests their hatred for the United States as being so culturally deep that even children are among their ranks. In the next scene, the White House confirms that the culprits are indeed bin Laden and his associates, and the president announces that these attacks carried out deliberately against "our country" are more than terrorism—they are acts of war. The Arab bin Laden is now officially marked as America's enemy for the narrative, the Taliban are marked as his associates and his devious protectors. Wolf Blitzer adds to this by informing us that the president was forceful in his statement, shocked like all of us, and angry. Blitzer's explanation tells the audience that the new "normalcy" means an official acceptance of our own anger toward the enemy and a confident commitment to fight him.

While up to this point we were afraid of the Arabs because they threatened and overturned certain myths, we now have to find things that they did so that we have something to which to attach our anger, something for which to hate them. A large number of dead was, earlier in the film, something to desire secretly in imaginations of disaster. The tide is now turned on September 13, 2001, when we see that these victims had faces, names, and families, although most of these are quickly panned by the CNN camera. *America Remembers* demonstrates how the families tried to locate their loved ones by posting snapshots and hanging posters of the "missing" in public places and by standing in lines for information. This quick camera pan is partially successful in enlisting our awe and deep emotion for the number of dead and the drama of their demise. Family members are singled out as they tell of how they talked to their loved ones who were trapped in the World Trade Center towers and awaiting their deaths or of how their loved ones began their "normal days" and were never seen again. But the scarcity of names, descriptions, and full details prevents us from hearing the stories of September 11th. Elizabeth Cohen, CNN correspondent, talks of how she and her colleagues did not want to thrust themselves on these people in an informational feeding frenzy, but rather wanted to stand to the side with journalistic professionalism and not get in the way of those who were grieving. Nevertheless, it was the need of the families to try to locate their missing loved ones that led them to seek out CNN and tell their stories. When Cohen talks to Vinny Camaj, who lost his father, a World Trade Center window washer, and hears what Vinny wants his father to know if he is listening, Cohen breaks into tears but still continues to report. Tears of loss are shown running down the cheeks of a woman who pleads to know if anyone has seen her daughter. A mother is shown crying as she pleads for a son to come home. A woman who commits herself to continue to search for a family member and a man who talks of a loved one who has a daughter at home cry as well. Cohen talks of how she has dealt with such stories for two days. Special people, "fathers, mothers, sisters, wives, husbands, children," have all been lost to these people, according to Cohen. In encouraging us to cry with these people and to accept the emotional wounds of the tragedy as our own, Cohen adds, "I don't know how you can help but cry."

The sense of familial loss and tragedy is also shown to have affected the president of the United States. On September 14, the designated National Day of Prayer, the nation's political elite gather in the National Cathedral to attend a presidential ceremony. Sandra Silberstein discusses the importance of this ceremony and the rhetoric of the speech in establishing

George W. Bush as the national chaplain, one of the many important roles of the president of the United States.[28] CNN's presentation shows how important this event was in terms of how the president delivered his sermon and less in terms of what he actually said. We are told that the touching ceremony, highlighting the emotional tie between former president George H. W. Bush, his father, and the presidential son, "was the most interesting moment of the day." After George W. Bush gives his sermon, his father reaches over to grab his hand — a scene played in slow motion — as if to say, "Good for you."

The president also encourages us to be angry with the enemy when he tours Ground Zero later that day. The "I can hear you" speech was a moment when the president not only saw the devastation of the World Trade Center himself, but felt the pain, anger, and resolve of the American rescue workers. His statement that he can hear the American people is followed with the statement "And the people who knocked these buildings down will hear all of us soon." The crowd roars with cheers and chants of "USA! USA! USA!" because, as John King notes, the people understood him. What they obviously also understood was the presidential call to violence, and their reaction was an approval of such violence. While in a press conference held on September 17, 2001, the president demands justice. In a later scene showing him addressing Congress on September 20, 2001, he announces,

> [1] Tonight we are a country awakened to danger and called to defend freedom. . . . [2] Our grief is turned to anger, and anger to resolution. . . . [3] Whether we bring our enemies to justice or bring justice to our enemies, justice will be done. [Applause]

While these words were part of a continuous paragraph in real time, *America Remembers* breaks the sentences apart, showing the reaction each one symbolizes. To visualize the president's first sentence, CNN shows the activity, technology, muscularity, preparedness, ferocity, and professionalism of America's Special Forces. To illustrate his second sentence, CNN shows the painstaking efforts of rescue workers at Ground Zero and Giuliani's statement "These terrorist cowards are not going to be allowed to break our spirit. In fact, they made a very big mistake." And in response to the third sentence, CNN shows senior analyst Jeff Greenfield saying "It was a perfect speech. I don't know that any president has ever given a speech where more of the country wanted him to succeed." The president gives us confidence in wanting the most decisive form of punishment for the Arab enemy. He promotes the rawest, and now purest, form of justice. As America was feminized in its passivity during the sneak attack, the president now establishes his masculinity and that of America, adopting the Wild Western style of "Dead or Alive." Such a call for practices of the Wild West represents a sanctioning of "cowboy" or vigilante-style violence for himself and his administration. This Wild Western call to justice sanctions aggressive action that "def[ies] public law and constitutional principles in order to 'do what a man's gotta do.' "[29] His call taps what Slotkin describes as the "savage war," a characteristic episode of the Myth of the Frontier, where violence must become absolute, exacted more savagely than the savage himself can do, and where the savage enemy must be exterminated. The return to "normalcy" will only come as a regeneration through violence.[30] Therefore, it is not surprising to see CNN's presentation of a "Dead or Alive" poster of bin Laden. The poster is partially defaced, and foul-languaged graffiti and the words "Kill, Kill, Kill!" are written on it.

The presidential call for action against the Arab enemy and his Taliban cronies is absorbed by the American culture. The New York Stock Exchange (NYSE), on September 17, reopens with a resounding commitment to defeat bin Laden and to avenge what he did to the nation. The American economy was put on hold with the symbolic closure of the stock exchanges. While the American economy had been strong and surging forward in the years prior to September 11, 2001, the Arab attacks were effective enough to close the stock exchanges down for a number of days. The NYSE chairman Dick Grasso makes a boisterous pledge, as shown to the film's audience, "We are one country today committed, unified in the pursuit to find and punish and obliterate those who committed that horrible act against this great nation." Those on the bell platform and on the trading floor applaud him and his stance. "Our heroes," members of the rescue teams, are seen opening the marketplace with the ringing of the bell. A blond policeman with bulging and tattooed biceps, the visual epitome of superhero strength, masculinity, male aesthetics, and over-determined phallic power, stands out as he seemingly blesses the resurrection of America's economic might.[31] He stands as a visual representation of anchorman Lou Dobbs's words that there was an absolute determination to not let terrorists shut down our financial system.

And while this may make us feel good for the moment, the Arab attacks and the fear, loss, and uncertainty they caused became a catalyst for the market's devastating free fall. At the time when Grasso's bellicose speech was being made, CNN's Dobbs was on the floor and sensed the nervous tension of the traders. The film shows Dobbs reporting on this mood. The American capital markets, once the locomotive of all economies in the world, now lost a trillion dollars over the next five days. CNN shows the distraught look of a civilian as the dollar amount is announced as "ripped out" of the economy. While this news sets the tone of an imagined 1929 crash, CNN stops short and does not show frenzy or the panic on the trading floor that such a crash would likely entail. Instead, CNN encourages us to believe that America can absorb and endure a crash like this. A final aerial view of Ground Zero, before this segment, closes with a screen fade-out implying that bin Laden and his Arab hijackers were able to bring down the once unbeatable American economy just as they did the World Trade Center towers. CNN reminds us that the Arab enemy can destroy American lives, landmarks, and the economy. The Arab enemy can make Americans afraid for their lives and the lives of their children. And the Arab enemy would like to drive us from modernity to an anachronistic way of life similar to that from which he sprang in the Third World.

At long last, we are shown the recoveries of some dead bodies from Ground Zero and glimpses of funerals, which, as we are told, were in the hundreds. The scene of Ground Zero was enough to make CNN's Paula Zahn sick to her stomach, as she stated earlier in the film. Aaron Brown notes that what he remembers most is the unidentifiable smell, a possible blend of jet fuel, burning steel, and human flesh. He describes the smell as horrible and as lasting for months. New York City became spiritually small as everyone dealt with the same tragedy, and it was, we are told, sad. "Oh God, it was sad," says Brown. The pictures of countless invited funeral attendees are shown along with those who seem to be unconnected with the deceased and just choose to look on and give their respect. Children who are too small and still too innocent to understand are shown to have to deal with the realities of death. The funerals, Zahn states, were a part of the healing that went on in America at the time. On September 23, 2001, people pack Yankee Stadium to partake in another memorial, "A Prayer for America," where Mayor Giuliani reminds us that "we have met the worst of humanity with the best of humanity." And he reminds us to assure our children not to be afraid, because it is safe to live your life in America. It is, in other words, safe to return to "normalcy."

"Normalcy" begins with the spiritual camaraderie of American patriotism and the affinity of all Americans with "New Yorkers." The identities, as noted by Silberstein's study, of being American and being a New Yorker merged; American pride and New York pride were synonymous.[32] CNN also presents images of the American flag accompanied by voices singing patriotic songs in conjunction with images of New York and the presence of Mayor Giuliani. Aaron Brown talks of how he is reborn as a New Yorker. He now admires the city's people and has fallen in love with the city itself. New Yorkers have committed themselves to rebuild the American city.

"Normalcy" also begins with the reestablishment of boundaries and terms that position Americans on the side of "good" and the Arab enemies on the side of "evil." "Normalcy" is the erasure of postmodern blurriness and the establishment of categories of distinction, and a renewal of Orientalist discipline. This requires the Orientalist power of defining the Arab enemies as terrorists and cowards working against Americans defined as heroes and loved ones. This requires the clarity of American doctrine as newly defined by Bush: "Every nation in every region now has a decision to make. Either you are with us or you are with the terrorists." This means building a coalition of nations against bin Laden and his Taliban cronies. This brings back the "normalcy" of wartime conduct from the first Bush administration based on a coalition of nations that is committed to fight the savage enemy, who does not use or respect the civilized conduct of war. Amanpour talks of how the administration knew that it needed a coalition to take military action and how remarkable this coalition-building was at achieving success, as it was quickly and seamlessly put together. CNN shows brief views of Bush meeting with heads of state. The film's narrative talks of the hard work of coalition-building while clips are presented showing Secretary of State Colin Powell enumerating to reporters a long list of countries that have been contacted or are in a diplomatic conference. CNN's John King announces that Powell made more than eighty phone calls to different countries in ten days. While most of the heads of state that meet with Bush are dressed in Western-style business suits or military uniform (representing Western democratic states and even Arab states), those that are with the terrorists are robed and bearded Taliban. The Taliban leadership refuses to give up bin Laden without evidence, if at all, and calls for *jihad* to be waged by all Muslims if the United States and its allies attack any Muslim state. The Taliban and their supporters are shown as mobs in the street burning Bush in effigy and destroying the American flag. They scream out bin Laden's name in reverence.

"Normalcy" also means that there must be a break with the multicultural utopianism that demeans America and elevates Others through cultural relativism. Bush is shown assuring the nation that it is in a fight against "evil" and not against Islam. No religion is being held accountable for September 11th, only "evil" is being taken to task. To make this message the new "norm," John King reminds us that it requires applying the political rule of "repetition, repetition, repetition." And with this, Attorney General John Ashcroft presents the Arab faces of "evil" to the press. Each mug shot is correlated with the flight each individual commandeered and crashed. These Arabs become Others with the use of the disciplinary science of suicide bomber profiles. "These people," as CNN correspondent Mike Boettcher calls them, are rational killers with plans. The video clips of these "evil" Arabs are shown as the Arabs make their way through the security checkpoints of the American airports at this point in the narrative. The clips show that the Arabs are frightening because they can blend into our lives; and while we can see them, as the camera shots attest, we cannot distinguish them from ourselves. These Arabs are "scary," according to Boettcher, because they act rationally and are therefore hard to spot out in our world. And although they appear to act rationally, they are willing to take their own lives and those of thousands of innocent people.

"Normalcy" begins with getting back to work. Bush is shown addressing a crowd of airline workers in Chicago at O'Hare International Airport. While he speaks of America's spiritual strength, an airplane flies overhead with the sounds of thrusting jet engines, indicating a strong return to scheduled airline service, and the crowd cheers and waves American flags in affirmation. The Bush administration knew, as John King tells us, that it was imperative psychologically and economically to demonstrate that it was safe to fly again. Bush tells the crowd that his administration is serious about airline safety in America. "Get on the airlines," states Bush. "Get about the business of America." And Miles O'Brien, CNN anchor, tells how "You got the impression from listening to him that it was our patriotic duty to get back to work, to get in the air, to take that business trip even if you really don't want to."

"Normalcy" means accepting that those victims who have yet to be found will not be found. It is a sad time, we are told. "It is an inevitable stage. You have to reach it," consoles CNN correspondent Martin Savidge. Such an acceptance is admitting to ourselves that our dreams and fantasies of finding those missing must end. But as the film's scenes of recovery efforts and of a banner that overlooks Ground Zero show, there is the commitment "We will never forget!" As we labor to never forget, the quick camera pan of photographs posted to find loved ones is actually an act of forgetting. Such a pan and a montage of quick images of destruction limit detail and, at the very least, tell us nothing of who these people were. Instead, the CNN cameras attempt to package the "experience." Moreover, the call to "never forget" is actually a euphemism to justify the violence of the next scenes of *America Remembers:* "Operation Enduring Freedom."

"Normalcy" also becomes the desire for or acquiescence to the War on Terrorism, of which Operation Enduring Freedom is the opening chapter. We are reminded that this war is not something we asked for, but rather an answer necessitated by the acts of terrorists. Attesting to this, one soldier points out, "We train every day for war and pray for peace." American troops are shown practicing combat in a "prepare mode." They are in a state of readiness to answer the nation's call. This call can only be given when the commander-in-chief orders it. On October 7, 2001, the president of the United States did give this order, and we are shown his explanation to Americans that he has done so. Such action is an attempt to reestablish a portion of the "old paradigm," which Benjamin and Simon described: "Terrorists would be dealt with decisively . . . and every effort would be made to ensure that justice would be rendered when harm was done."[33] Moreover, CNN tells us that not only did the news agency anticipate the presidential order, but, like the military itself, CNN was on the air and prepared to report when the order was given. The American desire to exact violence is satiated through the aesthetics of war and military technology. Up-to-date radar screens appear to demonstrate our power of gaze over the enemy, high-flying bombers can be seen to manifest our reach over the enemy, a powerful missile launch and a daisy-cutter bomb drop prove our mighty punch, and the appearance of mushroom clouds on enemy land fills the screen to give us the pleasure of lethal and effective retaliation. The Pentagon provides gun-camera video footage of a building being isolated and decimated with precision, along with the interpretation "The video speaks for itself." Such an image of exactitude seems to stand in opposition to former cultural depictions of the Arabs' inability to kill with precision. And so, this Pentagon clip is played in juxtaposition to the wide view of Ground Zero, where devastation is widespread and still smoldering on November 1, 2001. The slow but resolute efforts of rescue workers, almost two months later, seem to be minuscule compared to the vastness of destruction. The Arab enemy's interest in killing thousands only heightens the Arab spray of death, in contrast to the Americans' penetrating and single shot when killing. However, a different situation may have occurred here and may, therefore, upset the trope of Arab inaccuracy. The coordinated taking of American airliners, the precision penetration "like a spear" into the north tower, the likeness of one of the attacking aircraft to our own weaponry in being "a cruise missile with wings"—these characterizations actually fit into witness descriptions of the Arab attack and CNN's presentation of it. And yet, here CNN reverts to the old representation of the Arabs in order to sugarcoat the promotion of American retaliation. Interestingly, CNN shows the American daisy-cutter bomb, notorious for its wide, indiscriminate devastation, being dropped, but CNN does not show its explosion or its effect.

Secretary of Defense Donald Rumsfeld reminds us that "normalcy" through military action will require patience. He states, "In the end, war is not about statistics, deadlines, short attention spans, or twenty-four-hour news cycles. It's about the will to see this through to certain victory." But that is not how CNN reproduces the war: we get quick glimpses of paratroop jumps, explosions, and military troop and vehicle movement. Within moments, Mazar-i-Sharif is taken on November 9, Kabul falls on November 13, hundreds are captured, and the Taliban are defeated. Only one significant American death (CIA agent Mike Spann) is noted. The CIA is honored for work done in its dealing with "very bad guys" overseas, and the shocking discovery of an American man, identified as John Walker Lindh, who had joined the Taliban and possibly adopted the ideology of Osama bin Laden, is cursorily presented. Within eight minutes, *America Remembers* spans months to show that America is able to absorb its grief, respond, and rout the Arab enemy and the Taliban. CNN's Amanpour assures us that the Taliban, as characteristically expected, "essentially turned tail and ran."

"Normalcy" is also liberating Afghanistan's people. The American victors are greeted by "liberated" crowds, something that did not happen in Vietnam. Returning to "normalcy" means a lifting of the draconian burdens imposed by the Taliban regime. The Afghani people are now free to come out into the streets, to open their marketplaces and shops, to play music, to clap and dance in the streets, to display sexy portraits of women, to drink Pepsi Cola, and to consume other American products. "Normalcy" means to reinstate the smile, to lift the veil, to let children be children again, and to shave the once compulsory beard. "Normalcy" means an imposed revaluation of life as expressed in the posted proverb "Whatever you don't like for yourself you must not like for others." And while the return to "normalcy" also brings the loss of an untold number of lives, and destroyed buildings and property, with it, "normalcy," we are promised, brings a "net positive effect" to Afghanistan. Amanpour assures us that even though life in Afghanistan may not be perfect, "it is incredibly and immeasurably better."

However, the regeneration of violence in the War on Terror is a vague venture because the war itself may have an indiscernible enemy. The enemy is, we are told, the Arab Osama bin Laden and his Taliban cronies, but they do not sport military uniforms. They are far away and, in some cases, within our borders in terrorist cells. Since they are hard to distinguish from among the mass of Third World Others and maybe from ourselves, their ambiguity is a threat to our Orientalist disciplinary gaze and knowledge. The Taliban may be bin Laden's associates, but they are only our collateral enemies. Without more information about them, CNN presents the problem of how to sweep all these enemies into one category. The enemy is summarily shown to be everywhere and surrounding us, as illustrated in the scene of a military marker that indicates their presence in every direction. But bin Laden is the man that needs to be destroyed. The American president must remind us that he will get him, and Bush demeans him by describing him as uncivilized and even beastly. "In terms of Mr. bin Laden himself, we'll get him running. We'll smoke him out of his cave. And we'll get him eventually." CNN adds to this description of the uncivilized enemy by showing portraits of a coldly staring bin Laden and by showing him walking into a cave and closely gathering with his lieutenants so they may eat from a communal dish with their hands, as if in an animalistic feeding frenzy. Here again, as in *The Exorcist,* the evil Arab emanates from the *vagina dentata* of the Third World land. The American unleashing of bombers and mushroom clouds in the Tora Bora mountain range where such caves exist is thereby justified and welcomed against this interstitial spirit/being of man/animal.

Despite the American efforts, bin Laden just fades away and his fate is still unknown. This, too, becomes a new "normalcy" in the post–September 11th era. Bin Laden may still exist, somewhere out there in the wilderness, and may still defy our disciplinary attempts. Moreover, most of the Taliban members just steal away to their villages and farmlands. They disappear into the population and countryside and continue harboring their beliefs and ideologies. We must accept bin Laden's presence as a new part of the "normalcy." We must understand that he and his deputies may come back to threaten us again one day.

As if our inability to find bin Laden and his associates were not enough to define a new "normalcy," the microbiologic threat of anthrax in America, represented in photographs produced by microscopy, creates more fear and panic. The anthrax scare is displayed as an alien microscopic invasion. We see images from Cold War, U.S. Army file-film footage showing American medical research teams struggling to isolate and contain millions of potentially fatal organisms in a single drop of liquid culture that can be easily ingested through breathing. The arrival of anthrax was a return to the biological concerns of twenty-five years earlier. CNN medical correspondent Dr. Sanjay Gupta tells us that anthrax was a topic mostly put to rest in modern medical education until now. Tommy Thompson, Health and Human Services secretary, is shown telling the public that a diagnosed case of contamination in Florida seems to be an isolated one. Bob Stevens, an American tabloid journalist, had contracted the virus and died, and the pictures of CNN's *America Remembers* show the resulting closure of his newspaper offices, the arrival of FBI figures in white body suits and respiratory masks and tanks to investigate the offices, and the need to supply medical treatment to those who might have been exposed by affiliation with Stevens. CNN correspondent Susan Candiotti tells us that she learned that "this is serious."

The subsequent mailings of anthrax in letters to NBC, the *New York Post,* and Senate Majority Leader Tom Daschle further spread the scare. CNN's Paula Zahn talks of how the tainted letters affected those in the journalistic profession, and Aaron Brown relates how they made all Americans question their normal routines of touching things and opening letters. This new scare disrupting our "normal day" required the president to make the statement "Our nation is still in danger, but our government is doing everything in our power to protect our citizenry. The American people need to go about their lives." The presence of anthrax in our postal system also spreads fear that CNN helps create. As the bacillus travels through the post offices, CNN shows voluminous stacks of mail being rapidly sorted by machines. The audience's gaze cannot focus on any particular letter because of the rapid sorting system and because many of the letters are similar in size and color. Second, CNN dramatizes the scenario of an envelope held in human hands against a black backdrop. One hand taps it repeatedly, and with each tap the envelope emits a white powder, meant to simulate spores of *Bacillus anthracis* being emitted in the air (but remaining purely fictional) from "normal" handling. The images show that this was a scenario never anticipated in our "normal" lives, methods, and thoughts. And while the American government was busy treating those in the higher echelons of the government offices and the media corporations, it was not treating those who worked in what was being used as the distribution network of the anthrax: the post offices. Many clips of CNN reports are replayed to show how the crisis was spreading. There was even concern that the president of the United States might have been exposed, and Bush is shown stating "I don't have anthrax." Not knowing how many letters were out there and not knowing who was next to receive one, the American people are shown to be changing their lives by not accepting mail. A picture of a picket fence gate, a symbol of suburban American bliss, with a note posted and stating "No mail, please. Thank you," is intended to show how the fear and "normalcy" of abnormalcy had reached from government buildings and corporations to the American suburban landscape.

The presentation of the anthrax attacks is interesting because, while the Bush administration cannot explicitly place the blame on Arab enemies, Arab culpability is implied. CNN chooses to highlight the threats in the letters that imply Arab anger: "Death to America. Death to Israel. Allah is great." The letters are addressed in English. Although the English writing may play on fears of mimicry, Arab culpability is never proven in *America Remembers*. In fact, the incident is dropped without further investigation because it is shown to have a victorious ending for America. The idea seems to be that the Arabs can be the culprits because of their threats and because of their recent attacks on America. Arab culpability for anthrax is further bolstered because of our realization that the enemies may be living among us, maybe even have been for years, and may be hiding behind the English language. But more than this, Arab culpability finds its greatest support in the belief that the Arabs are dangerous because they are effective in overturning the myths of "normalcy" in America. The upsets in our daily routines of mail delivery, in the business of government and corporations, and in human correspondence match with the previous upsets of all the daily routines in American life as shown in *America Remembers*'s narrative. The anthrax incidents come just after seeing military movement against bin Laden, his jihadist fighters, and his Taliban associates and therefore imply the possibility of a devious counterattack on their part. CNN then assures us that there were only five deaths and only eighteen were infected. Meanwhile, America proves able to contain the problem: thirty thousand people are treated, and the Arab-like desires to turn back the scientific clock and to kill masses of people, if those were the motives, are frustrated. The victory lies in the fact that a portion of the myth of "normalcy" is defended—American science prevails.

The post–September 11th era, as shown by *America Remembers,* requires a new "normalcy" in America, where daily routine must accommodate the possibility of the Arab enemies living among us and readily poised to attack us. American routines are shown to include a stepped-up police and military presence, the presence of guns in public places, long lines at airport security checkpoints and more intrusive body searches, airport terminal shutdowns over security breaches and subsequent travel delays, and reports of possible anthrax scares. Vice President Dick Cheney is quoted as saying "The enemy is resourceful and ruthless. We have to assume there will be more attacks." Airplanes and post offices are shown to be new points of vulnerability. Also shown are American monuments, nuclear power plants, chemical plants, shipping ports, bridges, and even our borders. Attorney General John Ashcroft is quoted as saying "We urge Americans, in the course of their normal activities, to remain alert and to report unusual circumstances or inappropriate behavior." Director of Homeland Security Tom Ridge announces, "We think it is very important since September 11th for America to remain on the highest possible alert." And Ashcroft also says, "We will be on alert indefinitely." Americans on the street claim that their lives are now filled with anticipation, vulnerability, uncertainty, fear, and a sense of being overwhelmed. When CNN correspondent Martin Savidge adds that paranoia became part of our life as we sensed the enemy was on every street corner, the film shows two men with dark and swarthy complexions under a streetlight, seemingly having the capability of making us vulnerable. The fear of sleeper cells, those who come into America, blend in, and dare to lead normal lives until they are ready to strike at us, spurs the government to round up suspicious people and those in violation of immigration law and to hold them incommunicado. Fear of news itself becomes part of life as the White House asks news agencies not to indiscriminately play messages from Osama bin Laden because he may be speaking in code to such sleeper cells. But as CNN Homeland Security correspondent Jeanne Meserve points out during an aerial view of New York City, "The thing that is so scary is that it is impossible to protect all the things they need to protect." In essence, the Orientalist hope to discipline and control the Arabs is dashed.

However, CNN is able to prove the usefulness of such news video not only as good news information, but also as journalism's effort to fight bin

Laden. The tape showing Osama bin Laden and his lieutenants gloating over the destruction of the World Trade Center towers becomes a smoking gun that proves his culpability for masterminding the attacks on September 11 and his evil character in his celebration of killing Americans. This tape becomes a possible weapon against bin Laden because it is the evidence that he might not want to have shown. In it, Arab men, whom Aaron Brown calls "toadies," kiss bin Laden and sit dressed in their robes and head covers. They revere him as a hero because he killed three thousand Americans. Bin Laden is shown bragging about the preparations, calculations, and optimism that were necessary in order to kill the most Americans possible. Brown says bin Laden's boasting makes you want to retch. CNN is able to show the American public that bin Laden is not only the culprit but absolutely evil. This tape acts as a point of closure for the American psyche.

Such closure also comes when on December 22, 2001, American Airlines Flight 63, en route from Paris to Miami, is almost blown up by Richard Reid, who tried to ignite a bomb carried in the sole of his shoe. The foiling of his plan to destroy the airplane and to kill Americans becomes a new symbol of alertness and reaction to those who wish to do Americans harm. Courageous passengers and crew members are said to have wrestled Reid to the ground, immobilized him, and not allowed him "to get away with it." The upshot, as this response is intended to show, is that Americans have adapted to the new "normalcy" without crippling fear, without leniency, and with heroism.

Americans today live their new "normalcy" as a result of a historical rift that was created from what is known as "September 11th." Secretary of Defense Rumsfeld is shown reminding us that on September 11, the Pentagon and World Trade Center towers were burning, the Taliban were in power, and Afghanistan was a safe haven for terrorists. Today, the fires are finally out, the Taliban are driven from power, and their leaders are on the run. The president is quoted as saying that this is a year that will never be forgotten and that those lost in the attacks and on the battlefields will remain in our prayers. Mrs. Spann, wife of the CIA agent killed in Afghanistan, reminds us that her husband, assumably like other Americans, was heroic not because of the way in which he died, but because of the way in which he lived his "normal" life. September 11th, according to Paula Zahn, had shaken the core of who we are as a people. She points out that Americans will never live with the degree of innocence they once had, and Aaron Brown states that Americans are no longer protected by the historical myth of the isolation and protection given by the oceans. CNN anchorman Bill Hemmer reminds us that the people in the towers could have been any one of us. But September 11th also was a time when, as Elizabeth Cohen states, hope and love of the human spirit in America prevailed even in the most difficult of times. No matter where you live or who you are, Aaron Brown points out, you will know where you were on September 11, 2001, and what you thought.

CNN's *America Remembers* uses some of the very characteristics of the "evil" Arabs that the fictional narratives of the "evil" Arabs used before September 11, 2001. The "evil" Arabs attacked America and remain elusive to our gaze. They are destructive, fearsome, and backward. They are willing to break all boundaries of civilization, try to turn America into an image of their abode, and care nothing about how we may suffer. Most of all, *America Remembers* purports to lay bare the heinous motivation of the "evil" Arabs, whose efforts are directed at threatening and usurping American myths. In this film, such myths are the many myths of "normalcy" in our American lives and practices. Meanwhile, the American hero is also devised. Silberstein talks of how September 11th established George W. Bush as a legitimate president of the United States. She uses the rhetoric of his speeches to prove her point. But the real hero portrayed in the narrative of *America Remembers* is not George W. Bush, but CNN itself.

Silberstein points out that in the post–September 11th era, returning to "normalcy" also meant that consumerism had to be encouraged and so consumerism became a patriotic activity. Instead of planting victory gardens, as Americans did in World War II, it was more patriotic to buy material items in this recent era. While conspicuous consumption seemed trivial and self-absorbed, buying things American meant that you were defeating the enemy.[34] The DVD of *America Remembers* is one of those very consumer items that helped encourage such patriotism. CNN journalists are no longer the antipatriotic and feminizing culprits of America in wartime depictions. Instead, they prove themselves as supporters of the War on Terror and help America defeat the Arab enemies. Theories of representation borrowed from Holocaust studies tell us that attempts to represent are destined to fall short and thereby diminish the totality, importance, and tragedy of the experience. However, the Orientalist project, as Ella Shohat reminds us, must name, discipline, and categorize that which is encountered in order to remove ambiguity; to exercise power; to possess, to master, and to defeat Otherness with a masculinizing effort.[35] The events of September 11th were so new, overwhelming, and unbelievable that while CNN's Sanjay Gupta states that they cause one to be at a loss for words, *America Remembers* attempts to map that terra incognita of experience. Hence, CNN appropriates September 11th. And although this film purports to be about September 11th, it falls terribly short and rather creates a subjective narrative that excludes the totality of the event itself and legitimates CNN as a voice having authority over the events. The story-as-it-is-told is about CNN and not about the story-as-it-happened. While CNN professes to be an ultimate source of information, it never answers the American questions that Amanpour poses: "Who are these people? Why are they doing this?" To do so would require much more than a ninety-minute DVD. It would require, as Ziauddin Sardar and Merryl Wyn Davies suggest, self-reflection about our American culture, our political and commercial methods, and our egocentric narrative practices.[36] Sara R. Horowitz points out that our narratives of historical events create heroes to whom we cling and villains from whom we disassociate ourselves. They thereby free us of questioning our own racism and complicity in the events.[37] *America Remembers* constricts us to the narrative of the "evil" Arabs. To accept CNN's rendition of September 11th as historical documentary without critical investigation and examination is to be complicit with the narrative and to dismiss the racism and prejudice against Arab peoples found in our tales about them and ourselves.

Conclusion

*S*OUTH *Park,* the animated comedy series of life in a "quiet little red-neck, ho-dunk, white-trash mountain town" of Colorado, is known for its vulgar characters, violent scenarios, and appeal to America's Generation X. *South Park* can also be, and I hail it as endearingly such, an informative barometer and lampoon of when the discourse of popular culture has just gone too far, taken itself too seriously, and lost sight of its real status. Many times it seems that nothing is sacred on *South Park.* Environmentalism, race and religion, harassment and political correctness, sex and sexuality, poverty and famine, SARS, WMD (weapons of mass destruction), Christ and Christianity, patriotism, bodily noises and defecation, murder and death, and even Barbra Streisand, to name but a few, are lampooned seemingly unmercifully by the jumpy, rigid, and simply animated characters. As a good rule of thumb, if a topic makes it to *South Park,* then its popularity in American culture has probably reached levels of absurdity and deserves a reality check. If a topic has become entrenched in our cultural discussions, then it begs to be dismantled, and *South Park* will assist. While *South Park* may seem juvenile and cruel in dismantling serious and important cultural topics, the show in reality is brilliant when it forces us to see that the discourse about these highly sacred icons may be just paper tigers with as little dimension to them as the images of the characters in the series themselves. *South Park* shows us firsthand that lampooning these icons, and laughing in the process, will not blind us, deform our appearance, or strike us dead on the spot. Best of all, *South Park* makes us stop, reflect, and question how the topics emerged in our cultural discourse with such popular acclaim as to make us reverent, concerned, or fearful of them in the first place. And to show the good-naturedness of *South Park,* the animated series is aware of itself as becoming too popular as well. *South Park* scripts often lampoon the frenzied marketing and overly hyped popularization of cartoons, television shows, and movies, as in their treatment of *Terrence and Phillip,* a fictional Canadian television

South Park: Bigger, Longer & Uncut (1999). Kenny, Cartman, Kyle, and Stan go to the skating pond to tell the other kids of South Park that they have just seen the amazing new R-rated Terrence and Phillip movie: *Asses of Fire*. Photo courtesy of the Academy of Motion Picture Arts and Sciences.

show without which the kids of South Park, Colorado, who will go to great lengths to be able to see it, just cannot live.

The Comedy Central program series *South Park* is so successful that a cinematic film was produced in 1999. To convey to the American audience that all limits were off in this film, because some things just cannot be shown on television, the film has the sexually suggestive title *South Park: Bigger, Longer & Uncut*.[1] In this film, the kids find a way to sneak into the newly released, R-rated movie version of Terrence and Phillip's *Asses of Fire*. This is a jape on the hype surrounding *South Park*'s own movie version, and the boys — Stan, Kyle, Kenny, and Cartman — are a reflection of the very audience members now watching *Bigger, Longer & Uncut*. Terrence and Phillip's R-rated movie is filled with "nothing but foul language and toilet humor," and the easily impressionable boys become so elated with their experience that they indiscriminately take on the vocabulary, sometimes unconsciously. While the other kids in the town are impressed with the boys' experience, the South Park parents are horrified and quickly convince themselves that their children have been adversely influenced by the movie and are now addicted to swearing. "This is what happens when toilet humor is allowed to run rampant!" states Kyle's mother. The parents organize themselves against the movie and, in their frenzy, look further outward to a more powerful source of villainy: Canada. In the meantime, the children are forced to go through deprogramming, and an experimental "V-chip" invented by Dr. Vosknocker is implanted into Cartman's brain as a way to curb his swearing impulses. Every time he swears, the V-chip gives him a painful, high-voltage shock.

The movement Mothers Against Canada (MAC) takes on momentum and reaches the point at which the U.S. government kidnaps Terrence and Phillip for corrupting America's youth and condemns them to death in a televised forum that also includes a star-studded USO (United Service Organization) show hosted by Big Gay Al. Since Terrence and Phillip generate most of the Canadian GNP, the Canadians attack the United States because the kidnapping of Terrence and Phillip is tantamount to an attack on Canada's national economy. The United States, in turn, declares war on its neighbor to the north and interns all Canadians living in America in death camps. The war becomes a fight for the children's future and the establishment of a smut-free environment. The boys, who are now sorry for all the trouble they caused, attempt to reason with the out-of-control adults, get involved in politics themselves, and try to stop the war.

The *South Park* movie also cleverly instructs the American Orientalist audience on the use of the "evil" Arab as character. Kenny, the poor boy of the town, is killed — he is also killed in every television episode — and finds himself condemned to Hell for throwing a rock at a bird, staring at women's breasts every day, and shirking his responsibilities to attend church and choosing to go to the *Terrence and Phillip* movie instead. During his fall into Hell, he encounters a host of frightening demons and tortured spirits, including Adolf Hitler, Mahatma Gandhi, and actor George Burns. Ultimately, he encounters the "evil" Satan himself, a red-toned, muscular, horned, bearded, and cloven-footed beast that chases, snatches, and binds him in preparation for being tortured. Satan's first appearance is a performance of terror in which his deep and bellowing voice and towering stature scare the daylights out of the poor boy. However, Satan himself, the most frightening spirit and purveyor of evil, is no match for the real evil that lurks in this horrific inferno: Saddam Hussein. Saddam Hussein has been killed by a pack of wild boars and now lives in Hell, and he has entered into — get this — a homosexual relationship with Satan.

The movie's narrative usurps the Christian myth that Satan is the seal of evil, the ultimate sinful spirit, and the most repulsive of all souls. The narrative ridicules the overly determined rhetoric and American myth of today that Saddam and the Arabs are the ultimate images of "evil" on Earth. Saddam's gay relationship with Satan is abusive, and not because Satan is so bad, but because Saddam is so very wicked. The big and buff Satan has, in reality, the temperament of a marshmallow, the sensitivity of a romantic, and the softness of a teddy bear. His voice is as mellow as can be, and in his big musical number he sings in the passionate falsetto of a pop singer. He admits that he is Saddam's "cream puff." Satan is sentimental and hungers for attention, love, and respect. He misses the romantic past when he and Saddam would stay up all night and just talk. Now Saddam only wants sex, and Satan questions Saddam's lovemaking preference for being always "from behind." Maybe, Satan wonders, Saddam is thinking of someone else when they make love.

Saddam, on the other hand, is more evil than Satan. He is ruthless, uncaring, and selfish. He is oversexed, more sexually impetuous than Satan himself, using Satan as a fuck-buddy rather than showing him the respect due to the master of Hell, let alone a lover, a partner, or a significant other. He says he loves Satan, but his deeds speak differently than his words. Satan accuses Saddam of spending "so much time convincing me I was weak and stupid, that I . . . believed it myself." Saddam is the top in the relationship, and Satan is the passive bottom and Saddam's "bitch." Saddam does not communicate well with the distraught Satan, and he does not nurture Satan's emotions. As Satan's self-help book states, "Saddam Is from Mars, Satan Is from Venus." Saddam demeans Satan in front of others, as in the scene in which Kenny is tortured. Saddam pushes Satan away from the controls of the torture machine to which Kenny is bound. He tortures the little boy himself, and, since torture turns on this "evil" Arab, he asks Satan to rub his nipples during the procedure. This disrespect toward Satan's work upsets Satan, and, rather than speaking in the frightening voice with which he first scared Kenny, he whines at Saddam, "I don't see why you have to belittle me in front of people like that. . . . Well, sometimes I don't think you have any respect for me."

With the war on Earth raging out of control, Satan sees his chance to rise out of Hell and take over the world in an apocalypse when Terrence and Phillip are executed. Saddam, who is always eager to take over the world, finds this biblical talk "hot" and just the type of words that really "turn[s] my [Saddam's] crank." Later, Kenny, now released from the tor-

South Park: Bigger, Longer & Uncut (1999). The war between the USA and Canada rages on Earth. The clash makes way for Armageddon and becomes an opportunity for the gay couple—Satan and Saddam—to emerge from Hell and rule the world. Photo courtesy of the Academy of Motion Picture Arts and Sciences.

turing apparatus, finds Satan crying after a fight with Saddam, and the boy encourages him to leave Saddam. Because of Kenny's words of encouragement, Satan finds the strength to tell Saddam that he is leaving him and going to rule Earth alone. But Saddam breaks Satan's resolve, and wins back Satan's love during his performance of the musical number "I Can Change," complete with dancing harem girls, nargileh, violence, and murder. And while he may have convinced Satan for the time being, when both do come to Earth, Saddam shows that he plans to rule Earth alone. He commands everyone to bow to him, declares that a giant statue of him be erected, and thereby upstages Satan as the ruler of the world for the next two million years.

However, Saddam is defeated in the end, or at least for the time being.[2] During the apocalyptic battle, Cartman receives a high-voltage charge that reverses the effects of the V-chip that once stopped his cursing. Instead of a painful zap to his brain, the V-chip gives him the power to zap others. His vulgar language, once the cause for the war, now saves the day. He begins to call Saddam names that would have curled the hair of MAC, and with his name-calling he exudes lightning bolts that enervate Saddam. Saddam pleads with Satan to help him, and then belittles Satan for his inaction by calling him a "weak, stupid cumbucket." At that point, Satan destroys Saddam by throwing him back into Hell and impaling him upon a pointed rock below. And although Saddam is shown as dead, he still comes back to life to sing with the chorus in the finale. Everyone is happy now. Satan finds his inner solace, he sets the world back to a time before the war, Terrence and Phillip are released and embraced by MAC, parents and children have better relationships, peace is reestablished between the two belligerent countries, and Kenny earns his wings in Heaven.

What does *Bigger, Longer & Uncut* bring to the discussion of Orientalist fear? It makes us reflect on our overuse, to the point of silliness, of the "evil" Arabs in order to produce fear in American popular film and even in daily political discourse. The construction of the "evil" Arabs has more to do with ourselves than the Arabs-as-they-are. We must contemplate how and why we use the "evil" Arabs and reflect on our prejudicial exploitation of them. In essence, our anxiety about ourselves is often reflected in the impotency of our ideological and mythic structures and our heroes. *Bigger, Longer & Uncut* ridicules us with our own cultural folly.

Saddam has become today's quintessential "evil" Arab, although he seems to be in a dead heat with Osama bin Laden, one bigger than the other depending on the political convenience of the moment. *Bigger, Longer, & Uncut* shows us how this "evil" construction of the Arab has gone so far that we have made him more "evil" than evil itself. In fact, the longtime purveyor of evil, terror, and fear in human culture, Satan, is a wimp in comparison to this "evil" Arab. As *South Park* shows, our rhetoric of good and evil, when it comes to the "evil" Arabs, may have gone so far that we ourselves have devalued the ideological structure of good and evil. Peter Stanford states that the Devil is supposed to be "the catch-all character to blame for actions too terrible to ascribe to a loving God and too frightening to put down to dark urges in the human psyche."[3] *Bigger, Longer & Uncut* shows us that we have upended this role of Satan with the character of the "evil" Arab. The South Park residents even invite Satan to feel free to come back and visit them anytime he wants now. And to jokingly convince us that Saddam is so evil that he has no equal, the closing credits tell us that the voice talent of Saddam Hussein was played by Saddam "himself."

Interestingly, *South Park* shows that there is a certain absurdity in our comfort in destroying the "evil" Arab and claiming victory for ourselves. While our Orientalist use of narrative and visual language can create a disciplined Arab, the Arab's wickedness comes to the fore when he defies it by challenging our ideological and mythic structures. And so, we must turn to the prejudicial act to contain him once again. Cartman can only overpower Saddam with language. But his language has to be taken to an extreme in order to overpower the "evil" Arab, and this extreme results in a juvenile silliness of saying bad words. Cartman spews forth a string of rambling and gratuitous words that makes no sense whatsoever: "Fuck! Shit! Cock! Ass! Titties! Boner! Bitch! Muff! Pussy! Cock! Butthole! Barbra Streisand!" The last of these gives him the most powerful of electrical zaps. Only this way of destroying the "evil" Arab will let the world live in peace, happiness, and carefree relationships with flowers, fireworks, and even a killer whale jumping for joy. Swearing, the casus belli, becomes acceptable and even good, and without the "evil" Arab the world performs as perfectly as the finale in a Vincent Minelli musical.

Our latest cultural discourse of national self, since the arrival of George W. Bush's administration and the events of September 11th, relies upon a world that is no longer multicultural, but rather strongly bifurcated between good and evil. The lines have been drawn once again in the latest military endeavor of the United States and its allies against the "evil" Arabs. The "evil" Arabs and the Middle East have become our antithesis, and may continue to be so as our national self is more and more compared to the Other through the nexus of foreign policy. For the foreseeable future, U.S. forces will continue to occupy Iraq, Palestinians will persist in struggling for statehood, and al-Qaeda will continue its call to attack the United States. Oil will continue to be imported from the Arab states, and oil embargoes, some thirty years after the first one, remain a frightening thought deep in the American psyche.[4] Nevertheless, to further deal with the tales of the "evil" Arabs, we are now armed with the awareness and knowledge of Orientalist fear, a way of identifying a discourse, and a new way of seeing our Orientalist inclinations and toleration for our own prejudices.

The illusion is made of at least two images: the easily discernible image of the "evil" Arab and the less obvious image of ourselves. Readers of *"Evil" Arabs in American Popular Film* should be able to look at other representations of the "evil" Arab and, I hope, find it impossible to accept these ethnic and global imaginaries without the other image, that of

SOUTH PARK AND ORIENTALIST FEAR | 255

ourselves, popping into their vision from time to time. Readers should now inquire as to the degree of the prejudicial act involved in the representations of the characters of "evil" Arabs, and I encourage readers to do so. Henry Krips points out that the scopic drive provides complete pleasure when the subject can see (voyeurism) and at the same time be seen (exhibitionism). Therefore, the pleasure in viewing the illusion of Arcimboldo's *The Water,* Ichthyoid Man, and the "evil" Arabs does not come from seeing through the first-level deception alone, but when "viewers look back at what they have seen, thus scrutinizing themselves, and specifically their own roles as viewers. Thus they place themselves and what they see on display."[5] The identification of stereotypes is a beginning foray into and an important part of such an inquiry. Nevertheless, to get closer to understanding how and why we use "evil" Arabs in our cultural narratives and to flesh out the prejudicial act further, we must include inquiries into our own ideological and mythic structures, a move beyond dissecting the stereotypes alone, as a new methodology from which to proceed. Karim H. Karim states in his important book *Islamic Peril,* "The self-awareness of one's own cognitive processes is the first step towards the production of less ethnocentric and more authentic accounts of events"[6] — and, if I may add, of human beings, their lands, and their cultures as well.

Notes

PREFACE

1. *Studium* and *punctum* are terms, borrowed from Roland Barthes, that relate to photography but are also applicable to all visual art. *Studium* is "an average affect, almost from a certain training ... [an] application to a thing, taste for someone, a kind of general, enthusiastic commitment, of course, but without special acuity. It is by *studium* that I am interested in so many photographs, whether I receive them as political testimony or enjoy them as good historical scenes: for it is culturally (this connotation is present in *studium*) that I participate in the figures, the faces, the gestures, the settings, the actions." *Punctum* "will break (or punctuate) the *studium*. This time it is not I who seek it out (as I invest the field of the *studium* with my sovereign consciousness), it is this element which rises from the scene, shoots out of it like an arrow, and pierces me.... A photograph's *punctum* is that accident which pricks me (but also bruises me, is poignant to me)." Roland Barthes, *Camera Lucida*, trans. Richard Howard, pp. 26–27.

2. As a matter of fact, Giuseppe Arcimboldo did paint more illusionary portraits. See, for example, his paintings *The Winter* (1563), *The Fire* (1566), *Herod's Head* (1566?), *The Genius of Cooking* (1569), and *Vertumnus as Rudolph II* (1591), which are reproduced and discussed in Giancarlo Maiorino, *The Portrait of Eccentricity*, pp. 31–83.

INTRODUCTION

1. Samuel Tolansky, *Optical Illusions*, p. 141.

2. Patricia Ann Rainey, *Illusions: A Journey into Perception*, p. 15.

3. J. R. Block and Harold E. Yuker, *Can You Believe Your Eyes? Over 250 Illusions and Other Visual Oddities*, p. 239.

4. Jack G. Shaheen, *Reel Bad Arabs: How Hollywood Vilifies a People*, p. 8. Add to this kit limousines and camels, as in his article "The Hollywood Arab (1984–1986)," *Journal of Popular Film and Television* 14 (1987): 148–149, and oil wells and buying power, as in his book *The TV Arab*, pp. 4–5.

5. Shaheen, *Reel Bad Arabs*, p. 4. Examples of such abuses are numerous and are further discussed in, but are not limited to, such works as Tom Engelhardt, *The End of Victory Culture: Cold War America and the Disillusioning of a Generation*, regarding Native Americans; Ed Guerrero, *Framing Blackness: The African American Image in Film*, regarding African Americans; and Robert G. Lee, *Orientals: Asian Americans in Popular Culture*, regarding Asian Americans.

6. Shaheen, *Reel Bad Arabs*, p. 6.

7. Ibid., p. 33.

8. Ibid., p. 192. Chapter 1 of *"Evil" Arabs in American Popular Film* investigates the narrative and scenes of *The Exorcist* more thoroughly.

9. William Greider, "Foreword," Shaheen, *Reel Bad Arabs*, p. viii. The temptation to use Muslims as replacement villains for the evil Soviet Union is discussed in more detail by John L. Esposito, *The Islamic Threat: Myth or Reality?*, p. 4.

10. Shaheen, *Reel Bad Arabs*, pp. 485-487, 550. Chapter 4 of *"Evil" Arabs in American Popular Film* discusses the racism in *Three Kings*.

11. Gordon W. Allport, *The Nature of Prejudice*, pp. 207-208.

12. Louis Althusser, "Ideology and Ideological State Apparatuses (Notes towards an Investigation)," in *Essays on Ideology*, pp. 1-60.

13. Henry Krips, *Fetish: An Erotics of Culture*, p. 75.

14. Kaja Silverman, *The Subject of Semiotics*, pp. 220-221.

15. Susan Mackey-Kallis, *The Hero and the Perennial Journey Home in American Film.*

16. Melani McAlister, *Epic Encounters: Culture, Media, and U.S. Interests in the Middle East, 1945-2000*, pp. 1, 8.

17. Edward W. Said, *Orientalism*, p. 12.

18. The "impression of universality," according to Allport, is "social support for one's views (whether the support is real or imaginary), [validating] these views and [protecting] the individual from harassing doubt and conflict." Allport, *The Nature of Prejudice*, p. 335.

19. Ibid., p. 403.

20. David D. Gilmore, *Monsters: Evil Beings, Mythical Beasts, and All Manner of Imaginary Terrors*, pp. 18-22.

21. Lee, *Orientals*, p. 3.

22. David Frum, *How We Got Here: The 70's, the Decade That Brought You Modern Life—For Better or Worse*, p. 4.

23. Daniel J. Boorstin, *The Image: A Guide to Pseudo-Events in America*, pp. 4-5.

24. Christina Klein speaks of a "global imaginary" as "an ideological creation that maps the world conceptually and defines the primary relations among peoples, nations, and regions.... In reducing the infinite complexity of the world to comprehensible terms, it creates a common sense about how the world functions as a system and offers implicit instruction in how to maneuver within that system; it makes certain attitudes and behaviors easier to adopt than others." Christina Klein, *Cold War Orientalism: Asia in the Middlebrow Imagination, 1945-1961*, pp. 22-23.

25. McAlister, *Epic Encounters*, p. 5.

26. Douglas Little shows that even American foreign policy leaders and makers were oftentimes victims of their Orientalist outlooks when dealing with the Arabs and the Middle East. Douglas Little, *American Orientalism: The United States and the Middle East since 1945*, pp. 9-42.

27. McAlister, *Epic Encounters*, p. 30.

28. Ibid., pp. 47-55.

29. Ibid., p. 35.

30. There are a number of notable studies providing examples of European and American portrayals of Arabs from the Middle Ages to the millennium years. These include the four works by Jack G. Shaheen noted in this book's bibliography. Others among them are: Matthew Bernstein and Gaylyn Studlar, eds., *Visions of the East: Orientalism in Film;* Steven C. Caton, *LAWRENCE OF ARABIA: A Film's Anthropology;* Norman Daniel, *Islam and the West: The Making of an Image;* Lawrence Davidson, *America's Palestine: Popular and Official Per-*

ceptions from Balfour to Israeli Statehood; Esposito, *The Islamic Threat;* Edmund Ghareeb, ed., *Split Vision;* Rana Kabbani, *Europe's Myths of Orient;* Karim H. Karim, *Islamic Peril: Media and Global Violence;* Little, *American Orientalism;* Cindy Arkelyan Lydon, "American Images of the Arabs," *Mid East* 9 (May/June 1969): 3–14; McAlister, *Epic Encounters;* Hamid Mowlana, George Gerbner, and Herbert I. Schiller, eds., *Triumph of the Image: The Media's War in the Persian Gulf—A Global Perspective;* Edward W. Said, *Orientalism,* and *Covering Islam: How the Media and the Experts Determine How We See the Rest of the World;* Fuad Sha'ban, *Islam and Arabs in Early American Thought: Roots of Orientalism in America;* Faegheh Shirazi, *The Veil Unveiled: The Hijab in Modern Culture;* Reeva S. Simon, *The Middle East in Crime Fiction: Mysteries, Spy Novels, and Thrillers from 1916 to the 1980's;* Abderrahman Slaoui, *The Orientalist Poster;* Linda Steet, *Veils and Daggers: A Century of NATIONAL GEOGRAPHIC's Representation of the Arab World;* and Michael W. Suleiman, *The Arabs in the Mind of America.*

31. Frum, *How We Got Here,* p. 312.

32. Daniel Yergin, *The Prize: The Epic Quest for Oil, Money & Power,* pp. 541–542.

33. "Oil: The Desert Foxes," *Time,* February 15, 1971, pp. 69–70.

34. "Oil: Power to the Producers," *Time,* March 1, 1971, pp. 74–76.

35. "New Reserves of Green," *Time,* January 31, 1972, p. 65.

36. "Facing a Powerful Cartel," *Time,* January 24, 1972, pp. 59–60.

37. "The Croesus of Crisis," *Time,* April 10, 1972, p. 31.

38. One article reports that churches are closed and made into mosques, "everywhere curling, zigzagging letters have supplanted the Latin alphabet," laws based upon Italian and British legal codes have been suspended and replaced with the commandments of Islam, witch hunting and book burnings are rampant, arrests are made without evidence, and professors are fired and bosses' desks are searched for pornography. "Libya: The People's Revolution," *Time,* June 4, 1973, p. 38.

39. "Cash Flood in the Middle East," *Time,* October 9, 1972, p. 78.

40. Ibid.

41. "Israel: The Dream after 25 Years: Triumph and Trial," *Time,* April 30, 1973, p. 45.

42. "The Energy Crisis: Time for Action," *Time,* May 7, 1973, p. 42.

43. "Middle East: Gasoline by Open Fire," *Time,* October 25, 1971, p. 29.

44. "Horror and Death at the Olympics," *Time,* September 18, 1972, p. 22.

45. Ibid., p. 30.

46. "Deadly Battle of the Spooks," *Time,* February 12, 1973, p. 29.

47. "Terrorism: Fatal Error," *Time,* August 6, 1973, pp. 31–32; and "Terrorism: The Wrong Passengers," *Time,* August 20, 1973, pp. 28–31.

48. "Middle East: Terror to End Terror?" *Time,* April 23, 1973, p. 23.

49. Frum, *How We Got Here,* p. 340.

50. "Israel: The Dream after 25 Years," p. 45. In a cartoon in the later November 5, 1973, issue of *Time,* an Arab sheikh, in one hand, holds up an American man (identified as the United States on his hat) with the gas tank nozzle and, with the other, takes U.S. dollars from the American (see Figure I.2 in this book). The caption states, "So much for your bankroll. . . . now fork over your Israeli policy . . !" "Still Tightening the Blockade," *Time,* November 5, 1973, p. 55.

51. "Oil: Libya's 100-Percenter," *Time,* May 28, 1973, p. 70.

52. "Policeman of the Persian Gulf," *Time,* August 6, 1973, pp. 30–31.

53. Stephen Paul Miller, *The Seventies Now: Culture as Surveillance,* pp. 4, 126.

54. "The Superpower Search for a Settlement," *Time,* October 29, 1973, p. 21.

55. "Are the Russians the Real Winners?" *Time,* November 5, 1973, p. 38.

56. "The Arabs' New Oil Squeeze: Dimouts, Slowdowns, Chills," *Time,* November 19, 1973, p. 88.

57. "The Life and Times of the Cautious King of Araby," *Time,* November 19, 1973, pp. 90–95; "We'd Like You to Know," Exxon's eight-page ad in *Time,* November 19, 1973; "Stepping on the Gas to Meet a Threat," *Time,* November 26, 1973, pp. 24–31; "A Time of Learning to Live with Less," *Time,* December 3, 1973, pp. 29–38; "Toward a Winter of Discontent," *Time,* December 3, 1973, pp. 48–49; "Cold Comfort for a Long, Hard Winter," *Time,* December 10, 1973, pp. 33–34; "Euphoria in Algiers, Trouble at the Canal," *Time,* December 10, 1973, pp. 55–56; and "Panic at the Pump," *Time,* January 14, 1974, pp. 15–16.

58. "Cold Comfort," p. 34.

59. "A Time of Learning to Live with Less," p. 38.

60. Ibid., pp. 37–38.

61. "The Souring of the Dutch," *Time,* December 3, 1973, p. 53.

62. "Squeeze on Poor Lands," *Time,* January 14, 1974, p. 18.

63. "The Emissary from Arabia," *Time,* December 17, 1973, p. 34.

64. "Oil Easier, Gas Tighter," *Time,* February 11, 1974, p. 28.

65. "A Time of Learning to Live with Less," p. 37.

66. When *LaStampa,* an Italian magazine, called Gaddafi a homosexual who had forty-eight wives and an ulcer, and slept on a bed of tobacco leaves, the Arab League Boycott Committee threatened to boycott *LaStampa*'s parent company Fiat. "Arabs Slap *LaStampa,*" *Time,* January 14, 1974, p. 29.

67. "Oil Easier, Gas Tighter," p. 28.

68. "Arab Pride and Power," *Newsweek,* February 18, 1974, p. 40.

69. "Letters—Mary Toy, Boston," *Time,* December 10, 1973, p. 4.

70. "Cold Comfort," p. 33.

71. McAlister, *Epic Encounters,* pp. 158–159.

72. Note, too, that the Shah adamantly refused to join the Arabs in the oil embargo against the United States. Little, *American Orientalism,* p. 221.

73. Yergin, *The Prize,* p. 689.

74. "Dance of the Oil Dervishes," *Time,* January 1, 1979, pp. 57–58; and "OPEC's Dangerous Game," *Time,* April 9, 1979, p. 56.

75. Yergin, *The Prize,* pp. 689–690.

76. The Arab caricature as signifier of OPEC is often seen in political cartoons during this period. The kaffiyeh-wearing, bearded, and Semitic-nosed Arab, marked somewhere on his corpus as "OPEC," is often doing something inimical to the multifarious signifiers of the United States. See, for example, the OPEC Arab playing and winning at strip poker with the U.S. Energy Non-Policy bumpkin in "OPEC's Dangerous Game," p. 60, or the OPEC Arab plucking the U.S. eagle in "The Great Energy Mess," *Time,* July 2, 1979, p. 14. Sometimes the Arab caricature is not marked as OPEC or OPEC is not personified as an Arab. However, the correspondence is implied on the same page. See the case where three Arabs, not marked as OPEC per se, are depicted standing in front of a gas line and jubilantly singing to the Americans "This land is your land. . . . This land is my land. . . . From California to the New York Islands." OPEC is the topic of this article: "Oil: The Blackmail Market," *Time,* November 19, 1979, p. 85. In another instance, a screw, marked as OPEC, penetrates the back of Uncle Sam. Accompanying this caricature on the same page are photographs of Arab OPEC ministers in "Here They Come Again," *Time,* December 17, 1979, p. 69.

77. "OPEC's Painful Squeeze," *Time,* July 9, 1979, p. 12.

78. "The Great Energy Mess," pp. 14–22, and "OPEC's Painful Squeeze," p. 17.

79. "More Woes on the Oil Front," *Time,* October 29, 1979, p. 71.

80. "The Crescent of Crisis," *Time,* January 15, 1979, p. 18.

81. "Searching for the Right Response," *Time,* March 12, 1979, p. 28.

82. "Bombs and Ugly Rhetoric," *Time,* April 2, 1979, p. 28.

83. "Iran: The Test of Wills," *Time,* November 26, 1979, p. 20.

84. "The Storm over the Shah," *Time,* December 10, 1979, p. 24.

85. Ibid.

86. "Precautions against Muslim Anger," *Time,* December 10, 1979, pp. 42–47.

87. Engelhardt, *The End of Victory Culture,* p. 270.

88. McAlister, *Epic Encounters,* pp. 199–200.

89. Ronald Reagan, "Address to the Nation on the United States Air Strike against Libya, April 14, 1986," in *The Public Papers of President Ronald W. Reagan.*

90. McAlister, *Epic Encounters,* p. 242.

91. Another such incident that Emerson cites occurs in Oklahoma City. Steven Emerson, *American Jihad: The Terrorists Living among Us,* pp. 1–3, 6.

92. Homi K. Bhabha, "The Other Question: The Stereotype and Colonial Discourse," in *Visual Culture: The Reader,* ed. Jessica Evans and Stuart Hall, pp. 370–378.

93. Bernstein and Studlar, *Visions of the East.*

94. Silverman, *The Subject of Semiotics,* pp. 220–221.

95. A final film, *South Park: Bigger, Longer & Uncut,* will be incorporated into my concluding remarks.

96. Francesco Casetti, *Inside the Gaze: The Fiction Film and Its Spectator,* trans. Nell Andrew with Charles O'Brien, pp. 1–15.

1. *THE EXORCIST*

1. *The Exorcist,* prod. William Peter Blatty, dir. William Friedkin, 112 min., Warner Bros. Inc., 1973, videocassette.

2. William Peter Blatty, *William Peter Blatty on* THE EXORCIST *from Novel to Film,* p. 349.

3. Shaheen, "The Hollywood Arab (1984–1986)."

4. The "Arab kit" includes belly dancers' outfits, veils, *kaffiyehs* (headdresses), flowing gowns and robes, scimitars, limousines, and camels. Ibid., pp. 148–149.

5. Examples include Thomas S. Frentz and Thomas B. Farrell, "Conversion of America's Consciousness: The Rhetoric of *The Exorcist,*" *Quarterly Journal of Speech* 61 (February 1975): 40–47; Herbert J. Gans, "*The Exorcist:* A Devilish Attack on Women," *Social Policy* 5 (1): 71–73; Mark Kermode, *The Exorcist,* 2nd ed.; Marsha Kinder and Beverle Houston, "Seeing Is Believing: *The Exorcist* and *Don't Look Now,*" in *American Horrors: Essays on the Modern American Horror Film,* ed. Gregory A. Waller, pp. 44–61; Bob McCabe, THE EXORCIST: *Out of the Shadows, The Full Story of the Film;* William Van Wert, "*The Exorcist:* Ritual or Therapy?," *Jump Cut* 1 (May–June 1974): 3–5; and Tony Williams, *Hearths of Darkness: The Family in the American Horror Film.* Susan Wloszczyna even cites puberty as a reason in "*The Exorcist:* True Evil Endures," *USA Today,* September 22, 2000.

6. These 102 minutes include those short, but still important, scenes that take place in New York.

7. Kermode, *The Exorcist,* pp. 23–28.

8. Williams, *Hearths of Darkness*, pp. 106–115.

9. James Monaco also notes that paradigmatic and syntagmatic are terms film theorists borrow from linguistics to help explain the connotative richness of film images and narratives. Viewers can grasp connotative meanings from connections and comparisons, not necessarily consciously, of images in context. Paradigmatic structure is considered a vertical structure of choosing "what goes with what" (e.g., white hat with hero/black hat with villain). Syntagmatic structure is conceptualized as a horizontal structure that deals with linear narrative and concerns "what follows what" (e.g., rescue follows capture). James Monaco, *How to Read a Film: The Art, Technology, Language, History, and Theory of Film and Media*, pp. 131–132, 341.

10. Will Wright, *Sixguns and Society*, p. 129.

11. This version is provided in William Peter Blatty, *William Peter Blatty on THE EXORCIST from Novel to Film*, pp. 43–270. An Iraq prologue does exist in Blatty's novel *The Exorcist*, pp. 1–8.

12. Shohat cites many character examples like Indiana Jones, Robinson Crusoe, Phileas Fogg, and Lawrence of Arabia. Ella Shohat, "Gender and Culture of Empire: Toward a Feminist Ethnography of the Cinema," in *Visions of the East*, ed. Matthew Bernstein and Gaylyn Studlar, pp. 19–66.

13. Piero Camporesi, *The Fear of Hell: Images of Damnation and Salvation in Early Medieval Europe*, trans. Lucinda Byatt, p. 75.

14. Dante Alighieri, *The Divine Comedy: Inferno*, Canto VIII, 65–75. Interestingly enough, deep in the city center and farther down into the circles of Hell, Dante finds the Arab Mohammad and his son-in-law Ali residing (Canto XXVIII). They suffer eternal punishment for sowing schism in human religious unity on Earth. Dante witnesses their bodies being repeatedly split in two—a punishment Dante sees as fitting their transgression—by a demon with a bloody sword.

15. Camporesi, *The Fear of Hell*, p. 6.

16. Shohat, "Gender and Culture of Empire," p. 27.

17. Ibid., p. 32.

18. I use the term "gaze" to mean the power to arrest, capture, and subjugate the outer world and its inhabitants to the visual control of the seeing agent.

19. Steet, *Veils and Daggers*, pp. 103–104.

20. John Ellis, *Visible Fictions: Cinema, Television, Video*, pp. 45–47.

21. Steet, *Veils and Daggers*, pp. 124, 141–143.

22. Shohat, "Gender and Culture of Empire," p. 21.

23. Daniel, *Islam and the West*, p. 17.

24. Paul Oppenheimer, *Evil and the Demonic: A New Theory of Monstrous Behavior*, p. 6.

25. Ibid., pp. 5–7.

26. Kinder and Houston, "Seeing Is Believing," p. 47.

27. Camporesi, *The Fear of Hell*, pp. 78–79.

28. Blatty, *William Peter Blatty on THE EXORCIST from Novel to Film*.

29. Van Wert, "*The Exorcist*: Ritual or Therapy?," p. 4.

30. Homi K. Bhabha, "Of Mimicry and Man," in Homi K. Bhabha, *The Location of Culture*, p. 89.

31. Bart Moore-Gilbert, *Postcolonial Theory: Contexts, Practices, Politics*, p. 132.

32. Shohat, "Gender and Culture of Empire," pp. 41–45.

33. Said, *Orientalism*, pp. 315–316.

34. Shirazi, *The Veil Unveiled*, pp. 42–43, 185–186.

35. Ibid., pp. 48–55.

36. Stephen E. Bowles, "*The Exorcist* and *Jaws*," *Literature Film Quarterly* 4 (3): 209.

37. Wright, *Sixguns and Society,* p. 32.

38. Like Propp, Wright points out that not all functions need be present. He adds that the functions may not appear in exactly the same order. Ibid., pp. 40–49.

39. Lee Clark Mitchell, *Westerns: Making the Man in Fiction and Film,* p. 166.

40. Ibid., pp. 163–168.

41. Michael Coyne, *The Crowded Prairie: American National Identity in the Hollywood Western,* pp. 1–15.

42. Wright, *Sixguns and Society,* p. 121.

43. Thomas Sutcliffe, *Watching: Reflections on the Movies,* p. 66.

44. Mitchell, *Westerns,* p. 187.

45. "The Plausible Impossible," *The Wonderful World of Disney* (television series), Episode 55, NBC (October 31, 1956).

46. "Arab Pride and Power," *Newsweek,* February 18, 1974, p. 40.

47. Blatty, *William Peter Blatty on THE EXORCIST from Novel to Film,* p. 37.

48. McCambridge was the voice of the demon in the Georgetown scenes. According to McCabe, Friedkin wanted to keep the demon a secret, and so he did not give her credit, either. Mercedes McCambridge went public with the information and demanded credit. Later, after about the first thirty prints of the film, her name appeared in the credits for her work as the "origin of the Devil." McCabe, *THE EXORCIST: Out of the Shadows,* pp. 112–115, 142–144.

49. Ibid., pp. 34–42.

50. Susan Wloszczyna, " 'Exorcist' Spews Out Challenge for Our Times," *USA Today,* September 21, 2000. The 2000 version of the film uses the muezzin's call to prayer at the end of the film as the camera looks down on the boarded window of Regan's empty bedroom while Father Dyer and Detective Kinderman walk away in lighthearted dialogue. This scene ties the narrative back to the Iraq prologue and further associates the demon that was in the bedroom with its origins in the Middle East and with the Arab. As the two men walk away, they are deaf to the voice and, unknown to them, are watched by the gaze of a spirit that "wails" as it did before.

2. ROLLOVER

1. *Rollover,* prod. Bruce Gilbert, dir. Alan J. Pakula, 118 min., Orion Pictures, 1981, video-cassette.

2. Matthew Josephson, *The Robber Barons: The Great American Capitalists, 1861–1901.*

3. Thomas V. DiBacco, *Made in the U.S.A.: The History of American Business,* p. xi.

4. Ibid., p. 15.

5. Ibid., p. 120.

6. Ibid., p. 235.

7. Burton W. Folsom, Jr., *The Myth of the Robber Barons: A New Look at the Rise of Big Business in America;* and George Gilder, *The Spirit of Enterprise.*

8. In using biographies of famous American capitalists (among them are Henry Ford, James J. Hill, John D. Rockefeller, Charles M. Schwab, Philip Scranton, Donald Trump, and Cornelius Vanderbilt), we can develop the "classical plot" of the American entrepreneur (syntagmatic structure) and an inventory of his classical characteristics (paradigmatic structure).

9. Gilder, *The Spirit of Enterprise*, p. 157.

10. Ibid., p. 213.

11. Donald Trump is a fine example of one who, in playing up his masculine, phallo-centric entrepreneurial character in his book *Trump: The Art of the Deal*, fits this profile. Trump proudly thinks big and belittles those who think small. He looks for leverage over others and insists that bravado is highly important to win people over to his side. He fights back when necessary and is as rock hard as he needs to be. He aims very high, "and then I just keep pushing and pushing and pushing to get what I'm after." Donald J. Trump with Tony Schwartz, *Trump: The Art of the Deal*, p. 32.

12. Wright, *Sixguns and Society*, pp. 25–26.

13. Paul Fussell, *Class: A Guide through the American Status System*, pp. 16, 171.

14. Stuart Hall, "Ethnicity: Identity and Difference," *Radical America* 23 (1989): 16.

15. Jeremy Black, *Maps and Politics*, pp. 88–89.

16. Peter Burke, *The Fabrication of Louis XIV*, p. 87.

17. Stella Bruzzi, *Undressing Cinema: Clothing and Identity in the Movies*.

18. Shaheen, "The Hollywood Arab (1984–1986)," pp. 148–149.

19. Bill Ashcroft, Gareth Griffiths, and Helen Tiffin, *Post-Colonial Studies: The Key Concepts*, p. 139.

20. W. J. T. Mitchell, *The Last Dinosaur Book*, pp. 157–161.

21. William K. Klingaman, *1929: The Year of the Great Crash*, p. 262.

22. Kim Newman, *Millennium Movies: End of the World Cinema*.

3. BLACK SUNDAY

1. *Black Sunday*, prod. Robert Evans, dir. John Frankenheimer, 143 min., Paramount Pictures, 1976, DVD.

2. Richard Slotkin, *Gunfighter Nation: The Myth of the Frontier in Twentieth-Century America*, pp. 625–627.

3. McAlister, *Epic Encounters*, p. 183.

4. Ibid., p. 187.

5. Slotkin, *Gunfighter Nation*, p. 10.

6. Here Slotkin quotes *Buffalo Bill's Wild West* programs from 1886 and 1893. Ibid., p. 77.

7. The present War on Terror seems to involve some aspects of the savage war concept. These aspects include the replacement of the "prisoner of war" designation, and its inherent protections under international agreements, with "terrorists" and "enemy combatants"; the inhumane treatment reported at Abu Ghraib and Camp X-Ray and Delta prisons; the delay of counsel and suspension of visitation rights to U.S. citizens considered to be "terrorists"; and the Bush administration's refusal to recognize the humanity of enemies through rhetorically stigmatizing them as "terrorists." How U.S. soldiers are actually engaging the "terrorists" on the ground in Iraq and Afghanistan is difficult to assess for certain, but the Bush administration boasts of "hunting them down" and "smoking them out," which provides an imaginary of savage warlike engagement for us.

8. For discussions on the cowboy and the corporate manager as heroic figures, readers should recall my previous analyses of *The Exorcist* and *Rollover*. For discussions of the military man as a heroic figure, readers should see subsequent chapters analyzing *Three Kings* and *Rules of Engagement*.

9. Slotkin, *Gunfighter Nation*, pp. 431, 462.

10. Ibid., pp. 489–623.

11. Susan Jeffords, *The Remasculinization of America: Gender and the Vietnam War*, p. 167.

12. Martin Rubin, *Thrillers*, pp. 25–30.

13. I borrow slightly from John Updike's proposal to conceptualize the male body, in reproduction, as a "delivery system" for the sperm that rams "home his seed into the gut of the chosen woman." Complementarily, the female body is "a mazy device for retention." While he does not discuss the female body in the action of giving birth, the breaking of water and finally pushing the infant out are less concerned with precision. John Updike, "The Disposable Rocket," in *The Male Body: Features, Destinies, Exposures*, ed. Laurence Goldstein, p. 8.

14. Davidson, *America's Palestine*, pp. 39, 51, 65.

15. Suleiman, *The Arabs in the Mind of America*, p. 10.

16. Roy Harvey Pearce, *The Savages of America: A Study of the Indian and the Idea of Civilization* p. 229.

4. THREE KINGS

1. *Three Kings*, prod. Charles Roven, dir. David O. Russell, 115 min., Warner Bros. Inc., 1999, DVD.

2. Actually, *Three Kings* was filmed in Casa Grande, Arizona. The American desert was a set made to conform (with a constructed village, military base, fortress, and international border) to an imaginary Iraq. See supplemental documentary provided in DVD version of *Three Kings*.

3. On March 20, 2003, U.S. and British forces actually did cross into southern Iraq and began the present occupation of Iraq.

4. Paul Fussell has provided excellent insight into the meaning of "chickenshit." The term refers to "behavior that makes military life worse than it need be: petty harassment of the weak by the strong; open scrimmage for power and authority and prestige; sadism thinly disguised as necessary discipline; a constant 'paying off of old scores'; and insistence on the letter rather than the spirit of ordinances." The term refers to the small fowl as opposed to larger animals because "it is small-minded and ignoble and takes the trivial seriously. Chickenshit can be recognized instantly because it never has anything to do with winning the war." Furthermore, Fussell writes about soldiers' uses of the expletive "fuck." "If you couldn't oppose the chickenshit any other way, you could always say, 'Fuck it!' " Paul Fussell, *Wartime: Understanding and Behavior in the Second World War*, pp. 80, 95.

5. Engelhardt, *The End of Victory Culture*.

6. Robin Moore, *The Green Berets*.

7. Engelhardt, *The End of Victory Culture*, pp. 3–4.

8. Ibid., p. 3.

9. John Hellmann, *American Myth and the Legacy of Vietnam*, p. 21.

10. Engelhardt, *The End of Victory Culture*, p. 39.

11. Ibid., p. 159.

12. Ibid., p. 10.

13. Jeffords, *The Remasculinization of America*.

14. Ibid., p. 51.

15. Herbert I. Schiller, "Manipulating Hearts and Minds," in *Triumph of the Image: The Media's War in the Persian Gulf—A Global Perspective*, ed. Hamid Mowlana, George Gerbner, and Herbert I. Schiller, p. 25.

16. Antony Easthope, *What a Man's Gotta Do: The Masculine Myth in Popular Culture,* p. 2.

17. Ibid., p. 6.

18. Judith Roof, *Come as You Are: Sexuality and Narrative,* pp. 1–40.

19. Mackey-Kallis, *The Hero and the Perennial Journey Home in American Film,* p. 1.

20. Tom Brokaw, *An Album of Memories: Personal Histories from the Greatest Generation,* p. 354.

21. Myra MacPherson, *Long Time Passing: Vietnam and the Haunted Generation.*

22. Ibid., p. 487.

23. Ibid., p. 315.

24. Jeffords, *The Remasculinization of America,* p. 54.

25. H. Bruce Franklin, *Vietnam and Other American Fantasies,* pp. 191–192.

26. Jean Baudrillard, *The Gulf War Did Not Take Place,* trans. Paul Patton, pp. 61–87. Furthermore, I suggest that much of the film's special effects of surreal coloring, point-of-view shots, and slow motion, and the use of commercial brand names, materials, and products playfully highlight the hyperreality of the Gulf War experience far out in the Arab landscape and the "authenticity" of the film as portraying experience of the Gulf War.

27. Asu Aksoy and Kevin Robins, "Extermination Angels: Morality, Violence, and Technology in the Gulf War," in *Triumph of the Image: The Media's War in the Persian Gulf—A Global Perspective,* ed. Hamid Mowlana, George Gerbner, and Herbert I. Schiller, pp. 202–212.

28. Fussell, *Wartime,* p. 115.

29. Easthope, *What a Man's Gotta Do,* pp. 95–97.

30. Linda Blandford, *Super-Wealth: The Secret Lives of the Oil Sheikhs.*

31. My pun, not theirs.

32. Franklin, *Vietnam and Other American Fantasies,* p. 14.

33. Ibid.

34. Aksoy and Robins, "Exterminating Angels."

35. Easthope, *What a Man's Gotta Do,* p. 15.

36. Roof, *Come as You Are,* p. 29.

37. Larry H. Addington, *America's War in Vietnam: A Short Narrative History,* p. 152.

38. Richard Slotkin, *The Fatal Environment: The Myth of the Frontier in the Age of Industrialization, 1800–1890,* pp. 34–35.

39. Shaheen, *Reel Bad Arabs,* pp. 11, 485–487.

40. Bush quoted in Brian Balogh, "From Metaphor to Quagmire: The Domestic Legacy of the Vietnam War," in *After Vietnam: Legacies of a Lost War,* ed. Charles E. Neu, p. 31.

5. *RULES OF ENGAGEMENT*

1. *Rules of Engagement,* prod. Richard D. Zanuck and Scott Rudin, dir. William Friedkin, 127 min., Paramount Pictures, 2000, DVD.

2. Addington, *America's War in Vietnam,* p. 119.

3. Ibid., pp. 121–123.

4. Alvin J. Schmidt, *The Menace of Multiculturalism: Trojan Horse in America,* p. 139. For further condemnation of Clinton as leading multiculturalist, see also Lynne V. Cheney, *Telling the Truth: Why Our Culture and Our Country Have Stopped Making Sense—and What We Can Do about It,* pp. 182–191.

5. For the benefit of the reader, I shall use the terminology of the film ("new/old ball-

game" or "new/old") in the rest of this discussion when referring to multiculturalism and its theoretical and ideological cousins, on the one hand, and their antithesis, on the other. The reader should keep in mind, however, that conservative critics may not use this term, but rather may individually refer to multiculturalism, postmodernism, deconstructionism, or relativism, or may just condense them into the term "political correctness."

6. David Thibodaux, *Political Correctness: The Cloning of the American Mind*, p. 82.

7. Cheney, *Telling the Truth*, pp. 86, 204.

8. Keith Windschuttle, *The Killing of History: How Literary Critics and Social Theorists Are Murdering Our Past*, pp. 36–37.

9. Richard Bernstein, *Dictatorship of Virtue: How the Battle over Multiculturalism Is Reshaping Our Schools, Our Country, Our Lives*, p. 4.

10. Conservatives' fear of and crusade against multiculturalism seem to emulate Richard Hofstadter's description of "the paranoid style in American politics." Their fear may be another "successive episodic wave" in which "the paranoid disposition is mobilized into action chiefly by social conflicts that involve ultimate schemes of values and that bring fundamental fears and hatreds, rather than negotiable interests, into political action. Catastrophe or the fear of catastrophe is most likely to elicit the syndrome of paranoid rhetoric." Hofstadter also states, "The paranoid tendency is aroused by a confrontation of opposed interests which are (or are felt to be) totally irreconcilable, and thus by nature not susceptible to the normal political processes of bargain and compromise." Richard Hofstadter, *The Paranoid Style in American Politics and Other Essays*, p. 39.

11. John K. Wilson, *The Myth of Political Correctness: The Conservative Attack on Higher Education*, p. 8.

12. See MacPherson's discussion of Project 100,000. MacPherson does note that in frontline combat, racism was a minor issue. Nevertheless, she declares, the actual placement onto the battlefield did involve racism. Myra MacPherson, *Long Time Passing*, pp. 30, 558–562.

13. Engelhardt, *The End of Victory Culture*, p. 39.

14. Interestingly enough, Colonel Jon T. Hoffman's history of the USMC states that this is a narrative of legend. "In reality, the Mameluke-style sword first came into the Corps when the Marine quartermaster ordered a batch from England in 1825. Except for a brief period during and immediately following the Civil War, it has remained the sword of Marine officers ever since." Colonel Jon T. Hoffman, *USMC: A Complete History*, p. 37.

15. Actually, *Rules of Engagement* was filmed in northern Morocco. The North African landscape, a Moroccan village, and its inhabitants became sets and cast chosen and made to conform to an imaginary Yemen, its capital San'a, and Yemenis. See supplemental documentary provided in DVD version of *Rules of Engagement*.

16. Karim, *Islamic Peril*, p. 68.

17. Ziauddin Sardar and Merryl Wyn Davies, *Why Do People Hate America?*, pp. 193–211.

18. Operation Eagle Claw was President Jimmy Carter's unsuccessful attempt to rescue the American hostages from the American embassy in Tehran, April 1980. The mission failed when the rescue aircraft carrying troops collided at Desert One in the Iranian landscape. *Rules of Engagement* provides a successful version of this type of rescue attempt in a new and fantastic context.

19. Schmidt defines "white man's guilt" as "a feeling of remorse that many white Americans have regarding their nation's past sins, relative to the discrimination against racial minorities and women, for example." Schmidt, *The Menace of Multiculturalism*, p. 7.

20. Windschuttle, *The Killing of History*, pp. 1–37.

21. Windschuttle makes this point. Cultural relativists "endorse as legitimate other cultures that do not return the compliment. Some other cultures, of which one of the best known is Islam, will have no truck with relativism of any kind." Ibid., p. 301.

6. CNN'S *AMERICA REMEMBERS*

1. *America Remembers*, prod. Ken Shiffman and Brian Rokus, dir. not noted, 90 min., Time, Inc. Home Entertainment, 2002, DVD.

2. Barbie Zelizer, "Every Once in a While: *Schindler's List* and the Shaping of History," in *Spielberg's Holocaust: Critical Perspectives on SCHINDLER'S LIST*, ed. Yosefa Loshitzky, p. 30.

3. Omer Bartov, "Spielberg's Oskar: Hollywood Tries Evil," in *Spielberg's Holocaust: Critical Perspectives on SCHINDLER'S LIST*, ed. Yosefa Loshitzky, pp. 41–60 (his observation about stories of the murdered from p. 47).

4. Miriam Bratu Hansen, "*Schindler's List* Is Not *Shoah*: Second Commandment, Popular Modernism, and Public Memory," in *Spielberg's Holocaust: Critical Perspectives on SCHINDLER'S LIST*, ed. Yosefa Loshitzky, p. 81.

5. Sara R. Horowitz, "But Is It Good for the Jews?: Spielberg's Schindler and the Aesthetics of Atrocity," in *Spielberg's Holocaust: Critical Perspectives on SCHINDLER'S LIST*, ed. Yosefa Loshitzky, p. 137.

6. Sandra Silberstein, *War of Words: Language, Politics, and 9/11*, pp. 1–17.

7. These descriptions can be found in President Bush's remarks in Sarasota, Florida, after he learned of the attacks on the World Trade Center (September 11, 2001, 9:30 A.M. EDT), at his later arrival at Barksdale Air Force Base (September 11, 2001, 1:04 P.M. EDT), in his address to the nation (September 11, 2001, 8:30 P.M. EDT), and in his address to a joint session of Congress and to the American people (September 20, 2001, 9:00 P.M. EDT). Ibid., pp. 18–28.

8. Barbie Zelizer describes an "interpretive community" as "a group that authenticates itself through its narratives and collective memories." Barbie Zelizer, *Covering the Body: The Kennedy Assassination, the Media, and the Shaping of Collective Memory*, p. 9.

9. The DVD's back cover jacket bills *America Remembers* as a compilation of "CNN's incomparable coverage of 9/11 and the months that followed. This comprehensive documentary gives you a powerful, minute-by-minute account of the events of 9/11 as they developed, as well as a compelling look at the aftermath: a time of reflection, resolve, and retaliation."

10. By the term "9/11 literature," I mean those books that have appeared since that date and purport to tell the "full story" of September 11, 2001. Many of these books are "current events" books based upon journalists' reports and interviews, conspiracy theories, patriotic declarations, insider information, and party ideology. They tend to fulfill popular tastes and the demands in publishing for collective memory and bereavement, rather than adhere to the standards of scholarly inquiry or the discipline of historiography. For good examples, see Richard Bernstein, *Out of the Blue: The Story of September 11, 2001 from Jihad to Ground Zero;* Emerson, *American Jihad;* Jere Longman, *Among the Heroes: United Flight 93 and the Passengers and Crew Who Fought Back;* Bill Sammon, *Fighting Back: The War on Terrorism—from Inside the Bush White House;* and Lance Wubbels, *September 11, 2001—A Time For Heroes: A Tribute to American Faith, Guts, and Patriotism.*

11. Daniel Benjamin and Steven Simon, *The Age of Sacred Terror*, p. 219.

12. Ibid., p. 220.

13. Ibid., pp. 350–351.

14. Ibid., p. 385.

15. As another example of how CNN has not adhered to the event-as-it-happened, it uses the same pictures of the guards in the streets to depict the heavily protected route in Bush's departure from Florida and the heavily protected route on his arrival in Nebraska.

16. Gilmore, *Monsters*, pp. 174–189.

17. Susan Sontag, "The Imagination of Disaster," *Commentary* 40, no. 4 (October 1965): 44.

18. Ibid.

19. Bartov, "Spielberg's Oskar," p. 47.

20. Gilmore, *Monsters*, pp. 4–5.

21. Ibid., p. 36.

22. Silberstein, *War of Words*, pp. 39–55.

23. H. G. Wells, *The Time Machine*, pp. 78–79.

24. *The Day After* (1983) is a made-for-television film about a nuclear missile battle between the United States and Soviet Union. The film deals with the destruction, death, and quality of life that are imagined to result from the initial explosions and in the nuclear fallout aftermath.

25. Sontag, "The Imagination of Disaster," p. 42.

26. This desire to liken the event to nuclear disaster is also found in 9/11 literature and becomes part of the September 11th discourse. Benjamin and Simon, for example, compare the explosions of the two airplanes flying into the World Trade Center towers with U.S. military tactical nuclear weapons that can "be calibrated to deliver this explosive yield—of nearly a quarter kiloton. Of course, the attacks did not cause any radioactive fallout, but the energy release was nonetheless extraordinary, off the charts of comparison with all other terrorist attacks." Benjamin and Simon, *The Age of Sacred Terror*, p. 34.

27. Newman, *Millennium Movies*, pp. 10–11, 219.

28. Silberstein, *War of Words*, pp. 39–59.

29. Slotkin, *Gunfighter Nation*, p. 651.

30. Ibid., p. 12.

31. Kenneth R. Dutton, *The Perfectible Body: The Western Ideal of Male Physical Development*, pp. 338–345.

32. Silberstein, *War of Words*, p. 91.

33. Benjamin and Simon, *The Age of Sacred Terror*, p. 219.

34. Silberstein, *War of Words*, p. 124.

35. Shohat, "Gender and Culture of Empire," pp. 20–35.

36. Sardar and Davies, *Why Do People Hate America?*, pp. 193–211.

37. Horowitz, "But Is It Good for the Jews?," p. 137.

CONCLUSION

1. *South Park: Bigger, Longer & Uncut*, prod. Trey Parker and Matt Stone, dir. Trey Parker, 81 min., Warner Bros. Inc., 1999, DVD.

2. Saddam Hussein shows up again in the television series. In one episode ("Do the Handicapped Go to Hell?," Episode 410, July 19, 2000), he returns to Satan and tries to come between Satan and his new lover, Chris. In another ("A Ladder to Heaven," Episode 612, November 6, 2002), Saddam is building weapons of mass destruction in Heaven, which gives President George W. Bush a reason to contemplate bombing Heaven.

3. Peter Stanford, *The Devil: A Biography*, p. 233.

4. In late 2000, *Business Week* printed an article about Saddam Hussein as a "hidden cul-

prit" and a "master manipulator" behind the rise in oil prices. "Saddam might," according to the article, "unleash potentially the scariest weapon in his depleted arsenal: oil blackmail." John Rossant and Stan Crock, "Saddam May Soon Unleash His Best Weapon: Oil Blackmail," *Business Week,* October 2, 2000, p. 72.

5. Krips, *Fetish,* p. 27.
6. Karim, *Islamic Peril,* p. 177.

Bibliography

Adair, Gilbert. *Hollywood's Vietnam: From* The Green Berets *to* Apocalypse Now. New York: Proteus Publishing Company, 1981.

Addington, Larry H. *America's War in Vietnam: A Short Narrative History.* Bloomington: Indiana University Press, 2000.

Ahmed, Nafeez Mosaddeq. *The War on Freedom: How and Why America Was Attacked, September 11, 2001.* Joshua Tree, Calif.: Tree of Life Publications, 2002.

Aksoy, Asu, and Kevin Robins. "Extermination Angels: Morality, Violence and Technology in the Gulf War." In *Triumph of the Image: The Media's War in the Persian Gulf—A Global Perspective,* ed. Hamid Mowlana, George Gerbner, and Herbert I. Schiller, pp. 202–212. Boulder, Colo.: Westview Press, 1992.

Alger, Horatio. Ragged Dick and Mark, the Match Boy: *Two Novels by Horatio Alger.* Orig. 1868; New York: Scribner Paperback Editions, 1998.

Allport, Gordon W. *The Nature of Prejudice.* 25th anniversary ed. Orig. 1954; Cambridge, Mass.: Perseus Books, 1979.

Althusser, Louis. *Essays on Ideology.* London: Verso, 1971.

America Remembers. Produced by Ken Shiffman and Brian Rokus, director not noted. 90 min. Time, Inc. Home Entertainment, 2002. DVD.

Anderegg, Michael, ed. *Inventing Vietnam: The War in Film and Television.* Philadelphia: Temple University Press, 1991.

"Arab Pride and Power." *Newsweek,* February 18, 1974, pp. 40–46.

"The Arabs' New Oil Squeeze: Dimouts, Slowdowns, Chills." *Time,* November 19, 1973, pp. 88–95.

"Arabs Slap *LaStampa.*" *Time,* January 14, 1974, p. 29.

"Are the Russians the Real Winners?" *Time,* November 5, 1973, p. 38.

Ashcroft, Bill, Gareth Griffiths, and Helen Tiffin. *Post-Colonial Studies: The Key Concepts.* London: Routledge, 2000.

Balogh, Brian. "From Metaphor to Quagmire: The Domestic Legacy of the

Vietnam War." In *After Vietnam: Legacies of a Lost War,* ed. Charles E. Neu, pp. 24–55. Baltimore: Johns Hopkins University Press, 2000.

Barthes, Roland. *Camera Lucida: Reflections on Photography.* Trans. Richard Howard. New York: Hill and Wang, 1981.

———. *Mythologies.* Trans. Annette Lavers. New York: Hill and Wang, 1974.

Bartov, Omer. "Spielberg's Oskar: Hollywood Tries Evil." In *Spielberg's Holocaust: Critical Perspectives on SCHINDLER'S LIST,* ed. Yosefa Loshitzky, pp. 41–60. Bloomington: Indiana University Press, 1997.

Baudrillard, Jean. *The Gulf War Did Not Take Place.* Trans. Paul Patton. Orig. 1991; Bloomington: Indiana University Press, 1995.

Benjamin, Daniel, and Steven Simon. *The Age of Sacred Terror.* New York: Random House, 2002.

Bennett, William J. *The De-Valuing of America: Our Fight for Our Culture and Our Children.* Colorado Springs, Colo.: Focus on the Family Publishing, 1994.

Bernstein, Matthew, and Gaylyn Studlar, eds. *Visions of the East: Orientalism in Film.* New Brunswick, N.J.: Rutgers University Press, 1997.

Bernstein, Richard. *Dictatorship of Virtue: How the Battle over Multiculturalism Is Reshaping Our Schools, Our Country, Our Lives.* New York: Vintage Books, 1994.

———, and the staff of *The New York Times. Out of the Blue: The Story of September 11, 2001, from Jihad to Ground Zero.* New York: Times Books, 2002.

Bhabha, Homi K. *The Location of Culture.* London: Routledge, 1994.

———. "The Other Question: The Stereotype and Colonial Discourse." In *Visual Culture: The Reader,* ed. Jessica Evans and Stuart Hall, pp. 370–378. London: Sage Publications, 1999.

Black, Jeremy. *Maps and Politics.* London: Reaktion Books, 1997.

Black Sunday. Produced by Robert Evans and directed by John Frankenheimer. 143 min. Paramount Pictures, 1976. DVD.

Blandford, Linda. *Super-Wealth: The Secret Lives of the Oil Sheikhs.* New York: William Morrow and Company, 1977.

Blatty, William Peter. *The Exorcist.* New York: Bantam Books, 1972.

———. *William Peter Blatty on THE EXORCIST from Novel to Film.* New York: Bantam Books, 1974.

Block, Bruce. *The Visual Story: Seeing the Structure of Film, TV, and New Media.* Boston: Focal Press, 2001.

Block, J. R., and Harold E. Yuker. *Can You Believe Your Eyes? Over 250*

Illusions and Other Visual Oddities. New York: Brunner/Mazel Publishers, 1992.

"Bombs and Ugly Rhetoric." *Time,* April 2, 1979, pp. 28–33.

Boorstin, Daniel J. *The Image: A Guide to Pseudo-Events in America.* Orig. 1961; New York: Vintage, 1992.

Bowles, Stephen E. *"The Exorcist* and *Jaws." Literature Film Quarterly* 4 (3): 196–214.

Brasted, Howard. "The Politics of Stereotyping: Western Images of Islam." *Manushi* 98 (1997): 6–16.

Brokaw, Tom. *An Album of Memories: Personal Histories from the Greatest Generation.* New York: Random House, 2001.

———. *The Greatest Generation.* New York: Random House, 1998.

———. *The Greatest Generation Speaks: Letters and Reflections.* New York: Random House, 1999.

Brooks, Peter. *Reading for the Plot: Design and Intention in Narrative.* New York: Alfred A. Knopf, 1984.

Bruzzi, Stella. *Undressing Cinema: Clothing and Identity in the Movies.* London: Routledge, 1997.

Buchanan, Patrick J. *The Death of the West: How Dying Populations and Immigrant Invasions Imperil Our Country and Civilization.* New York: St. Martin's Press, 2002.

Buckland, Warren. *Film Studies.* London: Hodder & Stoughton, Ltd., 1998.

Burke, Peter. *The Fabrication of Louis XIV.* New Haven, Conn.: Yale University Press, 1992.

Burkett, B. G., and Glenna Whitley. *Stolen Valor: How the Vietnam Generation Was Robbed of Its Heroes and Its History.* Dallas, Tex.: Verity Press, 1998.

Cameron, Kenneth M. *Africa on Film: Beyond Black and White.* New York: Continuum, 1994.

Campbell, Joseph. *The Hero with a Thousand Faces.* Orig. 1968; Princeton, N.J.: Princeton University Press, 2004.

———. *The Power of Myth with Bill Moyers.* Ed. Betty Sue Flowers. Orig. 1988; New York: Anchor Books, 1991.

Camporesi, Piero. *The Fear of Hell: Images of Damnation and Salvation in Early Medieval Europe.* Trans. Lucinda Byatt. University Park: Pennsylvania State University Press, 1991.

Carroll, Noël. *The Philosophy of Horror or Paradoxes of the Heart.* London: Routledge, 1990.

Cartmell, Deborah, et al. *Alien Identities: Exploring Differences in Film and Fiction*. London: Pluto Press, 1999.

Casetti, Francesco. *Inside the Gaze: The Fiction Film and Its Spectator*. Trans. Nell Andrew with Charles O'Brien. Bloomington: Indiana University Press, 1998.

"Cash Flood in the Middle East." *Time*, October 9, 1972, pp. 78–79.

Caton, Steven C. *LAWRENCE OF ARABIA: A Film's Anthropology*. Berkeley and Los Angeles: University of California Press, 1999.

CBS News. *What We Saw: The Events of September 11, 2001—In Words, Pictures, and Video*. New York: Simon and Schuster, 2002.

Chancer, Lynn S. *Sadomasochism in Everyday Life: The Dynamics of Power and Powerlessness*. New Brunswick, N.J.: Rutgers University Press, 1992.

Cheney, Lynne V. *Telling the Truth: Why Our Culture and Our Country Have Stopped Making Sense—and What We Can Do about It*. New York: Simon and Schuster, 1995.

Chomsky, Noam. *9-11*. New York: Seven Stories Press, 2002.

Chowdrhy, Prem. *Colonial India and the Making of Empire Cinema: Image, Ideology, and Identity*. Manchester, England: Manchester University Press, 2000.

Clarke, John R. *Looking at Lovemaking: Constructions of Sexuality in Roman Art, 100 B.C.–A.D. 250*. Berkeley and Los Angeles: University of California Press, 1998.

"Cold Comfort for a Long, Hard Winter." *Time*, December 10, 1973, pp. 33–34.

Coyne, Michael. *The Crowded Prairie: American National Identity in the Hollywood Western*. London: I. B. Tauris, 1997.

Crane, Jonathan Lake. *Terror and Everyday Life: Singular Moments in the History of the Horror Film*. London: Sage Publications, 1994.

"The Crescent of Crisis." *Time*, January 15, 1979, pp. 18–25.

"The Croesus of Crisis." *Time*, April 10, 1972, p. 31.

"Dance of the Oil Dervishes." *Time*, January 1, 1979, pp. 57–58.

Daniel, Norman. *Islam and the West: The Making of an Image*. Reprint from 1960. Oxford, England: Oneworld Publications, 2000.

Dante Alighieri. *The Divine Comedy of Dante Alighieri*. Trans. Melville Best-Anderson. Norwalk, Conn.: Easton Press, 1978.

Davidson, Lawrence. *America's Palestine: Popular and Official Perceptions from Balfour to Israeli Statehood*. Gainesville: University of Florida Press, 2001.

"Deadly Battle of the Spooks." *Time*, February 12, 1973, pp. 28–29.

Derry, Charles. *Dark Dreams: A Psychological History of the Modern Horror Film.* South Brunswick, N.J.: A. S. Barnes and Company, 1977.

DiBacco, Thomas V. *Made in the U.S.A.: The History of American Business.* New York: Harper and Row, 1987.

Dorfman, Ariel. *The Empire's Old Clothes: What the Lone Ranger, Barbar, and Other Innocent Heroes Do to Our Minds.* Trans. Clark Hansen. New York: Pantheon Books, 1983.

————, and Armand Mattelart. *How to Read Donald Duck: Imperialist Ideology in the Disney Comic.* Trans. David Kunzle. Orig. 1971; New York: International General, 1991.

Doty, Alexander. *Flaming Classics: Queering the Film Canon.* London: Routledge, 2000.

Douglas, Mary. *Purity and Danger: An Analysis of Concepts of Pollution and Taboo.* 2nd ed. Orig. 1966; London: Routledge, 2000.

D'Souza, Dinesh. *What's So Great about America.* Washington, D.C.: Regnery Publishing, 2002.

Dunne, Michael. *Intertextual Encounters in American Fiction, Film, and Popular Culture.* Bowling Green, Ohio: Bowling Green State University Popular Press, 2001.

Dutton, Kenneth R. *The Perfectible Body: The Western Ideal of Male Physical Development.* New York: Continuum Books, 1995.

Easthope, Antony. *What a Man's Gotta Do: The Masculine Myth in Popular Culture.* London: Routledge, 1990.

Ellis, John. *Visible Fictions: Cinema, Television, Video.* London: Routledge, 2000.

Emerson, Steven. *American Jihad: The Terrorists Living among Us.* New York: Free Press, 2002.

"The Emissary from Arabia." *Time,* December 17, 1973, p. 34.

Emmison, Michael, and Philip Smith. *Researching the Visual.* London: Sage Publications, 2000.

Emmott, Bill. *Japanophobia: The Myth of the Invincible Japanese.* New York: Times Books, 1993.

"The Energy Crisis: Time for Action." *Time,* May 7, 1973, pp. 41–49.

Engelhardt, Tom. *The End of Victory Culture: Cold War America and the Disillusioning of a Generation.* New York: Basic Books, 1995.

Esposito, John L. *The Islamic Threat: Myth or Reality?* 2nd ed. Orig. 1992; Oxford, England: Oxford University Press, 1995.

"Euphoria in Algiers, Trouble at the Canal." *Time,* December 10, 1973, pp. 55–56.

The Exorcist. Produced by William Peter Blatty and directed by William Friedkin. 112 min. Warner Bros. Inc., 1973. Videocassette.

"Facing a Powerful Cartel." *Time,* January 24, 1972, pp. 59–60.

Fink, Rychard. "Horatio Alger as a Social Philosopher." Introduction to *RAGGED DICK and MARK, THE MATCH BOY: Two Novels by Horatio Alger.* Orig. 1962; New York: Scribner Paperback Editions, 1998.

Finlay, Anthony. *Demons! The Devil, Possession & Exorcism.* London: Blandford, 1999.

Folsom, Burton W., Jr. *The Myth of the Robber Barons: A New Look at the Rise of Big Business in America.* Herndon, Va.: Young America's Foundation, 1996.

Foucault, Michel. *Discipline and Punish: The Birth of the Prison.* Trans. Alan Sheridan. New York: Vintage Books, 1977.

Franklin, H. Bruce. *Vietnam and Other American Fantasies.* Amherst: University of Massachusetts Press, 2000.

Frentz, Thomas S., and Thomas B. Farrell. "Conversion of America's Consciousness: The Rhetoric of *The Exorcist.*" *Quarterly Journal of Speech* 61 (February 1975): 40–47.

Frum, David. *How We Got Here: The 70's, the Decade That Brought You Modern Life—For Better or Worse.* New York: Basic Books, 2000.

Fussell, Paul. *Class: A Guide through the American Status System.* New York: Simon and Schuster, 1983.

———. *Wartime: Understanding and Behavior in the Second World War.* Oxford, England: Oxford University Press, 1989.

Gabler, Neal. *Life: The Movie: How Entertainment Conquered Reality.* New York: Vintage Books, 1998.

Gans, Herbert J. "*The Exorcist:* A Devilish Attack on Women." *Social Policy* 5 (1): 71–73.

Ghareeb, Edmund, ed. *Split Vision: The Portrayal of Arabs in the American Media.* Washington, D.C.: American-Arab Affairs Council, 1983.

Gilder, George. *The Spirit of Enterprise.* New York: Simon and Schuster, 1984.

Gilmore, David D. *Monsters: Evil Beings, Mythical Beasts, and All Manner of Imaginary Terrors.* Philadelphia: University of Pennsylvania Press, 2003.

Gold, Judith Taylor. *Monsters & Madonnas: The Roots of Christian Anti-Semitism.* Ed. Joseph Gold. Rev. ed. Syracuse, N.Y.: Syracuse University Press, 1999.

Goldstein, Laurence, ed. *The Male Body: Features, Destinies, Exposures.* Ann Arbor: University of Michigan Press, 1994.

Grant, Barry Keith, ed. *The Dread of Difference: Gender and the Horror Film.* Austin: University of Texas Press, 1996.

"The Great Energy Mess." *Time,* July 2, 1979, pp. 14–22.

Guerrero, Ed. *Framing Blackness: The African American Image in Film.* Philadelphia: Temple University Press, 1993.

Hall, Stuart. "Ethnicity: Identity and Difference." *Radical America* 23 (1989): 8–20.

Halliwell, Leslie. *The Dead That Walk: DRACULA, FRANKENSTEIN, THE MUMMY, and Other Favorite Movie Monsters.* New York: Continuum, 1988.

Hansen, Miriam Bratu. *"Schindler's List* Is Not *Shoah:* Second Commandment, Popular Modernism, and Public Memory." In *Spielberg's Holocaust: Critical Perspectives on SCHINDLER'S LIST,* ed. Yosefa Loshitzky, pp. 77–103. Bloomington: Indiana University Press, 1997.

Hellmann, John. *American Myth and the Legacy of Vietnam.* New York: Columbia University Press, 1986.

"Here They Come Again." *Time,* December 17, 1979, p. 69.

Hoffman, Bruce. *Inside Terrorism.* London: Indigo, 1999.

Hoffman, Colonel Jon T. *USMC: A Complete History.* Hong Kong: Hugh Lauter Levin Associates, 2002.

Hofstadter, Richard. *The Paranoid Style in American Politics and Other Essays.* New York: Alfred A. Knopf, 1965.

Hoge, James F., Jr., and Gideon Rose, eds. *How Did This Happen? Terrorism and the New War.* Oxford, England: Public Affairs, Ltd., 2001.

Horner, William R. *Bad at the Bijou.* Jefferson, N.C.: McFarland Classics, 1982.

Horowitz, Sara R. "But Is It Good for the Jews?: Spielberg's Schindler and the Aesthetics of Atrocity." In *Spielberg's Holocaust: Critical Perspectives on SCHINDLER'S LIST,* ed. Yosefa Loshitzky, pp. 119–139. Bloomington: Indiana University Press, 1997.

"Horror and Death at the Olympics." *Time,* September 18, 1972, pp. 22–30.

"Iran: The Test of Wills." *Time,* November 26, 1979, pp. 20–32.

"Israel: The Dream after 25 Years: Triumph and Trial." *Time,* April 30, 1973, pp. 26–45.

Jahoda, Gustav. *Images of Savages: Ancient Roots of Modern Prejudice in Western Culture.* London: Routledge, 1999.

Jeffords, Susan. *The Remasculinization of America: Gender and the Vietnam War.* Bloomington: Indiana University Press, 1989.

Josephson, Matthew. *The Robber Barons: The Great American Capitalists, 1861–1901.* New York: Harcourt, Brace and Co., 1934.

Kabbani, Rana. *Europe's Myths of Orient.* Bloomington: Indiana University Press, 1986.

Kaminsky, Stuart M. *American Film Genres.* 2nd ed. Chicago: Nelson-Hall, 1985.

Karim, Karim H. *Islamic Peril: Media and Global Violence.* Montreal: Black Rose Books, 2000.

Kermode, Mark. *The Exorcist.* 2nd ed. London: British Film Institute, 1998.

Kinder, Marsha, and Beverle Houston. "Seeing Is Believing: *The Exorcist* and *Don't Look Now.*" In *American Horrors: Essays on the Modern American Horror Film,* ed. Gregory A. Waller, pp. 44–61. Urbana: University of Illinois Press, 1987.

King, Geoff. *Spectacular Narratives: Hollywood in the Age of the Blockbuster.* London: I. B. Tauris, 2000.

Klein, Christina. *Cold War Orientalism: Asia in the Middlebrow Imagination, 1945–1961.* Berkeley and Los Angeles: University of California Press, 2003.

Klingaman, William K. *1929: The Year of the Great Crash.* New York: Harper and Row, 1989.

Krips, Henry. *Fetish: An Erotics of Culture.* Ithaca, N.Y.: Cornell University Press, 1999.

Lanning, Michael Lee. *Vietnam at the Movies.* New York: Fawcett Columbine, 1994.

Lee, Robert G. *Orientals: Asian Americans in Popular Culture.* Philadelphia: Temple University Press, 1999.

Lesonsky, Rieva, and Gayle Sato Stodder. ENTREPRENEUR MAGAZINE'S *Young Millionaires.* Irvine, Calif.: Entrepreneur Media, 1998.

Levy, Emanuel. *Small-Town America in Film: The Decline and Fall of Community.* New York: Continuum, 1991.

"Libya: The People's Revolution." *Time,* June 4, 1973, p. 38.

"The Life and Times of the Cautious King of Araby." *Time,* November 19, 1973, pp. 90–95.

Little, Douglas. *American Orientalism: The United States and the Middle East since 1945.* Chapel Hill: University of North Carolina Press, 2002.

Longman, Jere. *Among the Heroes: United Flight 93 and the Passengers and Crew Who Fought Back.* New York: HarperCollins, 2002.

Loshitzky, Yosefa, ed. *Spielberg's Holocaust: Critical Perspectives on SCHINDLER'S LIST.* Bloomington: Indiana University Press, 1997.

Luckiesh, M. *Visual Illusions: Their Causes, Characteristics, and Applications.* New York: Dover Publications, 1965.

Lydon, Cindy Arkelyan. "American Images of the Arabs." *Mid East* 9 (May/June 1969): 3–14.

McAlister, Melani. *Epic Encounters: Culture, Media, and U.S. Interests in the Middle East, 1945–2000.* Berkeley and Los Angeles: University of California Press, 2001.

McCabe, Bob. *THE EXORCIST: Out of the Shadows, the Full Story of the Film.* London: Omnibus Press, 1999.

McCallum, Dennis, ed. *The Death of Truth: What's Wrong with Multiculturalism, the Rejection of Reason, and the New Postmodern Diversity.* Minneapolis: Bethany House Publishers, 1996.

Mackey-Kallis, Susan. *The Hero and the Perennial Journey Home in American Film.* Philadelphia: University of Pennsylvania Press, 2001.

McLeod, John. *Beginning Postcolonialism.* Manchester, England: Manchester University Press, 2000.

McNamara, Robert S., with Brian Van De Mark. *In Retrospect: The Tragedy and Lessons of Vietnam.* New York: Vintage Books, 1996.

MacPherson, Myra. *Long Time Passing: Vietnam and the Haunted Generation.* Orig. 1984; New York: Anchor Books, 1993.

Maiorino, Giancarlo. *The Portrait of Eccentricity: Arcimboldo and the Mannerist Grotesque.* University Park: Pennsylvania State University Press, 1991.

Mastai, M. L. d'Otrange. *Illusion in Art: Trompe l'Oeil. A History of Pictorial Illusionism.* New York: Abaris Books, 1975.

Memmi, Albert. *The Colonizer and the Colonized.* Expanded ed. Boston: Beacon Press, 1965.

Messadié, Gerald. *A History of the Devil.* Trans. Marc Romano. Orig. 1993; New York: Kodansha International, 1997.

Messaris, Paul. *Visual Literacy: Image, Mind, and Reality.* Boulder, Colo.: Westview Press, 1994.

"Middle East: Gasoline by Open Fire." *Time,* October 25, 1971, pp. 29–30.

"Middle East: Terror to End Terror?" *Time,* April 23, 1973, pp. 19–23.

Miller, Stephen Paul. *The Seventies Now: Culture as Surveillance.* Durham, N.C.: Duke University Press, 1999.

Milman, Miriam. *The Illusion of Reality: Trompe L'Oeil Painting.* New York: Rizzoli, 1982.

Mirzoeff, Nicholas. *An Introduction to Visual Culture.* London: Routledge, 1999.

Mitchell, Lee Clark. *Westerns: Making the Man in Fiction and Film.* Chicago: University of Chicago Press, 1996.

Mitchell, W. J. T. *The Last Dinosaur Book.* Chicago: University of Chicago Press, 1998.

Monaco, James. *How to Read a Film: The Art, Technology, Language, History, and Theory of Film and Media.* Oxford, England: Oxford University Press, 1981.

Moore, Robin. *The Green Berets.* New York: Crown Publishers, 1965.

Moore-Gilbert, Bart. *Postcolonial Theory: Contexts, Practices, Politics.* New York: Verso, 1997.

"More Woes on the Oil Front." *Time,* October 29, 1979, pp. 70–71.

Mowlana, Hamid, George Gerbner, and Herbert I. Schiller, eds. *Triumph of the Image: The Media's War in the Persian Gulf—A Global Perspective.* Boulder, Colo.: Westview Press, 1992.

Neu, Charles E., ed. *After Vietnam: Legacies of a Lost War.* Baltimore: Johns Hopkins University Press, 2000.

Neupert, Richard. *The End: Narration and Closure in the Cinema.* Detroit: Wayne State University Press, 1995.

Newman, Kim. *Millennium Movies: End of the World Cinema.* London: Titan Books, 1999.

"New Reserves of Green." *Time,* January 31, 1972, p. 65.

O'Brien, Tom. *The Screening of America: Movies and Values from Rocky to Rain Man.* New York: Continuum, 1990.

O'Connor, John E., and Martin A. Jackson, eds. *American History/American Film: Interpreting the Hollywood Image.* Foreword by Arthur M. Schlesinger, Jr. New York: Frederick Ungar Publishing Co., 1979.

"Oil: Libya's 100-Percenter." *Time,* May 28, 1973, pp. 70–75.

"Oil: Power to the Producers." *Time,* March 1, 1971, pp. 74–76.

"Oil: The Blackmail Market." *Time,* November 19, 1979, p. 85.

"Oil: The Desert Foxes." *Time,* February 15, 1971, pp. 69–70.

"Oil Easier, Gas Tighter." *Time,* February 11, 1974, pp. 27–28.

"OPEC's Dangerous Game." *Time,* April 9, 1979, pp. 56–60.

"OPEC's Painful Squeeze." *Time,* July 9, 1979, pp. 12–15.

Oppenheimer, Paul. *Evil and the Demonic: A New Theory of Monstrous Behavior.* New York: New York University Press, 1996.

Pagels, Elaine. *The Origin of Satan*. New York: Vintage Books, 1995.

"Panic at the Pump." *Time*, January 14, 1974, pp. 15–16.

Pearce, Roy Harvey. *The Savages of America: A Study of the Indian and the Idea of Civilization*. Baltimore: Johns Hopkins University Press, 1953.

Pipes, Daniel. *Militant Islam Reaches America*. New York: W. W. Norton, 2002.

"The Plausible Impossible." *The Wonderful World of Disney* (television series), Episode 55, NBC, October 31, 1956.

"Policeman of the Persian Gulf." *Time*, August 6, 1973, pp. 30–31.

"Precautions against Muslim Anger." *Time*, December 10, 1979, pp. 42–47.

Propp, V. *Morphology of the Folktale*. 2nd ed. Austin: University of Texas Press, 1994.

Rainey, Patricia Ann. *Illusions: A Journey into Perception*. Hamden, Conn.: Linnet Books, 1973.

Reagan, Ronald. "Address to the Nation on the United States Air Strike against Libya, April 14, 1986." In *The Public Papers of President Ronald W. Reagan*. Online at http://www.reagan.utexas.edu/archives/speeches/1986/41486g.htm. Simi Valley, Calif.: Ronald Reagan Library.

Rollover. Produced by Bruce Gilbert and directed by Alan J. Pakula. 118 min. Orion Pictures, 1981. Videocassette.

Roof, Judith. *Come as You Are: Sexuality and Narrative*. New York: Columbia University Press, 1996.

Rose, Gillian. *Visual Methodologies*. London: Sage Publications, 2001.

Rossant, John, and Stan Crock. "Saddam May Soon Unleash His Best Weapon: Oil Blackmail." *Business Week*, October 2, 2000, p. 72.

Rubin, Martin. *Thrillers*. Cambridge, England: Cambridge University Press, 1999.

Rules of Engagement. Produced by Richard D. Zanuck and Scott Rudin and directed by William Friedkin. 127 min. Paramount Pictures, 2000. DVD.

Said, Edward W. *Covering Islam: How the Media and the Experts Determine How We See the Rest of the World*. New York: Vintage Books, 1997.

———. *Orientalism*. New York: Vintage Books, 1979.

Sammon, Bill. *Fighting Back: The War on Terrorism—from Inside the Bush White House*. Washington, D.C.: Regnery Publishing, 2002.

Sanello, Frank. *Reel vs. Real: How Hollywood Turns Fact into Fiction*. Lanham, Md.: Taylor Trade Publishing, 2003.

Sardar, Ziauddin, and Merryl Wyn Davies. *Why Do People Hate America?* New York: Disinformation Company, Ltd., 2002.

Sartre, Jean Paul. *Anti-Semite and Jew.* Trans. George J. Becker. New York: Schocken Books, 1948.

Schiller, Herbert I. "Manipulating Hearts and Minds." In *Triumph of the Image: The Media's War in the Persian Gulf—A Global Perspective,* ed. Hamid Mowlana, George Gerbner, and Herbert I. Schiller, pp. 22–29. Boulder, Colo.: Westview Press, 1992.

Schlesinger, Arthur M., Jr. *The Disuniting of America: Reflections of a Multicultural Society.* New York: W. W. Norton & Company, 1992.

Schmidt, Alvin J. *The Menace of Multiculturalism: Trojan Horse in America.* Westport, Conn.: Praeger, 1997.

"Searching for the Right Response." *Time,* March 12, 1979, pp. 28–31.

Sha'ban, Fuad. *Islam and Arabs in Early American Thought: Roots of Orientalism in America.* Durham, N.C.: Acorn Press, 1991.

Shaheen, Jack G. *Arab and Muslim Stereotyping in American Popular Culture.* Washington, D.C.: Center for Muslim-Christian Understanding, 1997.

———. "The Hollywood Arab (1984–1986)." *Journal of Popular Film and Television* 14 (1987): 148–157.

———. *Reel Bad Arabs: How Hollywood Vilifies a People.* Brooklyn, N.Y.: Olive Branch Press, 2001.

———. *The TV Arab.* Bowling Green, Ohio: Bowling Green State University Popular Press, 1984.

Sharp, Robert M. *The Lore and Legends of Wall Street.* Homewood, Ill.: Dow Jones–Irwin, 1989.

Shirazi, Faegheh. *The Veil Unveiled: The Hijab in Modern Culture.* Gainesville: University of Florida Press, 2001.

Shohat, Ella. "Gender and Culture of Empire: Toward a Feminist Ethnography of the Cinema." In *Visions of the East: Orientalism in Film,* ed. Matthew Bernstein and Gaylyn Studlar, pp. 19–66. New Brunswick, N.J.: Rutgers University Press, 1997.

———. "The Media's War." *Social Text* 28 (Spring 1991): 135–141.

———. *Unthinking Eurocentrism: Multiculturalism and the Media.* London: Routledge, 1994.

———, and Robert Stam. "The Cinema after Babel: Language, Difference, Power." *Screen* 26 (May–August 1985): 35–58.

Silberstein, Sandra. *War of Words: Language, Politics, and 9/11.* London: Routledge, 2002.

Silverman, Kaja. *The Subject of Semiotics.* Oxford, England: Oxford University Press, 1983.

Simon, Reeva S. *The Middle East in Crime Fiction: Mysteries, Spy Novels, and Thrillers from 1916 to the 1980's.* New York: Lilian Barber Press, 1989.

Simpson, Mark. *Male Impersonators: Men Performing Masculinity.* London: Routledge, 1994.

Slaoui, Abderrahman. *The Orientalist Poster.* London: I. B. Tauris, 1998.

Slotkin, Richard. *The Fatal Environment: The Myth of the Frontier in the Age of Industrialization, 1800–1890.* Norman: University of Oklahoma Press, 1985.

———. *Gunfighter Nation: The Myth of the Frontier in Twentieth-Century America.* Norman: University of Oklahoma Press, 1998.

———. *Regeneration through Violence: The Mythology of the American Frontier, 1600–1860.* Norman: University of Oklahoma Press, 1973.

Sobchack, Vivian. *Screening Space: The American Science Fiction Film.* 2nd ed. Orig. 1987; New Brunswick, N.J.: Rutgers University Press, 1998.

Sorlin, Pierre. *The Film in History: Restaging the Past.* Totowa, N.J.: Barnes and Noble Books, 1980.

Sontag, Susan. "The Imagination of Disaster." *Commentary* 40, no. 4 (October 1965): 42–48.

"The Souring of the Dutch." *Time,* December 3, 1973, p. 53.

South Park: Bigger, Longer & Uncut. Produced by Trey Parker and Matt Stone and directed by Trey Parker. 81 min. Warner Bros. Inc., 1999. DVD.

"Squeeze on Poor Lands." *Time,* January 14, 1974, p. 18.

Stanford, Peter. *The Devil: A Biography.* New York: Henry Holt and Company, 1996.

Steet, Linda. *Veils and Daggers: A Century of NATIONAL GEOGRAPHIC's Representation of the Arab World.* Philadelphia: Temple University Press, 2000.

"Stepping on the Gas to Meet a Threat." *Time,* November 26, 1973, pp. 24–31.

"Still Tightening the Blockade." *Time,* November 5, 1973, p. 55.

Storey, John. *Cultural Studies & the Study of Popular Culture: Theories and Methods.* Athens: University of Georgia Press, 1996.

"The Storm over the Shah." *Time,* December 10, 1979, pp. 24–27.

Sturgis, Alexander. *Optical Illusions in Art: Or—Discover How Paintings Aren't Always What They Seem to Be.* New York: Sterling Publishing Co., 1996.

Suleiman, Michael W. *The Arabs in the Mind of America.* Brattleboro, Vt.: Amana Books, 1988.

"The Superpower Search for a Settlement." *Time,* October 29, 1973, pp. 20–21.

Sutcliffe, Thomas. *Watching: Reflections on the Movies.* London: Faber and Faber, 2000.

Taves, Brian. *The Romance of Adventure: The Genre of Historical Adventure Movies.* Jackson: University Press of Mississippi, 1993.

"Terrorism: Fatal Error." *Time,* August 6, 1973, pp. 31–32.

"Terrorism: The Wrong Passengers." *Time,* August 20, 1973, pp. 28–31.

Thibodaux, David. *Political Correctness: The Cloning of the American Mind.* Lafayette, La.: Huntington House Publishers, 1992.

Three Kings. Produced by Charles Roven and directed by David O. Russell. 115 min. Warner Bros. Inc., 1999. DVD.

"A Time of Learning to Live with Less." *Time,* December 3, 1973, pp. 29–38.

Tolansky, Samuel. *Optical Illusions.* Oxford, England: Pergamon Press, 1964.

"Toward a Winter of Discontent." *Time,* December 3, 1973, pp. 48–53.

Trump, Donald J., with Tony Schwartz. *Trump: The Art of the Deal.* New York: Random House, 1987.

Updike, John. "The Disposable Rocket." In *The Male Body: Features, Destinies, Exposures,* ed. Laurence Goldstein, pp. 8–11. Ann Arbor: University of Michigan Press, 1994.

VanDerBeets, Richard. *The Indian Captivity Narrative: An American Genre.* Lanham, Md.: University Press of America, 1984.

Van Wert, William. "*The Exorcist:* Ritual or Therapy?" *Jump Cut* 1 (May–June 1974): 3–5.

Waller, Gregory A., ed. *American Horrors: Essays on the Modern American Horror Film.* Urbana: University of Illinois Press, 1987.

Warner, Marina. *Managing Monsters: Six Myths of Our Time.* London: Vintage, 1994.

Weiss, Richard. *The American Myth of Success: From Horatio Alger to Norman Vincent Peale.* Urbana: University of Illinois Press, 1988.

Wells, H. G. *The Time Machine.* New York: Barnes & Noble Books, 1994.

———. *The War of the Worlds.* New York: Barnes & Noble Books, 1994.

Williams, Tony. *Hearths of Darkness: The Family in the American Horror Film.* Orig. 1995; London: Associated University Presses, 1996.

Wilson, John K. *The Myth of Political Correctness: The Conservative Attack on Higher Education.* Durham, N.C.: Duke University Press, 1995.

Windschuttle, Keith. *The Killing of History: How Literary Critics and Social*

Theorists Are Murdering Our Past. Orig. 1996; San Francisco: Encounter Books, 2000.

Wloszczyna, Susan. "*The Exorcist:* True Evil Endures." *USA Today,* September 22, 2000.

————. " 'Exorcist' Spews Out Challenge for Our Times." *USA Today,* September 21, 2000.

Woods, Tim. *Beginning Postmodernism.* Manchester, England: Manchester University Press, 1999.

Wright, Will. *Sixguns and Society.* Orig. 1975; Berkeley and Los Angeles: University of California Press, 1977.

Wubbles, Lance. *September 11, 2001—A Time for Heroes: A Tribute to American Faith, Guts, and Patriotism.* Shippensburg, Pa.: Treasure House, 2001.

Yergin, Daniel. *The Prize: The Epic Quest for Oil, Money & Power.* Orig. 1991; New York: Touchstone Books, 1992.

Zelizer, Barbie. *Covering the Body: The Kennedy Assassination, the Media, and the Shaping of Collective Memory.* Chicago: University of Chicago Press, 1992.

————. "Every Once in a While: *Schindler's List* and the Shaping of History." In *Spielberg's Holocaust: Critical Perspectives on SCHINDLER'S LIST,* ed. Yosefa Loshitzky, pp. 18–35. Bloomington: Indiana University Press, 1997.

————. *Remembering to Forget: Holocaust Memory through the Camera's Eye.* Chicago: University of Chicago Press, 1998.

Index